D1570972

DAY BY DAY
THROUGH THE
GOSPEL
OF JOHN

DAY BY DAY
THROUGH THE
GOSPEL
OF JOHN

365 TIMELESS DEVOTIONS
FROM CLASSIC WRITERS

EDITOR AND COMPILER

LANCE WUBBELS

a division of Baker Publishing Group
Minneapolis, Minnesota

Published by Bethany House Publishers
11400 Hampshire Avenue South
Bloomington, Minnesota 55438
www.bethanyhouse.com

Bethany House Publishers is a division of
Baker Publishing Group, Grand Rapids, Michigan

Printed in the United States of America

ISBN 978-0-7642-3073-8

Library of Congress Control Number: 2018935315

Unless otherwise indicated, all Scripture quotations are taken from the Holy Bible, New International Version®. NIV®. Copyright © 1973, 1978, 1984, 2011 by Biblica, Inc.™ Used by permission of Zondervan. All rights reserved worldwide. www.zondervan.com

Scripture quotations labeled AMP are from the Amplified® Bible, copyright © 2015 by The Lockman Foundation. Used by permission. (www.Lockman.org)

Scripture quotations labeled AMP-CE are from the Amplified® Bible, copyright © 1954, 1958, 1962, 1964, 1965, 1987 by The Lockman Foundation. Used by permission. (www.Lockman.org)

Scripture quotations labeled KJV are from the King James Version of the Bible.

Scripture quotations labeled NKJV are from the New King James Version®. Copyright © 1982 by Thomas Nelson, Inc. Used by permission. All rights reserved.

Scripture quotations labeled NLT are from the Holy Bible, New Living Translation, copyright © 1996, 2004, 2015 by Tyndale House Foundation. Used by permission of Tyndale House Publishers, Inc., Carol Stream, Illinois 60188. All rights reserved.

Cover design by LOOK Design Studio

18 19 20 21 22 23 24   7 6 5 4 3 2 1

INTRODUCTION

During the second half of the nineteenth century, Great Britain was home to some of the greatest expository preachers, biblical scholars, and Christian leaders and writers in all of church history. Legendary names such as Charles Spurgeon, Alexander Maclaren, Joseph Parker, Hudson Taylor, Catherine Booth, George MacDonald, Alexander Whyte, Frances Ridley Havergal, and others stand out as giants of the church. Their predecessors, including John Wesley, Matthew Henry, and Adam Clarke, left them a rich tradition of biblical and evangelical excellence to follow, and follow they did. On the American side, R. A. Torrey, S. D. Gordon, and Charles Finney were cut from the same cloth, as well as South African Andrew Murray.

Over my thirty-five years of working in Christian publishing, I have been delighted to discover a wealth of rich expositions from the classic writings of these revered saints. However, much of what they wrote is not easily accessible, hidden away in out-of-print books or in large, expensive pastoral volumes (some of these writings are now available online). It has remained my passion for years to make these writings available in a popular format and provide readers with the wisdom that lies buried in the old volumes.

In this book, I have compiled and edited "the very best of the best" of their inspirational insights on the Gospel of John. Verse by verse, following the biblical text consecutively through the life of Jesus Christ, here are 365 devotional readings packed with profound biblical commentary, sound wisdom, and practical application for a Christian's daily walk. Readers will reap an unforgettable understanding into the life, words, and ministry of our Lord and Savior.

It is my hope and prayer that these readings will help bring alive for you the Word of God. May they be a source of biblical inspiration that leads to thoughtful meditation, reflection, and abundant worship.

LANCE WUBBELS

CONTRIBUTORS

CHARLES SPURGEON (1834–1892) was the remarkable British "Boy Preacher of the Fens" who became one of the greatest preachers of all time. Coming from a flourishing country pastorate in 1854, he accepted a call to pastor London's New Park Street Chapel. This building soon proved too small and so work on Spurgeon's Metropolitan Tabernacle was begun in 1859. Through Spurgeon's ministry, the Metropolitan Tabernacle grew into a congregation of more than six thousand, and added well over fourteen thousand members during his thirty-eight-year London ministry. The combination of his clear voice, his mastery of the language, his sure grasp of Scripture, and a deep love for Christ produced some of the noblest preaching of any age. An astounding number of sermons (3,561) have been preserved, from which the readings in this book have been selected and edited.

During his lifetime, Spurgeon is estimated to have preached to 10 million people. He remains history's most widely read preacher. There is more material written by Spurgeon than any other Christian author, living or dead. His sixty-three volumes of sermons stand as the largest set of books by a single author in the history of Christianity, comprising the equivalent to the twenty-seven volumes of the ninth edition of the *Encyclopedia Britannica*.

ALEXANDER MACLAREN (1826–1910) was a Scottish Baptist minister who pastored the Portland Chapel, Southampton (1846–1858) and Union Chapel, Manchester (1858–1903), where he acquired the reputation of "the prince of expository preachers." Next to Charles Spurgeon, Maclaren's sermons have been the most widely read sermons of their time. His preaching drew vast congregations and his sermon methods of subdivision and analogies drawn from nature and life have been widely imitated ever since.

The eleven volumes of Maclaren's *Expositions of Holy Scripture*, from which the devotional readings in this book are derived, are still available today. Of these expositions, W. Robertson Nicoll, a noted New Testament Greek scholar, said, "Will there ever be such a combination of spiritual insight, of scholarship, of passion, of style, of keen intellectual power? He was clearly a man of genius. So long as preachers care to teach from the Scriptures, they will find him their best guide and help."

JOSEPH PARKER (1830–1902) was an English Congregational preacher who was ordained in 1853 to the ministry in Banbury Congregational Church, though his formal education had ceased when he was sixteen. In 1869 he moved to Poultry Chapel in London, which congregation built the City Temple, opening in 1874. There Parker ministered until his death, preaching twice each Sunday and every Thursday morning, earning a reputation as one of the city's greatest pulpit masters, alongside Spurgeon and Liddon. With an impressive appearance, regal personality, commanding voice, and impeccable diction, he preached authoritatively and appealingly. Only Spurgeon exceeded him in attracting crowds. During 1885–1892, he preached through the Bible. Those sermons were published in the twenty-five volumes of *The People's Bible*, from which these devotional readings were selected and edited.

S. D. GORDON (1859–1936) was a prolific author and evangelical lay minister active in the latter part of the nineteenth and early twentieth centuries. He served as assistant secretary of the Philadelphia YMCA from 1884 to 1886 and then became state secretary for the YMCA in Ohio, serving from 1886 to 1895. An incessant and tireless itinerant speaker, his quiet style of devotional speaking and writing, always illustrated with parabolic stories, had gripping power to hold the attention and stir the heart. He is perhaps best known for his series of books "Quiet Talks about . . . ," which have their own unique style, very different from that of other writers of his day and from which these devotional readings were selected and edited.

ANDREW MURRAY (1828–1917) was born in South Africa. After receiving his education in Scotland and Holland, he returned to South Africa and spent his life there as a pastor, missionary, and author of many devotional books. He was a champion of the South African Revival of 1860 and one of the founders of the South African General Mission.

ALEXANDER WHYTE (1836–1921) was a Scottish minister often described as "the last of the Puritans." Educated at King's College, Aberdeen, and at the Free Church of Scotland's New College, Edinburgh, he was called to Edinburgh as successor to R. S. Candlish at St. George's Free Church. During nearly forty years there, he established a reputation as a graphic and compelling preacher to an extent probably unparalleled even in a nation of preachers, and was the author of numerous devotional books.

GEORGE MACDONALD (1824–1905), Scottish novelist, poet, and pastor, was one of the most original and influential writers of Victorian Britain. His more than fifty books—including fantasy, fairy tales, short stories, sermons, essays, poems, and some thirty novels—sold in the millions and made him one of the most popular authors of the day. His writing profoundly influenced the lives of many well-known Christians, including C. S. Lewis, G. K. Chesterton, and Oswald Chambers.

JOHN WESLEY (1703–1791) was the founder of Methodism. Educated at Charterhouse and Christ Church, Oxford, he was elected in 1726 to a fellowship at Lincoln College at the same university. He embarked upon his life work with a clear object: "to reform the nation, particularly the church, and to spread Scripture holiness over the land." To conserve the gains of his prolific evangelism outreach, he formed societies that became the organization of Methodism.

R. A. TORREY (1856–1928) was both an evangelist and Bible scholar. Long associated with D. L. Moody, he became most prominent during world preaching tours in 1902 and 1921. His preaching in Wales in 1902 has been noted as one of the causes of the Welsh revivals of the early 1900s. He was the first superintendent of the Moody Bible Institute and the author of numerous devotional and theological books.

HUDSON TAYLOR (1832–1905) was a pioneer missionary to the almost closed empire of China, founding the China Inland Mission in 1865. Amazingly, by 1895, Taylor led 641 missionaries, about half of the entire Protestant force in China. Few men have been so powerful an instrument in God's hands, proclaiming the gospel to such a vast population and bringing so many Christian churches into being.

CHARLES FINNEY (1792–1875), lawyer, college professor, pastor, and evangelist, left behind a record of a half-century of revival that is unparalleled in

America and gave birth to a new evangelistic movement that is still employed today. He spearheaded the Second Great Awakening in America, influenced the course of history, and is often directly or indirectly credited with the conversions of around five hundred thousand people.

MATTHEW HENRY (1662–1714) studied at a Nonconformist academy in London and was privately ordained a Presbyterian minister. His first pastorate was in Chester (1867–1712), followed by Hackney (1712–1714). Greatly influenced by the Puritans, he made the exposition of Scripture the central concern of his ministry. In 1704 he began the seven-volume *Commentary on the Bible* for which he is remembered.

FRANCES RIDLEY HAVERGAL (1836–1879) was an English religious poet and hymn writer. "Take My Life and Let It Be" and "Like a River Glorious" are two of her best-known hymns. She wrote a set of five "Royal" books from which these devotional readings were selected and edited.

CATHERINE BOOTH (1829–1890) was cofounder of The Salvation Army, along with her husband, William Booth. She was a successful preacher at a time when women preachers were a rare phenomenon and women had few civil rights. She is also highly celebrated for her commitment to social reform.

ADAM CLARKE (1760–1832) was a British Methodist theologian, preacher, and biblical scholar. He is chiefly remembered for writing his *Commentary on the Bible* that took forty years to complete, and was a primary Methodist theological resource for two hundred years.

In the beginning was the Word, and the Word was with God, and the Word was God.

John 1:1

John, fisherman's son and all, was born with one of the finest minds that have ever been bestowed by God's goodness upon any of the sons of men. He had a profoundly intuitive mind—an inward, meditating, contemplative, imaginative, spiritual mind. His mind was by nature extraordinarily rich and deep and lofty. John has the immortal honor of having conceived and meditated and inscribed the most magnificent passage ever written with pen and ink. The first fourteen verses of his Gospel stand alone and supreme over all other literature. "The Word was with God, and the Word was God." These two phrases contain far more philosophy, far more grace and truth and beauty and love, than all the rest that has ever been written by pen of man or spoken by tongue of man or angel. The Word, spoken of John, is a divine person in human nature—a revelation, an experience, and a possession—of which John himself is the living witness and the infallible proof.

How did John sink so deep into the unsearchable things of his Master? What was it in John that lifted him so high, making him an apostle of wisdom and love? For one thing it was his gift of meditation. John listened as none of the other disciples listened to all that Jesus said, and then he thought on it continually. Meditation with imagination combined in John to stir up the most profound insights into the person of Jesus Christ that were ever written.

I encourage you to meditate on these divine things that John wrote. Meditation is the true root and sap of all faith and prayer and spiritual obedience. Why are our minds so impaired and barren in the things of God? Why do we have so little faith? Why have we so little hold of the reality, and nobility, of divine things? The reason is plain. Occasionally, we read our New Testament, but we do not take time to meditate. We seldom consider who we are and what we are, who and what Jesus is to us, and what we are to say, do, ask, and receive. If we allow the thought of Jesus Christ to delight and overawe our hearts, He will become more to us than our nearest friend, more real to us than our morning papers and all our business dealings. Meditate on John's Gospel.

ALEXANDER WHYTE

In the beginning [before all time] was the Word (Christ),
and the Word was with God, and the Word was God
Himself.

John 1:1 AMP

The other Gospels begin with Bethlehem; John begins with eternity. Luke dates his narrative by Roman emperors and Jewish high priests; John dates his "in the beginning." To attempt an exposition of these verses in our narrow limits is absurd. We can only note the salient points of this, the profoundest page in the New Testament.

The threefold utterance in this verse carries us into the depths of eternity, before time or creatures were. Genesis and John both start from "the beginning," but, while Genesis works downward from that point and tells what followed, John works upward and tells what preceded—if we may use that term in speaking of what lies beyond time. Time and space and creatures came into being, and, when they began, "the Word was." Surely no form of speech could more emphatically declare absolute, uncreated being, outside the limits of time. Clearly, too, no interpretation of the words fathoms their depth, or makes worthy sense, that does not recognize that the Word is a person.

"The Word was with God" asserts the eternal communion of the Word with God. The preposition used here means, more accurately, "toward" and expresses the thought that in the Word there was motion and tendency toward, and not merely association with, God. It points to mutual, conscious communion, and the active going out of love in the direction of God.

"And the Word was God" asserts the community of essence, which is not inconsistent with distinction of persons, and makes the communion of active Love possible; for none could, in the depths of eternity, dwell with and perfectly love and be loved by God, except One who himself was God.

This verse stands apart as revealing the essential nature of the Word before the beginning of time. In it the deep ocean of the divine nature is partially disclosed, though no created eye can either plunge to discern its depths or travel beyond our horizon to its boundless, shoreless extent. But we can bow in worship before the One who was with God and who was God.

ALEXANDER MACLAREN

In the beginning was the Word.

John 1:1

In the beginning there was a wondrous One. He was the mind of God thinking out to man. He was the heart of God throbbing love out to man's heart. He was the face of God looking into man's face. He was the voice of God, soft and low, clear and distinct, speaking into man's ears. He was the hand of God, strong and tender, reaching down to take man by the hand and lead him back to the old tree of life, down by the river of water of life.

He was the person of God wearing a human coat and human shoes, walking in freely among us that we might get our tangled-up ideas about God and ourselves and about life untangled, straightened out. He was God wrapped up in human form, coming close so that we get acquainted with Him all over again.

John could have written the common name of Jesus here. If he had, people would immediately have said, "Yes, we know Him." But they didn't know Him. So John uses a new word and so floods in new light. And then we come to see whom he was talking about. It's a bit of diplomacy of God so as to get in through dulled ears and truth-hardened minds down into the heart.

Jesus was God coming in such a way that we could know Him by the feel of Him. We had gone blind to His face. We couldn't read His signature plainly autographed by His own hand on all of nature around us. But when Jesus came, men knew God by the feel of Him. They didn't understand Jesus. But the wounded, hungry crowds reached out groping, trembling fingers, and they knew Him. They began to get acquainted with their gracious King.

All this gives the simple clue to this Word that John uses as a new name for Jesus. Man had grown deaf to the music of God's voice, blind to the beauty of His face, slow-hearted to the pleading of His presence. His hand was touching us, but we didn't feel it. So He came in a new way and walked down our street, into our own doors, that we might be captivated by the beauty of His face, thrilled by the music of His voice, and enthralled by the beauty of His presence.

S. D. GORDON

In him was life, and that life was the light of all mankind.

John 1:4

The life of which John spoke became light to men in the appearing of Him in whom it came into being. The life became light that men might see it and themselves live by choosing that life also, by choosing so to live, such to be.

There is always something deeper than anything said—a something of which all human, all divine words, figures, and pictures are but the outer layers through which the central reality shines more or less plainly. Light itself is but the poor outside form of a deeper, better thing, namely, life. The life is Christ. The light, too, is Christ, but only the body of Christ. The life is Christ himself. The light is what we see and shall see in Him; the life is what we may be in Him. The life is the unspeakable unknown; it must become light such as men can see before men can know it. Therefore, the Word appeared as the obedient divine man, doing the works of His Father—the things, that is, which His Father did—doing them humbly before unfriendly brethren. The Son of the Father must take His own form in the substance of flesh, that He may be seen of men, and so become the light of men—not that men may have light, but that men may have life—that, seeing what they could not originate, they may, through the life that is in them, begin to hunger after the life of which they are capable, and which is essential to their being; that the life in them may long for Him who is their life, and thirst for its own perfection, even as root and stem may thirst for the flower for whose sake, and through whose presence in them, they exist. That the child of God may become the son of God by beholding the Son, the life revealed in light; that the radiant heart of the Son of God may be the sunlight to His people; that the idea may be drawn out by the presence and drawing of the perfect Son of the Father sent to His children.

The whole being and doing of Jesus on earth is the shining out of divine life that men might see it. It is an unveiling of the Father in the Son, that men may know Him. It is the prayer of the Son to the rest of the sons to come back to the Father, to be reconciled to the Father, to receive His life as their own.

GEORGE MACDONALD

In Him was life, and the life was the light of men.

John 1:4 NKJV

Out of the Word came life. Out of Him comes life. There was no life, there is none, except that which was in this One, and what came and comes out from Him all the time. How patient God is! There walks a man who has left God out of his life. Beside him walks a woman whose whole life is spent walking in the dark shadow of the streets of life. They have life—of the body, mind, and spirit. Listen softly, for all the life is there, coming out all the time from this One of whom John writes. It is not given once, as a thing to be taken and stored. It is being given, coming constantly with each breath, from this wondrous One.

"In Him was life." Out of His hand and heart come to us all the time all we are and all we have. We may leave God practically out, but He never leaves us out. The sustaining touch of His hand is ever upon us, upon the entire world. Yet this is the smaller part. John would have us know the fuller part. Out of Jesus, and into us, will come the abundant quality of life, if He may have His way with us.

"And the life was the light of men." He was what we have. He gives himself; not things, but a person. With God everything is personal. We go for the impersonal so much, or we try to. We have a genius for organizations and technologies. Yet deep down in our hearts we hunger for the human touch, the warm, personal touch. We all feel that. Yet the whole action of life is to crowd it out.

With God everything is personal. The life is the light of men. What He is in himself is what He gives. And this is all the light and life we ever have. Men make botany and astronomy. Man makes theology, and theology has its place, when it is kept in its place. God gives us Jesus.

I don't know much about botany or astronomy, and the more I read of theology the more I stand perplexed. But I confess to a great fondness for flowers, for stars, and a love for Jesus that deepens ever more into reverential awe and in tenderness and grateful devotion. The life was the light of men. He himself is all that we have. We go to things. We count worth and wealth by things. He gives himself. And He asks of us not things, but ourselves.

S. D. GORDON

The light shines in the darkness, and the darkness has not overcome it.

John 1:5

This is God's way of treating darkness: let the Light shine. The darkness can't stand the light. In a pitch-black room, strike a match and instantly the little flame drives away some of the darkness. The darkness flees like a frightened dog before the real thing of light.

Let me ask you a question. Come close and listen quietly, for this is tremendously serious. Is it a bit dark down where you live? Is it morally dark? Spiritually dark? Is it even a bit dark? Because if it is, does it not suggest that the light has not been shining as it was meant to? For where the light shines the darkness departs.

For, you see, this is still God's plan for treating darkness. It is meant to be true today of each of us—"the light shines in the darkness." Of course, we are not the light. He is the Light. But we are the light holders. I carry the Light of the world around inside of me. And so do you, if you know Him. It is not because of me, of course, but because of the great patience and faithfulness of Him who is the Light. A lantern may carry a clear light that brightens the world, and so may our lives with the true Light.

You and I are meant to be the human lanterns carrying the Light, and letting it shine clearly, fully. The lantern must be kept clean and clear so the light within can be seen freely. The great thing is that when we live clean, transparent lives, the Light within may shine out clearly. We may live unselfish, clean, Christlike lives by His grace.

Our Lord's great plan, bearing the stamp of its divinity in its sheer human simplicity, is this: we who know Jesus are to live out His life through Him. We're to let the whole of a Jesus—crucified, risen, living—shine out of the whole of our lives.

Is it a bit dark down where you are? Let the Light shine. Let the clear, sweet, steady Jesus-light shine out through your true, clean, quiet, Jesus-controlled life. Then the darkness must go. It can't withstand the purity of the Light's clear and steady shining. This is our Lord's wondrous plan through His own people.

S. D. GORDON

There was a man sent from God whose name was John.
He came as a witness to testify concerning that light,
so that through him all might believe.

John 1:6–7

The John spoken of here is John the Baptist, who we're told was sent from God. Ordinary biographies begin at another point. In John's case, parentage, birth, and training are omitted altogether as the very beauty of God lights up the face of the man. Men have different ways of looking at themselves. In some cases, they look downward toward "the slimy pit, out of the mud and mire" (Psalm 40:2) from whence they came. They keep the memory of "the quarry from which [they] were hewn" (Isaiah 51:1).

Others look at life and claim the dignity and the privilege of the sons of God. The influence of this view upon our strength and upon every aspect of our life must be intense and productive. We degrade life when we omit God from its plan. On the other hand, we enter into our work with fullness of power when we realize that it is God who works in us to will and to do of His good pleasure. What is our view of life? Have we but a physical existence, or are we the messengers of the Most High? When Moses went to his work, he was enabled to say, "I AM has sent me to you" (Exodus 3:14). So when John undertook his mission, he boldly claimed to be the appointed servant of God. In God, His omnipotence is the source of our strength.

John came as a witness. God reveals himself to us little by little as we are able to bear the light. He has set forth a long and wonderful procession of witnesses, from Moses even until John, who was the last of the illustrious line. It is well when a man distinctly knows the limit of his vocation. We are strong within our own bounds. John, as a professed Savior, would have been weak and contemptible, but as a witness he was a burning and a shining light, the morning star. He was a man standing on the highest mountain, who, catching a glimpse of the first solar ray, exclaimed, "Behold, the day comes!" And is not such an exclamation the only originality of which we are capable?

JOSEPH PARKER

He himself was not the light; he came onl
to the light. The true light that gives ligh
was coming into the world.

John the Baptist was but a temporary ray of light. T
that the hand of man can generate is instantly pal
shines in its strength. Beautiful indeed is the moon's li
alone, and not beautiful only, but exceedingly precious to m
it, would be in darkness. Yet, if it could speak, it would say, '
of another fire. Your admiration of my splendor will cease
sun." Such is the speech of the most luminous men. Our li
solar; or solar only because Christ is in us, and according to the measure of
our capacity, He sheds His glory through our life.

As the sun shines for every man, so Jesus Christ lives for every man. The
light in the house belongs to the homeowner, and the light in the street is a
public convenience, but the sun pours its morning and its noontide into every
valley and into the humblest home; that is the true light—the possession of
every man, yet the private property of none! And every man knows that the
sun is the true light—feels it to be such—and without hesitation affirms it
to be supreme. There is no debate whether the sun or the moon is the light
of the world. Imagine a dark night, and an observer who has never seen the
sun watches the sky. A star suddenly appears, and the observer hails it with
delight. Soon the moon shines in all her gentle strength, and the observer
says, "This is the fulfillment of the promise. What could be lovelier? Can
the sky possibly be brighter?" In due course the sun comes up and fills every
cloud with light, crowns every mountain with a strange glory, silvers every
leaf in the forest, burnishes the sea as glass, and chases all secrecy from the
face of the earth. Under such a vision, the observer knows that this is the true
light—the sovereign, all-dominating flame.

It is so with the revelation of Jesus Christ. When the eyes of men are opened
to Him in all His grace and wisdom and sympathy—in all the sufficiency of
His sacrifice and the comfort of His Spirit—the heart is satisfied, and every
rival light is lost in the infinite splendor of God the Son.

JOSEPH PARKER

*The true light that gives light to everyone was coming
into the world.*

John 1:9

Every person in the world is lighted by this Light. Through nature, the twinkling stars in the wondrous blue overhead, the unfailing freshness of the green out of the brown earth underfoot; through the unceasing wonders of these bodies of ours, so awesomely and skillfully made and kept going; through that clear, quiet, inner voice that speaks in every human heart amidst all the noises of earth and of passion; through these the light is shining, noiselessly, softly, endlessly, by day and by night.

It is the same identical light that John speaks of here that so shines upon every man, and always has. There is no light but His. His later name is Jesus. From the first, and everywhere still, it is the light that shines from Him that lights all men. He was with the Father in that creation week. He gave and sustained all life of every sort everywhere, and still does today.

But the light was obscured, clouded over, hindered by earth fogs and swampy mist rising up, until we are tempted to think there was no light, and is none, only darkness. Then He came closer and yet closer. He came in nearer form so as to get the light closer, and let it shine, through fog and clouds, for the sake of the darkened crowd.

And then—ah! still your heart—then He let the Light Holder, the great human Lantern, be broken, utterly broken, so that the light might shine out through broken lanterns in its sweet, soft, wondrous clearness into our blinded, blinking eyes, and show us the way back home. It was in that breaking that it acquired that wondrous, exquisite red tinge that becomes the unfailing hallmark, the unmistakable evidence of the real light.

And it is only as men know of this latest coming of the light, this tremendous, tragic, Jesus-coming of the light, that they can come into the full light. It's the reason He came the way He did. It's the reason when He gets possession of us there's the passion to take the full light of Jesus out to everyone we know. And this passion burns in us and through us in the sweep of its tender, holy flame. In this way, every man may be full of light, and so in following the light of Jesus, he shall not walk any longer in the darkness, but in the sweet, clear light of life.

S. D. GORDON

He was in the world, and though the world was made
through him, the world did not recognize him.

John 1:10

We come to the first of John's heartbreaking sentences. John had a hard time writing his Gospel. He was not simply writing a book. He was telling about his dearest Friend. And the telling makes his heart throb harder, and his eyes fill up, and the writing looks dim to him, as he tries to put the words down.

Read the verse again. It was His world, His child, His creation. He made it. But it failed to acknowledge Him. He came walking down the street of life. He met the world going the other way, and though it knew fully who He was, it turned its face aside and walked by with no return greeting.

He looked into the face of His world, as a mother does her child, for the look of recognition. But there was none. And He was heartbroken. And He devoted all His strength and time, himself, for those human years to—what? One thing, just one thing, a very simple thing: to get a look of recognition in the eyes of His child.

But there's more here. He looks into our faces, eager for that simple, direct, answering look into His face and out of our eyes, yours and mine. And we give Him things—church membership, orthodox belief, aggressive mission programs, money in good measure, tireless and then tired-out service—just things! Good things. But the direct look into His face, answering His own hungry, searching look, that look that reveals the inner heart that He waits for so often, is not there.

For you know the eyes are the true face. They are the doorway into the soul, out through which the soul, the person within, looks. I look at you; the person in me looks out at you through my eyes. And I look at the real you through your eyes. The real person is hidden away within but looks out through the eyes and is looked at only through the eyes. We truly give ourselves to Jesus as we look directly into His face. That tells Him all, and through that He transforms us.

S. D. GORDON

*He came to that which was his own, but his own did
not receive him. Yet to all who did receive him, to those
who believed in his name, he gave the right to become
children of God.*

John 1:11–12

Faith, the principal matter in our salvation, is described as receiving Jesus. It is the empty cup placed under the flowing stream, the penniless hand held out for heavenly alms. It is also described in the text as believing in His name. And this reception, this believing, is the main thing in real godliness. Faith is the simplest thing imaginable. It may be performed by a little child, and it has often been performed by individuals who are almost incapable of any other intellectual act.

And yet faith is as sublime as it is simple, as potent as it is plain. It is the connecting link between impotence and omnipotence. To lay hold of God by faith is the simplest and yet the grandest act of the mind. Faith is apparently so small a matter that many who hear the gospel can hardly believe that we really mean to teach that it brings salvation to the soul. They have even imagined that we mean to teach that it brings salvation to the soul. But it is not so; faith in Jesus as our Savior is a very different thing from *persuading* ourselves to believe that we are saved when we are not. We believe that we are saved by faith alone, but not by a faith that *is* alone. We are saved by faith without works, but not by a faith that is without works.

The faith that saves is the most operative principle known to the human mind; for he who believes in Jesus loves Him who saved him, and that love is the key of the whole matter. The loving believer ceases from everything that would displease Him whom he loves. He tries to abound in that which will please his beloved Redeemer. So salvation becomes the great reason for gratitude and changes the heart; and, the heart being turned, all the issues of life are changed. Faith is so simple that the little child who believes soon becomes strong in the Lord. It is a vital force that gets such mastery over individuals that it makes them new people, and as it grows it lifts them up from being mere men and women to being men and women of God. Faith the grain of a mustard seed develops into faith that moves the mountain. Faith the child increases into faith the giant. May we know how true this is by personal experience.

CHARLES SPURGEON

The Word became flesh and made his dwelling among
us. We have seen his glory, the glory of the one and only
Son, who came from the Father, full of grace and truth.

John 1:14

The words *made his dwelling* literally mean "to dwell in a tent," or if we may use an old word, "to tabernacle," and there is no doubt a reference to the Old Testament tabernacle in which the divine presence dwelt in the wilderness and in the land of Israel. The word is only found here and in two wonderful verses in the book of Revelation that express the culmination of all things that God desires to do in redemption. "He who sits on the throne will spread His tabernacle over them and shelter and protect them [with His presence]" (Revelation 7:15 AMP). "Look! God's dwelling place is now among the people, and he will dwell with them" (Revelation 21:3).

The human nature, the visible, material body of Jesus Christ, in which the everlasting Word enshrined itself—and which from the beginning was the agent of all divine revelation—that is the true temple of God. When we begin to speak about the special presence of omnipresence in any one place, we soon lose ourselves and get into deep waters of glory, where there is no standing. The language of the text sets before us that one transcendent, wonderful, all-blessed thought that this poor human nature is capable of, and has only once in the history of the world received into itself, the real, actual presence of the whole fullness of the Divinity. What must be the kindred and likeness between Godhood and manhood when into the frail vehicle of our humanity that wondrous treasure can be poured, when the fire of God can burn in the bush of our human nature and not be consumed. So it has been in Christ.

When we come with our questions "How can it be? How can the lesser contain the greater?" we have to be content with the recognition that the manner is beyond our fathoming, and to accept that fact, pressed upon our faith, that our hearts may grasp it and be at peace. God has dwelt in humanity. The everlasting Word, who is the coming forth of all the fullness of deity into the realm of finite creatures, was made flesh and lived among us. It leaves us with little we can do except worship.

ALEXANDER MACLAREN

*And the Word (Christ) became flesh (human, incarnate)
and tabernacled (fixed His tent of flesh, lived awhile)
among us; and we [actually] saw His glory (His honor, His
majesty), such glory as an only begotten son receives from
his father, full of grace (favor, loving-kindness) and truth.*

John 1:14 AMP-CE

The Old Testament tabernacle was not only the dwelling place of God, it was also and, therefore, the place of revelation of God. So in our text there follows, "We [actually] saw His glory." As in the tabernacle there hovered between the outstretched wings of the cherubim, above the mercy seat, the brightness of the symbolic cloud that was named "the glory of God," and was the visible manifestation of His presence, so John states that in that lowly humanity there lay shrined in the inmost place the brightness of the manifest glory of God. "We [actually] saw His glory." The rapturous adoration of the remembrance overcomes John, and he breaks his sentence as the blessed memory floods into his soul. "Such glory as an only begotten son receives from his father." The manifestation of God in Christ is unique, as becomes Him who partakes of the nature of that God of whom He is the representative and the revealer.

And how did that glory make itself known to us? By a miracle? Yes. As we read in the story of the first that Christ worked, "He revealed his glory; and his disciples believed in him" (John 2:11). But blessed be His name, miracles are not the highest manifestation of Christ's glory or of God's. For, as our text tells us, the Word that dwelt among us was "full of grace and truth," and therein is the glory most gloriously revealed.

The clear light of stooping love that shone forth warning and attracting in His gentle life, and the bright white beam of unmingled truth that streamed from the radiant purity of Christ's life, revealed God to hearts that yearn for love and spirits that hunger for truth, as no others of God's self-revealing works have done. And that revelation of the glory of God in the fullness of grace and truth is the highest possible revelation. For the most divine thing in God is love, and the true glory of God is neither some symbolic flashing light nor the pomp of mere power and majesty, nor even those incommunicable attributes with names such as *omnipotence* and *omnipresence*. These are all but the fringes of the brightness. The true central heart and lustrous light of the glory of God lie in His love, and of that glory Christ is the unique representative and revealer.

ALEXANDER MACLAREN

. . . who came from the Father, full of grace and truth.

John 1:14

Real grace and truth are always coupled. They tell the exquisite poise that is in everything God does. Truth is the backbone of grace. Grace is the soft cushioning of flesh upon the bony framework of truth. It is the soft, warm breath of life in truth. Truth is grace holding up the one and only standard of purity and right and insisting upon it. And as we look, we know within ourselves we never can reach it. Grace is truth reaching a strong, warm hand down to where we are and helping us grasp it.

Here is a man in the gutter, the moral gutter. It may be the actual gutter. Or, there may be the outer trappings of refinement that culture and wealth bring. But morally and in spirit, it's a gutter. The slime of sin and low passion, of selfishness and indulgence and self-ambition, oozes over everything in full sight. The man is in the gutter.

Truth is Jesus stretching His hand up high, up to the limit of an arm's length, and saying, "Here is the standard—purity, righteousness, utter honesty of heart, and unyielding purity of motive and life. You must reach this standard. It can never be lowered. You must come up to it."

And the man in the gutter says, "I'll never reach it." And he is right. By himself he never will. Yet it is the truth. But wait, that's only half the story.

Grace is Jesus going down into the lowest gutter and taking the man by his outstretched hand, lifting him up until he reaches the standard, and is never content till He does. That was a tremendous going down and a more tremendous lifting up. Jesus broke His heart and lost His life to bring us up.

But out from His broken heart poured the blood that proved both cleansing and healing. And out of the grace that cost His life there came new life that proved a new incentive and dynamic. The blood cleans the inside of the man, heals his wounds, and restores his sight and hearing and sense of touch. The new life put inside the man makes him rise up and walk determinedly, out of the gutter to a new location. He is a new man, with a new life, in a new location. That is the exquisite diplomacy of the love of God.

S. D. GORDON

For out of His fullness [the superabundance of His grace and truth] we have all received grace upon grace [spiritual blessing upon spiritual blessing, favor upon favor, and gift heaped upon gift].

John 1:16 AMP

With so infinite a theme we can do no more than children do when they take up a little seawater in a shell; their tiny scoop cannot embrace the ocean. I stand on the narrow edge of a vast expanse and leave the boundless depths to your contemplation. His fullness—an inexhaustible reservoir! Our filling—an illimitable endowment! Beloved, the river of God, which is full of water, can well supply the little canals that are fed from such a fountain with grace for grace.

It is His fullness, the fullness of Jesus Christ the Son of God, of which John speaks. Note this well; forget it not. Our Redeemer is essentially God. By nature He is divine. He has condescendingly taken upon himself our nature, and He is most truly man. Very God! Very man! In Him dwells all the fullness of the Godhead bodily. He is the express image of the Father's person, the brightness of His Father's glory; no mere glory, but the brightness of His Father's glory. What confidence this should inspire in our hearts! The fullness from which we derive the grace we receive is none other than the infinite fullness of God! And throughout His lifetime on earth He rendered entire and undeviating obedience to the law of God, having taken upon himself the form of a servant. In always doing His Father's will, through His suffering, death, resurrection, and ascension, Jesus finished the redemptive work that His Father gave Him to do.

And so it is that grace comes to us. God gives grace in preparation for further grace—the grace of a broken heart to make room for deep repentance; the grace of hatred of sin to make way for the grace of holy and careful walking, humility, and faith in Jesus; the grace of careful walking to make room for the grace of close fellowship with Christ; the grace of fellowship with Jesus to make room for the grace of full conformity to His image; perhaps the grace of conformity to His image to make room for brighter view of Jesus and still closer incomings into the very heart of the Lord Jesus. Like waves of the sea, one grace has hardly come into your soul when there follows another. Oh, sing to Him a new song! Let Him have fresh praise for all of His fresh mercies!

CHARLES SPURGEON

Now this was John's testimony when the Jewish leaders in Jerusalem sent priests and Levites to ask him who he was. He did not fail to confess, but confessed freely, "I am not the Messiah."

John 1:19–20

John the Baptist had been creating a great sensation. All the people for miles around had been crowding to his ministry, and people were looking out for some marvelous event. John receives the deputies sent by the religious leaders in the capital, who reflect that expectation with their question "Who are you?" No doubt, there was a temptation to make a messianic claim, but John did not. Indeed, he refuted it instantly.

John knew who he was. That is one of the main points every man should understand about himself. He should be able to say who he is, what he has been called to do, and what he is qualified to perform. Be warned that a man who may have great power within a given circle may have only to step beyond the line of his limit to be utterly weak and useless. If John had said, "I am the Christ," he would have won a moment's victory and glory, but he would have opened himself up to a most dishonorable and humiliating destiny. Surely, the temptation was there to seize him and cause him to say, "I could be as great as Elijah! I have within me the spirit of the greatest prophet so often referred to in the Old Testament!" Let a man extend himself ambitiously beyond his proper function and calling in life, and the result is self-inflicted humiliation and shame; and he who might have done something really good and useful will go out of the world having wasted his little day.

Do you know yourself? Do you know the measure of your strength? Do you work within the circle that God has assigned to you? Or are you wasting your strength in those foolish ambitions that tempt us away from proper limitations and mock us, throwing us back and back again into the dust, so that at the end of the day a man who might have done some solid and substantial work in life has done nothing but followed the whims of a useless ambition? Who are you? Are you great? Are you unknown? Are you intended for public or private ministry? What is your calling in life? Come to understand your calling from God and work according to a sincere conviction, and your life cannot be spent in vain. Blessed is the man who will pursue his investigation until he reaches the truth.

JOSEPH PARKER

"I baptize with water," John replied, "but among you stands one you do not know. He is the one who comes after me, the straps of whose sandals I am not worthy to untie."

John 1:26–27

S o, if John the Baptist was not the expected One, where was He? Standing among them! They were looking far away for the blessing promised to the world, and behold, that blessing was in their very midst. It is in this way that we miss many of the great revelations and wonderful presences that God sends down to cheer us and soothe us by gentle ministries. We think the great blessings are far off, but God says, "My child, they are under your very hand and close beside your footprints." So throughout the whole of the revelations of God we are told that things precious to our best life are much nearer to us than we imagine, that God is close at hand. We have but to open our eyes and we shall see the light; but to breathe our prayer and all that is good for us will be done in our hearts. We have no long pilgrimages to make, no great penalties to undergo, no self-infliction or remorse to perform. Christ has done the work for us. He is within reach of the prayer of our love. He is among us.

Too many Christians struggle with this realization, looking far to the east for God's coming, when the morning light already shines. Do you expect God to come in thunder and lightning, whirlwind and stormy tempest, with the trumpet and the shoutings of angels? Behold, He is in that little spring of water at your back door. He is all around your bed. He is numbering the hairs on your head. He is putting His hand upon the head of your little child. He is at your table. He makes your feet steadfast in all your paths, watching over all your goings out and your comings in. He has totally encompassed you, and He lays His hand upon you. And yet you are looking as though you require some great telescope to see the distance of God. There He stands within your whisper reach. He can hear every throb of your heart. He sees every tear that drops from your eye. There is nothing hidden from the fire of His look. Believe this, and a great awe will descend upon your life. Believe this, and every mountain will be an altar, every star a door into heaven, every flower an autograph of God, and the whole scene of your life will be blessed with an assurance and consciousness that God is close at hand.

JOSEPH PARKER

The next day John saw Jesus coming toward him and said, "Look, the Lamb of God, who takes away the sin of the world!"

John 1:29

I f we only had the accounts of Matthew and Mark and Luke, we would only recall the warnings from John about the coming wrath and unquenchable fire for sin. This rugged preacher, with the voice of the whirlwind and a grim and terrible countenance, wanted nothing of our wines and luxuries. His food was locusts and wild honey, and his home was the wilderness. Look at him there. Look at his long locks, his leather belt, and his rugged bearing. He is standing there silently; when he speaks, I wonder what his lips will say? When he shuts his mouth, he seems to have made a resolution; it seems he may never open his mouth again but to condemn the world! Have you heard his words slice the air? At the sight of Jesus, we would expect him to say, "Behold the lion of the tribe of Judah who devours the sinners of the world!"

Yet John delivered the most vital gospel sermon ever given by the lips of man or angel. "Look, the Lamb of God, who takes away the sin of the world!" Remember, John spoke this gentle gospel in the sweetest, most persuasive tone. Not the sinners, he said, but the sin. This is redemption. The other course would have been destruction. It is easy to destroy; it requires God to redeem. It is easy to strike; it requires infinite grace to heal. By one strike of His lightning He could have taken away the sinners, but it required the blood of His heart to take away the sin. We are not redeemed with such corruptible things as silver and gold, but with the precious blood of Jesus Christ, the Lamb of God!

Christ came to take away sin. We cannot take it away ourselves. Here is the atonement; here is the sacrifice of the Son of God—complete, sufficient, and final. The priest himself becomes the victim. Great is the mystery of godliness! To have seen everything in life but the Lamb of God is to have seen everything in life but the one thing worth seeing. To have beheld glorious sights and not to have seen the Lamb is to have seen the light from the outside of the window and not to have gone in and found rest and welcome and home!

JOSEPH PARKER

*And John bore witness, saying, "I saw the Spirit
descending from heaven like a dove, and He
remained upon Him."*

John 1:32 NKJV

Why did Jesus go to John for baptism? The rite was a purifying
one. It signified confession of sin, need of cleansing, purpose in
turning from wrong and sin to lead a new life. Why did Jesus
accept such a rite for himself? Read in the light of the whole story of Jesus,
the answer seems simple. Jesus was stepping down into the ranks of man as
his Brother. The kingdom He would establish among men would be for their
salvation.

In accepting John's baptism, Jesus was allying himself with the race of
men He had come to lead from the place where they were. To be baptized as
they were was the true path of fellowship with them in their need. He was
taking hold of their hands that He might be their leader up to the highlands
of a new life. He stepped down to their level. He would get beside the man
lowest down and lift him up. It was the clear evidence from the start that He
was the true Messiah, the King. And He was their Brother.

And notice the point He chooses for getting into that contact with His
brothers. It is the point at which they are turning from sin. It is at that point
that Jesus comes forward to meet us, close up, with outstretched hand. He is
waiting eagerly and steps up quickly to the side of the one who turns from sin.

But there's more. Read in the afterlight cast upon it; there is much more.
This was the beginning of all that would come after. The road up the hill to
the cross not far away led out of those waters. This was the starting point.
Jesus calmly turned His face toward the cross.

It meant much, for it was the first step into the path marked out. What
the Father had chosen for Him, He now chooses for himself. So every bit of
service, every plan, must be twice chosen: by God for a man; by the man for
himself as from God. He entered eagerly, for this was His Father's plan. That
itself was enough for Jesus. But, too, it was the path His needy brothers were
on. It was the road wherein He would defeat the enemy. And with a fresh
prayer in His heart and a quiet confidence in His eye, He stepped onto the
road with the calmness that strong purpose gives.

S. D. GORDON

The next day John was there again with two of his disciples. When he saw Jesus passing by, he said, "Look, the Lamb of God!"

John 1:35–36

If we hope to comprehend the message of this Gospel, we must come to understand its writer. John was swayed by a passion. It was a fiery passion flaming through all his life. It burned through him as the fierce forest fire burns through the underbrush. Every ungodly thing was eaten up by its flame. Every less-worthy thing came under its heat. It melted and mellowed and molded his whole being.

It was the Jesus-passion. It was kindled that memorable afternoon early in his life down in the bottoms of the Jordan. John's namesake, the Baptist, applied the kindling match. From then on the flames never flickered or burned low. They increased steadily, and they increased in purity, until his whole life was under their holy heat.

John did not always understand his Master. Sometimes he misunderstood Him. But he never failed in his trust of Him or in his fidelity to Him. Of the chosen inner circle, John was the one who remained true through the greatest test on the night of betrayal. Judas betrayed; Peter denied; the other nine fled in terror down the road to save their cowardly lives; but John "went with Jesus into the high priest's courtyard" (John 18:15). That fiery nature of his, that early won for him the stormy name of one of the "sons of thunder" (Mark 3:17), came completely under the sway of this holier, tenderer, stronger flame and burned itself out in the passion of love for Jesus.

This Jesus-passion swayed John completely. This explains the man and his career. It explains this Gospel of his ripe old age. And only this can. One must read the book through John's own heart, and then you begin to understand it. This Jesus-passion is the key to the book, the human key.

And the distinctive message of the book is simply this: Jesus was God on a loving errand to the earth. That simple sentence covers fully all that is found in John's twenty-one chapters. Every line in this entire Gospel can be traced back to the great mission of Jesus to win the hearts of men.

S. D. GORDON

"Behold the Lamb of God!"

John 1:36 NKJV

No theme is sweeter, more refreshing, more inspiring, more purifying to the believer than the Lamb of God. The sinner needs Him for salvation, but the believer needs Him to persevere, advance, conquer, and attain perfection. Give me that harp and let my fingers never leave its strings. To harp upon the name of Jesus is the blessed repetitiveness of a true ministry—a repetitiveness with more variety than all other subjects beside.

As the Lamb of God, Jesus is the chief of all sacrifices, the first of all offerings by which atonement is made for sin. Every Old Testament sacrifice was God's ordaining, but these were but pictures, symbols, and shadows of Jesus. He is the Lamb of the morning slain from before the foundation of the world, and the Lamb of the evening offered up in these last days for His people. Atonement for sin is truly and in very deed to be found in the Son of God, for in His blood alone is there efficacy to satisfy the law.

So let us always contemplate Jesus as the Lamb of God, for He is the grandest subject of thought in the universe. What are the sciences, the classics, or the poets by way of comparison? Jesus alone is wisdom, beauty, eloquence, and power. Jesus is God allied to human nature, God the infinite incarnate among the sons of men, God in union with humanity taking human sin, out of stupendous love condescending to be numbered with the transgressors, and to suffer for sin that was not His own.

Oh, wonder and romance, if men desire you, they may find you here! Oh, love, if men seek you, here alone, they may behold you! Oh, wisdom, if men dig for you, here they shall discover your purest ore! Oh, happiness, if men yearn for you, you dwell alone with the Christ of God. *O Lord Jesus, you are all we need!*

You may search the heavens above and the earth beneath, but you will find more in the Lamb of God than in all else beside. He is the sum and substance of all truth, the essence of all creation, the soul of life, the light of light, the heaven of heavens, and yet He is greater far than all this. There is no subject in the world so sublime, so vast, so elevating, or so divine. Let me behold the Lamb of God, and my eye sees every precious thing.

CHARLES SPURGEON

When the two disciples heard him say this, they followed Jesus. Turning around, Jesus saw them following and asked, "What do you want?" They said, "Rabbi" (which means "Teacher"), "where are you staying?" "Come," he replied, "and you will see."

John 1:37–39

In these verses we see the headwaters of a great river, for we have before us nothing less than the beginnings of the Christian church. The two disciples of John the Baptist heard his words concerning Jesus and decided to follow Him. One disciple was Andrew and the other was surely John. Clearly it had sunk very deep into John's mind; and now as he writes, at the very end of his life, the never-to-be-forgotten voice sounds still in his memory, and he sees again, in sunny clearness, all the scene that had transpired on that day by the fords of the Jordan. The first words and the last words of those whom we have learned to love cut deep into our hearts.

It was not an accident that the first words the Master spoke in His messianic office were this profoundly significant question: "What do you want?" He asks it of us all; He asks it of us today. Most people have never answered that question, but live incoherent, instinctive, unreflective lives that are driven by circumstances. If we knew what we were really seeking in our lives, we should know where to go look for it. Let me tell you what you are seeking, whether you know it or not. You are seeking rest for your heart, a home for your spirit; you are seeking for perfect truth, perfect beauty, and perfect goodness. You are seeking for all these, gathered into one white beam of light, and you are seeking for it all in a person. Unfortunately, many of us have hunted in all manner of impossible places for that which we can only find in Christ.

The disciples' answer was simple and timid, but His answer is "Come, and you will see!" There is a distinct call to the personal act of faith here, the distinct call to a firsthand knowledge of Christ. Come to Him and He will vindicate His own character. The deepest and sweetest part of His character and of His gifts can only be known on condition of possessing Him and them; they can be possessed only on condition of holding fellowship with Him. Taste and see that the Lord is good! Come and see! So simply were the first disciples made, and so simply are disciples made today.

ALEXANDER MACLAREN

Andrew, Simon Peter's brother, was one of the two who
heard what John had said and who had followed Jesus.
The first thing Andrew did was to find his brother Simon
and tell him, "We have found the Messiah" (that is, the
Christ). And he brought him to Jesus.

John 1:40–42

Andrew is a picture of what every disciple of Christ should be. He was a sincere follower of Jesus, whose immediate passion was to bring his brother to the Savior. Men who have never seen the beauties of Immanuel are not fit persons to describe them to others, but Andrew had seen it. And though he was but a young follower, he spread abroad the good news with freshness and fullness of joy that were contagious. He first finds Peter, who is his first success, but how many afterward he found, who shall tell? Throughout a long life of service it is probable that Andrew brought many stray sheep to the Redeemer's fold.

Many, too, may be brought to Christ through your example. Believe me, there is no preaching in this world like the preaching of a changed life, a holy life. In proportion as a church is holy, in that proportion will its testimony for Christ be powerful. Oh, if the saints were perfect, our testimony would be like a flaming fire torching a meadow of dry grass. Were the saints of God less like the world, more loving, more prayerful, more godlike, the tramp of the armies of Zion would shake the nations, and the day of the victory of Christ would surely dawn. Freely might the church trade her golden-mouthed preacher if she received in exchange men of the apostolic church. I would be content that the pulpit should be empty if all the members of the church would preach Christ by their patience in suffering, by their endurance in temptation, by exhibiting the household of those graces that adorn the gospel of Jesus Christ.

Our object should be to bring men to Jesus, by prayer, by instruction, by example, and by occasionally, as time and opportunity may serve us, giving a word of purposeful witness. A few words from a tender mother may drop like gentle dew from heaven upon a son's heart. A few sentences from a kind father given to a daughter have the power to change her life forever. A kind word dropped by a brother to a sister may be God's arrow of grace. I have known such little things as a tear or an anxious glance to work wonders. Always take care through all that you do to bring others to Jesus.

CHARLES SPURGEON

Jesus looked at him and said, "You are Simon son of John. You will be called Cephas" (which, when translated, is Peter).

John 1:42

A revelation of our Lord's relation to His disciples is given in the fact that He changes Simon's name. As Jehovah changed the names of Abraham and of Jacob, our Lord's changing of Peter's name is the clear assertion of His mastery over Peter. It also implies Christ's power and promise to bestow a new character on this disciple. Peter was by no means a "Rock" then, as the name means. The name no doubt implies official function, but that official function was prepared for by personal character; and insofar as the name refers to character, it means firmness. Peter was rash, impulsive, headstrong, self-confident, proud, and, therefore, necessarily changeable. Like the granite, all fluid and hot, and fluid because it was hot, he needed to cool in order to solidify into rock. It was not until his self-confidence had been knocked out of him, and he had learned humility by falling; not until all his presumption had tamed down and steadied by years of difficulty and responsibilities, did he become the rock Christ meant him to be.

All that lay concealed in Peter's future, but in the change of his name, while he stood on the very threshold of his Christian career, there was preached to him, and there is preached to us, this great truth, that if you will go to Jesus Christ, He will make a new man of you. No man's character is so obstinately rooted in evil but that Christ can change its set and direction. No man's natural dispositions are so faulty and low but that Christ can develop counterbalancing virtues, and out of the weakness make strength. He reads all of our character with all its weaknesses, and then with assured confidence on His face, He promises us a new nature and new dignities.

The process will be long and painful. There will be a great deal trimmed off. The sculptor makes the marble image by chipping away the superfluous marble. Simon did not know all that had to be done to make a Peter of him. We must thank God that we do not know all the sorrows and trials of the process of making us what He wills us to be. But we may be sure that if only we keep near our Master, and let Him have His way with us, and if only we will not shrink from the blows of His chisel, then out of the roughest block He will carve the fairest statue.

ALEXANDER MACLAREN

The following day Jesus wanted to go to Galilee, and
He found Philip and said to him, "Follow Me."

John 1:43 NKJV

Notice that Philip was not seeking Jesus. To him Christ reveals himself as drawing near to many a heart that has not thought of Him and laying a masterful hand of gracious authority on their lives in His invitation and command to "Follow Me." So we have a gradual heightening revelation of the Master's graciousness to all souls, to them that seek and to them that seek Him not. It is a revelation of the seeking Christ.

Everyone who reads the surrounding verses with even the slightest attention must observe how "seeking" and "finding" are repeated over and over again. Andrew and John are introduced to Jesus by John the Baptist, and Christ turns to them with the invitation to "Come and see." Andrew finds his brother Simon and brings him to Jesus. Then, again, Jesus finds Philip, who then finds Nathanael. It is a reciprocal play of finding and seeking all through these verses.

As it was in His miracles upon earth, so it has been in the sweet and gracious works of His grace ever since. Sometimes He healed in response to the yearning desire that looked out of sick eyes or that spoke from parched lips. Sometimes He healed in response to the entreating of those who, with loving hearts, carried their dear ones and laid them at His feet. But sometimes, to magnify the spontaneity and the completeness of His own love and to show us that He is bound and limited by no human cooperation, sometimes He reached out the blessing to a hand that was not extended to grasp it; and by His question "Do you want to get well?" kindled desires that otherwise had lain dormant (John 5:6).

And so in this story: He will welcome and always answer Andrew and John when they come seeking. And when Andrew brings his brother to Him, He will go more than halfway to meet him. But when these are won, there still remains another way by which He will have disciples brought into His kingdom, and that is by His going out and laying His hand on the man and drawing Him to His heart by the revelation of His own. But He really is seeking us all, whether through human agencies or not, whether our hearts are seeking Him or not. There is no heart upon earth that Christ does not desire, no man or woman within the sound of His gospel whom He is not seeking that He may draw them to himself.

ALEXANDER MACLAREN

*Jesus saw Nathanael coming toward Him, and said of
him, "Behold, an Israelite indeed, in whom is no deceit!"*

John 1:47 NKJV

There is a Man walking toward you in John's Gospel. Turn where you will, there Jesus is, always facing you, with a gentle eagerness in His face and in the forward leaning of His body. There is always warmth and gentleness radiating from His presence. This is the thing you feel most, the warmth. But it isn't the only thing. There is purity. There are ideals that seem out of reach in their great height. There's insistence on these ideals, stern, unbending insistence. Nathanael saw this. You see it too. You can't help it. You feel the tremendous pull. They seem to be almost beyond your imagining; they are so high up. But there's the warmth, drawing, awakening, calling.

You come to find that the warmth of that presence is as irresistible as the ideals and the insistence are unbending. And the warmth woos you. It warms you, till there comes the intense admiration of the ideals, and then the eager reaching of the whole being toward them.

This is John's picture of Jesus. This is God, in human garb, as He comes to us in John's pages. Jesus is God brooding over us to woo us toward His love and purity by the touch of His own dear presence.

John's book is put together as simply as his sentences. And as you take it up, it falls apart almost of itself, so simple and natural are its divisions. We had a look at the opening paragraphs of the Gospel, those eighteen brief verses that open the doorway into all the gospel holds for us. There is given chiefly John's vivid tremendous picture of a Person, coming with swift long strides and outreached hands. Now we see the great winsome wooing of this great God-man. He woos individuals by His personal touch. He devotes himself to one person, now here, now there. His skill and tact in personal dealings are matchless.

Someday we shall recognize the meaning of that modest but tremendous sentence—"God is love." Christ's love comes, gentle as the dawning light in the gray east, fragrant as the dew of the new morning, irresistible in its pervasive, persuasive presence as the rays of the growing sun, giving to us warmth, and life, and drawing out from within us warmth and life and beauty and strength, all in its own image. As we know it, we are getting acquainted with Him.

S. D. GORDON

Jesus said, "You believe because I told you I saw you under the fig tree. You will see greater things than that."

John 1:50

I f we demand to see first, we will never believe; but if we are willing to believe, we will see eventually. There is a growth in faith that renders it not the less faith, whereby we simply believe the declaration of God and later come to believe upon our personal experience of it. We believe until we realize the object of faith; we look at the things that are not seen and see Him who is invisible. From this we go further still, until we both taste and handle the good Word of Life, and faith becomes the substance of things hoped for. From looking to Christ we come to live and move and have our being in Him. The eye of faith gathers strength. At first it sees Christ through its tears, and that look saves the soul, though it perceives comparatively little of Him; but in later days the eye of faith becomes so powerful that it rivals that of the eagle, which can gaze upon the sun at midday.

Nathanael had seen something of the omniscience of Christ, yet he is promised to discover greater things than this. He would see more of the Godhead revealed. He would discover that not only could Christ read his heart, but Christ could change his heart through His omnipotence. He would see Christ casting out demons, healing the sick, and hushing the tempests. He had seen Christ's eye entering into his secrets, but he was to see communications established between the lowly hearts of men and the secrets of heaven. He saw how Christ as the Son of God dwelt among men; he is now to see how the abode of God and man shall be blended into one, and high communion maintained between earth and heaven.

What a great joy to the believing heart that heaven is laid open to all its citizens, even to those who dwell below. The franchise of the New Jerusalem is extended to these low-lying regions in which we live. The veil is rent, and we have access to the holiest; the abode of the church below is an adjunct of heaven, a suburb of the metropolitan city of the New Jerusalem. In the person of Christ, heaven is opened to earth, and earth laid open to communications with heaven. Do you know that, beloved? As you sit under that fig tree of yours, you are risen and reigning with Christ even now? May the Lord give us honest, simple faith, and then we will see greater things than these and eternal love will work wonders among us.

CHARLES SPURGEON

He then added, "Very truly I tell you, you shall see 'heaven open, and the angels of God ascending and descending on' the Son of Man."

John 1:51

This seems to be a figurative expression. Christ may be understood by this saying to mean that a clear and abundant revelation of God's will would be now made unto men. Heaven itself would be laid open as it were, and all the mysteries that had been shut up and hidden in it from eternity, relative to the salvation and glorification of man, would be now fully revealed. And by the angels "ascending and descending" we are to understand that a perpetual communion would now be opened between heaven and earth, through the person of Christ, who was God manifested in the flesh.

Our blessed Lord is represented in His mediator role as the ambassador of God to men; and the angels represent a metaphor taken from the custom of dispatching couriers or messengers from the prince to his ambassador in a foreign land, and from the ambassador back to the prince. This metaphor is especially highlighted when we consider 2 Corinthians 5:19–20: "And he has committed to us the message of reconciliation. We are therefore Christ's ambassadors, as though God were making his appeal through us." From this time on, Christ says, the whole concerns of man's salvation shall be carried on through the Son of Man, and a constant communion shall be established between heaven and earth.

What a glorious view this gives of the gospel dispensation! It is heaven opened to earth, and heaven opened on earth. The church militant and the church triumphant become one, and the whole heavenly family sees and adores their common Lord. Neither the world nor the church is left to the whims of time and chance. The Son of Man governs as He upholds all. Wherever we are praying, studying, hearing, or meditating, His gracious eye is upon us. He notes our needs, our weakness, and our petitions; and His eye affects His heart. Let us be without guile, deeply, habitually sincere, serious, and upright; and then we may rest assured, that not only the eye, but the hand of our Lord will be ever upon us for good. Happy is the man whose heart can rejoice in the thought, *My God sees me!*

ADAM CLARKE

*On the third day a wedding took place at Cana in Gali-
lee. Jesus' mother was there, and Jesus and his disciples
had also been invited to the wedding. When the wine
was gone, Jesus' mother said to him, "They have no
more wine." "Woman, why do you involve me?" Jesus
replied. "My time has not yet come."*

John 2:1–4

The first point that John makes all but as emphatic as the miracle itself is
the new relation between Mary and Jesus, the lesson she had to learn,
and her sweet triumphant trust. Now that she sees her Son surrounded
by His disciples, the secret hope that she had nourished silently for so long
bursts into flame, and she turns to Him with beautiful faith in His power to
help, even in the small present need. What an example her first word to Him
sets for us all! Like the two sad sisters of Lazarus, she is sure that to tell Him
of trouble is enough, for His own heart will compel Him to action. Let us tell
Jesus our needs and leave Him to deal with them as He knows how.

That Jesus did not call her *Mother*, but *Woman*, told her that she has to
learn that the assumption of the position of Messiah in which her mother's
pride so rejoiced, carried necessarily a consequence, the first of the swords that
were to pierce her heart (see Luke 2:35). The old days of Jesus being subject to
her were past forever, and now she was to take the role of a disciple—a cutting
thought, which many parents have similarly to taste when their children step
away from home for their own vocation. Jesus' "hour" is not to be prescribed
to Him, but His own consciousness of the time must determine His action.
Jesus would act, but He would act in His freedom with His infallible accuracy.

Mary's sweet humility and strong trust are seen clearly in her direction to
the servants, which is the exact opposite of what might have been expected
to the cold water dispensed upon her eagerness to prompt Jesus. Her faith
laid hold of the little spark of promise in that "not yet," and fanned it into a
flame. "Do whatever He tells you." How firm must have been the faith that
did not falter even at the stinging lesson and the apparent rebuff, and how it
puts to shame our feebler confidence in our better known Lord, if ever He
delays our requests! Mary left all to Jesus; His commands were to be implicitly
obeyed. Do we submit to Him in that absolute fashion both as to the time
and the manner of His responses to our prayers?

ALEXANDER MACLAREN

When the wine was gone, Jesus' mother said to him,
"They have no more wine."

John 2:3

The world's banquet runs out; Christ supplies an infinite gift. The great water jars that stood there, if the whole contents of them were changed, contained far more than sufficient for the modest needs of the wedding feast. The water that flowed from them, in obedience to the touch of the servant's hand, if the change were effected then, would flow as long as any thirsted. And Christ gives to each of us, if we so choose, a fountain that will spring unto life eternal. And when the world's platters are empty, and the world's cups are all drained, He will feed and satisfy the immortal hunger and thirst of every spirit that longs for Him.

The speech of the master of the banquet lends itself to another aspect of this same thought. He said in jesting surprise, "You have saved the best till now" (v. 10), whereas the world gives its best first, and when the palate is dulled and the appetite diminished, "then the cheaper wine." How true that is; how tragically true in some of our lives! In the individual, the early days of hope and vigor, when all things were fresh and wondrous, contrast miserably with the bitter experience of life that most have had. We drag remembrance, like a lengthening chain, through all our life; and with remembrance comes sorrow and regret. The splendid vision no longer attends our life, and we plod on our way through the weariness of middle life, or pass down into the deepening shadows of advancing and solitary old age. The best comes first, for the men who have no good but this world's.

But Jesus Christ keeps the best till the last. His gifts become sweeter every day. Time does not diminish them. Advancing years make them more precious and more necessary. The end is better in this course than the beginning. And when life is over, and we pass into heaven, the word will come to our lips with surprise and thankfulness, as we find how much better it all is than we had ever dreamed it could be: "You have saved the best till now."

Do not touch the cup that is offered to you by the world, spiced and fragrant and foaming. In the end its bite is like a serpent and its sting is like an adder. But take the pure joys that the Christ—loved, trusted, obeyed, summoned to your feast and welcomed into your heart—will bring to you. These shall grow and multiply until the perfection of the heavens.

ALEXANDER MACLAREN

His mother said to the servants, "Whatever He says to you, do it."

John 2:5 NKJV

Mary, with the best intentions, had run ahead of Jesus by putting to the front her motherly relationship at a time when it was necessary that it should be in the background. His gentle rebuke that He was not there to please her was met with the quiet silence that He was right. And then observe her admonition to the servants. Inasmuch as she had run before Him, she would have them to follow after Him, and she very wisely and kindly says to them, "Whatever He says to you, do it. Do not go to Him with any of your comments. Do not try to force His hand. He knows best. Stand back and wait till He speaks, and then be quick to obey His every word."

Notice that the servants did nothing till He instructed them. A great part of obedience lies in *not doing*. I believe that in the anxiety of many a trembling heart, the very best faith will be seen in not doing anything. Many a person has aggravated his trouble by doing something, when, if he had bravely left it alone, believingly left it in God's hands, it would have been infinitely better for him. Do not do what every whim or fancy in your poor brain urges you to do! Do not run before you are sent. They who run before God's cloud will have to come back again! Where Scripture is silent, you be silent! If there is no command, you had better wait till you can find some guidance. Blunder not on with a headlong anxiety lest you tumble into the ditch! "Whatever He says to you," do that. But until He speaks, sit still.

I think that our own experience goes to show us that our highest wisdom, our very best prosperity, will lie in our cautiously keeping behind Christ and never running before Him, never forcing His hand, never tempting Him as they did who tempted God in the wilderness—prescribing to Him to do this or that (see Numbers 14:22)—but, in holy, humble obedience, taking these words as our life motto henceforth, "Whatever He says to you, do it." True obedience is not always seen in what we do or do not do, but it is manifest in the perfect submission to the will of God—and the strong resolve that saturates the spirit through and through that what He bids us, we will do! My soul, be patient before God and wait until you know His bidding!

CHARLES SPURGEON

Nearby stood six stone water jars . . . each holding from twenty to thirty gallons. Jesus said to the servants, "Fill the jars with water"; so they filled them to the brim. Then he told them, "Now draw some out and take it to the master of the banquet." They did so, and the master of the banquet tasted the water that had been turned into wine. He did not realize where it had come from, though the servants . . . knew.

John 2:6–9

Notice how simple and unostentatious this miracle was. One might have expected that when the great Lord of all came here in human form He would inaugurate His miraculous career by summoning the scribes and Pharisees at least, if not kings and princes of the earth, to see the marks of His calling and the guarantees of His commission; gathering them all together to work some miracle before them, as Moses did before Pharaoh, that they might be convinced of His messiahship. He does nothing of the kind. He goes to a simple wedding, and there in the simplest and most natural way displays His glory. He does not call for the master of the feast, or for the bridegroom, or for any of the guests and begin to say, "You clearly perceive that your wine is all gone. Now, I am about to show you a great marvel, to turn water into wine." No, He does it quietly with the servants, using only water and the ordinary jars, making no fuss or parade. He works the miracle in the most commonplace and natural style; and that is just the style of Jesus. He could have hyped it by making it mysterious, theatrical, and sensational; but, being a genuine miracle, it is done just as nearly after the course of nature as the supernatural can go. He takes water, which naturally flows through roots into clusters with reddish juice and is then made into wine, and speeds up the process of His providence. He does it so smoothly that only the servants are aware of what has happened.

Now, whenever you try to serve Jesus Christ, do not make a fuss about it, because He never made a fuss about what He did, even when He was doing amazing miracles. If you want to do a good thing, go and do it as naturally as you can. Be simplehearted and simpleminded. Be yourself. Do not be affected in your godliness, as if you were going to walk to heaven on stilts. Walk on your own feet, and bring your faith to your own door and to your own kitchen. If you have a grand work to do, do it with that genuine simplicity that is next akin to sublimity. Nothing but simple naturalness has about it a genuine beauty; and such a beauty there is about this miracle of the Savior.

CHARLES SPURGEON

Jesus said to them, "Fill the waterpots with water." And they filled them up to the brim.

John 2:7 NKJV

As a general rule, when Christ is about to bestow a blessing, He challenges men's obedience by first giving a command, which is not to be questioned but to be obeyed. Christ says, "Fill the waterpots with *water*," though what you need is wine! Christ sees a connection between the water and the wine, though you do not. He has a reason for the pots being filled with water, which reason, as yet, you do not know—it is not yours to ask an explanation, but to yield obedience! You are to just do what Jesus bids you, as He bids you, how He bids you, and because He bids you! And you shall find that in your obedience there is a great reward.

I know that sometimes the path of obedience seems as if it could not lead to the desired result. We want to be doing something more, as if we could, and thereby complete our design more easily and directly. For instance, I know that many a troubled conscience thinks that simply to believe in Jesus for eternal life is too little a thing. The deceitful heart suggests it would be more effectual if certain works were added to it. Jesus simply commands, "Believe." It does appear to be too little a thing to be done, but when Jesus Christ is about to give a blessing, He issues a command that is not to be questioned. If you add something to believing, you will not be established.

In the service of Christ, use such abilities as you have. Jesus used what He found ready to His hand—the waterpots and water. Our Lord is accustomed to employing His own people and such abilities as they have rather than angels or a novel class of beings created fresh for the purpose. If you have no golden chalice, fill your earthen vessel. If you cannot consider yourself to be a vessel of rarest workmanship in silver, it does not matter—fill the vessel that you have. If you cannot, with Elijah, bring fire from heaven, and if you cannot work miracles with the apostles, do what you can! If you have no silver and gold, let such as you have be dedicated to Christ. Bring water at His bidding, and it will be better than wine! The most common gifts can be made to serve Christ's purpose. Just as He took a few loaves and fishes and fed the crowd with them, so will He take your waterpots and the water and do His winemaking!

CHARLES SPURGEON

The master of the banquet tasted the water that had been turned into wine. He did not realize where it had come from, though the servants who had drawn the water knew.

John 2:9

Mary expected that her son would, by majesty of power, appeal to the wedding guests and arouse their enthusiasm for Him. How far that was from our Lord's thoughts may be well seen in the fact that the miracle was not noticed even by the master of the banquet. So quietly was it done, so entirely concealed, as it were, in the two simple ordered acts, the filling of the water jars with water and the drawing of it out again, as to make it manifest that it was done for the sake of serving them. He did not do it even for the display of His goodness, but to be good. This alone could show His Father's goodness and glory. It was done because here was an opportunity in which all circumstances combined with the bodily presence of the powerful and the prayer of his mother to render it fit that the love of His heart should go forth in giving His merrymaking brothers and sisters more and better wine to drink.

And herein we find another point in which this miracle of Jesus resembles the working of His Father. For God ministers to us so gently, so secretly, as it were, with such a quiet, tender, loving absence of display, that men often drink of His wine, as these wedding guests drank, without knowing whence it comes—without thinking that the Giver is beside them, yes, in their very hearts. For God will not compel the adoration of men: it would be but idol worship that would bring to His altars. He will rouse in men a sense of need, which shall grow at length into a longing; He will make them feel after Him, until by their search becoming able to behold Him, He may at length reveal to them the glory of their Father. He works silently—keeps quiet behind His works, as it were, that He may truly reveal himself in the right time. John says that Jesus thus "revealed his glory; and his disciples believed in him" (v. 11). I doubt if any except His disciples knew of the miracle; or of those others who might see or hear of it, if any believed in Him because of it. It is possible to see a miracle and not believe in it; while many of those who saw a miracle of our Lord believed in the miracle, and yet did not believe in Him.

George MacDonald

*What Jesus did here in Cana of Galilee was the first of
the signs through which he revealed his glory; and his
disciples believed in him.*

John 2:11

What a tremendous contrast there is between the simple gladness of the rustic village wedding and the tremendous scene of the temptation in the wilderness that had preceded it only by a few days! What a contrast between the sublime heights of John's preceding chapter to this quaint incident that opens the ministry! What a contrast between the rigid asceticism of John the Baptist and the Son of Man, who enters freely and cheerfully into the common joys and relationships of human nature! How unlike the scene at the marriage feast must have been to the anticipation of the half-dozen disciples who had gathered around Him, all tingling with expectation as to what would be the first of His messianic power! The last thing they would have dreamed of would have been to find Him in the humble home in Cana of Galilee.

Let us learn the lesson that all life is the region of His kingdom; that the sphere of His rule is everything that a man can do or feel. Let us refuse that division of life that separates the sacred and secular. Jesus protests against the notion that religion has to do with another world rather than with this one. He protests against any narrowing conception of His work that would remove from its influence anything that touches our humanity. Let us learn that where His footsteps have trod is hallowed ground. If a prince shares for a few moments in the festivities of his gathered people, how magnificent the feast seems! Yet we have had our King in the midst of all our family life, in the midst of all our common duties; therefore are they consecrated. Let us learn that all things done with the consciousness of His presence are sacred. He has hallowed every corner of human life by His presence; and the consecration, like some spicy and perennial perfume, lingers for us yet in the otherwise scentless air of daily life, if we follow His footsteps.

Sacredness is not singularity. There is no need to withdraw from any region of human activity and human interest in order to develop the whitest saintliness, the most Christlike purity. The saint is to be in the world, but not of it; like the Master, who went straight from the wilderness and its temptations to the homey gladness of the rustic marriage.

ALEXANDER MACLAREN

This beginning of signs Jesus did in Cana of Galilee, and manifested His glory; and His disciples believed in Him.

John 2:11 NKJV

It was "the beginning of signs," and the first is the keynote for the rest; happy are we that the first miracle is full of blessing! The mission of Jesus is a happy one and so it opens at a marriage feast. It is intended to bring joy and gladness to heavy hearts, and so it begins with a deed of royal bounty. All our Lord's actions toward men are full of royal benevolence and grace.

All our Lord's miracles were worked to meet a need. The wine had run out at the wedding feast, and our Lord had come in at the time of the pinch, when the bridegroom would have been made embarrassed. That need was a great blessing. If there had been sufficient wine for the feast, Jesus would not have worked this miracle and they would never have tasted this purest and best of wines! It is a blessed need that makes room for Jesus to come in with miracles of love. It is good to run short that we may be driven to the Lord by our necessity, for He will more than supply it. If your needs stand before you like huge empty waterpots, or if your soul is as full of grief as those same pots were filled with water up to the brim, Jesus can, by His sweet will, turn all the water into wine, the sighing into singing! Be glad to be very weak that the power of God may rest upon you! He has an eye to our failures and needs, and He makes our distress the platform upon which He manifests His glory by supplying all our needs.

Jesus Christ will come and visit such as you are! He is willing to go to common men's houses even when they have a feast going on. See how He is able to bless human joy! You think, perhaps, that you will go to Jesus next time you are in sorrow, but come to Him at once, while you are in joy. You who are getting on in business, you who rejoice over a newborn child, you who are lately married, you who have moved into a new house: come to Jesus in your joy and ask Him to raise your happiness to a higher degree and quality and elevate it till it touches the joy of the Lord! Jesus is able to raise you from what you now are into something better, fuller, grander, nobler, and holier! May He do it now! Believe in Him and it shall be done!

CHARLES SPURGEON

When it was almost time for the Jewish Passover, Jesus
went up to Jerusalem. In the temple courts he found
people selling cattle, sheep and doves, and others sitting
at tables exchanging money. So he made a whip out of
cords, and drove all from the temple courts, both sheep
and cattle; he scattered the coins of the money changers
and overturned their tables.

John 2:13–15

The abuse in the temple had many practical grounds on which it could be defended. It was convenient both to buy sacrifices on the spot as well as exchange foreign money. It was profitable for the sellers, and no doubt to the priests, who were probably silent partners in the matter and rented out the space on which the stalls stood. And so, being convenient for all and profitable to many, the thing became a recognized institution, and no one thought of any incongruity in it until this young Nazarene felt a flash of zeal for the sanctity of His Father's house consuming Him.

This was the first public appearance of Jesus before His nation as Messiah. He inaugurates His work by a claim—by an act of authority—to be the King of Israel and the Lord of the temple. If we recall the words from the last prophet, in which Malachi says that "the messenger of the covenant . . . will come . . . he will purify the Levites" (3:1, 3), we get the significance of the incident. It is His solemn, authoritative claiming to be God's Messenger, the Messiah long foretold.

We see in this incident a singular manifestation of Christ's unique power. How did it come about that all these despicable hucksters had not a word to say and did not lift a finger in opposition, or that the temple guard offered no resistance and did not try to stop the unruly disturbance, or that the very officials, when they came to question Him, had nothing harsher to say than "What sign can you show us to prove your authority to do all this?" (John 2:18)? The answer is simple: a man ablaze with holy zeal, and having a secret ally in the hearts of those whom He rebukes, will awe a crowd even if he does not change them. But that is not the full explanation. I see with it an overwhelming impression of His personal majesty, and perhaps some revelation of that hidden glory that swam up to the surface on the Mount of Transfiguration (see Mark 9:2) that bowed all these men before Him like reeds before the wind. And though there was no recognition of His claim, there was something in the Claimant that forbade resistance.

ALEXANDER MACLAREN

To those who sold doves he said, "Get these out of here!
Stop turning my Father's house into a market!" His dis-
ciples remembered that it is written: "Zeal for your house
will consume me."

John 2:16–17

What a revelation of Christ's capacity for righteous indignation, of being consumed with holy zeal for the sanctity of God. We may well take the lesson from this that there is no love worthy of a perfect spirit in which there does not lie dormant a capacity for wrath, and that Christ himself would not have been the Joy-Bringer of the wedding feast unless, side by side, there had rested in Him the power of holy indignation and, if need be, of stern rebuke. We must retain our comprehension of His anger if we are not to damage our comprehension of His love. There is no wrath like the wrath of the Lamb. Christ with a whip of cords in His hand is a revelation that this generation, with its exaggerated sentimentalism, shrinking from the very notion of a divine judgment based upon eternal antagonism between good and evil, most sorely needs.

We should not think that Christ would behave any differently today if He were to visit our churches. Abuses creep in gradually, and they need continual watchfulness if they are not to assume the mastery. Men who are paid for preaching have a sore temptation to preach for pay. There must be money to finance the outward business of the house of God, but what about people who run their churches as they run businesses? What about people whose test of the prosperity of a Christian community is its balance sheet? What about the people who serve churches for the sake of what they can get from them? Jesus will come in some tremendous and manifest fashion and overthrow the money changers' tables. If He had not thus come, over and over again, to His church, Christian men would have killed Christianity long ago.

The same is true of our own lives. We so allow the noise and pollution of the market to press in that we no longer value the inner sanctuary. The only way to keep the world out of my heart is to have Christ filling it. If we ask Him, He will come to us. And if He has the whip in His hand, welcome Him anyway. When He enters, it will be like the rising of the sun, when all the beasts of the forest slink away to their dark dens. Jesus will enter in, and by His entrance purify our inner life and make us the glorious temples of the living God.

ALEXANDER MACLAREN

Jesus answered them, "Destroy this temple, and I will raise it again in three days." But the temple he had spoken of was his body.

John 2:19, 21

Notice the marvelous and unique consciousness of our Lord as to His own dignity and nature. Christ, in inmost reality, is all that the temple was, though it was but a poor symbol. In the temple had dwelt, though no longer at the time when He was speaking, a material and symbolical brightness, the expression of something which, for lack of a better name, we call "the presence of God." But what was that fire that flashed between the cherubim that brooded over the mercy seat with a light as shimmering and radiant as the light of love and of life—that compared to the glory, molded in meekness and clothed in gentleness, merciful and hospitable and inviting—a tempered flame on which the poorest, blind eyes could look and not wince—from the face and character of Jesus Christ the Lord? He is greater than the temple, for in Him, not in symbol but in reality, dwelt and dwells the fullness of that unnamable Being whom we call Father and God.

And not only does the fullness abide, but in Him the infinite abyss and closed sea of divine nature has an outlet and becomes a "river of water of life." And as the ancient name of that temple was "the tent of meeting," the place where Israel and God, in symbolical and ceremonial form, met together, so in inmost reality, in Christ's nature, manhood and divinity cohere and unite, and in Him all of us—the weak, the broken, the sinful, the rebellious—may meet our Father.

Notice also Christ's distinct prevision of how His life was going to end. He had not gone half a dozen steps in His public career but that our Lord beheld and accepted His cross. Its shadow fell upon His path from the beginning, because the cross was the purpose for which He came. All His life long, with the cross distinctly before Him, He journeyed toward it of His own loving will. Every step He took on earth's flinty roads, taken with bleeding and pure feet, He took knowing where He was going. Therefore, let us love Him with a love as persistent as was His own, who willed to be born and live because He had resolved to die for every man. He is the Lord of the temple as well as the Temple. Worship before Him, the Lord of heaven, with all your heart and with all your confidence, trust, and love forevermore!

ALEXANDER MACLAREN

But Jesus would not entrust himself to them, for he knew all people.

John 2:24

The same word that is translated *faith*, or *belief*, when used in a saving sense, is here translated *entrust*. Jesus did not give himself over into their power or keeping, because He could see into their hearts and He knew what they would do with Him if He did.

From this, we see the apostolic idea of faith. Faith is the committal, the giving over of the soul and of the whole being to God. It is risking myself (if we may use such a term when there is no risk about it), my all, for this life and for the next, on the truthfulness and goodness of God, and daring to live and act contrary to everyone around me, as if all that God has said is absolutely true!

Faith, all through the Scriptures, is represented as a voluntary thing. It is a something you can exercise or not, or God must have been unjust to have made a man's everlasting salvation or damnation to depend on what you have no power to do. You have power over your will. You can say, "Here I am, Lord, troubled on this or that matter, but I refuse to wait until I can clear up all these difficulties. I will take my stand on your declaration, and I will pledge myself to follow you and to do your will as you reveal it to me." If you do that, God will send you light. He will bring you into a large place and flood your soul with His light, and those doubts, like birds of prey, will take their flight forever. But it must be a voluntary commitment of your heart to Him.

God wants your heart. Then He will enlighten your intellect. He wants you to come and take your stand alongside His throne and the cross of His Son, and commit yourself wholly and forever into His hands. I never knew a person come to that commitment—and I have seen the most desperate of people—who did not soon get flooded with light. You may bring Him your gifts and your head knowledge and your doctrines and your formal services, or whatever else you like, but He will not accept them. The head can believe facts while the heart remains in unrighteousness, in hypocritical professions and outward performances. But it is only with the heart that we believe unto righteousness. Bring your heart then, and the Holy Spirit will help you commit it to God. Come and commit yourself. Trust Him.

CATHERINE BOOTH

Now there was a Pharisee, a man named Nicodemus
who was a member of the Jewish ruling council. He
came to Jesus at night and said, "Rabbi, we know you
are a teacher who has come from God."

John 3:1–2

Nicodemus was a man who held an official position in the ruling council of the nation, to which the Romans had left some considerable shadow of power in religious matters. He chose the night because he could not compromise himself in the eyes of his fellow rulers, half-ashamed and wholly afraid of speaking out the conviction that was working in his heart. There is always something wrong with any conviction about Jesus Christ that lets itself be huddled up in secret. The true apprehension of Jesus is like a fire in a man's bones that forces him to speak. If Christians can be silent, there is something dreadfully wrong with their Christianity. If they do not regard Jesus Christ in such a way as to compel them to stand out in the world and say, "Whatever anyone says or thinks about it, I am Christ's man," then be sure that they do not yet know Him as they should.

"Rabbi, we know . . ." Nicodemus gives Jesus Christ a certificate, duly signed and sealed by rabbinical authority. He evidently thinks that it is no small matter that he and some of his fellows should be disposed to look with favor upon this new teacher. And so he comes, if not patronizing the young man, at all events extremely conscious of his own condescension in recognizing Him this way. Yes, they "knew" when He had not begun to tread upon their entitlements or drive His spear through their traditional professions of orthodoxy and scrupulous, erroneous reasonings. But when He stepped on their toes, when He ripped up their pretensions, when He antagonized their formalism and traditionalism, they did not know where He came from. And there are many of us who are very polite to Christ as long as He does not interfere with us, but who begin to doubt His authority when He begins to rebuke our sins.

The man who says, "We know," and then proceeds to tell Christ the ground upon which He is accepted by him, is not in a position to draw near to the Savior. The religionist's confession has the ring of complacency, whereas, "Jesus! Have mercy upon me!" wins the Master's heart. Let us beware lest our knowledge stand in our way of knowing the One who came from God to rescue us from our sins.

ALEXANDER MACLAREN

He came to Jesus at night and said, "Rabbi, we know that you are a teacher who has come from God. For no one could perform the signs you are doing if God were not with him."

John 3:2

Nicodemus was wise in coming to Christ, but he came on the wrong lines and for the wrong purpose. Jesus Christ does not want to talk about miracles as credentials for His ministry. The miracles are but the dust of His feet. He wants to talk upon a greater subject. He will not discuss with any man the miracles. We have begun by thinking that if we could understand the miracles, we could understand the cross, and so we begin a study of the miracles. Christ has nothing to say to such false thinking. He says, in effect, "If you will come and ask me about inward, spiritual, and vital subjects, I will stay with you till the rising of the sun."

If we come to Christ for the wrong purpose, we get nothing from Him but that which dazzles and bewilders us, so that the mind is lost in a new perplexity. Thus we see how possible it is to be near and yet far. Nicodemus may have been a master in Jewish circles, but he lacked spiritual insight. Literal learning there was in abundance, but he was blind. It is the heart that sees; it is love that pierces the veil. Who was it who saw the person on the shore and said, "It is the Lord!"? Was it Peter? Peter saw nothing until it was straight before him. It was John, the disciple of love, who said, "It is the Lord!" (John 21:7). Love sees clearest, furthest, and best. If we have not love, we do not know God, or Christ, or the cross, or anything Christian. What is needed to understand Christ is spiritual insight.

Many men suffer from looking for the wrong thing. They are looking for historical arguments, powerful demonstrations, and theological theories. They will be disappointed with Christ. He will have nothing but pureness of soul, love of heart, a desire after the very spirit of childhood. Where He sees these things, there He abides, and He makes the heart burn with new love and gives the eyes the delight of continually changing and brightening vision.

Lord, make us like little children; enable us to look for the right things, namely, the revelation of your heart, your love, your purpose of redemption. Deliver us from the temptation of wanting to understand miracles, signs, wonders, and impossibilities; and then when we get near the top we shall be able to look down and see the miracles as very little things; help us, Lord, and give us vision of soul. Spiritual insight can only come from spiritual life.

JOSEPH PARKER

Jesus replied, "Very truly I tell you, no one can see the kingdom of God unless they are born again."

John 3:3

Nicodemus was a member of the Jewish ruling council, the Sanhedrin, but was apparently destitute of that spiritual insight that sees the possibility of the very stones being raised up as children of Abraham (see Matthew 3:9)—that sensitive and hopeful vision that sees everywhere the throbbings of an inner life and believes instantly in every word that even remotely hints at immortality. He was a literalist who never could have written the book of Revelation—seals and trumpets were not for men such as Nicodemus. He who had been convinced by the miracle was now astounded by the metaphor. The answer of Jesus Christ was strikingly consistent with His whole method of teaching; the strangeness of His language excited attention, provoked thought, sometimes awakened controversy, and so, through a process of troubled inquiry and anxious strife, men often entered into the mystery of Christ. It is a hard way, but those who travel it come into great strength.

Nicodemus had been an attentive observer of the public life of Jesus Christ. He was one of those people who always set their course upon facts; they never throw themselves completely upon great principles or risk themselves upon the strength of an argument; they only believe history, they never make it. The facts led him to reason that Jesus had come from God because of the miracles He did. Can the worker have found his way to omnipotence except through omniscience? Yet Jesus returned an answer that Nicodemus must be born again. The subject that Nicodemus introduced was miracles; the subject that Jesus Christ introduced was new life. Jesus showed that the miracles were symbolic and illustrative of one great miracle—namely, the second birth of men and women who had fallen into sin.

Jesus taught Nicodemus that unless every man himself became the subject of a miracle—the miracle of regeneration—his belief in other miracles would not admit him into the kingdom of heaven. Other miracles were to be looked at; this miracle was to be felt. Other miracles were material; this one was moral. Other miracles give new views; this miracle gives new life. This miracle of regeneration is the only explanation of all other miracles; and until a man has undergone its power, the other miracles may possibly be stumbling blocks to his reason. The new birth is the only way into the kingdom of God.

JOSEPH PARKER

*Jesus replied, "Very truly I tell you, no one can see the
kingdom of God unless they are born again." "How
can someone be born when they are old?" Nicodemus
asked. "Surely they cannot enter a second time into their
mother's womb to be born!" Jesus answered, "Very truly
I tell you, no one can enter the kingdom of God unless
they are born of water and the Spirit."*

John 3:3–5

Here we are told that men are born of the Spirit, or born anew through the Holy Spirit's power. Exactly the same truth is set forth in Titus 3:5, "He saved us, not because of righteous things we had done, but because of his mercy. He saved us through the washing of rebirth and renewal by the Holy Spirit." It is the work of the Holy Spirit to renew men, to make men anew, to regenerate men.

What is regeneration? "God, who is rich in mercy, made us alive with Christ even when we were dead in transgressions" (Ephesians 2:4–5). Regeneration is the impartation of life to men who are morally and spiritually dead because of their trespasses and sins. Every man, woman, and child was born into this world spiritually dead. We are by nature moral and spiritual corpses. In regeneration, the Holy Spirit imparts to us His own life.

Of course, the Word of God is the instrument that the Holy Spirit uses in imparting life: "For you have been born again, not of perishable seed, but of imperishable, through the living and enduring word of God" (1 Peter 1:23). The mere written Word will not produce the new birth, no matter how faithfully preached or taught, unless the Spirit of God makes it a living thing in the hearts of those to whom it is given. This comes out plainly in 2 Corinthians 3:6: "The letter kills, but the Spirit gives life." What did Paul mean? He had just contrasted the Word of God written on parchment with pen and ink to when it is written by the Spirit of God on the hearts of men. The Word written or printed in a book kills, brings condemnation and death; but that Word written by the Spirit in our hearts brings life. It is only the Holy Spirit who can take the heart of an individual and write the Word of God into it, making that person alive.

R. A. TORREY

"How can someone be born when they are old?" Nico-
demus asked. "Surely they cannot enter a second time
into their mother's womb to be born!"

John 3:4

Nicodemus seems to have come to the Savior with a general notion of his obligation to serve God, and a desire to do so. I daresay he thought he was a good man, who wanted to be a better one. There was the same dissatisfaction, the same disquiet in his soul that there is in every human soul until it finds God, and which nothing else can ever satisfy. God has made us for himself, and until we find the purpose for our being, we can never rest. We are like Noah's dove, wandering about and finding nowhere to rest. It was just so with Nicodemus. He wanted something. He had heard of this Teacher, had probably heard Him speak, and felt He was a teacher come from God. Like a great many other Nicodemuses since, he felt the words of the Teacher to be true, but he had a great many ifs and buts about it. So he sought a private discussion, no doubt thinking that he could bring out his own personal difficulties and get more light in that way.

But Jesus stopped Nicodemus right in the middle of his introduction with a doctrine that utterly confounded him; it was so adverse to all his preconceived notions and so utterly beyond any of his present conceptions. One can imagine Nicodemus fairly gasping as he looks at this wonderful doctrine, for he seems to have comprehended its magnitude, its importance, and its definiteness a great deal better than most people. But he stumbles at the difficulty and begins immediately, as people do now, to ask, "How can this be?" The Savior does not retract or explain it away, but rather says, in effect, "Do not be surprised. I admit there are difficulties. You cannot understand, and I cannot explain how this great spiritual change is wrought. But I tell you that it must take place for anyone who wants to be in my kingdom."

Such is the nature of Jesus' kingdom. It is a spiritual kingdom, and its subjects are spiritual people, energized by holy motives, holy desires, and purposes. We should not marvel at this doctrine or other biblical doctrines because we cannot comprehend them. We count the natural wind as a great mystery, yet we know the wind blows because we see its results and feel its power. It is just so with the operations of the Spirit: we see His results and feel His power and know that we are under His influence.

CATHERINE BOOTH

Jesus answered, "Very truly I tell you, no one can enter the kingdom of God unless they are born of water and the Spirit."

John 3:5

This, I feel sure, is not the first time that Jesus of Nazareth and Nicodemus of Jerusalem have met. The sudden and direct way in which our Lord receives the cautious ruler's diplomatic certificates and civilities, and every single word of the whole subsequent conversation, all point unmistakably to some previous meeting. Perhaps he had been to the Jordan and witnessed the baptism of Jesus but had been unable to enter in himself. Nicodemus saw the pearl, and knew something of the value of it, but he could not make up his mind to sell all he possessed so as to pay the price. He did not feel free and able to act as his conscience told him he should immediately act. He simply could not extricate himself from the duties, the responsibilities, and the entanglements of his Pharisaic office. And yet he could not get away from the question of who and what Jesus of Nazareth was, or might turn out to be. So he slipped out of the city that night and determined to see in secret this mysterious man who had perplexed his mind.

It did not take long for the ruler's breath to be taken away by Jesus' piercing words: "No one can enter the kingdom of God unless they are born of water and the Spirit." The divine doctrine sliced down into Nicodemus's self-deceiving heart and cut it open to the daylight. Water clearly pointed to a baptism of repentance, but Nicodemus had not been willing. He stood ready for his regeneration, and for his first entrance into the kingdom of heaven, and he was within one short step of its gate, but that step was far too hard for Nicodemus to take. "No," our Lord essentially said to Nicodemus, "we do not need to talk about my mighty works. You know your first duty in this whole matter, and you refused. To enter the kingdom you must join the ranks of the sinners and confess your sins."

And yet Jesus lovingly continues to press Nicodemus to come to the light, and his history shows that Jesus was effective (see John 19:39). Perhaps you have been a friend of truth by night as well. When God in His goodness gives yet another offer, seize it on the spot. Like Nicodemus, take your stand with Jesus in your own Sanhedrin. The whole seventy council members will turn against you, but what of it? What place will they have when Jesus is suddenly revealed in all His glory at His second coming?

ALEXANDER WHYTE

"You should not be surprised at my saying, 'You must be born again.'"

John 3:7

We need not wonder that there are some mysteries in our holy faith, for there are mysteries everywhere. In nature, and in our own bodies, there are ten thousand things we do not understand. We observe that the wind blows; we know it blows, for we feel it, but where it comes from or where it goes to we do not know. It is not remarkable, therefore, that there should be mysteries in the kingdom of God.

Yet Christ, by using the metaphor of the wind, shows us that though the mystery is a matter of fact, it can be turned to practical account, for though we do not understand the wind, we can make use of it. The wind, though not understood, has been employed in a thousand ways in the service of man. Similarly, it is altogether beyond my powers to explain the mystery of the new birth, how the Spirit of God transforms a sinner into a new creature in Christ Jesus. But keep in mind that it was the King of kings who said, "You must be born again." This is a truth that cannot be put aside, whether we feel we understand it or not.

But what is it to be born again? While I cannot explain its mystery, I can explain its results. I know that the Holy Spirit usually operates through the Word, through the proclamation of the truth of the gospel. So far as we know, He works upon the mind according to the laws of the mind by first illuminating the understanding. He then influences the will and changes the affection, but over and above all that we can describe there is a marvelous power that He exerts, which must remain among the inscrutable mysteries of this finite state. By this power, such a wondrous effect is produced that a man becomes a new man as much as if he had been born again in an altogether higher sphere. A new nature is created within him, a nature that hates what the old nature loved and loves what the old nature hated, a nature akin to the nature of God. That is a wonderful phrase in Peter's second epistle: "that through them you may participate in the divine nature" (2 Peter 1:4). In his first epistle, he writes that "you have been born again, not of perishable seed, but of imperishable, through the living and enduring word of God" (1 Peter 1:23). The new birth is the creation within us of that new, divine, immortal life that is a true miracle of the Spirit of God.

CHARLES SPURGEON

"Do not marvel that I said to you, 'You must be born again.'"

John 3:7 NKJV

While a man is in a mere natural state, before he is born of God, he has, in a spiritual sense, eyes and sees not; he has ears, but hears not. His spiritual senses are all locked up: he is in the same condition as if he did not have them. Hence he has no communion with God. He has no true knowledge of the things of God, either of spiritual or eternal things; therefore, though he is a living man, he is spiritually dead. But as soon as he is born of God, there is a total change in all these particulars. The "eyes of your understanding" are opened (Ephesians 1:18 NKJV). His ears being opened, he is now capable of hearing the inward voice of God, saying, "Be of good cheer; your sins are forgiven" (Matthew 9:2 NKJV). He is conscious of "the peace of God, which surpasses all understanding" (Philippians 4:7 NKJV). He many times feels such a joy in God as is "inexpressible and full of glory" (1 Peter 1:8 NKJV). He knows "the love of God has been poured out in our hearts by the Holy Spirit" (Romans 5:5 NKJV), and all his spiritual senses are then exercised to discern spiritual good and evil. He is alive to God through Jesus Christ. Grace is descending into his heart, and prayer and praise are ascending to heaven. And by this communion between God and man, this fellowship with the Father and the Son, the life of God in the soul is sustained; and the child of God grows up, till he comes "to the measure of the stature of the fullness of Christ" (Ephesians 4:13 NKJV).

The nature of the new birth is that great change that God works in the soul when He brings it into life; when He raises it from the death of sin to the life of righteousness. It is the change wrought in the whole soul by the almighty Spirit of God when it is created anew in Christ Jesus, when it is "renewed in knowledge according to the image of Him who created him" (Colossians 3:10 NKJV), when the love of the world is changed into the love of God; pride into humility; passion into meekness; hatred, envy, malice, into a sincere, tender, unselfish love for all mankind. In a word, it is that change whereby the earthly, sensual, devilish mind is turned into the "mind . . . which was also in Christ Jesus" (Philippians 2:5 NKJV). "So is everyone who is born of the Spirit" (John 3:8 NKJV).

JOHN WESLEY

"The wind blows wherever it pleases. You hear its sound, but you cannot tell where it comes from or where it is going. So it is with everyone born of the Spirit."

John 3:8

The wind is air in motion and is material; but air is apparently more spiritual than any of the other elements, except fire, since it cannot be grasped by the hand or seen with the eye. It is certain that wind truly exists, for we hear its sound and observe its various effects. We may watch the clouds hastened along like the birds, but the wind that drives them is beyond our sight. We observe the waves aroused to fury in the tempest, but the breath that so excites them we cannot see. Hence the word becomes all the more excellent a figure of that mighty power—the Holy Spirit—of whose existence no person ever doubts who has come under His influence, but who nevertheless is not to be traced in His movements or seen as to His divine person, for He is mysterious, incomprehensible, and divine.

The Holy Spirit is absolutely free in His operations, but He is not arbitrary; He does as He wills, but His will is infallible wisdom. The wind, though we have no control over it, has a law of its own, and the Holy Spirit is a law unto himself. He does as He wills, but He wills to always do what is for the best. Moreover, we know with regard to the wind that there are certain places where you will almost always find a breeze: not here in the crowded city, or down in the valley shut in by the mountains, or on the distant steaming marsh; but lift up your eyes to the hills and mark how the breeze courses along the downs and sweeps the summits of the mountain ranges. In the morning and the evening, when the inland air is hot as an oven, gentle winds come to and from the sea and fan the fisherman's cheek. You may find places where the air seems always stagnant and men's hearts grow heavy amid the feverish calm, but there are elevated hillsides where life is easy, for the air exhilarates by its perpetual freshness. Mark this well: among God's saints, in the use of the means of grace, in private prayer, in communion with the Lord, you will find the wind that blows where it wills always in motion.

CHARLES SPURGEON

"The wind blows where it wishes, and you hear the sound of it, but cannot tell where it comes from and where it goes. So is everyone who is born of the Spirit."

John 3:8 NKJV

We hear the sound of the wind from the little whisper among the young soft leaves of the opening beeches in our woods, up to the hurricane that spreads devastation over hundreds of miles of the ocean. That voice, now a murmur, now a roar, is the only manifestation of the unseen force that sweeps around us. And if you are a Christian, your new life should be thus perceptible to others, in a variety of ways and in many degrees of intensity. You cannot show its roots; you are compelled to show its fruits. You cannot lay bare your spirit and say to the world, "Look! Here is the presence of divine life in me," but you can go among people and witness to the possession of it by the life you live. There are a great many church members from whom, if you were to listen ever so intently, you would not hear a sigh or a ripple. There is a dead calm: the "sound like the blowing of a violent wind . . . from heaven" (Acts 2:2) has died down; and there is nothing but a gradual swell upon the windless ocean. "The wind blows," and the "sound" is heard. The wind ceases, and there is a hideous silence. And that is the condition of many a person who has a name to live and is dead. Does anyone hear the whisper of that breath in your life? It is not for me to answer the question; it is for you to ask it and answer it for yourself.

Christians should be in the world, as the very breath of life in the midst of stagnation. When the Christian church first sprung into being, it did come into that corrupt, deadly marsh of ancient heathenism with healing on its wings and like fresh air from the pure hills into some fever-stricken district. Wherever there has been a new outburst, in the experience of individuals and churches, of that divine life, there has come, and the world has felt that there has come, a new force that breathes over the dry bones, and they live. Alas, that so frequently the church has ceased to perform its obvious purpose, to breathe on the slain that they may live (see Ezekiel 37:1–10).

The world does not know where the Christian life comes from. If you are a believer, you should bear in your character a certain indefinable something that will suggest to those around you that the secret of your life is divine. A Christian life should be the manifestation to the world of the supernatural.

ALEXANDER MACLAREN

"You are Israel's teacher," said Jesus, "and do you not understand these things?"

John 3:10

So many people, like Nicodemus, read only the letter of the Bible, and so are afraid the Bible may be taken from them. No man can take love from the heart, devotion from the soul, or trust from the spirit. You may steal a document, but you cannot steal a revelation. If we have only a theologian's Bible, it may be taken from us any day. If we have God revealed to the heart through the medium of the Bible, we are independent of all criticism, all hostility; we have a sanctuary into which we can retire and within whose walls we can be forever safe.

Even many Christians have hold of the wrong Bible; that is, they hold the Bible by the wrong end. They are constantly troubled by any assault that is made upon the sanctuary of revelation. They go to the Bible timidly, anxious when they discover that there is more than one theory about the first chapters of Genesis, or that some people doubt whether the serpent really spoke to Eve. These people live in gloom and apprehension, thinking that any criticism of the Bible is another attack of the devil.

I go to the Bible to see if the fresh air blows there, if there is some word to be spoken to my soul, if there is any touch that makes me alive again. Criticisms come and go regarding Scripture, but what is the inner, eternal, redeeming spirit of the Book? That man's Bible can never be taken from him; he has laid up riches where moth and rust do not consume, and where thieves do not break in and steal. That Bible is hidden in the heart; that revelation is an eternal treasure; the Spirit himself bears witness with our spirit that this is the very revelation of God. In this sense, the Bible asks only to be read—to be read patiently, thoroughly, sensitively, to see if it covers not the whole breadth of life, answering all its deepest questions, and breathing good news upon its brokenhearted repentance. Are you a teacher in Israel and seeking to bolster up some book simply because you are afraid that if its mechanical structure is altered its spirit will evaporate? This is not mastery; this is bondage. The Bible outlives all assailants and breathes its blessings upon awakening souls. It is because the spirit of the Book is the Spirit of God, because the message of the Book is a message of righteousness, atonement, reconciliation, spiritual purification, and the ultimate triumph of grace over sin.

CHARLES SPURGEON

"Just as Moses lifted up the snake in the wilderness, so the Son of Man must be lifted up, that everyone who believes may have eternal life in him."

John 3:14–15

The people of Israel in the wilderness, who spoke out against God and were attacked by the fiery serpents, are clear representatives of mankind under sin (see Numbers 21:4–9). Can you imagine the terror that spread through the camp from such a report? Can you picture their sufferings and contortions when the poison infected their veins, a hot fire running through every nerve and muscle of the person? How awful must have been the deaths! How much like the effects of sin! Fiery snakes, you are nothing when compared with fiery lust, fiery greed, fiery selfishness, or fiery jealousy. Snakes may inject poison into the blood, but sin permeates the soul with condemnation, shame, and corruption. When sin has had its perfect work and fully developed itself in a person's life, we have a picture that snake-bitten Israel would not set forth to us in all its horrors.

The remedy for the Israelites was a brazen serpent; and the remedy for sinners is Christ crucified. The raising of a brass snake may have been considered a ridiculous hope, impossible to bring healing, something to be despised, yet there was no other means of cure. And so the cross of Christ also does in its outward appearance seem to be the simplicity of simplicities, foolishness to the world, to be despised and rejected of men. But when you come to study and understand the marvelous plan of God's justice upheld, and man pardoned through the atoning blood of the cross, I say that not even the mighty intellect of God could have conceived a wiser plan than the wisdom of God displayed in Christ Jesus crucified.

What were the Israelites to do? What are sinners to do? The Israelites were to look; sinners are to believe. Can you see Moses lifting up the brass snake and marching through the camp boldly crying out, "Look, look, look!"? Can you conceive of one dying person after another glancing up and receiving miraculous healing? So it is for those who believe in Jesus! The devil may claim that you are shut out from grace, but Jesus says that whoever believes in Him—no matter how great their sin—will be saved. Your character may be as black as the darkest night, but Christ Jesus is your only merit. Jesus invites you to believe. Look to Him; look to Him and live.

CHARLES SPURGEON

". . . so the Son of Man must be lifted up."

John 3:14

Why *must* Jesus go to the cross? It was because of the requirements of the divine righteousness and the necessities of sinful men. And so Christ's was no martyr's death, like one who had to die as the penalty of the faithful carrying out of His duty. It was not the penalty that He paid for doing His work, but it was the work itself. Not that gracious life, nor His words of sweet wisdom, nor His acts of power, completed His task, but He came to give His life as a ransom for many.

Must is a hard word. It sounds like an unwelcome necessity. Was that the case? When He said those words, was He shrinking back? No! He must die because He would save us, and He would save us because He loved us. His loving obedience to God coincided with His pity for men; and not merely in obedience to the requirements of the divine righteousness, but in compassion for the necessities of sinners, necessity was laid upon Him. Nothing held Christ to the cross but His own desire to save us. Oh, if we think of that sweet life as having clear before it from the very first steps that grim end, how infinitely it gains in heartrending beauty! He *must* die for our sakes.

Thus Christ stands before us, the pattern for the only obedience that is worth calling so, the obedience that would be pain unless it was doing the work of God. Our faith is meant to make it a second nature, or, as I venture to call it, an instinct—a spontaneous, uncalculating, irrepressible desire—to be in fellowship with God and to be doing His will. That is the meaning of our Christianity. There is no obedience in reluctant obedience; forced service is slavery, not service. Christianity is given for the specific purpose that it may bring us so into touch with Jesus Christ that the mind that was in Him may be in us, and like Him, we find our very life's breath in doing the Father's will.

If my Christianity does not make me withdraw from what it forbids, and spring eagerly to what it commends, my Christianity is of very little use. Glad obedience is true obedience. When duty is delight, that delight will never become disgust, nor will joy pass away.

ALEXANDER MACLAREN

"For God so loved the world that he gave his one and only Son, that whoever believes in him shall not perish but have eternal life."

John 3:16

B efore Jesus Christ came into this world, almost no one ever dreamed of saying "God loves." Some of the Old Testament psalmists had glimpses of that truth and came near to expressing it, but among the foreign gods it was unknown. Once it was a new and almost incredible message, but we have grown accustomed to it. But if we try to think of what it means, the whole truth would flash up into fresh newness, and all the miseries and sorrows and perplexities of our lives would drive away down the wind, and we should be no more troubled with them. "God loves" is the greatest thing that can be said.

"God so loved the world." Now, when we speak of loving a number of individuals—the broader the stream, the shallower it is, is it not? The most intense patriot in England does not love her one ten-thousandth part as well as he loves his own little girl. We speak of wide generalities with our love, but God loves all because He loves each. Every person is isolated, getting as much of the love of God as if there was not another creature in the whole universe. It is very good to say He loves the world, but it is a great deal better to say what Paul said: "who loved me and gave himself for me" (Galatians 2:20).

Keep in mind that the world God loves is made up of sinful mankind, men separated from Him. The great and blessed truth taught here is that, however I may drag myself away from God, I cannot drive Him away from me, and that however little I may love or think about Him, it does not make one ounce of difference as to the fact that He loves me. I know if a man does not love Him back, God's love has to take shapes that it would not otherwise take, which may be inconvenient for the man. But though the shape may alter, the fact remains, and every sinner on earth has God's love resting upon him.

God not only sent His Son, but far more tenderly, wonderfully, heartbreakingly, God gave His one and only Son. There is no love that does not delight in giving, and there is no love that does not delight in depriving itself, in some fashion of what it gives. "God so loved"—so deeply, so purely, so perfectly—that He gives the gift of His Son to every soul in the world.

ALEXANDER MACLAREN

"For God so [greatly] loved and dearly prized the world, that He [even] gave His [One and] only begotten Son, so that whoever believes and trusts in Him [as Savior] shall not perish, but have eternal life."

John 3:16 AMP

M en who love much will give much, and you may usually measure the truth of love by its self-denials and sacrifices. The love that spares nothing, but spends itself to help and bless its object, is love indeed, and not the mere name of it. Little love forgets to bring water for the feet, but great love breaks its box of alabaster and lavishes its precious ointment (see Mark 14:3).

Consider, then, what this gift was that God gave. It was His one and only Son. None of us have ever had such a son to give. Ours are the sons of men; His was the Son of God. The Father gave His other self, one with himself. When the great God gave His Son, He gave God himself, for Jesus is not in His eternal nature less than God. When God gave God for us, He gave himself. What more could He give? God gave His all: He gave himself. Who can measure this love?

Could you give your son to die for your enemy? Yet God seemed to so love us that, to put it very strongly, He seemed to love us better than His only Son and did not spare Him that He might spare us. He sent Jesus to be afflicted with base slanders by scribes and Pharisees, to hunger and thirst amid poverty so dire that He had nowhere to lay His head, to be scourged and crowned with thorns, to hang on a criminal's cross, and then seemed to turn His face from Jesus as He died. Can you understand that love? I can well imagine you giving your son to a dangerous missionary cause, where he may die an honorable death, but could you think of parting with him to die a criminal's death? Oh, wondrous stretch of love, that Jesus Christ should die!

O that you may have faith to lay hold on Jesus, for so He will be yours. He is God's free gift to all receivers; a full Christ for empty sinners. Nothing is freer than a gift. Nothing more worth having than a gift that comes from the hand of God, as full of effectual power as ever it was. The fountain is eternal, but the stream from it is as fresh as when first the fountain was opened. There is no exhausting this gift. I call upon you from this point to admire the love of God because of His transcendent gift to us all.

CHARLES SPURGEON

"Whoever believes in him is not condemned."

John 3:18

You are aware that in our courts of law, a verdict of "not guilty" amounts to an acquittal, and the prisoner is immediately set free. So is it in the language of the gospel; a sentence of "not condemned" implies the justification of the sinner. It means that the believer in Christ receives now a present justification. Faith does not produce its fruits eventually, but now. We are today accepted in the Beloved, today pardoned from sin, today innocent in the sight of God. We are now forgiven; even now are our sins put away; even now we stand in the sight of God as though we had never been guilty. There is neither spot nor wrinkle remaining upon any believer in the matter of justification in the sight of the Judge of all the earth. Oh, ravishing, soul-transporting thought! There are some clusters of this vine that we shall not be able to gather until we go to heaven; but this is one of the first ripe clusters and may be plucked and eaten here.

Come, my soul, think of this. You are actually and effectually cleared from guilt. You are led out of your prison. You are delivered from the bondage of the law. You are freed from sin and can walk at liberty. The Savior's blood has secured your full emancipation. Once you were unable to see the Father's face, but you can see it now. You have access to the throne of grace and can speak with Him boldly and He with you. Once there was a fear of punishment, but you have been pardoned. All the love and the acceptance that a perfectly obedient being could have obtained of God, belong to you, because Christ was perfectly obedient on your behalf and has credited all His merits to your account!

Oh, that the Holy Spirit would enlarge our hearts, that we might draw sweetness out of these thoughts! There is no condemnation. Moreover, there never shall be any condemnation. The forgiveness is not partial but perfect. And it will last in eternity as well as in time. Today we stand clothed in the righteousness of Christ, and we shall wear this same wedding dress at the great wedding feast. Heaven and earth shall pass away, but this righteousness shall never grow old. Because Jesus is our righteousness, there will be no end to our righteousness, and of its perfection and of its beauty there shall be no end.

CHARLES SPURGEON

John answered and said, "A man can receive nothing unless it has been given to him from heaven."

John 3:27 NKJV

A dispute had arisen between John's disciples and the Jews about purifying (v. 25). We may suppose that John's disciples argued boldly that his baptism was superior to all the purifications of the Jews. It is likely that they had more zeal than discretion. The truths of God have often suffered by the brashness of those who have undertaken to defend them. That dispute was followed by a complaint that John's disciples made concerning Christ and His baptizing (v. 26). It is common for men, when they find themselves in the heat of contention, to extend their quarrel to others. They suggest that Christ's setting up a baptism of His own was a piece of presumption; as if John, having first set up this rite of baptizing, must have the monopoly of it. They suggest that it reflected ingratitude to John and conclude that it would be a total eclipse to John's baptism. Aiming at the monopoly of honor and respect has been in all ages the blight of the church, as also a vying of interests and a jealousy of rivalship and competition. We are mistaken if we think the excelling gifts and graces and labors of one are a diminution and belittling to another who has obtained mercy to be faithful; for the Spirit is a free agent, "distributing to each one individually as He wills" (1 Corinthians 12:11 NKJV).

John's disciples expected that he resented this matter as they did; but in his response, the first minister of the gospel (for so John was) is an excellent pattern to all believers to humble themselves and to exalt the Lord Jesus. John submits to the divine assignment and satisfies himself with that. Different roles of service are according to the direction of divine providence, different endowments according to the distribution of divine grace. We should not envy those who have a larger share of gifts than we have or move in a larger sphere of usefulness. John reminds his disciples that Jesus would not have thus excelled him except He had received it from heaven; shall they begrudge it? If God is pleased to give to others more ability and success than to us, shall we be displeased at it? John was ready to own that it was the free gift of heaven that made him a preacher, a prophet, a baptist: it was God who gave him the role he had toward the people; and, if now his role were to decline, God's will be done!

MATTHEW HENRY

"He must become greater; I must become less."

John 3:30

I have often wondered how John the Baptist, the forerunner of Jesus Christ, was able to be content with being no more than the forerunner. Why did he not leave behind the ministry of calling people to repentance and take up the ministry of reconciliation? When he said to his disciples, "Look, the Lamb of God," why did the Baptist not leave the Jordan and become a disciple and then an apostle of Jesus Christ? Well, to begin with, Jesus did not call John any more than He called His own brother James. John was a great man and a great preacher, but this was not his calling. It was as if he said to his disciples, "Go with Him. I must work at the Jordan and preach repentance, and He will teach you to preach pardon. I shall not live to see Gethsemane, Calvary, Olivet, and Pentecost, but you will. He must become greater; I must become less."

These last words were by far the very best thing the Baptist ever said or did for his disciples. I would rather have had the grace from God to say that than have been the greatest man who ever lived. And yet, when I come up close to it and look it in the face, the great utterance of the Baptist is not as unapproachable as it first appears. John had, after all, been told over and over again by his parents that he was the forerunner of the Messiah. During all those years alone in the searing heat of the wilderness, John thought about no one other than the Lamb of God. And thus it was when Jesus of Nazareth came to the Jordan to be baptized by John, the Baptist refused and said, "I need to be baptized by you" (Matthew 3:14). John fully recognized Jesus for who He was, and thus there was no tinge of envy in his voice. The most envious-minded man in the entire world does not envy a lion, or an eagle, or an angel. If Jesus had been simply a carpenter of Nazareth, who had suddenly become a popular preacher with all men, I would stand in awe if John had said all this about his own decreasing. But John's theology was crystal clear in stating, "Look, the Lamb of God," which makes his "I must become less" simply a true affirmation of his faith.

ALEXANDER WHYTE

"He must increase, but I must decrease."

John 3:30 NKJV

There is nothing that I know in biography anywhere more beautiful, more striking, than the contrast between the two halves of the character and demeanor of the Baptist: how, on the one side, he faces all men fearlessly and recognizes no superior, and how neither threats nor flatteries nor anything else will tempt him to lessen one inch of the claims for repentance that he urges; and, on the other hand, like some tall cedar, touched by the lightning's hand, he falls prone before Jesus Christ and says, "He must increase, and I must decrease." He is all boldness on one side, all submission and dependence on the other.

You remember how, in the face of many temptations to assert himself, he repeatedly denied that he was the Messiah, and how he stuck by that infinitely humble and beautiful saying, "I am the voice"—that is all. You remember how the whole nation "reasoned in their hearts about John, whether he was the Christ *or* not" (Luke 3:15 NKJV) and how his own disciples tried to get him to assert himself above Jesus (see John 3:26). And you remember the lovely answer that opened such depths of unexpected tenderness in the rough nature: "He who has the bride is the bridegroom; but the friend of the bridegroom, who stands and hears him, rejoices greatly because of the bridegroom's voice. Therefore this joy of mine is fulfilled" (John 3:29 NKJV).

And what conceptions of Jesus Christ had John that he thus bowed in his lofty calling before Him and softened his heart into submission? He knew Him to be "the Lamb of God who takes away the sin of the world" (John 1:29 NKJV). Therefore he fell before Him. Thomas à Kempis says somewhere, "He is truly great who is small in his own sight and thinks nothing of the giddy heights of worldly honor." You and I know far more of Jesus Christ than John the Baptist did. Do we bow ourselves before Him as he did? Let us begin with the recognition of the Lamb of God who takes away the world's sin, and with it ours. Let the thought of what He is and what He has done for us bow us in heartfelt submission. Let it shatter all dreams of our own importance or our own worth. The vision of the Lamb of God and that alone will crush in our hearts the serpent's eggs of self-esteem and self-regard.

ALEXANDER MACLAREN

But He needed to go through Samaria.

John 4:4 NKJV

I t is true that through Samaria was the nearest way from Judea to Galilee, yet Jesus might have gone around this region that was despised by the Jews. But He would not do so, for there were souls in Samaria who were to be blessed by His presence. He had a constraint upon Him, an inward impulse, and we quickly discover why.

With the eyes of faith, I can see Jesus Christ, very weary, sitting on the well. Let me look at Him awhile. I like the picture so; it seems to comfort me, for I perceive that He is waiting. There is a woman coming—a poor, fallen woman—and He is waiting to bless her. Jesus is weary, but He waits. That is just the attitude of my Lord toward you! He waits to be gracious. He is in no hurry. He patiently waits.

Jesus is also watching. I can see that He is turning His eyes toward the city gate. "She will be out very soon," He says to himself. "She must come here, and I know that she is coming." He is not looking around at the scenery. That is not the chief thing to Him, just now—He is looking for this wounded soul that is coming. Oh, my dear friend, Jesus is still waiting and watching for you!

At last Jesus spies out the person for whom He is waiting and watching. Here she comes! And now I perceive how willing He is. His heart seems to beat more quickly; His eyes are brighter than usual; He is not half as weary as He was. That woman was coming, and Christ was "all there," as we say. He was ready to speak the right words—a word in season to one who was weary—to speak the word of admonition, or of comfort, or of invitation. And He is "all here" at this moment. His heart is so full of love for you!

He was at the well, waiting and watching and willing. And though He was very weary, yet when the woman came to Him and she believed His message, He saved her right away. Yes, He will blot out your sins and put them away, even now, the moment you put your trust in Him! And even with His weary hands He will wipe away your transgressions. He is so sick of your wanderings that He will end them and receive you into His heart that you may never wander again!

CHARLES SPURGEON

Jacob's well was there, and Jesus, tired as he was from the journey, sat down by the well. It was about noon. When a Samaritan woman came to draw water, Jesus said to her, "Will you give me a drink?"

John 4:6–7

Try to see this for a moment through the woman's eyes. She comes down from her little village, up among the hillside cliffs, across the narrow, hot valley, beneath the sweltering sunshine, and she finds, in the midst of the lush vegetation around the ancient well, an evidently exhausted Jew looking in the well, but having no vessel by which to get any of its cool treasure. Jesus' request was the utterance of a felt and painful necessity. We see Jesus the true man, fully subject to physical necessities and dependent on kindly help just as we are. But why this humiliation? He who turned the water into wine could easily have found a miraculous way of quenching His thirst. Ah, the wonder is that the eternal Word chose the filial spirit of dependence on His Father, which forbids Him here to use other means of securing a drink that He so needed than the appeal for help from the Samaritan woman. He did not need to ask the woman to give it, but He chose to do so, and He chose to live this way His entire lifetime on earth. Let us always remember that the motive of this willing acceptance of the limitations and weaknesses of humanity is, in the deepest analysis, simply His love of us.

In that lonely Traveler, worn, exhausted, thirsty, craving for a drink of water from a stranger's hand, is set forth "the glory of the one and only Son . . . full of grace and truth" (John 1:14). A strange manifestation of divine glory this is! But if we understand that the glory of God is the lustrous light of His self-revealing love, perhaps we shall understand how, from that faint voice "Will you give me a drink?" that glory sounds forth more than in the thunders that rolled about the rocky peak of Sinai in the giving of the law. Strange to think that the same voice was also the voice that spoke to the sea, "Peace, be still," and there was calm; that said to demons, "Come out of him!" and they evacuated their fortress; that cast its command into the grave of Lazarus, and he came forth; and which one day all who are in the grave shall hear, and hearing shall rise to life eternal. May we join the Samaritan woman and allow His voice to continue to speak to us until He reveals himself as the reader of the secrets of the heart.

ALEXANDER MACLAREN

The Samaritan woman said to him, "You are a Jew and I am a Samaritan woman. How can you ask me for a drink?" (For Jews do not associate with Samaritans.)

John 4:9

Our Lord's first words to the woman were simply the expression of a real physical thirst. But it was nonetheless what the woman felt it to be, a strange overleaping of a barrier that towered very high. A Samaritan, a woman, a sinner, is the recipient of the first clear confession from Jesus Christ of His messiahship and dignity. She was right in her feeling that something lay behind His sweeping aside of the barriers and coming so close to her with His request. These two, the prejudices of race and the contempt for women, two of the crying evils of the world, were overpassed by our Lord as if He never saw them. And therein lay a symbol, if you like, but nonetheless a prophecy that will be fulfilled, of the universal adaptation and destination of the gospel, and its independence of all distinctions of race and sex, condition, moral character. "There is neither Jew nor Gentile, slave nor free, nor is there male and female, for you are all one in Christ Jesus" (Galatians 3:28).

If Jesus had been but a Jew, it was wonderful that He should talk to a Samaritan. But there is nothing in the character and life of Christ, as recorded in Scripture, more remarkable and plain than the entire absence of any racial peculiarities or of characteristics owing to His position in space and time. So unlike His nation was He that the very elite of His nation snarled at Him and said, "Aren't we right in saying that you are a Samaritan and demon-possessed?" (John 8:48). So unlike them was He that one feels that a character so vibrantly human to its core, and so impossible to explain from its surroundings, is inexplicable except on the basis of the New Testament theory that He is not a Jew or man only, but the Son of Man, the divine embodiment of the ideal humanity, whose dwelling was on earth, but His origin and home in the heart of God. Therefore, Jesus Christ is the world's Christ, your Christ, my Christ, everyone's Christ; the Tree of Life that stands in the midst of the garden, that all men may draw near to it and gather its fruit.

Answer His offer of the gift as this woman did: "Give me this water so that I won't get thirsty" (John 4:15); and He will put into your heart that indwelling spring of water welling up to eternal life!

ALEXANDER MACLAREN

Jesus answered her, "If you knew the gift of God and who it is that asks you for a drink, you would have asked him and he would have given you living water."

John 4:10

All through Scripture we hear the sound of this living water as it runs. If we look closely, we see that the living water is eternal life (v. 14), which becomes like a spring of water welling up within the life of the believer. "For with you is the fountain of life" (Psalm 36:9). And so, in the end, the gift of God is God himself. Nothing else will suffice for us. We need Him, and we need none but Him.

Jesus says that the water will "become in them"—something that we carry about with us in our hearts, inseparable from our being, free from all possibility of being torn away by violence or sorrow, or even being parted from us by death. What a man has outside of himself he only seems to have. Our only real possessions are those that have passed into the substance of our souls. All else we shall leave behind. The only good is inward good; and this water of life satisfies our thirst because it flows into the deepest place of our being and abides there forever.

Oh, you who are seeking your satisfaction from springs that remain outside of you despite all your efforts, learn that all of them, by reason of their externality, will sooner or later be broken pots that hold no water. I beseech you, if you want rest for your souls and satisfaction for your yearnings, look for it there, where only it can be found, in Him, who not only dwells in the heavens to rule and shower down blessings, but enters into the waiting heart and abides there, the inward, and therefore the only real possession and riches.

It is springing up—with an immortal energy, with ever fresh fullness, by its own inherent power, needing no pumps or generators, but ever gushing forth its refreshment, an emblem of the joyous energy and continual freshness of vitality that is granted to those who carry God in their hearts, and therefore can never be depressed beyond measure, nor ever feel that the burden of life is too heavy to bear or its sorrows too sharp to endure. It springs up to eternal life, for water must seek its source and rise to the level of its origin, and this spring within a man that reaches up ever toward the eternal life from which it came, and which it gives to its possessor, will bear him up toward the eternal life that is native to it, and therefore native to him.

ALEXANDER MACLAREN

Jesus answered, "Everyone who drinks this water will be thirsty again, but whoever drinks the water I give them will never thirst. Indeed, the water I give them will become in them a spring of water welling up to eternal life."

John 4:13–14

The thirst of the body is a type of the worldly experience of all mankind. It is satisfied for a moment, and then comes back with a strong craving. And, unfortunately, what we drink to try to satisfy the thirst of our souls too often creates a deeper thirst that nothing can ever satisfy.

You may have, if you will, in your own heart, a springing fountain of delight and of blessedness that will ensure that no unsatisfied desires shall ever torment you. Christ in His fullness, His Spirit, the life that flows from both and is planted within our hearts, these are offered to us all; and if we have them, we carry enclosed within ourselves all that is essential to our joy. We can say, "I have learned the secret of being content in any and every situation" (Philippians 4:12), not with the proud, stoical independence of a man who does not know God, but with the humble independence of a man who can say, "I can do all this through him who gives me strength" (v. 13).

No independence of externals is possible, or wholesome if it were possible, except that which comes from absolute dependence on Jesus Christ.

If you have Christ in your heart, life is possible, peace is possible, and joy is possible, under all circumstances and in all places. Everything that the soul can desire, it possesses. You will be like the garrison of a besieged castle, in the courtyard of which is a sparkling spring, fed from some source high up in the mountains, and finding its way in there by underground channels that no besiegers can ever touch. Sorrows will come and make you sad, but though there may be much darkness around you, there will be light in the darkness. The trees may be bare and leafless, but the sap has gone down to the roots. The world may be all wintry and white with snow, but there will be a bright little fire burning in your fireplace. You will carry within yourself all the essentials to blessedness. If you have Christ in your vessel, you can smile at the storm. Those who drink from the world's fountains shall thirst again, but those who have Christ in their hearts will have a fountain within that will not freeze in the bitterest winter or fail in the fiercest heat.

ALEXANDER MACLAREN

"But whoever drinks the water that I give him will never be thirsty again. But the water that I give him will become in him a spring of water [satisfying his thirst for God] welling up [continually flowing, bubbling within him] to eternal life."

John 4:14 AMP

There is matchless music in these words of Jesus. They are words that held a fascination for me like almost no other declaration of our Lord. They seemed to me like a marvelous strain of music from some faraway, heavenly world. And as I came to understand their meaning and to experience for myself the great truth they set forth, there was in them a preciousness that I cannot put into words.

Jesus spoke these words to the Samaritan woman when He was extremely weary and thirsty. Desiring to draw her into spiritual life, Jesus pointed down to Jacob's ancient well and said, "Everyone who drinks this water will be thirsty again" (v. 13). And how true it is of every earthly fountain of satisfaction or joy; no matter how deeply one drinks, he soon thirsts again. Drink as deeply as you will of the fountain of wealth, you are not satisfied long. Drink of worldly fame or honor or power, but how long will you be content? Drink of worldly pleasures, you will soon want to drink again, only deeper next time. Drink as deeply as you will of the fountain of human knowledge, science, philosophy, literature, music, or art, and you will thirst again. Yes, drink even of that most nearly divine of all human fountains, the fountain of human love, you soon thirst again. Not one of these things fully satisfies and they do not satisfy for long.

Then our Lord added the wonderful words that if you drink of the water He gives, the Holy Spirit (see John 7:37–39), you will be fully and forever satisfied. I wish that you would sit and ponder these words in silence until their full meaning and full force take entire possession of your mind and heart. Anyone who really receives the Holy Spirit as an indwelling presence will be fully and forever satisfied, and that is the only possible way to be fully and forever satisfied.

R. A. TORREY

The woman said to him, "Sir, give me this water so that I won't get thirsty and have to keep coming here to draw water."

John 4:15

Just as the man who drinks water has his thirst satisfied, so the man who receives the grace of God in his heart gets that which his nature wants. In Christ our deepest desires are fully satisfied. It is a grand thing for a man to be able to say, "I am content," but the believer in Christ can say that. They carry the pearl of contentment in their hearts. Jesus takes away the restless spirit and gives us rest. Jesus is the door that fits the heart, and when He is near to us, He shuts out the world's cold and heat and gives us sweet contentment. Oh, you ambitious one, you who run after something to satisfy your inner soul, turn to the cross, for at the foot of it there springs a sacred fountain of soul-satisfying delight, and if you will but drink, your ambition shall be over, and you will desire it no more. There is satisfaction for the deepest longings of the heart, mind, and conscience, in the fountain that springs from the wounds of Jesus. Faith is the silver cup. Dip it into the overflowing stream and drink.

This water is also life-preserving. In the waterless desert, where the mouth burns like a fire, oh, for a drink of water! A bag of diamonds could not buy a cup there! Priceless is the pure, clear water that sustains life. Such is the grace of God to the soul of man. The whole world over, there is nothing that can save a soul apart from the grace of God. Your good works and ceremonies can no more fill your heart with peace than the hot sand of the desert can quench the thirsty traveler. You must get grace through Jesus Christ or hope will never dawn upon you, but despair's midnight shall be your everlasting portion. Oh, soul, if you receive God's grace, you shall never die! You shall bid defiance to the grave and sing in the very jaws of death.

And water is filth-purging. This fountain can wash out the worst of sin—the stain of blasphemy and lust, the pollution of theft and murder. All manner of sin shall be forgiven to the man who comes to the cross and trusts in Jesus. Friend, this can all be yours by faith, trusting in the blood of God's dear Son.

CHARLES SPURGEON

"God is spirit, and his worshipers must worship in the Spirit and in truth."

John 4:24

When God created man and breathed into him of His own spirit, man became a living soul. The soul stood midway between the spirit and the body and had to either yield to the spirit to be lifted up to God or to the flesh and its lusts. In the fall, man refused to listen to the spirit and became a slave of the body. The spirit in man became utterly darkened.

In regeneration, it is the spirit that is made alive and born again from above. In the regenerate life and in the fellowship with God, it is the spirit of man that has ever to yield itself to the Spirit of God. The spirit is the deepest, inward part of the human being, which is stated clearly in Psalm 51:6 (NKJV), "Behold, You desire truth in the inward parts, and in the hidden part You will make me to know wisdom," or in Jeremiah 31:33, "I will put my law in their minds and write it on their hearts." It is of this also that Isaiah says: "My soul yearns for you in the night; in the morning my spirit longs for you" (Isaiah 26:9). The soul must sink down into the depths of the hidden spirit and call upon it to stir itself up to seek God.

God is a Spirit, most holy and most glorious. He gave us a spirit with the sole purpose of holding fellowship with Him. Through sin, that power has been darkened and nearly quenched. There is no way for its restoration except through presenting the soul in stillness before God for the working of His Holy Spirit in our spirit. Deeper than our thoughts and feelings, God will, in our inward parts, in our spirits within us, teach us to worship Him in the Spirit and in truth.

"For they are the kind of worshipers the Father seeks" (John 4:23). He will by the Holy Spirit teach us this if we wait for Him. In this moment, be still before God and yield yourself with the whole heart to believe in and to receive the gentle working of His Spirit. And breathe out such words as these:

My soul, be silent before the Lord. With my soul I have desired you in the night; yes, and with my spirit within me I seek you early. On you, O God, do I wait.

ANDREW MURRAY

Just then his disciples returned and were surprised to find him talking with a woman. But no one asked, "What do you want?" or "Why are you talking with her?"

John 4:27

Study this story and note how our Master with divinely skillful art sought after a single soul! What a contrast to today when our habit is to do nothing but what is showy; every work must be with the beat of drums or the sound of tambourines. May the Lord work in us the steadfast desire to always reach out, even when no one else sees it; when not a single disciple is in view. Oh, that we may have such an estimate of the value of one person that we count whole days spent to bring that person to the Savior's feet. Blessed is he who works on though he is never heard of and looks for his reward from his Master. In the heat of the day the Lord Jesus found rest and refreshment in speaking to one whom many would hardly look upon, except with scorn. We may not be surprised today that He spoke with the Samaritan woman, but we do wonder with a higher kind of astonishment that He would ever speak to the likes of us, who have so sadly fallen and grieved His heart. Oh, the compassion of the Redeemer's heart!

Then study the reaction of the disciples. Talking with a woman went against the cultural grain of the day, but that she was a Samaritan caused them to marvel. Above all things, Jews hated Samaritans, as foreigners and heretics, who dared to call Jacob their father and to believe themselves orthodox. She was even one of those Samaritan heretics who had dared to set up a rival temple to the one in Jerusalem and say that they also were the people of God. How could so good a man mix himself up with such a person?

Look at the disciples! See that sweet-souled John, and yet he is surprised. There is Peter, good but faulty, and he marvels. They were all good men. Oh, Peter and John and the rest of you, look into your own hearts and let a glance of the Holy Spirit lighten up the darkness of your spirits, and you will renounce this self-righteous marveling that grieves the woman, and you will enter into deeper sympathy with your Lord's love. I am sorry when believers claim a marvelous spirituality and yet turn away from such as Jesus would have welcomed. Dear friends, let us never disdain the worst of men or women, but seek with all our might to win them for our Lord.

CHARLES SPURGEON

*Then, leaving her water jar, the woman went back to the
town and said to the people, "Come, see a man who told
me everything I ever did. Could this be the Messiah?"*

John 4:28–29

The Samaritan woman could have looked at the disciples' intrusion into her discussion with Christ as another evil hardship suffered at the hands of men, but instead she gave herself to a holy task: she goes her way to try to persuade others to meet this divine One who had unveiled her heart. Always be prepared, whenever your usual course of life is interrupted, that the Lord has some special work for you to do. Do not fret or try to back the train engine to get on the old lines again. No, if the switch is turned by the divine hand, go on. He who has the management of all the railroads of your life knows better which way your soul should go than you yourself can know. If you are led away from the church where your soul has flourished, you may feel like one banished and orphaned. But if you are sent to some church where everything is dreary and dead—go there like a coal of fire to set them aflame. Your Lord would not have permitted the breaking up of your peace unless He had some high service for you.

And go she did, so quickly that she left her water jar behind. The Spirit of God thought well to record this fact, and I think there must be a measure of teaching in it. She left her water jar, first, for speed. When the King's business requires haste, it is wise to leave behind everything that hinders. A man has hardly felt the power of eternal things unless at times he forgets some earthly matters. So then go and try to do all that you possibly can. When in faith you attempt what you cannot alone accomplish, God will be at your back, and in your weakness His strength shall be made clear.

So it is significant that she left behind her water jar. Sometimes you have to leave your place of business to win a soul to Christ. It may even set you back a few steps or cause you to lose some dollars, but if your heart is filled with a longing to find the lost sheep, go and do it. I daresay that the Samaritan woman got her water jar back again, and you will get back to business soon enough and make all matters right. If a person comes to faith in Christ, you will have made a profit by any loss you may have sustained.

CHARLES SPURGEON

"Come, see a Man who told me all things that I ever did. Could this be the Christ?"

John 4:29 NKJV

Yes, it is not merely a vague general belief in Christ as the Teacher who "will tell us all things" that suffices for heart conviction of the reality of Jesus Christ, but the individual knowledge of Christ the Searcher who "told me all things that I ever did." This was what led the woman of Samaria to exclaim, "Could this be the Christ?" This was to her the irresistible proof of His messiahship.

What about us? If we know anything of true fellowship with the Lord Jesus, our experience will not be unlike hers. When He turns the keen flame of His eyes upon the dark corners of our hearts and flashes their far-reaching, all-revealing beam upon even the far-off and long forgotten windings of our lives; when in His light we see the darkness, and in His purity we see the sin that has been, or that is, then we know for ourselves that He is indeed the Christ.

He does not merely show us; it is something more than that. It is not merely an invisible hand drawing away the veil from hidden scenes and a light brought to bear upon them so that we can see them if we will. It is more personal, more disturbing, and yet more tender than that. He tells us what we have done; and, if we listen, the telling will be very clear, very thorough, and unmistakable.

At first we are tempted not to listen at all. We shrink from the still, small voice that tells us such startlingly unwelcome things. Oh, do not stifle the voice! Instead, ask Him to let His voice sound louder and clearer, and believe that the goodness of God will lead you to repentance. Only listen; and He will tell you not only all the things that you have ever done, but all the things that He has done for you. He never leaves off in the middle of all He has to tell, unless we willfully interrupt Him. We must simply say, "Master, speak on." Never shrink from the probings of our beloved Physician. Dearer and dearer will the hand become as we yield to it. Sweeter and sweeter will be the proofs that He is our faithful friend, who only wounds that He may perfectly heal.

FRANCES RIDLEY HAVERGAL

"My food," said Jesus, "is to do the will of him who sent me and to finish his work."

John 4:34

G od's will was also the will of Jesus; not only passively, but actively, He wished to do it. God's work was His work completely, so that He wished to finish it. He longed to go the full length of God's eternal purpose and carry it out as far as that purpose concerned himself. Now, when a man feels, "My one desire is that I may do God's will, I have no other will but His will; my own will has fallen into God's will as a brook falls into a river," then he is at peace. It is a blessed thing to rejoice in being crossed in our own purpose, in order that the purpose of the Lord may be more completely fulfilled. When a man wants to do God's work, and to get through with it whatever it may cost, he is sure to feel strength in his heart. He who will glorify God, whatever it may cost him, is a happy man. He who serves God in body, soul, and spirit, to the utmost of his power, finds new powers given to him hour by hour, for God opens to him fresh springs of living water.

Perhaps you do not see this truth; but if you have ever experienced what it is to lay your whole soul on the altar, and feel that for Christ you will live and for Christ you would die, you will know by experience that I speak the truth. If your heart's desires were as ravenous as that of the young lions when they howl for their prey, they would be abundantly satisfied by your soul's being tamed into complete submission to the will of God. When your will is God's will, you will have your will: when your will rings out in harmony with the will of God, there must be sweetest music all around our steps. Our chief sorrows spring from the roots of our selfishness. Hang up self upon the cross of Calvary, and your soul will no longer be consumed with the hunger and thirst of discontent. When you are tuned to perfect harmony with God, you begin your heaven upon earth, even though you may find yourself in poverty or in sickness. I know by experience that the way to renew your strength for suffering or for service is to become more and more at one with the will and the purpose of the Most High; as God's glory becomes the one object of life, we find in Him our all in all.

CHARLES SPURGEON

Jesus said to them, "My food is to do the will of Him who sent Me, and to finish His work."

John 4:34 NKJV

Jesus had hidden food that He received from His Father, and that was the secret of His power. No one could have discovered what it was; but when He tells us, it appears so simple that many are puzzled over it. His food was to do the will of God.

Food meets a felt need. Jesus' hunger was for one thing: to please His Father. Without that He could not rest; in that one thing He had all He needed. And when He found the will of God, He did it, and thereby fed His soul with its appropriate food and was satisfied.

Food involves appropriation, like the exercise of fellowship. The weak soul who truly surrenders himself to the will of God becomes wonderfully strengthened by it. Obedience to God, instead of exhausting the energies, renews them. The doing of God's will was Jesus' food.

Food brings both quickening and joy. Eating is not only necessary for strength but also enjoyable. To observe a feast in the Spirit is itself equivalent to food. Obedience to God's will was Jesus' highest joy.

Jesus has become my food, and He dwells in me as the power of my life. Now I know the means by which this life must be fed and strengthened within me. The doing of God's will is my food. The doing of God's will was for Jesus the bread of heaven; and since I have now received Jesus as my heavenly Bread, He teaches me to eat what He ate; He teaches me to do the will of the Father. And so the feast of the Supper is prolonged in the continued life of obedience to the will of God.

ANDREW MURRAY

"We know that this man really is the Savior of the world."

John 4:42

Omnipotence and omnipresence are what are called natural attributes of God. They have their true worth only when linked to and inspired by His moral attributes, holiness, and love. When our Lord spoke of the omnipotence having been given to Him—"all authority in heaven and on earth" (Matthew 28:18)—and the omnipresence—"I am with you always" (v. 20)—His words pointed to that which lies at the root of all: His divine glory as the Savior of the world and Redeemer of men. It was because He humbled himself and became obedient to death, the death of the cross, that God so highly exalted Him (Philippians 2:6–11). His share as the man Christ Jesus in the attributes of God was owing to the work He had done in His perfect obedience to the will of God and the finished redemption He had accomplished for the salvation of men.

It is this that gives meaning and worth to what He says of himself as the omnipotent and omnipresent One. Between His mention of these two attributes, He gave His command that they should go out into all the world and preach the gospel and teach men to obey all that He has commanded. It is as the Redeemer who saves and keeps from sin, as the Lord Christ who claims obedience to all that He has commanded, that He promises His divine presence to be with His servants.

It follows as a matter of necessity that it is only when His servants show in their lives that they obey Him in all His commands, that they can expect the fullness of His power and His presence to be with them. It is only when they themselves are living witnesses to the reality of His power to save and to keep from sin that they can expect the full experience of His abiding presence, and that they will have power to train others to the life of obedience that He asks.

Yes, it is Jesus Christ who saves His people from their sin, who rules over a people willing in the day of His power, proves in them that He enables them to say, "I delight to do your will, O my God," and who says, "I am with you always." The abiding presence of the Savior from sin is promised to all who have accepted Him in the fullness of His redeeming power, and who preach by their lives as well as by their words what a wonderful Savior He is.

ANDREW MURRAY

Once more he visited Cana in Galilee, where he had turned the water into wine. And there was a certain royal official whose son lay sick at Capernaum. When this man heard that Jesus had arrived in Galilee from Judea, he went to him and begged him to come and heal his son, who was close to death.

John 4:46–47

This being Jesus' second miracle, we cannot fail to notice how remarkably these two miracles are contrasted. The one takes place at a wedding, a neighborhood scene of festivity and gladness. But life has deeper things in it than gladness, and a Savior who preferred the house of feasting to the house of mourning would be no Savior for us. With this miracle Jesus turns to the darker side of human experience. The happiest home has its saddened hours; the truest marriage joy has associated with it many cares and anxieties. Therefore He who breathed blessings over wedded joys goes on to answer the heartrending pleas of parental anxiety. It was fitting that the first miracle should deal with gladness, for that is God's purpose for His creatures, and that the second should deal with sicknesses and sorrows, which are additions to that purpose made needful by sin.

We also must note that it was a royal official's son who was sick. Disease finds its way into every rank of society. We need to remind ourselves of this lest we slip into skepticism by doubting the equality of divine rule. There are no magical lines beyond which death cannot come. The great sea of trouble roars and foams over every line of latitude, and the bleak wind and storm strikes the traveler in every land. Does the poor man suppose that pain cannot find a way through the strong walls of the palace or the castle? Does he think that great advantages have made a wall of defense around the man of wealth? Then he knows nothing of human history, nor can he be expected to know that the great advantages that he covets are themselves the sources of the great man's fiercest temptations. The poor man thinks that the high spire is a long way from the flood; so it is, but how much nearer the lightning!

JOSEPH PARKER

*Then Jesus said to him, "Unless you people see signs
and wonders, you will by no means believe."*

John 4:48 NKJV

A craving after signs and wonders was a symptom of the weak state of men's minds in our Lord's day; they refused solid nourishment and sought after mere wonder. The gospel that they so greatly needed they would not have; the miracles that Jesus did not always choose to give they eagerly demanded. Many nowadays must see signs and wonders or they will not believe. Some have said in their heart, "I must have a dream or a vision or hear a word or see an angel." Some believers hear of a revival or a movement of the Spirit in another place and then gather to pray, demanding the same exact manner of revival. Should we not always be seeking the Holy Spirit to be working in souls, but not dictating how He does it? Where the Spirit works in the soul, we are always glad to see true conversion, and if He chooses to work in the body too, we shall be glad to see it! If men's hearts are renewed, take it with or without the signs and wonders. For my part, let me see God's work done in God's own way—a true and thorough revival, but the signs and wonders we can readily dispense with.

Thus some undeserving mortals dream that my Lord is to be dictated to by them! They are beggars at His gate, asking for mercy, and they must draw up rules and regulations as to how He shall give that mercy. Do you think that He will submit to this? My Master is of a generous spirit, but He has a royal heart, He rejects all dictation, and maintains His sovereignty of action.

Why, if such is your case, do you yearn for signs and wonders? Is not the gospel its own sign and wonder? Is not this a miracle of miracles, that "God so loved the world that He gave His only begotten Son, that whoever believes in Him should not perish but have everlasting life" (John 3:16 NKJV)? Surely that precious word, "Whoever desires, let him take the water of life freely" (Revelation 22:17 NKJV), and that solemn promise, "the one who comes to Me I will by no means cast out" (John 6:37 NKJV), are better than signs and wonders! A truthful Savior ought to be believed. He is truth itself. Why will you ask proof of the truthfulness of One who cannot lie? The demons themselves declared Him to be the Son of God; will you mistrust Him?

CHARLES SPURGEON

Then Jesus said to him, "Unless you [people] see [miraculous] signs and wonders, you [simply] will not believe." The royal official pleaded with Him, "Sir, do come down [at once] before my child dies!" Jesus said to him, "Go; your son lives!" The man believed what Jesus said to him and started home.

John 4:48–50 AMP

These words must have come like a dash of cold water upon the hot anxiety of the royal official. In them we see our Lord's singular calmness and majestic rest, who never needed to hurry because He was conscious of absolute power. He puts aside the apparently pressing necessity to deal with a far deeper, more pressing one. It was worthy of His care to heal the boy; it was far more needful that He should train and lead the father to faith. The one can wait much better than the other.

And there is in the words, too, something like a sigh of profound sorrow. It is Christ's own pained heart that speaks. He reads the man's heart with that divine omniscience that pierces beyond the surface and sees in him the very same evil that has affected all his countrymen. Jesus' sorrowful gaze sees the wide-reaching spirit of blindness of His people that is to their own impoverishing. The official and his fellows were blind to all the beauty of His character. The graciousness of His character was nothing to them. They failed to see His tenderness and wisdom, His glory and love, but raced after Him for a miracle. It is a disease that still affects us deeply and still drives a knife into the loving heart of the Savior.

When the official persists in his request, Jesus refuses to comply because He knows it will strengthen the man's feeble faith. Asked to "come" to weak faith, He rewards it with less, which is actually more. He refuses to come that He may heal at a distance, and thus manifests still more wondrously His power and His grace. His wise treatment is effective, and he who was sense-bound turns and goes away having believed the Lord's bare word and carrying a confidence that the Healer has worked a wonder.

And that is what you and I have to do. We have Christ's bare word, and no more, to trust to for everything. We must be content to go out of His presence with only His promise and to cling to that. A feeble faith needs something tangible and visible. A strong faith strides away from the Master, happy and peaceful in its assured possession of a blessing based solely on Christ's word. That was enough for this man, who sprang from infancy of faith to maturity. Is it enough for you?

ALEXANDER MACLAREN

"Unless you people see signs and wonders," Jesus told him, "you will never believe." The royal official said, "Sir, come down before my child dies."

John 4:48–49

N otice in the royal official's case that seeking faith did not simply make him sincere in prayer but made him persistent in prayer. He asked once, and the only answer he received was an apparent rebuff. He did not turn away in a sulk. "Sir," he said, "come down." I cannot tell you how he said it, but I have no doubt it was expressed in soul-moving terms, with tears forming in his eyes and hands placed together in an attitude of entreaty. He seemed to say, "I cannot let you go unless you come and save my child. Please, do come. Is there anything I can say that can get you to come? Let a father's affection be my best argument. If my lips are not eloquent, let the tears of my eyes supply the place of the words of my tongue."

What mighty prayers are those that seeking faith will make a person pray! I have heard the seeker sometimes plead with God with all the power that Jacob ever could have had at Jabbok's brook (see Genesis 32:24–32). I have seen the sinner under distress of soul seem to take hold of the pillars of the gate of mercy and rock them to and fro as though he would sooner pull them up from their deep foundations than go away without effecting an entrance. I have seen sinners pull and tug, strive and fight and wrestle rather than not enter the kingdom of heaven. No wonder that those who come before God with cold prayers do not find peace. Heat them red hot in the furnace of desire and they will burn their way upward to heaven. Those who merely say in the chill form of orthodoxy, "God be merciful to me a sinner," will never find mercy. It is the person who cries in the burning anguish of heartfelt emotion: "O God, be merciful to me a sinner! Save me or I perish!" who gains his plea. It is the person who concentrates his soul in every word and flings his very being into every sentence that wins his way through the gates of heaven. Seeking faith can make a person do this.

CHARLES SPURGEON

Now there is in Jerusalem near the Sheep Gate a pool, which in Aramaic is called Bethesda and which is surrounded by five covered colonnades. Here a great number of disabled people used to lie—the blind, the lame, the paralyzed.

John 5:2–3

The five porches around the pool of Bethesda were once places used by rich people for purposes of luxurious indulgence and self-enjoyment. In the process of time, the porches became hospitals, and in these hospitals lay a great multitude of people who had been disabled—the blind, the lame, the paralyzed. They were gathering places of human pain, need, and sorrow. Think of sorrow focalized, of pain, suffering, distress brought to a head—a multitude of sufferers. Surely the place would be a place of weeping! And understand that the people referred to in this census of sorrow were not afflicted with one affliction. We have a great multitude of people representing a great multitude of diseases.

Most of us seldom see numbers, multitudes of suffering, sorrowing, dying creatures. But it does us good to look into one of those places; it makes us sober, thankful; it sometimes makes us sad. Pain has always been in the majority. We live in a world of pain! There are easily a thousand diseases that can strike a man to pieces, a thousand ways of whipping him to the grave. The man who is in robust health today may be smitten before the setting of the sun with a fatal disease. In the midst of life, we are in death; our breath at best is in our nostrils. Man breathes and then cannot get his breath again, and he is gone—we call him dead. Life is a perpetual crisis. We are always walking on the cobweb string; it is snapped at any moment.

Like this invalid, we are all waiting, groaning, sighing for the Savior. We can be waiting in our own anxiety, distress, impatience, distrust, and complaining—the kind of waiting that wears the soul out. Or we can be waiting in patience, hope, contentment, assurance that God will, in His own time, redeem His promises and make the heart strong. God desires that we always live and wait upon Him in expectation. Expectation will save us from earthiness and lift us from the dust, just as the presence of Jesus at the pool brings with it a healing in His wings.

JOSEPH PARKER

When Jesus saw him lying there, and knew that he already had been in that condition a long time, He said to him, "Do you want to be made well?"

John 5:6 NKJV

I t seems a strange question to ask. Would the poor man have been lying at the pool if he had not been anxious for healing? Must there not have been in the very look of his face, as he gazed upon the Savior, an answer to that question, superseding all necessity of saying it? Yet it may be that our Lord perceived that the paralysis of the man's body had to a very painful degree numbed his mind and brought on a paralysis of his will. He had hoped until his heart was sick, and now it had almost come to this, that he scarcely cared whether he was made whole or not. The bow had been bent so long that all its elasticity was gone. The Savior touched a chord that needed to vibrate when He inquired as to his will; He awakened by that question a dormant faculty whose vigorous exercise, it may be, was one of the first essentials to a cure.

Would you be willing now to be made whole? I can imagine your saying, "Yes, I want to be like Jesus," and yet permit me to ask if you know what that means and whether you are willing for the process that carries you on toward making you whole as Christ is whole. If a man is made whole before God, he is made thoroughly, absolutely honest before men—no more lying, half-truths, or taking advantage of others. A man who is made whole must forgive others. A man who is made whole must make a complete break with sin in whatever shape it takes in his life. Let me also remark, if a man is made whole, there are not only moral virtues that will abound in him, but spiritual graces, for a man who is whole is sound in spirit as well as in outward character. What then would happen to you if you were made whole in your spirit?

Come, do not shirk the question! Will you be made whole? Would you be set free from the lusts and sins that have been your darlings? Would you be delivered from the desires of your flesh? Be honest with yourself, and see yourself in the true light; but if indeed you would be purified from sin, and be made holy, say so. Rest assured, God, who has made you to long after holiness, has prepared holiness for you, and the instrument by which He will work it in you now is your faith.

CHARLES SPURGEON

"Sir," the invalid replied, "I have no one to help me into the pool when the water is stirred. While I am trying to get in, someone else goes down ahead of me." Then Jesus said to him, "Get up! Pick up your mat and walk."

John 5:7–8

Jesus entered the Bethesda pool and picked out the most helpless man in the whole world. That is a true gospel sentence. Jesus always loves to give His mercy to those who need it most. There lay that man, and he did not think of Christ, but Christ stood and looked at him; he did not know Jesus Christ, but Jesus Christ knew him, and He knew that the man had been a long time in this condition. Jesus knew that the man had been sick for thirty-eight years. He knew that before the man told Him he had been often disappointed. The man had tried many times, as well as his paralyzed body would allow him, to get into the water, but someone else always plunged into the water first and received their healing. He had seen many others healed, and that had made his own condition all the more painful. He was, or perhaps had become through the years, the most ambivalent, weakminded man that you ever met. You know people like him. You cannot help them. Whatever they do, it never succeeds. They are the type of person who needs to be put in a basket and carried on somebody else's back all through the world. Rather than saying, "Yes, Lord, I desire to be made well with all my heart," he rambled on and on about why he hadn't been. Indecisive and insecure, he was a hopeless case.

Now, my Lord and Master picked out this very man to be the subject of His healing energy. Wonders of grace to God belong! He who chooses the weak and despised ones in this world to confound the wise pitied this helpless invalid who was almost as paralyzed in his mind as he was in his body. Jesus Christ comes to the lost and ruined man and commands him to rise up—words that must have sounded like thunderclaps. The gospel came to the man, and comes to us, as a command. Although we are too ruined to rise, if we believe in Jesus Christ, we can rise. In the command there is gospel power. The man believed in Jesus; that was all he did. As pitifully irresolute as he had been, he had enough sense, and God gave him enough grace, simply to believe in Jesus. And the transformation that swept through his body is like the mighty change that God works in us by His blessed Spirit as we simply believe in Jesus.

CHARLES SPURGEON

*The invalid answered, "Sir, I have no one to put me in the
pool when the water is stirred up, and while I am coming
[to get into it myself], someone else steps ahead of me."*

John 5:7 AMP

This reminds us that there is a tremendous amount of selfishness in the world. Although many others have been cured, they have forgotten that their cure binds them in God's law of love to see that other sufferers are aided in their attempts at recovery. Of all who had been cured at the pool, not one remained to give this man the benefit of his strength. What a world this would be without one man finding joy in helping another! Selfishness makes the world a very little place, a very cold, fruitless, gloomy corner. It may seem to be a grand thing to write one's own name everywhere as owner and lord, but if the name is not written on recovered and thankful human hearts, it will soon be rubbed out and forgotten. Love is the only ink that does not fade; love is the only memory that strengthens with time; love is the bond that never corrodes. We have only as much as we have given; by as much as we have helped other people, we have laid up reserves of strength that will give us mastery and honor in time to come.

We see that Jesus Christ always went about doing good—not waiting for the lost, but seeking them; not standing still, but going after them till they were found. The stream of His most merciful help poured from an inexhaustible fountain, and no poor, brokenhearted soul was ever excluded from the healing waters. The same field of loving service lies before us all. What if we were to resolve that every day we would make a point of assisting one person toward the pool of healing? Being healed by God's grace, our place is to help others on to recovery. It is an infallible sign that a man has not undergone Christian healing if he has no care about healing others. The divinely vitalized energy of God's love warms and stirs the heart with all the impulses of far-reaching charity. It moves the believer beyond a conscience that tells him what to do, and by an almost omnipotent constraint love makes him do it. You will find love at the poolside, offering to help the poorest sufferer step into the healing waters; and long after conscience is satisfied, love will add something that far exceeds such a limited sway. Love has dominion over the whole man.

JOSEPH PARKER

Jesus said to him, "Rise, take up your bed and walk."

John 5:8 NKJV

Like many others, the sick man had been waiting for a sign to be given. What must it be like to be an invalid for thirty-eight years? Wearily did he watch the pool, but no angel came; yet he waited still and knew not that there was One near him whose word could heal him in a moment. Many are in the same plight today: they are waiting for something—a stirring emotion, a remarkable "word" or impression, or a dream or vision; they wait and watch in vain. It is a very sad reflection that many are now looking for something, but not looking to Christ and to Him alone, forgetting the present Savior, who bids them look to Him and be saved. He could heal them at once, but they prefer to wait for an angel and a wonder. To trust Him is the sure way to every blessing, and He is worthy of the most implicit confidence; but unbelief makes them prefer the cold porches of Bethesda to the warm bosom of His love.

Well, what did Jesus Christ do for the sick man? *He gave him a command.* "Rise, take up your bed and walk." The words sounded like three thunderclaps. "But he cannot! He is paralyzed, good sir." Yes, but it was a gospel command that implied faith. The man could not walk of himself, but if he believed in Jesus Christ, he could rise and walk. So it was really a command to exercise faith in Jesus and to prove it by practical works. "But the man could not do it." That has nothing to do with it. The power is not in the person, but in the command. Jesus Christ could make him rise. By His power, through the simple act of believing in Him, he was made whole. The man believed in Jesus. That was all he did. He resolved that he would try his legs, and to his astonishment those poor legs worked.

There was a look about Jesus, a majestic gleam about His eyes, a wonderful force in the tone of His voice that was very different from what the man had ever seen before. He knew not who He was, yet somehow confidence was born in his soul. How much more, then, may faith come to you who know that Jesus Christ is the Son of God? Rise up and walk directly. You will be surprised to find the mighty change that God is working in you by His blessed Spirit through that simple act of faith.

CHARLES SPURGEON

*The Jewish leaders said to the man who had been healed,
"It is the Sabbath; the law forbids you to carry your
mat." But he replied, "The man who made me well said
to me, 'Pick up your mat and walk.'"*

John 5:10–11

The Pharisees had no eyes for the miracle, paying no attention to the fact that it was a paralyzed man who carried the mat, and so laid hold only of the broken rabbinical restriction. The man responds as if to say, "He who gave me the power to walk, has He not a right to tell me what to do with the mat? Was I not bound to walk when and where He commanded me?"

And if you generalize that, it comes to this: the only person who has a right to command you is the Christ who saves you. He has the absolute authority to do as He will with your restored spiritual powers, because He has bestowed them all upon you. His dominion is built upon His benefits. He is the King because He is the Savior. He rules because He has redeemed. He begins with giving, and it is only afterward that He commands; and He turns to each of us with that smile upon His lips and with tenderness in His voice that will bind any man, who is not ungrateful, to Him forever. "If you [really] love Me, you will keep and obey My commandments" (John 14:15 AMP).

There is always something hard and distasteful to the individual will in the tone of authority assumed by any man whatsoever. We always more or less rebel and shrink from it. There is only one thing that makes the commandment sweet, and that is when it drops like honey from the honeycomb, from lips that we love. So does it in the case of Christ's commands to us. It is a joy to know and to do the will of One to whom the whole heart turns with gratitude and affection. And Christ blesses and privileges us by the communication to us of His pleasure concerning us, that we may have the gladness of yielding to His desires, and so meeting the love that commands with the love that obeys.

The things that require a Christian response are often very painful. There is always self-sacrifice in Christian virtue, and self-sacrifice has always a sting to it, but "My yoke is easy and my burden is light" (Matthew 11:30). This is true because His yoke is padded with the softest velvet of love and lies upon our neck lightly because He has laid it there. All the rigid harshness of the command is done away when the command comes from Christ's lips, and His command turns duty into joyful service.

ALEXANDER MACLAREN

*Later Jesus found him at the temple and said to him,
"See, you are well again. Stop sinning or something
worse may happen to you."*

John 5:14

Here we have the Healer who is also the Judge, warning the healed one of the possibility of a relapse. The man's thirty-eight years of illness had apparently been brought on by depravity. Perhaps it was a sin of the flesh—avenged in the flesh—that had given him a miserable life. One would have thought he had received warning enough, but Christ seeks the man out and warns him that should he enter into sin again, something worse could happen to him. Why the warning? Because the first one had apparently done him no good. So here are the lessons for us. There is always the danger that we will fall back into our old sins, even if we think we have overcome them. The powerful influence of habit, a weak will, familiarity, imagination, memory, and sometimes—as in the case of an alcoholic—the physical effect of the odor upon one's senses—all these factors make it extremely likely that one who has once been under the condemnation of any evil will be tempted to fall under its sway again.

And such a fall is not only more criminal than the former but is also more deadly than the former. "It would have been better for them not to have known the way of righteousness, than to have known it and then to turn their backs on the sacred command that was passed on to them. Of them the proverbs are true: 'A dog returns to its vomit'" (2 Peter 2:21–22)—a crude metaphor to express a far worse reality. Dear reader, there is no condemnation blacker, no spiritual eminence from which we cannot walk away, and thus the warning!

Christian men and women, you have been made whole. A mighty hand lifted you out of the pit of despair and set you in the sweet path of hope. Your heart may have gotten back all its best hopes, yet it is possible that all might be forgotten. "Stop sinning or something worse may happen to you." And turn to the Lord and say, "Hold me up, and I shall be saved." Then the enemies will not be able to recapture you, and the chains that have dropped from your wrists will never enclose them again.

ALEXANDER MACLAREN

Afterward Jesus found him in the temple, and said to him, "See, you have been made well. Sin no more, lest a worse thing come upon you."

John 5:14 NKJV

Besides appearing to be listless, discouraged, and depressed, the man whom Jesus healed was by no means an attractive character. Our Lord said to him after he was healed, "Sin no more, lest a worse thing come upon you," from which it is not an improbable inference that his first infirmity had come upon him by some deed of vice or course of excess. The man apparently had been guilty of that which brought upon his body the suffering that he was enduring. Some people consider it to be a point beyond all disputing that we should help the worthy, but that when a man brings a calamity upon himself by wrongdoing, we are justified in letting him suffer that he may reap what he has sown. This cold Pharisaic idea is very congenial to minds that are bent upon saving their money. It springs up in many hearts—or rather in places where hearts should be—and it is generally regarded as if it is an axiom infallible and universal.

I venture to say that our Savior never taught us to confine our giving to the deserving. He would never have bestowed His grand gift of grace on any one of us had He carried that rule. We cannot afford to cramp our compassion and charity into a sort of petty justice and sour our giving into a miniature court of law. When a man is suffering, let us pity him, however the suffering has come. When a man is found to be in misery, it is time that his infirmity should be more considered than his iniquity and that his present sorrow should be thought upon more than his former folly. So Jesus thought, and therefore He came to the sinner, not with reproach but with restoration. Jesus saw the disease rather than his depravity and gave him pity instead of punishment.

Our God is kind to the unthankful and to the evil; be therefore merciful, as your Father is merciful. Remember how our Lord said, "Pray for those who spitefully use you and persecute you, that you may be sons of your Father in heaven; for He makes His sun rise on the evil and on the good, and sends rain on the just and on the unjust" (Matthew 5:44–45 NKJV). Let us imitate Him in this, and wherever there is pain and sorrow, let it be our joy to relieve it.

CHARLES SPURGEON

MARCH

27

"Very truly I tell you, whoever hears my word and believes him who sent me has eternal life and will not be judged but has crossed over from death to life."

John 5:24

Here are two distinct states of existence—death and life—with nothing between. No broad space between where we may stand, leading to the one or to the other; only a boundary line too fine to balance upon. Not even two or three from one to the other, but one step from death to life. The foot lifted from the hollow crust over the volcanic fire and set upon the Rock of salvation.

How tremendously important it is to know whether this step has been taken, yet how clear and simple the test. Are you trembling and downhearted, wanting some very strong support for your very weak faith? Lay hold of this. See how the rope is let down low enough to meet the hand that you can hardly lift?

"Whoever hears my word . . ." Can you say you have not heard? You have heard His word as His word, recognizing it as such and receiving it as such. The word of Jesus is heard by your innermost self, and you would not be hearing and recognizing it if you were still dead. A marble statue hears not.

". . . and believes him who sent me." Do you not believe that the Father sent the Son? Did He not so love the world? Let the very recoil from such plain English of unbelief show you the sin and folly of doubting anymore. You do hear His word, you do believe in the Father who sent the Son to be your Savior. Will you not now believe the fact that you have passed from death to life? The fact and the full blessedness of this reality are not changed by varying degrees of realization.

See your position, take His word for what it is, and give Him thanks for having lifted you in your blindness and helplessness over that solemn boundary line when you could not even step over it. Sing to the Lord for He has done it, and the shadowy hosts of fears and doubts shall flee away. From death—cold, dark, hopeless, useless, loveless; the death in our trespasses and sins—unto life with its ever-increasing abundance; life crowned with light and love; life upon which only a shadow of death can ever pass, and that only the shadow of the portal of eternal glory; life in Jesus, life for Jesus, life with Jesus. This is your position now!

FRANCES RIDLEY HAVERGAL

"Do not marvel at this; for the hour is coming in which all who are in the graves will hear His voice and come forth—those who have done good, to the resurrection of life, and those who have done evil, to the resurrection of condemnation."

John 5:28–29 NKJV

The immortality of the soul is amazing, but men could not have imagined so great a wonder that the body should rise again. This hope of the resurrection that is brought to light by the revelation of Christ Jesus is one of the brightest gems in His crown. If it is so that all the dead shall rise at the voice of Christ, let us worship Him! How gloriously is He now exalted! If we could even but see the hem of this truth that He shall raise all the dead out of their graves; if we did but begin to perceive its grandeur of meaning, we would fall at the Savior's feet as John did when he said, "I fell at His feet as dead" (Revelation 1:17 NKJV).

What consolation for our wounded spirits concerning our departed loved ones! We never mourn with regard to the souls of the righteous; they are forever with the Lord. But we find much consolation with regard to that which is "sown in dishonor," but shall be "raised in glory" (1 Corinthians 15:43 NKJV). Your dead shall live! Weep not as though death is the end; you shall look again with your own eyes into those eyes that have spoken love to you so often, which are now closed in the darkness of the grave. Your departed friend shall come back to you, and having loved his Lord as you do, you shall rejoice with him in the land where we die no more! It is but a short parting; it will be an eternal meeting; forever with the Lord, we shall also be forever with one another!

And you will not be forgotten; your separated spirit shall have its appointed place, and that body that once contained it shall have its Watcher to guard it till by the power of God it shall be restored to your spirit again at the sounding of Christ's voice. You shall rise again and stand before the once crucified Son of Man! It is not possible that you should be forgotten; you must, you shall rise! It is a wondrous truth of God, and yet we may not marvel at it so as to doubt it, though we may marvel at it and adore the Lord who shall bring it to pass.

Oh, what amazing power is yours, my Lord and my Master! All hail, Immanuel! You have the keys of death and of hell; my soul loves and adores you, you ever great enthroned Prince, the Wonderful Counselor, King of kings and Lord of lords!

CHARLES SPURGEON

"John was a lamp that burned and gave light, and you chose for a time to enjoy his light. I have testimony weightier than that of John. For the works that the Father has given me to finish—the very works that I am doing—testify that the Father has sent me."

John 5:35–36

Jesus Christ is now speaking contrastively, not paying a compliment, to John. John was a burning lamp—the best light you could have at the time. But when there is a better light to see by, the lamp is put out. John was a burning and shining lamp only until the dawn made the eastern sky white with young splendor and promised the noonday. He was only burning and shining because the darkness was so dense around him—a lamp before the dawn, a little light to be going on with until the impartial sun filled all heaven with His glory. Thus Jesus Christ indicates the effectiveness of John the Baptist until the true Light came. The lamp is of necessity local and limited, but very useful; so every man that came before Jesus Christ, however great in prophetic genius and noble in prophetic function, was a lamp that was only waiting until the sun shone.

What, then, does Jesus Christ say of himself? He says, "I am the light of the world" (John 8:12). How arrogant, how intolerable, if He were but a man! The very contrast that He establishes is but an exhibition of infinite disrespect, if it is the contrast of man against man. The deity of Jesus Christ is not to be established by little grammatical discussions. So long as you have grammar as your demigod, you will have very skillful controversies, word-fencing most agile and keen and wonder-striking. The deity of Christ runs through His whole spiritual action—every touch was the touch of God; every word had about it some glint of a light higher than the brightness of the sun. The deity of Jesus Christ may be established by this very instance. All other men are lamps, shining only until the moment Jesus Christ comes into the world, and the glory is that of noontide—infinite and cloudless. We could not allow any man the use of such poetry; it is not poetry, it is blasphemy. He puts himself in a wrong relation to God and to us, if He is but talking blank verse. Do not find the deity of the Savior in a Greek preposition, or in the sudden turn of some verb in its mazy conjugation. Christ is God by His deeds, by His claims. He does not hesitate to correct men's notions of God, and in the act of humbling himself He leads men to worship Him. This is the mystery of godliness.

JOSEPH PARKER

"I have testimony weightier than that of John. For the works that the Father has given me to finish—the very works that I am doing—testify that the Father has sent me."

John 5:36

The Jews were unrelenting in their blind demand that Jesus establish the credibility of His authority. Looking only for some merely technical standard, they seemed altogether unable to move from effect to cause. They saw a lame man leaping with exuberant strength, or a bent and broken woman bloom with health; yet, when they turned to the great Worker, their eyes were dimmed by a puzzled and even angry prejudice. That worker, who was only Mary's son, was too flawed to substantiate His great claims.

Jesus appealed to His works as the verification of His claims on more than one occasion. "Go back and report to John what you hear and see: The blind receive sight, the lame walk, those who have leprosy are cleansed, the deaf hear, the dead are raised, and the good news is proclaimed to the poor" (Matthew 11:4–5). Both in His personal and spiritual life, as well as in ours, the grand and final appeal as to authority is to works. The whole quality of the worker will be shown in his whole conduct and service among men. A man's testimony, as a professed servant of God, is to be found in his works. Let a man prove his salvation by his holiness. If a man should say that God sent him, let him prove his mission by his life—having heard his word, we await his works.

Take the case of a church. You profess to be divinely called, but what is the proof? Do not refer me to a long line of illustrious preachers or a splendid sanctuary. Are you considered in the neighborhood to be a power for good? Do you visit the widow and the fatherless in their affliction? Are you eyes to the blind and feet to the lame? Do the poor bless you, and those who are ready to perish hold you in grateful reverence? Is Jesus Christ crucified the inspiration of your labor, and Jesus Christ risen the source of your power? Where are the proofs of our love? What light have we shed on the world? Prove your call by your works. Show that the love of Christ is the all-compelling power of your lives, and by holiness, patience, and charity set up a claim too strong to be overthrown, too lofty to be defied. Away with the system that believes much and does nothing about it. Blessed are those who are drawn toward self-sacrifice, the service that comes of love.

JOSEPH PARKER

"You have never heard his voice nor seen his form, nor does his word dwell in you, for you do not believe the one he sent. You study the Scriptures diligently because you think that in them you have eternal life."

John 5:37–39

How is it possible that these Jews did not see that Jesus Christ was the Messiah of the Old Testament and the very Son of God? They had the right book in their hands. And they took infinite pains to master the particulars of it; thus they got their living, their eminence, their fame, their influence. Yet they missed the point. They could tell you how many books were in the Bible, how many words were in each division, how many consonants and vowels were in the literary composition of the Scripture—still they had no revelation. They handled every letter as if they contained eternal life, yet they missed the wisdom, the poetry, the hope. What music will you get out of a wooden alphabet, perfectly correct in every letter and in the number of the whole, and turning them upside down—when will the music come? Their Old Testament was torn to pieces by grammarians, who wrenched it until it bled, through rough handling; yet there was no Christ in it. It was the right book, and it held the right doctrine, but it was a murdered book.

Jesus said that "his word" did not "dwell" in them. A man must himself be a Bible before he can understand God's Bible. The Jews handled the Bible with a superstitious reverence, but there was nothing in themselves to which the Bible could speak—no connection between the thing written and the heart reading it. So it is today. You will get out of the Bible what you bring to it. If you want to find God's word in the Bible, you will find it. If the word is already in you in some dim, unconscious, but surely felt way, the book will talk to you, and you will talk to the book, and you will seem to have met one another in a mysterious kinship of soul. No mere critic can understand the Bible; no word-chopper can preach the Bible; no grammarian can so analyze the words that he will ever reach the genius of any revelation from the heavens. We may have committed the whole Bible to memory and yet know nothing about God's revelation. When His word dwells in you, every verse of Scripture is an angel, every discourse a revelation, and every history a tragedy. Wonder of wonders it must have been to the great heart of Christ that men should read about Him and not recognize Him. May we never come under such a curse.

JOSEPH PARKER

"You search and keep on searching and examining the Scriptures because you think that in them you have eternal life; and yet it is those [very Scriptures] that testify about Me."

John 5:39 AMP

The Greek word here rendered *search* signifies a strict, close, diligent, curious search, such as men make when they are seeking gold or hunters when they are in pursuit of game. We must not rest content with having given a superficial reading to a chapter or two, but with the candle of the Spirit we must deliberately seek out the hidden meaning of the word. Holy Scripture requires searching—much of it can only be learned by careful study. There is milk for babes, but also meat for strong men. The rabbis wisely say that a mountain of matter hangs upon every word, yes, upon every title of Scripture. Tertullian, one of the early church fathers, exclaims, "I adore the fullness of the Scriptures."

No man who merely skims the book of God can profit thereby; we must dig and mine until we obtain the hidden treasure. The door of the word only opens to the key of diligence. The Scriptures claim searching. They are the writings of God, bearing the divine stamp and approval—who shall dare to treat them with lightness? He who despises them despises the God who wrote them. God forbid that any of us should leave our Bibles to become swift witnesses against us in the great day of account.

The Word of God will repay searching. Why do men go into the fields if there is no grain to harvest? Why do they dig in the mines if they do not find precious metals? God does not bid us sift a mountain of chaff with here and there a grain of wheat in it, but the Bible is a granary of wheat, and we have but to open the door and find it. Scripture grows upon the student. It is full of surprises. Under the teaching of the Holy Spirit, to the searching eye it glows with the splendor of revelation, like a vast temple paved with wrought gold and roofed with rubies, emeralds, and all manner of gems. No merchandise is like the merchandise of Scripture truth.

Lastly, the Scriptures reveal Jesus, "that testify about Me." The more you search them the better, but it is not *the* thing—*it* is not the saving work. The Scriptures (with all reverence of them) are but the mine—Christ is the treasure! They are the fields, but He is the harvest! No more powerful motive can be urged upon Bible readers than this: he who finds Jesus finds life, heaven, all things. Happy is he who, searching his Bible, discovers his Savior.

CHARLES SPURGEON

"These are the very Scriptures that testify about me, yet you refuse to come to me to have life."

John 5:39–40

Christ is a person, a living person, full of power to save. His salvation is kept in himself; and if you want to have it, you must come to Him. He is still the one source and fountain of eternal mercy. There is no getting it by going around Him or by only going near Him. You must come to Him, actually to Him, and there must be a personal contact established between the Lord Jesus and your spirit. It must be a spiritual contact, by which your mind, heart, and thought shall come to Christ, and faith, like a hand, shall touch Him spiritually, grasp Him by believing upon Him, and receive life and grace from His divine power.

"Come to me to have life" includes all that is absolutely needful for salvation. It is the lowest stage of grace, and yet the term comprehends the very highest condition of the soul, even when it enters into glory and enjoys life at the right hand of God. The grace that enables you to overcome sin, the joy that enables us to master trouble, the light that helps us to look into divine mysteries, the inward spiritual principle given in regeneration, by which we have fellowship with God and with His Son Jesus Christ—these are the main ingredients in the life that you need.

O dear friend, life—the life of God in the soul—is to me the one thing needful, the one thing without which all the world were not worth the having. It would be better to be poor and hungry and naked than to be without this inner life. It is true life in this world to live by faith upon the Son of God. And it is the life that shall qualify you to dwell with cherubim and seraphim and join their songs, the life that will enable you to stand before the throne of God and cast your crown at His feet in ecstasy of grateful joy.

Infinite mockery to have the Bible but not the revelation, to have the shell but not the kernel, to have His book, but in it we never see the shape and hear His voice. O sweet, sweet word, *come*! It means the toddle of a little child; it means the running of an eager servant; it means the hurrying of one who is thirsty because he hears somewhere the splash of fountains. There is no dragging, no holding back; it is all "coming." Come your own way—but always come.

CHARLES SPURGEON

"You search the Scriptures, for in them you think you have eternal life; and these are they which testify of Me. But you are not willing to come to Me that you may have life."

John 5:39–40 NKJV

Scripture is not given to us merely to make us know something about God in Christ, nor only in order that we may have faith in the Christ thus revealed to us, but for a further end—great, glorious, but not distant—namely, that we may "have life." *Life* is deep, mystical, and inexplicable by any other words than itself. It includes pardon, holiness, well-being, immortality, and heaven, but it is more than all of these.

This life comes into our dead hearts and quickens them by union with God. Who is joined to God lives. Union with Christ in His sonship will bring life into dead hearts. He has come from heaven with fire, the fire of the divine life in union with His humanity, and He imparts it to us all if we will. He touches our death, and it is quickened into life. And the condition on which that great name will bring to us life is simply our faith. If you trust Him as the Son of God who comes down to earth that we in Him might have the immortal life He is ready to give, then the end that God has in view in all His revelation, that Christ had in view in His passion, has been accomplished for you. If you do not, it has not. You may think highly of Him, you may be ready to call Him by many great and appreciative names, but oh! Unless you have learned to see in Him the divine Savior of your soul, you have not seen what God means for you to see.

But if you have, then all other questions about this Book, important as they are in their places, may settle themselves as they will; you have got the essence, the thing that it was meant to bring you. Many a scholar has studied the Bible all his life and yet has missed the purpose for which it was given; and many uneducated men and women have found it. It is not meant to be disputed over, it is not meant to be read as an interesting product of the religious consciousness, it is not to be admired as a great example of sacred literature, but it is to be taken as being God's great Word to the world, the record of the revelation that He has given us in His Son. The eternal Word is the theme of all the written Word.

Make the jewel that is brought us in this treasury your own. Come to Jesus that you may have life.

ALEXANDER MACLAREN

"How can you believe, who receive honor from one another, and do not seek the honor that comes from the only God?"

John 5:44 NKJV

The promises made to faith are free and sure; the invitation and encouragement strong; the mighty power of God close at hand and free. All that hinders the blessing being ours is pride or a lack of faith. In our text, Jesus reveals to us that it is indeed pride that makes faith impossible: "How can you believe, who receive honor from one another?" As we see how in their very nature pride and faith are irreconcilably at odds, we learn that faith and humility are at their root one, and that we can never have more of true faith than we have of true humility. It is possible to have strong intellectual convictions and assurance of the truth while pride is still in the heart, but it makes living faith, which has power with God, impossible.

Humility is simply the disposition that prepares the soul for living in trust. Even the most secret breath of pride, in self-seeking, self-will, self-confidence, or self-exaltation, is only the strengthening of that self that cannot enter the kingdom or possess the things of the kingdom because it refuses to allow God to be who He is.

"How can you believe, who receive honor from one another?" Nothing can cure you of the desire to receive glory from men or of the sensitiveness and pain and anger that come when it is not given, but seeking alone the glory and honor that comes from God. Let the glory of the all-glorious God be everything to you. You will be freed from the glory of men and of self and be content and glad to be nothing. Out of this nothingness you will grow strong in faith, giving glory to God, and you will find that the deeper you sink in humility before Him, the nearer He is to fulfill every desire of your faith.

ANDREW MURRAY

*A great crowd of people followed him because they saw
the signs he had performed by healing the sick.*

John 6:2

T hat word *because* opens the door to a thousand reasons. Every man who
follows Christ follows Him for some reason of his own. Nicodemus came
to Jesus and declared that "no one could perform the signs you are doing
if God were not with him" (John 3:2). There are those who need all kinds of
wonders to be done before their eyes, and through the gate of amazement
they will come to Jesus. Others, like the Samaritans, are convinced by argument and theological persuasion (see John 4:42). Others believe in Christ
because of known cases of spiritual conversion that defy any explanation
but the power of God. Every man must begin where he can, but by all means,
let us encourage him to come in. All kinds of people are in the church, and
they have come as a result of all kinds of approach. One has an argument;
another has a miracle, a personal revelation, a grand conversion, a prophecy,
or a psalm. Do not seek to bring all these ministries and operations into a
dead monotony. We are meant to have within the church unity with diversity,
and we ought to celebrate it.

But woe to the soul who has not the true Christ, but one that is outward,
appointed by some skilled hand, preached by some eloquent tongue, imposed
by some lofty authority. That is not Christ at all. Any so-called Christ will
wither, will peel off the frescoed wall, or topple on the throne made for him by
some cabinetmaker. Every man must lay hold of Christ with his own hand, for
his own reason, and see Christ with His own eyes, and have a part or aspect
of Christ that belongs to himself in an almost exclusive sense. Let the heart
say how it sees Christ, lays hold of Christ, for what reason in particular it
clings to Christ: that is enough. You cannot shake a man out of what he is
really persuaded of in his own heart. If he trusts in certain writings, he may
lose them; if he is persuaded emotionally to nod his head to certain propositions, he will soon forget the propositions; but if Christ is born in a man,
He remains there the hope of glory—his own Christ, not some other man's
Christ. Let the despised and banished soul say, "I have seen one flash of His
glory, one view of His beauty, and I have heard one tone of His music, and
to that, what I have seen and known, I cling."

JOSEPH PARKER

*When Jesus looked up and saw a great crowd coming
toward him, he said to Philip, "Where shall we buy bread
for these people to eat?" He asked this only to test him,
for he already had in mind what he was going to do.*

John 6:5–6

Jesus had gone away to snatch a brief moment of rest, but the hurrying crowds come pressing with their common curiosity after Him for another miracle. No movement of impatience passes across His mind; no reluctance as He turns away from the vanishing prospect of a quiet afternoon with His friends. He looks on the crowd, and His first thought is that of sympathy. Before they even realized their needs, Christ was there to supply them. Even with the careless He shows His care, and His heart was prophetic of their necessities.

But, further, He selects for the question Philip, a man whom we would declare an intensely practical person, who seems to have had little faith in anything that he could not get hold of by his senses. Jesus hoped that the question might shape itself in the hearer's mind into a promise, and that Philip might have been able to say, "You can supply it, Master. We need not buy it." Jesus puts problems before His followers to settle; takes us, as it were, into His confidence with questionings that test us, whether we can rise above the level of the material and visible, and whether all our conceptions of possibilities are bounded by these. And though we may fail to see the answer at first, it works to help us rise to a clear faith.

Philip scans the multitude and makes a rough calculation of the cost. He was a man of numbers, who believed in what could be put into tables and statistics. But, like a great many of us, he left out one element in his calculation, and that was Jesus Christ, and so his answer went dragging itself like a wounded bird, when it might have risen on the wings of faith into the heavens and soared and sung.

When we have to deal with Christ's working, probabilities that can be tabulated are not altogether the best bases upon which to rest our calculations. Learn that the audacity of a faith that expects great things, though there is nothing visible upon which to build, is wiser and more prudent than the creeping common sense that adheres to facts that are shadows and forgets that the chief fact is that we have an almighty Helper and Friend at our side.

ALEXANDER MACLAREN

*Another of his disciples, Andrew, Simon Peter's brother,
spoke up, "Here is a boy with five small barley loaves
and two small fish, but how far will they go among
so many?"*

John 6:8–9

Just a boy. We don't know his name or why he brought this slender provision. But in the providence of God, he was the right boy in the right place that day. Christ never is in need but He has somebody at hand to supply that need. If we will but believe, the same is true in our lives. He will never desert His people. He will find men when He needs them. Thus it has been in the history of the saints, and thus it shall ever be. Before the Reformation there were many learned men who knew something of Christ's gospel, but they communed with one another and with Christ very quietly. What was needed was an untamable fellow who would upset the old state of things. The God who made Luther knew what He was doing when He made him; He put within him a great burning fire that could not be restrained, and it burst forth and set the nations ablaze. Never despair about providence. David will come forth to slay Goliath.

But the boy's provision was nearly despised away—what could be the use of such a small stock? Now, I daresay that some of you have had Satan saying to you, "What is the use of your trying to do anything?" To you, dear mother, with a family of children, he has whispered, "You cannot serve God." He knows very well that, by sustaining grace, you can; and he is afraid of how well you can serve God if you bring up those dear children in the fear of God. He says to you, "You have very little ability. What can you do?" Ah, dear friend, he is afraid of what you can do, and if you will only do what you can do, God will help you to do what now you cannot do. But the devil is afraid of even the little that you can do now; and many a child of God seems to side with Satan in despising the day of small things. The things that God will honor, man must first despise. You run the gauntlet of the derision of men, and afterward you come out to be used of God.

Our blessed Master, now that He has ascended into the heavens, has more rather than less power. He is not baffled because of our lack, but can even now use insignificant means to accomplish His own glorious purposes. He will never desert you in your spiritual need any more than He failed that hungry crowd.

CHARLES SPURGEON

Jesus then took the loaves, gave thanks, and distributed to those who were seated as much as they wanted. He did the same with the fish.

John 6:11

Note the transformation of the loaves and fish when placed in the blessed hands that one day would bear the nail prints. Is it not a wonderful thing that Christ, the living God, should associate himself with our feebleness, with our lack of talent, with our ignorance, with our little faith? And yet He does so. If we are not associated with Him, we can do nothing; but when we come into living touch with Him, we can do all things. Those barley loaves in Christ's hand became pregnant with food for the multitude. Out of His hands they are nothing but barley loaves; but in His hands, linked to Him, they are in contact with omnipotence. Have you thought of bringing all that you possess to Him, that it may be joined to Him? There is that brain of yours; it can be associated with the teachings of the Holy Spirit. There is that heart of yours; it can be warmed with the love of God. There is that tongue of yours; it can be touched with the live coal from off the altar. I do not say that every man of common ability can rise to high ability by being associated with Christ through faith. But I do say this, that his ordinary ability, in association with Christ, will become sufficient for the occasion to which God has called him. Never number your deficiencies; bring what you have, and let all that you are—body, soul, and spirit—be associated with Christ. The talents you have will have new power, for they will come into a new condition toward Him. And what may not be hoped for by association with such wisdom and might?

Only let us make sure that we have truly given ourselves over to Christ. If you have made that full transfer, there lies great power at your disposal. Oh, that we had more real placing of our lives in Christ's hands! The time that you have not used for self, but given to Christ, the knowledge that you have not stored, as in a bottle, but given to Christ, the ability that you have not wielded for the world, but yielded to Christ, your influence and position, your money and home, all put into Christ's hands, and reckoned to be not your own, but His. Be like the lad and give your all. Do not think of reserving some for yourself or for another occasion. If you can believe that God can feed five, believe that He can feed five thousand.

CHARLES SPURGEON

When they had all had enough to eat, he said to his disciples, "Gather the pieces that are left over. Let nothing be wasted."

John 6:12

Here we are taught to think of the large surplus in Christ's gifts over and above our need. Our Lord has himself given us a commentary upon this miracle. All of Christ's miracles are parables, for all teach us, on the level of natural and outward things, lessons that are true in regard to the spiritual world. And here we have Christ, on the day after the miracle, commenting upon it in His long and profound discourse upon "the bread of life" (John 6:32–59), which plainly intimates that He meant His office of feeding the hungry crowds to be a picture and a guide that might lead to the apprehension of the higher view of himself as "the bread of God . . . that comes down from heaven and gives life to the world" (v. 33) by His broken body and shed blood.

So, we are not inventing an interpretation of this passage when we say that the abundance far beyond what the eaters could make use of at the moment really represented the large surplus of inexhaustible resources and unused grace that is treasured for us all in Christ Jesus. Those whom He feeds will have a feast. His gifts answer our need, and over-answer it, for He is "able to do immeasurably more than all we ask or imagine" (Ephesians 3:20), and neither our conceptions, nor our petitions, nor our present powers of receiving are the real limits of the illimitable grace that is laid up for us in Christ, and which, potentially, we have each of us in our hands whenever we lay our hands on Him.

Oh, dear friend, what you and I have ever had and felt of Christ's power, sweetness, preciousness, and love is as nothing compared with the infinite depths of all that lies in Him. The sea fills the little creeks along its shore, but it rolls in unfathomed depths, boundless to the horizon. And all the present experience of all Christian people, of what Christ is, is like the experience of the first settlers in some great undiscovered continent, who timidly plant a little fringe of population around its edge and grow their scanty crops there, while the great prairies of miles, with all their wealth and fertility, are lying unknown in the heart of the unexplored continent. Christ is a great deal more than all mankind have yet found Him to be. Let us see that nothing of that infinite preciousness of His is lost to us.

ALEXANDER MACLAREN

So they gathered them and filled twelve baskets with the pieces of the five barley loaves left over by those who had eaten.

John 6:13

These men had given the crowds this miraculously made bread, but they had to exercise ordinary carefulness in the preservation of the supernatural gift. Christ has been given to you by the most stupendous miracle that ever was or can be wrought, and the Spirit of Christ has come to dwell in your heart to make you wise and fair, gentle and strong, and altogether Christlike. But you must take care of these gifts. You have to use wisely and not waste the Bread of Life that came down from heaven, or the Bread of God will not feed you. You have to provide the basket in which to carry the surplus bounty of the divine gift, or you may stand hungry in the midst of plenty.

Be watchful stewards of Christ by being diligent in your use of the grace given. See that you use to the very full, in the measure of your present power of absorbing and your present need, the gift bestowed upon you. Be sure that you take in as much of Christ as you can contain before you begin to think of what to do with the surplus. If we are not careful to take what we can, and to use what we need, of Christ, there is little chance of our being faithful stewards of the surplus. Many believers seem to have much more given to them in Christ than they need because they are doing no work to use up the gift.

Be careful to guard the grace given from whatever would deplete it. Let not worldliness, business, cares of the world or the sorrows of life, its joys, duties, anxieties, and pleasures—let not these so come into your heart that they will elbow Christ out of your heart and dull your appetite for the true Bread that came down from heaven.

Not only by use and by careful guarding but also by earnest desire for greater gifts of Christ shall we receive more and more of His sweetness and preciousness into our heart as well as His beauty and glory into our transformed character. The basket that we carry, this recipient heart of ours, is elastic. It can stretch to hold any amount that you would like to put into it. The desire for more of Christ's grace will stretch its capacity, and as its capacity increases, the inflowing gift grows, and Christ fills the larger room of my poor heart.

ALEXANDER MACLAREN

Jesus, knowing that they intended to come and make him king by force, withdrew again to a mountain by himself.

John 6:15

These words enable us to come to some understanding of the role or place of force in the gospel of Jesus Christ. It is a common saying that some men have greatness thrust upon them. From all such men Jesus Christ separates himself, knowing that what is done by force or compulsion may by force or compulsion be undone. So He would not have a kingdom that was forced upon Him, nor would He be forced upon a kingdom. Wonderful words are written upon the blood-red banner of this King. Read some of them: "Put your sword away" (John 18:11). "My kingdom is not of this world" (John 18:36). "He made himself nothing, but taking the very nature of a servant . . ." (Philippians 2:7). "Here I am! I stand at the door and knock" (Revelation 3:20). Are these kingly words? Jesus would not be a man-made king; in some other way He would come to the throne. The leader of the masses must live by popular favor; this man must rule by a deeper and nobler law. So He passes away from the impulsive crowd.

This is the second time that Jesus declined to be a king. It is not every man who has two such chances in one lifetime—Jesus had them and despised them. Once He was shown all the kingdoms of the world and the glory of them and was told that they might be His if He would bend His knee to the devil, and He said no (see Matthew 4:8–10). Everything, you see, depends upon how you get hold of your kingdom. If you have offered false worship for your kingdom, it will rot in your grip, and if you have been forced upon a reluctant heart, that heart will cast you off in the springtime of its returning power. Jesus came to be a king, yes; King of kings and Lord of lords, but His kingdom has nothing to do with force or compulsion.

Jesus Christ reigns by distinct consent of the human mind. This King knocks at our door and offers himself as the gospel for our soul. When I look at Him speaking these words, there glows through His carpenter's garments a light that supersedes the sun. We love Him because He first loved us. He lays hold of our entire loves, leaves no element of it unclaimed, dominates the whole sphere of our purified and sanctified desires—that means an everlasting reign. When I put these things together, I cannot tell how my heart glows with love to this wondrous Nazarene. Even so, come and reign over us, Ancient of Days!

JOSEPH PARKER

Then Jesus, knowing that they were going to come and take Him by force to make Him king, withdrew again to the mountainside by Himself.

John 6:15 AMP

Man needs God. God made man for himself, for man to find his life and happiness in God alone.

Man needs to be alone with God. Man's fall consisted in his being brought, through the lust of the flesh and the world, under the power of things visible and temporal. His restoration is meant to bring him back to the Father's house, the Father's presence, the Father's love and fellowship. Salvation means being brought to love and to delight in the presence of God.

Man needs to be alone with God. Without this, God does not have the opportunity to shine into his heart, to transform his nature by His divine working, to take possession and to fill him with the fullness of God.

Man needs to be alone with God to yield to the presence and the power of His holiness, of His life, and of His love. Christ on earth needed it; He could not live the life of a Son here in the flesh, without at times separating himself entirely from His surroundings and being alone with God (see Luke 9:18). How much more must this be indispensable for us!

When our Lord Jesus gave us the blessed command to enter a private place, to shut the door, to pray to our Father in secret, all alone, He gave us the promise that the Father would hear such prayers and mightily answer them in our life before men (see Matthew 6:6).

Alone with God—that is the secret of true prayer, of true power in prayer, of real living, face-to-face fellowship with God, and power for service. There is no true, deep conversion, no true, deep holiness, no clothing with the Holy Spirit and with power, no abiding peace or joy, without being daily alone with God. What an inestimable privilege is the institution of private prayer to begin every morning. Let it be the one thing our hearts are set on, seeking and finding and meeting God.

Take time, oh, my soul, take time, to be alone with God.

ANDREW MURRAY

He departed again to the mountain by Himself alone.

John 6:15 NKJV

Throughout the Gospels we see our Savior's intense desire to meet with God, to commune with the Father. Herein there is a living likeness between His prayers and ours. Yet His devotions must have been very different from ours because He had no sin or personal weakness to confess or lament as we often do. I can conceive that much of His devotion was shown in conversation with the Father, when His blessed mind, forever in agreement with the mind of God, spoke to God, and God revealed himself to Him. Intimate communication must have been the main ingredient of the Savior's prayers. The Savior would tell the Father all His love for Him, how He desired nothing but the salvation of those whom the Father gave Him, and He would listen to the Father speaking to Him heart-to-heart. His prayers in solitude must have been marvelous communications. How simple, yet how spiritual! How full! How deep! How intense! The Master's prayers were a free, outspoken talk with the Most High.

Our Lord loved to put prayer first of all. He would go nowhere or attempt nothing till He had prayer. He would not preach a sermon or work a miracle, however necessary, however profitable, until first of all He had drawn near to God. Take heed to yourself to follow the same rule. Look no man in the face till you have seen the face of God. Speak with no one till you have spoken with the Most High. Take not to running till you have in prayer laid aside every weight, lest you lose the race. We cannot, we must not, think of entering upon a day or upon an enterprise without our God; let us attempt nothing without Him.

We are always in need, and therefore our daily devotion must consist largely of petitions. But yet we are by divine grace the children of God, and the child says many things to his father beside that which takes the form of a request. Have we not with joyful reverence told our heavenly Father that we love Him? How we long to be with Him? How we long to be more like Him? How we desire to serve Him? That is how we talk with God alone. Our heart is to the heart of God as the echo to the Father's voice that calls us.

So the Savior departs and gets alone with God. Dear friend, take care that you also pray. If our Lord needed to pray, how much more do we require it?

CHARLES SPURGEON

When evening came, his disciples went down to the lake,
where they got into a boat and set off across the lake
for Capernaum. By now it was dark, and Jesus had not
yet joined them. A strong wind was blowing and the
waters grew rough.

John 6:16–18

The miracle had worked up the excitement of the crowd to a very dangerous point. Crowds are always the same, and this crowd thought that the prophet who could make bread at will was the kind of prophet whom they wanted. Christ, seeing the danger and not desiring that His kingdom should be furthered by such revolting motives, withdrew into the loneliness of the bordering hills. It was wise to divide the little group. It would save the disciples from being affected by the boisterous enthusiasm of the crowd and from revealing the place where Jesus had gone. So they are sent across to the other side of the lake, some five or six miles. But suddenly one of the gusts of wind that are frequently found upon mountain lakes rose and soon became a gale with which they could not battle.

Is it not the history of the church in a nutshell? Is it not the symbol of life for us all? The solemn law under which we live demands persistent effort and imposes continual opposition toward us. There is no reason why we should regard that as evil, because we are not fair-weather sailors. The purpose of life is to make men; the meaning of all events is to mold character. Anything that makes me stronger is a blessing; anything that develops my character and confidence is the highest good that can come to me. And so be thankful when a sudden gust thrashes the sails and sends you to the helm and takes all your effort to keep from sinking. Do not murmur or think that God's providence is strange. Recognize Him as the Lord who, in love and kindness, sends all the different kinds of weather that make for the complete year.

In the darkness, in the fight against the tempest, and in the absence of the Master, no doubt the disciples looked up in vain and wondered where Jesus was. Mark gives us one sweet touch when he tells us that Christ on the hillside saw them toiling at rowing, but they did not see Him (see Mark 6:48). No doubt they felt themselves deserted, but Jesus' calm and loving gaze looked down, pitying all their fear and toil. The darkness did not hide from Him, nor His own security on the steadfast land make Him forget, nor His communion with the Father so absorb Him as to exclude them, or us, from His thoughts.

ALEXANDER MACLAREN

When they had rowed about three or four miles, they
saw Jesus approaching the boat, walking on the water;
and they were frightened.

John 6:19

Here we have a revelation of Christ as the Lord of the material universe, a kingdom wider in its range and profounder in its authority than that which the shouting crowd had sought to force upon Him. His will combined with the yielding wave sustained His material body on the tossing surges. The miracle is a manifestation of the glory of Christ and of His power over the physical order of things. In it we have a wonderful picture that is true for all ages of the mighty Christ, to whose gentle footstep the unquiet surges are as a marble pavement; and who draws near in the purposes of His love, unhindered by opposition, and using even opposing forces as the path for His triumphant progress.

In His marvelous providence, Christ uses all the tumults, the opposition and tempests that surround the boat that bears His followers, as achieving His purposes. We stand before a mystery to which we have no key when we think of these two certain facts: first, the omnipotent redeeming will of God in Christ; and, second, the human opposition that is able to rear itself against that. And we stand in the presence of another mystery when we think that in some mysterious fashion He works His purposes by the very antagonism to His purposes, making even the head winds fill the sails, and planting His foot on the white crests of the angry, surging waves. How often in the world's history has this scene repeated itself, and by a divine irony the enemies have become the helpers of Christ's cause, and what they plotted for destruction has turned out rather for the furtherance of the gospel!

Remember that Christ, in His gentle sustaining help, comes near to us all across the sea of sorrow and trouble. A more tender, a more gracious sense of His nearness to us is ever granted to us in the time of our darkness and our grief than is possible to us in the sunny hours of joy. It is always the stormy sea that Christ comes across, to draw near to us; and those who have never experienced the tempest have yet to learn the inmost sweetness of His presence. When it is night, and it is dark, at the hour that is the keystone of night's black arch, Christ comes to us, striding across the stormy waters. Sorrow brings Him near to us. Do you see that sorrow does not drive you away from Him?

ALEXANDER MACLAREN

They saw Jesus approaching the boat, walking on the water; and they were frightened. But he said to them, "It is I; don't be afraid." Then they were willing to take him into the boat.

John 6:19–21

These disciples had fought gallantly with the storm; then possibly in the chill uncertain light of the gray dawn breaking over the eastern hills, a questionable shape coming across the water freezes their heart blood with terror. The average man, if he believes that anything out of the unseen is near him, shrinks in fear. And so they mistook the coming Master.

I ask you if we do not often make the same mistake. We are often so absorbed with our work and life, so busy tugging at the oar, that we have no time and no eyes to look across the waters and see who it is coming to us through the tempest. Tears fill our eyes and weave a veil between us and the Master. And when we do see that there is something there, we are often afraid of it. And sometimes when a gentle whisper of consolation, or some light air, as it were, of consciousness of His presence breathes through our souls, we think it is only a phantom of our making, and that the coming Christ is nothing more than a figment of our thoughts and imaginations.

Let no absorption in cares and duties, let no unchildlike murmuring, no selfish abandonment to sorrow, blind you to the Lord who always comes near troubled hearts if they will only look and see! Let no reluctance to entertain spiritual ideas, no shrinking from the thought of Christ as a killjoy keep you from seeing Him as He draws near to you in your troubles. Let no sly, mocking doubt, nor any poisonous air, blowing off the foul and stagnant marshes of present materialism make you think that the living Reality, treading on the waves, is a dream or a projection of your imagination on to the void of space. He is real, whatever may be phenomenal and surface. The storm is not as real as the Christ. The waves will pass, but He abides forever.

Lift up your heart and be glad. "It is I; don't be afraid" is the true word of the Master. What a thrill of glad confidence must have poured itself into their hearts, when once they rose to the height of that wondrous fact! There is no fear in the consciousness of His presence. His coming is the banishment of danger and the exorcism of dread. Take Christ on board and let Him stand between you and the tempest.

ALEXANDER MACLAREN

But He said to them, "It is I; do not be afraid."

John 6:20 NKJV

The frightened disciples had only to hear Jesus speak, and without a name being mentioned, they perceived that it was the Lord. It is not possible for me to convey to you what richness of consolation lies at the thought that Jesus is Jesus, which is, being interpreted, the Savior. That one character and office is cheering, but the same is true of all the names He wears. It is Jesus who walks the water of your trouble and comes to you—Jesus the Son of God.

Jesus speaks to you: "It is I." Have you lost a loved one? Have your possessions failed? Is your health departing? Are your joys declining? Alas! It is a dying, fleeting world, but Jesus is always the same. Be comforted; whatever else is gone, wherever else the arrows of death may fly, Jesus still lives. "It is I" are blessed words of rich comfort to be heard in the darkness of the night by weary mariners whose spirits are sinking within them.

Jesus spoke this message to believers who were tossed with a tempest, and we need it when we are depressed and troubled by the surrounding of these evil times. In seasons of job loss, great sickness, wars and calamities, and public disasters, it is balm to the spirit to know that Jesus is still the same. Sin may abound yet more, the light of the gospel may burn low, and the prince of darkness may widely sway his destroying scepter, but Jesus is the same. Look through the darkness, and you will see your Lord amid the hurricane, walking the waters of politics, ruling national convulsions, governing, overruling, and restraining it according to His wisdom. When men's hearts sink for fear and the rowers feel their oars ready to snap from the strain of useless toil, I hear the word that is the soul of music: "It is I; do not be afraid. I am ruling all things. I am coming to the rescue of my church; she shall yet sail on smoother waters and reach her desired haven."

Forebodings fill the air, and our sinking spirits chill the very marrow of our life. Nothing will serve but the present and sure consolations of the Lord Jesus. We must hear Him say, "It is I," or we shall faint. Then is the soul braced to withstand the next billow. When Jesus is with us, troubles have lost their power to trouble.

CHARLES SPURGEON

Once the crowd realized that neither Jesus nor his disciples were there, they got into the boats and went to Capernaum in search of Jesus.

John 6:24

The crowd was searching after Jesus from a very selfish motive, not because of the gracious words He spoke, or to give Him thanks for the benefits received at His hand, but merely because they hoped to eat the loaves and fish again. From such wretched motives let us flee. May we all shun with detestation the very idea of making a profession of faith for the sake of worldly advantage; it is utterly detestable. Those who seek Jesus Christ with the groveling desire to make a gain of godliness are hypocrites of the lowest sort.

For those who truly seek Christ, there is a large amount of hopefulness in it, even if the motives for seeking have a mixture of darkness with the light. He would not be seeking Jesus unless he had some kind of faith—at any rate, a theoretical faith—in the Savior and in his need of Jesus. Men who are aroused and caused to think are on the road to conviction of sin, and conviction is on the way to faith in Christ. I am glad that Jesus is the object of the seeker, for nothing else is worth seeking. What a pleasing sight it is to see a man who has formerly been prayerless, falling upon his knees! How gratifying to see the unread Bible brought down from the dusty shelf!

But, alas, I may be disappointed. The early cloud of hope may melt into nothingness. Hope tells a flattering tale, but she may be deceived. It is possible for the seeker to look east and west to behold a wonder, while the Wonderful, the Savior, stands at his right hand ready to forgive. In seeking, then, there is some good, but oh, how much of evil! Here are gleams and flashes of light, but oh, how dense is the darkness of unbelief! Look not at salvation's cup, but drink of it. Stand not by the fountain's edge, but wash in it and be clean. Oh, may the Holy Spirit lead you to cease your search for fine pearls, for the pearl of great price is before you. Jesus is not to be discovered in secret; He stands before you openly. Jesus is Immanuel, "God with us." A prayer will reach Him, a wish will find Him, a groan will pierce His heart—only confide in Him and He is yours. Take the simple command of the gospel: "Believe in the Lord Jesus."

CHARLES SPURGEON

Then they asked him, "What must we do to do the works God requires?" Jesus answered, "The work of God is this: to believe in the one he has sent."

John 6:28–29

Note the difference between the works the crowd asks about and the work Christ speaks of. They thought of a great variety of religious observances and deeds. Christ gathers them all up into one. They thought of a pile, and that the higher it rose the more likely they were to be accepted. He unified the requirement and brought it all down to this one act, and on which alone the whole weight of man's salvation is to rest. "What must we do to do the works God requires?" is a question asked in all sorts of ways by the hearts of men around us; and what a babble of answers comes! One says, "Rites and ceremonies." Another says, "Culture and education." The moralist says, "Do this, that, and the other thing." Jesus brushes them all aside and says, "No. Not doing, but trusting." Insofar as that is an act, it is the only act that you need.

That is evidently reasonable. The man is more than his work; motive is more important than action; character is deeper than conduct. God is pleased, not by what men do, but by what men are. We must *be* first, and then we shall *do*. Such is true in all human relations. What would you care for a child who scrupulously obeyed but did not love or trust? What does a president care about a citizen who performs acts of loyalty and all the while is plotting and nurturing treason in his heart?

If doing separate acts of righteousness is the way to do the works God requires, then no man has ever done them. For it is a plain fact that every man falls below his conscience—and one's conscience is less scrupulous than the divine law. The worst of us knows a great deal more than the best of us; and our lives, universally, are, at best, lives of partial effort after unreached attainments of obedience.

The gospel is, first of all, trust; and then, set yourself to do the works of faith. It works by love, it is the opening of the heart to the entrance of the life of Christ, and, of course, when that life comes in, it will act in the man in a manner appropriate to its origin and source. He who has opened his heart to receive the life of Christ, will, as a matter of course, bring forth, in the measure of his faith, the fruits of righteousness.

ALEXANDER MACLAREN

Then Jesus declared, "I am the bread of life. Whoever comes to me will never go hungry, and whoever believes in me will never be thirsty."

John 6:35

Jesus Christ is the bread without which we cannot live. He never says He is a rare delicacy or luxury, a feast that the rich alone can afford. He likens himself to the necessities of life, and in so doing He shows wisdom, a reach of mind, a grasp of human nature, that should save Him from the attacks of malicious men. An adventurer would not have seen in metaphors so humble a philosophy so profound. Adventurers like big words and glaring figures; they speak great swelling words of vanity; they search heaven and earth for effective figures; they disdain the everyday. Not so with Jesus Christ. He is the Bread of Life, He is Water, He is Light, He is the Door, He is the Good Shepherd. These words, so simple, stretch their meaning around the whole circle of human life, and by their choice alone is the supreme wisdom of Jesus Christ abundantly attested.

Man needs Jesus Christ as a necessity and not as a luxury. You may be pleased to have flowers, but you cannot survive without bread. Jesus Christ is not a phenomenon, He is Bread; He is not a curiosity to be labeled as a remarkable specimen, He is Water. As surely as we cannot live without bread, we cannot live truly without Christ. If we do not know Christ, we are not living, our movement is a mechanical flutter, and our pulse is but the stirring of physical life. Only the holy Christ of God can satisfy the hunger and the thirst of the soul of man. He is the only Healer of my wounds, the one Savior of my soul.

Oh, the darkness of leaving the simplicity of Jesus Christ. I care not how rich our music, how magnificent our architecture, how impressive our method of worship, if all this is kept strictly in its proper place. I love beauty; I am moved to passion and heroism by inspiring music; I would make the Lord's house glad with every expression of love; but this done, I would write on the doorposts, on the roof, and on every wall, the words of Jesus: "Something greater than the temple is here" (Matthew 12:6). I prefer knowledge to ignorance, but I prefer holiness to either. Culture, when not a chattering and fussy show, may be noble and even majestic; but nothing is as cold as culture and nothing so mean, when not inflamed and impassioned by the Spirit of Christ. We must always go back to the bread of Christ and find all we need in His grace and truth.

JOSEPH PARKER

And Jesus said to them, "I am the bread of life. He who comes to Me shall never hunger, and he who believes in Me shall never thirst."

John 6:35 NKJV

C hrist compares the needs of men to hungering and thirsting. What pain can be worse beneath the skies than hunger and thirst? Now, Jesus has come to meet the deep, pressing, vital needs and pains of your nature. Your desire for a clear conscience, to be loved by someone, to be secure in this life, to not fear death, all these vast desires Jesus has come to meet, and all these He does meet in the case of all who come to Him, as everyone who has sought Him will bear witness.

He who is a believer in Jesus finds enough in his Lord to satisfy him now and to content him forevermore. The believer is not the man whose days are weary for lack of comfort, and whose nights are long from absence of heart-cheering thoughts, for he finds in his faith such a spring of joy, such a fountain of consolation, that he is content and happy. Put him in a dungeon and he will find good company; place him in a barren wilderness and he will eat the bread of heaven; drive him away from friendship and he will meet the "friend who sticks closer than a brother" (Proverbs 18:24 NKJV). Sap the foundation of his earthly hopes, but his heart will still be fixed, trusting in the Lord.

The heart is insatiable till Jesus enters it, and then it is a cup full to over-flowing. There is such a fullness in Christ that He alone is all to the believer. The true saint is so completely satisfied with the all-sufficiency of Jesus that he hungers and thirsts no more—except for deeper drinks from the living fountain. In that sweet manner shall you thirst; it shall not be a thirst of pain, but of loving desire; you will find it a sweet thing to be panting after a fuller enjoyment of Jesus' love.

Someone once said, "I have been lowering my bucket down into the well often, but now my thirst after Jesus has become so insatiable that I long to put the well itself to my lips and drink." Is this the feeling of your heart? Do you feel that all your desires are satisfied in Jesus, and that you have no want now, but to know more of Him and to have closer fellowship with Him? Then come continually to the fountain and take of the water of life freely. Jesus will never think you take too much, but will ever welcome you, saying, "Drink, yes, drink deeply, O beloved ones!" (Song of Solomon 5:1 NKJV).

CHARLES SPURGEON

"All those the Father gives me will come to me, and whoever comes to me I will never drive away."

John 6:37

This is one of the most generous gospel texts that I remember having seen between the covers of my Bible. It is generous, first, to the character to whom the promise is made—"whoever comes to me." The man may have been guilty of an atrocious sin, but if he comes to Christ, he shall never be driven away. To that atrocious sin he may have added many others, but if he comes to Jesus, he shall not be cast out. He may have made himself as dark as hell; yet, the Lord will not cast out the person who comes to Him. Be your character what it may, you shall not be turned away. Through Jesus Christ, if you but believe in Him, your whole past shall be rolled up and put away, as though it had never existed, and you shall be born again.

An old man took his fair-haired granddaughter on his knee, threaded his fingers through her locks, and said, "Child, God keep you from the sin into which I have plunged. My old life is almost over, and I am past hope. Would to God I were a child again!" Lo, the angel of mercy whispers to anyone in such a condition, "You may be a child again!" The man who is a graybeard in infamy may yet become a babe of innocence through the cleansing power of the blood of Jesus Christ. Go write it in new stars across the night sky: "Whoever comes to me I will never drive away." Let the sun cast all his beams upon it until it seems written in the splendor of God.

I would also have you notice the blessed certainty of this salvation: "I will never drive away." The negatives in the Greek language used here make it very strong. As much as to say, "On no account, or for no reason, or on no pretense, or from no motive whatever, will I ever in time or in eternity cast out the soul who comes to me." That is how it stands—a declaration of absolute certainty. What a blessed thing it is to get your foot on certainties. Let us look into the beautiful face of Jesus and believe that He does indeed receive us; and if He receives us, we are received into the heart of God; we are received into eternal life; and eventually we shall be received into everlasting blessedness. Oh, the joy that it is so absolutely certain!

CHARLES SPURGEON

*At this the Jews there began to grumble about him be-
cause he said, "I am the bread that came down from
heaven." They said, "Is this not Jesus, the son of Joseph,
whose father and mother we know? How can he now
say, 'I came down from heaven'?"*

John 6:41–42

I wish to bring before your notice the wonderful way to which our Lord, in this great dissertation concerning himself as the Bread of Life, gradually unfolds the depths of His meaning and of His offer. He began by saying that He, the Son of Man, will give to men the bread that "gives life to the world" (v. 33). And then when that saying is but dimly understood, and yet awakes some strange new desires in the hearers, and they come to Him and ask, "Sir, always give us this bread" (v. 34), He answers them with opening another finger of His hand, as it were, and showing them a little more of the treasure that lies in His palm. For He says, "I am the bread of life" (v. 35). That is an advance on the previous saying. He gives bread, and any man who was conscious of possessing some great truth or some great blessing that would refresh and nourish humanity might have said the same thing. But now we pass in the shadow of a greater mystery: "I am the bread of life." You cannot separate what Christ gives from what Christ is. You can take the truths that another man proclaims, altogether irrespective of him and his personality. You can take Plato's teaching and do as you like with Plato. But you cannot take Christ's teaching and do as you like with Christ. His personality is the center of His gift to the world.

Then notice how He draws us further into the circle of the light. Now He asserts, "I am the bread that came down from heaven." The listeners immediately laid hold of that one point, neglecting for the moment all the rest, and became fixed on the fact that they knew Jesus' parents, which seemed to contradict His declaration. Christ presses the point that you cannot get to the heart of His message unless you have accepted the truth concerning Him, that "in the beginning was the Word, and the Word was with God, and the Word was God" (John 1:1), and that at a definite point in time "the Word became flesh and made his dwelling among us" (John 1:14). Heaven must come, and has come, to earth, if earth is to rise to heaven. The ladder must be let down from above, if ever from the lower level men are to ascend to the summit where the face of God can be seen.

ALEXANDER MACLAREN

"I am the bread of life."

John 6:48

Herein Jesus teaches us to fix our eyes mainly upon His blessed person and to think of Him first and foremost. He is the center and soul of all. There is a tendency about us to get away from Jesus and to look rather to the streams than to the Fountainhead. Why are we more taken up with bits of glass that sparkle in the light than with the sun itself? That tree of life, in the midst of the paradise of God—we forget to eat of it, wandering to the border of the garden to pluck the fruit of the forbidden Tree of Knowledge of Good and Evil. Oh that our lives might be secured to the cross of Christ alone.

As manna was the perfect food for the Israelites in the wilderness, so Jesus Christ is to the soul. In Him is life for men, and no disease or death. If our souls live upon Christ, and nothing else but Christ, He will produce no disease within the heart; He will not inflame the imagination; He will not excite the passions. If we were to feed on Christ alone, we should become pure, holy, lowly, meek, gentle, and humble; in a word, we should be perfect even as He is. There is no sustenance for faith, love, patience, joy, as living daily upon Jesus, our Savior.

If we do but get hold of Jesus Christ and feed on Him, He is sufficient for us—sufficient for gigantic labors, sufficient for anguish, and grief, and sorrow; sufficient for the weakest of the babes, for He is pure milk; sufficient for the full-grown men among us, for He is the strong meat of the kingdom. His flesh is meat indeed. For your spiritual manhood there is bone, gristle, muscle, brain, everything that you need, in Christ. If you feed on Him, He will build you up, not in one direction only, but in all ways. For you are complete in Christ—thoroughly furnished for all your necessities. Christ Jesus meets all the needs of all His people with a divine sufficiency.

Oh, the sweetness that there is in the bread that came down from heaven! Do you know it? If you love Jesus, you wish for nothing new. Why leave this bread of heaven for the unsatisfying husks afforded by other sources? The first truth we are to remember is that Jesus Christ fully meets all the needs of the new life.

CHARLES SPURGEON

"I am the living bread that came down from heaven. Whoever eats this bread will live forever. This bread is my flesh, which I will give for the life of the world."

John 6:51

To feed upon Christ is to believe that which is revealed about Him, and then to appropriate Him to yourself by personal faith. Furthermore, it means to meditate much upon Him. There are sweet doctrines in the Bible that I delight to make my own by reading, marking, learning, and inwardly consuming them, for they are parts of the great circle of truth that is revealed of God. But I find that I am never so comforted, strengthened, and sustained as by deliberately considering Jesus Christ's precious death and atoning sacrifice. His sacrifice is the center of the circle, the focus of the light. There is a charm, a divine fascination, about His wounds.

O sacred Head once wounded! O dear eyes so red with weeping! O precious side, pierced for me! I could forever gaze, admire, and adore! There is no beauty in all of the world like that which is seen in Him who had "nothing in his appearance that we should desire him" (Isaiah 53:2). This one vision is enough for all eyes for all time. There is no sustenance to the heart like the sustenance that comes of His flesh and His blood given up in anguish and in death to work out our redemption. Beloved, this is the bread of heaven. "This is my body given for you; do this in remembrance of me" (Luke 22:19).

Oh, live near the cross! Build your house on Calvary! Frequent Gethsemane! Listen to the groans of your pleading Lord! Be much with a dying Christ. Be much with a risen Christ. Be much with a reigning Christ. Be much in anticipation of a coming Christ. For the more you are with Him, the more your soul will be filled with satisfaction and influenced to sanctification. He shall fill your soul as with marrow and with fatness, and your mouth shall praise Him with joyful lips, for He can say, and none other, "I am the living bread that came down from heaven."

Beloved, feeding upon Jesus we have an immortal blessedness: we shall never die. If we have fed on Christ, we shall fall asleep, but it will be in Jesus. We shall only pass into a higher stage of life: for that food on which we feed shall be in us the pledge of an immortality equal to the immortality of the Christ who has become our bread.

CHARLES SPURGEON

Jesus said to them, "Very truly I tell you, unless you eat the flesh of the Son of Man and drink his blood, you have no life in you. Whoever eats my flesh and drinks my blood has eternal life, and I will raise him up at the last day. For my flesh is real food and my blood is real drink."

John 6:53–55

It is evident that the Jews misunderstood the Savior and thought He referred to the literal eating of His flesh. It is no wonder that they stirred among themselves over such a saying, for, understood literally, it is horrible and revolting to the last degree. In this the Jews made the mistake of taking literally what Christ meant spiritually. Judicially blinded, as the result of unbelief, they stumbled at noonday as in the night and refused to see where all was plainly set forth. The veil was on their hearts. Ah, how prone is man to pervert the words of the Lord! Let us not fall into their error, but may divine grace lead us to see that our Lord's words are spirit and life.

This is a very beautiful and simple metaphor, when understood to refer spiritually to the person of our Lord. The act of eating and drinking is transferred from the body to the soul, and the soul is represented as feeding upon Jesus as the bread of life. Eating is the taking into yourself of something that exists externally, which you receive into yourself, and which becomes a part of you and helps to build you up and sustain you. It involves believing that Jesus was truly who He said He was, that He actually lived and died and was buried and rose again. It involves believing that Jesus' body was actually nailed to a tree, was really laid in the grave, and Thomas did in real deed put his finger into the print of the nails. There must be no doubts about these foundation facts. If we would feed upon Jesus, He must be real to us, for a man does not eat and drink shadows and fantasies.

Just as bread when it is eaten becomes dissolved and absorbed and afterward is turned into blood and flows through all the veins and goes to make up the body, even so Christ is to the soul. He becomes our life and through faith enters mysteriously into vital union with us. To feed upon Jesus Christ is to take Him in so that your life is hidden with Him, till you grow to be like Him, till your very life is Christ, and the great fact that Jesus lived and died becomes the mightiest truth under heaven, swaying your whole soul, subduing it to itself, and then elevating it to the highest degree.

CHARLES SPURGEON

"He who eats My flesh and drinks My blood abides in Me, and I in him."

John 6:56 NKJV

L ife must be fed with life. In a seed the life of nature is hidden, and we enjoy the power of that life in bread. As with the body, so it is with the spirit. The body is fed by the visible, the changeable life; the spirit must be fed with the invisible, unchangeable life of heaven. ·

It was to bring us this heavenly life that the Son of God descended to earth. It was to make this life accessible to us that He died like the seed in the earth, that His body was broken like the grain of wheat. It is to communicate this life and to make it our own that He gives himself to us in the Lord's Supper.

By His death Jesus took away the cause of everlasting hunger and sorrow, namely sin. The spirit of man, his part that does not die, can live only by God, who only has immortality. Sin separated man from God, and an eternal hunger and an eternal thirst of death are now his portion. He lost God, and nothing in the world can satisfy his infinite cravings. But Jesus comes and takes sin away and brings it to nothing in His body and gives us that body to eat and to do away with sin in us. Since "in Him dwells all the fullness of the Godhead bodily" (Colossians 2:9 NKJV), when I receive and enjoy Him, not only do I have the forgiveness of sins but I have the life of God.

Wonderful grace! May we come to understand it. The one who benefits from the Lord's Supper is the one who is distinguished from others by the fact that he or she has partaken of the Bread of Life.

Glorious food! Heavenly bread! It imparts heavenly life to us. Love to God, blessed rest, true holiness, and inward power, all that characterizes the life that is enjoyed in heaven. Let us be encouraged. We can do all things through Christ who strengthens us. He dwells in us. He is our food.

ANDREW MURRAY

"It is the Spirit who gives life; the flesh profits nothing. The words that I speak to you are spirit, and they are life."

John 6:63 NKJV

What is meant by "the flesh" here? The word *flesh*, in Scripture, has a dozen different modifications of its one abiding meaning. In this passage, it means that which is outward and appeals to the eye, or the ear, or to other powers of man's physical nature. There was much of this in the Jewish faith; but whenever the worshipers rested in it and did not reach to its spiritual teaching, it profited them nothing. Paul uses the same term when speaking to the Judaizing Galatians: "Having begun in the Spirit, are you now being made perfect by the flesh?" (Galatians 3:3 NKJV), which we understand to mean, having begun by God's Holy Spirit with a spiritual love to God, a spiritual faith in Jesus, and a spiritual life within, do you mean, now, to be made perfect by external ceremonial religion, resting and abiding in them as though they had a power to bless?

What is the meaning of the term *spirit*, which stands here in contrast with the *flesh*? Flesh is the external part of religion—that which the eye sees and the ear hears. Spirit is the inward part of religion—that which the soul understands, receives, believes, and feeds upon. It is this spiritual element that makes it a living thing. This spiritual religion is consistent with the spiritual nature that God the Holy Spirit gives to us, and as Christ's teachings are themselves living and spiritual, they are the proper food of spiritual men. The Jews commonly thought that religion lay in ceremonial observances, in eating certain foods, in hand washing, in going up to the temple to pray, and other outward performances. Jesus tells them that this flesh religion profits nothing; it is dead!

What, then, is the life of godliness? What is the essence of acceptable worship? His answer virtually is "It is your inward emotions, desires, beliefs, and adoration that are living worship." Then He adds, in effect, "My words are not concerning outward observances, but are of a spiritual character. I come not to you with 'Wash, vow, stand, sit, kneel.' My words deal with the inner life and spirit and are addressed to your spiritual natures. The words that I speak to you are spirit and life."

Be careful of any religion that is merely beautiful ritual performance or that tickles your fancy or stirs your feelings. True grace penetrates the very core of our nature, changes the heart, subdues the will, renews the passions, and makes us new creatures in Christ Jesus!

CHARLES SPURGEON

"This is why I told you that no one can come to me
unless the Father has enabled them."

John 6:65

f you were asked, "How do you know you have everlasting life?" you might
answer, "Because God has promised it" (see 1 John 2:25). But how do you
know He has promised it to you? If you answer, "Because I have believed
and have come to Jesus" (see John 3:16), this looks like you are resting your
hope of salvation upon something that you have done, upon the fact that you
have "come." And then, of course, any whirlwind of doubt will raise dust
enough to obscure that fact and all the comfort of it.

Yet there is grand comfort not in it, but in the glorious chain of which even
this human link is first forged and then held by Jehovah's own hand. Apart
from this, it is worth nothing at all.

Do not shrink from the words. Do not seek to explain them away. The
Faithful and True Witness spoke them, and the Holy Spirit has recorded them
forever. Jesus' words stand, even though many of His disciples murmured at
them at the time. Our coming to Jesus was not of ourselves; it was the gift
of God.

How did the gift operate? Not by coercing, but by drawing. "No one can
come to me unless the Father who sent me draws them" (John 6:44). Here
comes the great "Let the one who wishes take the free gift of the water of
life" (Revelation 22:17); for unless and until the Father drew them, no mortal
born of Adam ever wanted to come to Jesus. He had to draw us, or we never
would have thought of coming. Oh, the terrible depth of depravity revealed
by that keen sword-word: "Yet you *refuse* to come to me to have life" (John
5:40). Settle it, then, that no one ever had a glimmer of a will to come, but
that shining *whoever* flashed its worldwide splendor for their opening eyes
(see John 3:15–16).

But your will, now being acted upon more and more by His Spirit, the
Father drew you. Was it not so? Was it anything but loving-kindness that He
drew you? "I have loved you with an everlasting love; I have drawn you with
unfailing kindness" (Jeremiah 31:3). Our coming to Jesus was personal and
individual, but only because of God the Father's personal drawing of love.

FRANCES RIDLEY HAVERGAL

"You do not want to leave too, do you?" Jesus asked the Twelve. Simon Peter answered him, "Lord, to whom shall we go? You have the words of eternal life."

John 6:67–68

We are all tempted—sometimes tempted severely—to give up our faith and Christian hope. The hand that grasps spiritual treasures is not always equally strong. In dealing with the state of things that usually surround this painful experience, I ask this question: If we give up the faith, what shall we have instead?

Let me remind you that it is infinitely easier to ask questions than to answer them and to pull down than to build up. This rule applies to every area of life, but bears with special force upon the highest questions that engage the mind. Is it not easier, for example, to waste money than to earn it? Is it not easier to spoil a picture than to paint one? It is easier to tempt a man than to save him; easier to ruin life than to train it for heaven! There are skillful, articulate people who give themselves to the work of unsettling the human mind upon every subject. They have a genius for destruction. They lay no foundations. They teach no distinct and positive truth. They give the lie to all faith and throw distrust upon all spiritual experiences.

To all such people I put the practical question: If we go away from Christ, to whom shall we go? Will you give up the idea of the living, loving, personal God, ruling over all, which indeed is a mystery, and receive into your soul the greater mystery of godlessness? Shall we give up the notion of creation and receive the infinite absurdities of a world without a Creator? Convince me that a chair could not make itself, yet the sun is self-created. My coat had a maker, but my soul had none? Such a belief not only destroys faith, but it insults and dishonors reason itself. Faith displaced only brings intellectual insanity as well as moral licentiousness.

To believe in Jesus Christ speaks of deeper studies, of holy mysteries, of divine delights! It speaks with hallowed rapture of reunions, of immortal fellowship, of battles blessed with complete and imperishable victories, of hope perfected in ecstatic and cloudless vision! If you believe in this revelation, you draw water from the deep, cool well of its promises; your suffering becomes a joy through the support of its rich and inspiring grace. Who could be so foolish as to let go of such a hope?

JOSEPH PARKER

"We have come to believe and to know that you are the
Holy One of God."

John 6:69

In Jesus we see the incomparable excellence of the divine nature. "You have loved righteousness and hated wickedness; therefore God, your God, has set you above your companions by anointing you with the oil of joy" (Hebrews 1:9). God's infinite hatred of sin, and His maintenance of the Right, might appear to have little moral worth, as being a necessity of His nature. In the Son we see divine holiness tested. He is tried and tempted. He suffers, being tempted. He proves that holiness has indeed a moral worth: it is ready to make any sacrifice, to even give up life and cease to be rather than consent to sin. In giving himself to die rather than yield to the temptation of sin, in giving himself to die that the Father's righteous judgment may be honored, Jesus proved how righteousness is an element of the divine holiness, and how the Holy One is sanctified in righteousness.

But this is only one side of holiness. The fire that consumes also purifies: it makes partakers of its own beautiful Light-nature all that is capable of assimilation. So divine holiness not only maintains its own purity, it communicates it too. Jesus' holiness proved itself to be the very incarnation of Him who had spoken as the High and Lofty One who dwells with him who is of a contrite spirit. In Him was seen the affinity holiness has for all that is lost and helpless and sinful. He proved that holiness is not only the energy that in holy anger separates itself from all that is impure, but which in holy love separates itself from even what is most sinful to save and to bless. In Him we see how the divine holiness is the harmony of infinite righteousness with infinite love.

Jesus came to teach us that it was possible to be a man, and yet to have the life of God dwelling in us. We ordinarily think that the glory and the infinite perfection of the Deity are the proper setting in which the beauty of holiness is to be seen: Jesus proved the perfect adaptation and suitability of human nature for showing forth that which is the essential glory of the Deity. He showed us how, in choosing and doing the will of God, and making it his own will, man may truly be holy as God is holy.

ANDREW MURRAY

For even His brothers did not believe in Him.

John 7:5 NKJV

It is a very painful truth, that those who were the near relatives of the Savior were not believers in His divine mission—at first, at any rate. He was truly a prophet who was without honor in His own country and among His own family; and, on this occasion of the Feast of Tabernacles, they half taunted Him concerning His claims. In effect, they said to him, "If indeed you are a prophet, get out into the world and prove it. We hear that you profess to work miracles; then, why do you hide yourself away in this country place down here in Galilee? Go up to Jerusalem and perform your wonders before the crowds in the capital"—half hoping, perhaps, that His claims might prove to be true, yet not, at that time, being themselves willing to become His disciples.

See how perverse is the human heart. These men might even live in close companionship with Christ, and even be nearly related to Him after the flesh, and yet not believe Him. So the best of believers need not wonder why they have family members who are not believers, and we may not feel certain that there is any fault to be found in their example if others are not brought to faith by it; for, certainly, there was no fault in the example of Christ, yet "even His brothers did not believe in Him."

Note, also, though no earthly relationship is of any avail in the kingdom of heaven, "even His brothers did not believe in Him." So that although I may be the child of godly parents, and one born in a family long known for their strong faith, yet I am, because of that, no nearer to the kingdom, unless I become myself a believer in Christ. Remember what Peter said on the day of Pentecost; you may have often heard that passage of Scripture half-quoted; let me quote the whole of it to you: "For the promise is to you and to your children" (Acts 2:39 NKJV). If you stop there, you do not get the true sense of it. "The promise is to you and to your children, and to all who are afar off, as many as the Lord our God will call." Therefore, that text teaches that there is no distinction between the children of believers and any other children. Even the brothers of Christ need to experience the grace of God or else they shall not inherit eternal life.

CHARLES SPURGEON

And there was much complaining among the people concerning Him. Some said, "He is good"; others said, "No, on the contrary, He deceives the people." However, no one spoke openly of Him for fear of the Jews.

John 7:12–13 NKJV

The people differed much in their sentiments concerning Christ. The hatred of the rulers toward Christ, and their inquiries about whether He would come to the Feast of Tabernacles, caused Him to be so much more talked of and observed among the people. Much of the interest in Jerusalem regarding Christ revolved around the opposition to Him and the merits of His cause being the more searched into. This complaining or murmuring was not against Christ so much as concerning Him. Some complained to the rulers because they did not approve of Him or because they did not silence Him. Some complained that He had so great a following in Galilee; others, that He had so little following in Jerusalem.

Some people said, "He is good," which was true, but it was far short of being the whole truth. He was not only a good man; He was the Son of God. Many who have positive thoughts of Christ have yet low thoughts of Him and hardly honor Him, even when they speak well of Him, because they do not say enough. Other people said, "No, on the contrary, He deceives the people." If this had been true, He would have been a very bad man. Although the doctrine He preached was sound and could not be contested, His miracles were real and could not be disproved, and His conversation was manifestly holy and good, yet these people took it for granted, notwithstanding, that there was some undiscovered deception at the bottom of it, reflected in the fact that the chief priests wanted Him dead.

Meanwhile, the people were frightened into silence by their superiors from speaking much of Him. While anyone was at liberty to criticize Him, none dared to support Him. And because nothing could justly be said against Him, they would not allow anything to be said of Him. It was a crime to name Him.

Such complaining and censuring concerning Christ is still very much among us. Christ and belief in Him have been, and will be, the subject of much controversy and debate (see Luke 12:51–52). Some receive the light of Christ and others resolve against it; some depreciate Him, others abuse Him. Thus many have aimed to suppress truth, under color of silencing disputes about it, and would have all talk of faith in Christ hushed, in hopes thereby to bury it in oblivion. But the liberty of open discussion is preferable, surely, to the silence of censure.

MATTHEW HENRY

Not until halfway through the festival did Jesus go up to the temple courts and begin to teach. The Jews there were amazed and asked, "How did this man get such learning without having been taught?"

John 7:14–15

The Jews thought there was only one way of learning. Jesus Christ committed the crime of irregularity. Propriety can never forgive that offense; it cannot in medicine or in business, but above all it cannot in theology. There is a certain way in which things should be done; if they are not done in that particular way, they are not done at all. Jesus was a thorn in the sides of the devotees of regularity. He was born in the wrong place, associated with the wrong people, and supported the wrong causes (the poor, the helpless, and the blind). He turned upside down things that had for ages been regarded as sacred. Filled with narrowness, bigotry, sectarianism, and smallness, the Jews were incapable of understanding Christ. Yet, these were the men who had registered themselves as the ones who preserved faith and truth. For them there was only one way of learning, and they controlled the curriculum. Anyone who had not passed through their course, no matter what he said, what he sang, how much he knew and touched and blessed the human heart, was uncertified, was without rabbinic and official endorsement.

There are more schools than one. The mountain is not to be ascended by one path only. Some have learned by experience what they never could have learned by lectures. Experience is a costly teacher, forcing the truth home upon the mind and heart in many ways. Parts of the Bible can only be read through the eyes of experience. The broken heart knows what scholarship can never comprehend. Feeling has taught many men some of the higher and tenderer mysteries of the kingdom of God. Certain parts of the Bible are only learned through our tears, coming in through the gashes and breaks and fractures that sorrow has made in the disappointed and wounded heart.

True spirituality is not learned by letters. It is a divine action in the soul, a divine communion, the claiming of a kinship in love for the Father, which an inexpressible confidence clings to. Make room for this type of learning. There is a line beyond which language cannot go; it says to the mind, I must leave you at this point. The peace of God that passes understanding brings a joy unspeakable and full of glory. Learn the eloquence of silence. Learn to muse, to burn with holy glowing, and to sing with immeasurable rapture.

JOSEPH PARKER

Jesus answered, "My teaching is not my own. It comes from the one who sent me."

John 7:16

Jesus is not afraid to explain how it is that He had received such marvelous learning. By *teaching*, understand that Jesus is not referring to formal theology, not systematic godliness, not a thought shaped and thrust and consolidated in one form forever, but to that endless process, that mystery of progress that claims eternity for its completion. He is saying, in effect, "'Not my own'—it is not an invention, a theory, not something I have thought out and elaborated. I am but an errand bearer. I do but speak the word I have heard and learned from my Father. Know that my incarnation is but the object on which the infinite silence breaks into the fountain of speech."

Here is an inspired man. Behold a teacher who is teaching what He has heard in some other world! It is just there that so many teachers fail. They have only one world, and one world can hold nothing but its own grave. The teacher sent from God has all the worlds; He has the key to every mansion in His Father's house. What theories men have invented, what neat philosophies, what sublimities of powerlessness! Why? because they have had no eternity, no infinity, and no overshadowing greatness. So we have alphabet-makers and bookmakers with their beginning and ending, measurable, estimable. Where is the spirit of eternity, the ring of everlastingness? They have not that spirit; what they say is their own, and therefore it can all be said.

He who speaks from eternity halts, suddenly deflects, adapts himself to the capacities with which He has to deal. He says, "I have much more to say to you, more than you can now bear" (John 16:12). Know the Bible in a thousand ways, and no one ever had the Bible taken out of their hands. That is the mystery. He may have a book taken out of his hands of which he was making a fetish, an idol, a vain thing; but no man who ever grasped the Bible with his soul had it plucked from him. He does not hold it linguistically, but with his heart.

JOSEPH PARKER

"Anyone who chooses to do the will of God will find out whether my teaching comes from God or whether I speak on my own."

John 7:17

The divine knowledge of Jesus has a human aspect to it. Our translation does not give the fullness of the Greek emphasis: "If any man wills to do His will, he must resolutely will himself to it." Doing is learning, and this is true in all areas of life. No man learns to swim by standing on the shore. If any man wills to do the will, sets himself to do it, says, "In God's strength I will do this," he shall know the teaching, it will come to him little by little.

Do not make the mistake of supposing that there is only one set or class of spiritual teachers. The rabbis thought they only knew the law; the scribes thought they only knew what was written, and they alone could read it. But there are a thousand teachers. Nature says she will tell us a thousand things if we will sit down and listen to her. If we go into all the rooms she has, we shall come back with all the fresh winds blowing around us, with the light of the noonday in our eyes, with the fragrance of flowers. Little children are about the greatest theologians there are. The return of a prodigal son can shake the harshness of a father's theological propositions and usher in a theology of sacrifice, of love, the theology that carries with it the gospel of redemption.

Cry mightily to God to point out to you the teacher that will understand and teach you best, and for you work the miracle of a new life. Test your faith in the marketplace. Will your teaching go into the business place, and there talk righteousness, and deal honestly, and look fearlessly in the face of insincerity and fraud and dishonorableness? Cling to the spirit that is in you. Will your godliness go home and help the sick one, and sit up all night and bring help to the sufferer without increasing his agony? And will you in the morning say nothing about sleeplessness or hunger or concern, but smile upon the sufferer as if he had done you a great favor? Will to do the Father's will, and who knows but someday God will come to you and say, "In reward for your obedience, patience, self-sacrifice, here is the key: open My kingdoms and revel in them by divinely invested right."

JOSEPH PARKER

*Jesus said, "I am with you for only a short time, and
then I am going to the one who sent me. You will look
for me, but you will not find me; and where I am, you
cannot come."*

John 7:33–34

No greater contrast can be conceived than that between Jesus' response to this group of Jews sent to arrest Him and to the little company of His faithful followers in John 13:33. Nearly the same words are spoken, but with what a different tone, meaning, and application! The enemies are told that they will never find Him. All the antagonism that has stormed against Christ and His cause and words has been powerless and vain. The pursuers are like dogs chasing a bird, sniffing along the ground, while the bird sits out of their reach on a bough of a tree. Jesus' foes could not touch His person until He chose, and vainly did they seek when it pleased Him to hide from them. And so ever since, in regard to His cause and to all hearts that love Him, no weapon that is formed against them shall prosper (see Isaiah 54:17). They shall be wrapped, when need be, in a cloud of protecting darkness from the enemy.

While it is always true that a seeking heart finds Jesus, it is also true that things neglected once cannot be brought back. There is a sowing time allowed to pass that can never return. To turn a deaf ear to Christ who asks you to love and trust Him will lead to the wish that it had been otherwise. Beware of an intellectual seeking of Christ that lacks the preparation of the heart. There are many people who go on the quest for spiritual certainty and are not capable of discerning Him when they see Him, because their eye is not single or because their heart is full of worldliness or indifference. Some begin with a foregone conclusion and look for facts to establish it, while others will not put away sinful things that rise up between them and their Master.

My friend, if you go to look for Jesus Christ with a heart full of the world, if you go to look for Him while you wish to hold on to all the habits and lusts of your past, you will never find Him. The proud man seeks for Him, the covetous man seeks for Him, the passionate, bad-tempered man seeks for Him; the woman plunged in pleasure or immersed in daily cares—these may in some feeble fashion go to look for Him and will not find Him because they have sought Him with hearts overcharged with other things and filled with the affairs of this life.

ALEXANDER MACLAREN

On the last and greatest day of the festival, Jesus stood and said in a loud voice, "Let anyone who is thirsty come to me and drink."

John 7:37

The temple guards were after our Lord, and He knew it. He could see them in the crowd, but He was not the least afraid. He reminds me of the minister who, when he was about to preach, was stopped by a soldier who held a pistol to the minister's head and threatened that if he spoke he would be killed. "Soldier," he said, "do your duty. I shall do mine." And he went on with his preaching.

It was the final day of the festival, the last time Jesus would see many of the Jews who had traveled to Jerusalem for the occasion; thus the time had come for Jesus to speak boldly. Whereas His custom was to sit and teach the people who gathered about Him, on this closing day He sought a prominent place in one of the outer courts of the temple and stood. Behold, He stands and comes to meet those whom He invites, pleading with them in a loud voice that they come to Him. He gathered up all the forces of His soul, and His whole spirit was moved with intense passion for the good of men, and He preached the gospel of salvation with complete abandon. I think I see the Master's face beaming with holy affection, and His eyes streaming with tears as He pleads with the multitude.

Jesus is seeking out needy, restless, longing hearts. Have you any desire after God? Do you desire to be rid of your sin? Do you know the peace and rest that He alone can give? Do you desire to be made pure in heart? Are you discontented with the pleasures of the world? Do you long for a higher, holier, and more heavenly life? Beneath the arch of heaven that same call of Jesus sounds out to every thirsty soul. You may come to Him now. A prayer will bring you to Him. A sigh will find and reach Him.

Look to Jesus, and continue to look until the glance of faith on earth shall melt into the vision of blessedness in heaven. Jesus stands before you as the central sun of salvation, and from Him the true light radiates on all sides. All who will turn their eyes to look to Him shall behold the light of life. What a day this would be if we all hastened to Jesus and drank from Him as from the sparkling fountain of grace! Why should we not?

CHARLES SPURGEON

"If anyone is thirsty, let him come to Me and drink!"

John 7:37 AMP

There is only one true spiritual direction, and that one direction points solely to one source. All those who would have their thirst quenched must come to one fountain, to one Jesus, who directs us to come to Him personally. He does not say to come to doctrines and creeds. Jesus is set before us as the Son of God, the Son of Man, who lived, who took human sin upon himself and died for it, to bring us to God. Then He was laid in the tomb for three days, after which He arose from the dead into newness of life, and after forty days ascended on high, leading captivity captive! At this moment He sits at the right hand of God, all power being given to Him in heaven and in earth. In His glory He is able to save you completely. But you must come to Him who finished His redeeming work and ever lives to make intercession for us.

If you will come to Jesus, He will give you the full supply for all the great needs of your soul. Whatever your spiritual desire is, Jesus will grant it. Whatever, in fact, your soul requires between this moment and glory, He will give it to you. But you must come to Him and to Him alone. Do not expect to find it in a doctrine, or church, or ceremony, or a doing, or a feeling. Your salvation lies in that divine person, who is clothed in the splendor of heaven, yet still wearing the marks of His passion. He looks like a lamb that has been slain, and He presents a perpetually complete atonement to God. There lies your hope, and there alone.

Come to Jesus and drink from His limitless supply of grace for every spiritual need. Put your mouth down and take in that which flows to you in the river of Christ's love. See how a newborn babe drinks from its mother's breast; do as the babe in Christ and take in according to your capacity. He bids you to receive Him; why hesitate? You are not to bring anything to Him but to take everything from Him. Open wide your soul and drink in Christ. Let streams of mercy flow through you in glorious torrents. It is all He bids you do; it is, in fact, to do nothing but to receive your God. Oh, that His sweet Spirit would accompany these words, so that you might feel your heart melting toward the Savior with the consent to infinite love!

CHARLES SPURGEON

"If anyone is thirsty, let him come to Me and drink! He who believes in Me [who adheres to, trusts in, and relies on Me], as the Scripture has said, 'From his innermost being will flow continually rivers of living water.'" But He was speaking of the [Holy] Spirit, whom those who believed in Him [as Savior] were to receive afterward. The Spirit had not yet been given, because Jesus was not yet glorified (raised to honor).

John 7:37–39 AMP

H ere we have the first step toward the fullness of the Spirit in our lives, namely, faith in Jesus Christ: "who believes in Me." But we have also another step in the word *thirst*: "if anyone is thirsty." Our Lord Jesus evidently had Isaiah 44:3 in mind when He uttered these words: "For I will pour water on the thirsty land, and streams on the dry ground; I will pour out my Spirit on your offspring, and my blessing on your descendants." Note carefully the words *if anyone is thirsty*.

Were you ever really thirsty? I was among the sixty thousand troops at Chickamauga Park during the Spanish-American War, and where there was no rain for many days. The air was full of dust thirty feet high day and night, and we ate dust and drank dust and slept dust and dreamt dust, and no water was fit to drink. I know what it means to be thirsty. When a man really thirsts, it seems as if every pore in his body has just one cry: "Water! Water! Water!" And when a man thirsts spiritually, his whole being has just one cry: "Holy Spirit! Holy Spirit! Holy Spirit! O God, give me the Holy Spirit!" Then it is that God pours floods upon the dry ground and pours His Spirit upon us.

Within us there must be an intense desire that arises out of our utter need of power to do effective service for God, a desire that longs for it at any cost. And it may cost you a good deal. It may take you out of a nice home here in America to China or to India or to Africa. And your intense desire must spring for the glory of God and not for your own glory. Acts 8:20–22 records the solemn case of Simon the magician who desired the Holy Spirit out of an unholy desire. Be careful at this point. Get alone with God and ask Him to show you whether you desire the Holy Spirit that you may glorify God as you should.

R. A. TORREY

*"Let anyone who is thirsty come to me and drink. Who-
ever believes in me, as the Scripture has said, rivers of
living water will flow from within them."*

John 7:37–38

You come to Christ by faith, you come by love, by communion. You were thirsty yesterday, so you drank. That will not quench today's thirst or prevent its recurrence. You must keep on drinking if you are to keep from perishing of thirst. Day by day, drop by drop, sip by sip, you must drink. The river of grace flows right past your door, yet your lips may be cracked with thirst, even while you hear the tinkle of its music among the pebbles and rocks.

And as we drink, as we trust in Christ, we become like the Christ whom we trust. This is a universal law. Derivatively and by impartation, no doubt, but still the man who has gone to that Rock, to the springing fountain as it gushes forth, receives into himself an inward life by the communication of Christ's divine Spirit, so that he has in him "a spring of water welling up to eternal life" (John 4:14). The book of Proverbs says, "A good man will be satisfied with his ways" (14:14 AMP), but the good man is only satisfied with his ways when he can say, "I have been crucified with Christ and I no longer live, but Christ lives in me" (Galatians 2:20), and from that better self he will be satisfied.

So we may have a well in the courtyard, and may be able to bear in ourselves the fountain of water, and where the divine life of Christ by His Spirit has through faith been implanted within us, it will come out from us. There is a question for believers: Do any rivers of living water flow out of you? If they do not, it is doubtful whether you have drunk from the stream. There are many professing Christians who are like foul little rivers that pass under bridges, all impure, and covered over so that nobody sees them. "Rivers of living water will flow from within them"—that is Christ's way of communicating the blessing of eternal life to the world—by the medium of those who have already received it. If your faith has brought the life of Christ into you, see to it that approaching Christ, and appropriating Christ, and adhering to Christ, you become conformed to Christ, and in your daily life, God's grace streaming through you to all, are "like streams of water in the desert and the shadow of a great rock in a thirsty land" (Isaiah 32:2).

ALEXANDER MACLAREN

(When he said "living water," he was speaking of the
Spirit, who would be given to everyone believing in him.
But the Spirit had not yet been given, because Jesus had
not yet entered into his glory.)

John 7:39 NLT

I t has been said that while the holiness of God stands out more prominently in the Old Testament, in the New it gives way to the revelation of His love. The remark could hardly be made if it were realized that the Spirit who is God takes up the description *Holy* as His own proper name, teaching us that now the holiness of God comes nearer than ever and is specially revealed as the power that makes us holy. In the Holy Spirit, God the Holy One of Israel comes near for the fulfillment of the promise that He will make us holy (see Leviticus 21:8). The unseen and unapproachable holiness of God had been revealed in the life of Jesus Christ; all that hindered our participation in it had been removed by His death. In the Holy Spirit, the Holy One comes to impart it to us and make it our own.

There are some who pray for the Spirit because they long to have His light and joy and strength, but their prayers go unanswered. It is because they do not desire Him as the *Holy* Spirit. His burning purity, His searching and convicting light, His making dead of the deeds of the flesh, of self with its will and power, His leading into the fellowship of Jesus as He gave up His will and His life to the Father—of all this they have not thought. The Spirit cannot come in power on them because they receive Him not as the *Holy* Spirit, in *sanctification* of the Spirit (see 2 Thessalonians 2:13). In seasons of revival, as among the Corinthians, He may indeed come with His gifts and mighty workings, while His holiness may be hardly manifest. But unless that sanctifying power is acknowledged and accepted, His gifts will be lost. His gifts coming on us are only meant to prepare the way for the sanctifying power within us. We must learn the lesson that we can have as much of the Spirit as we are willing to have of His holiness. Being full of the Spirit means to be fully holy.

The converse is equally true. We can only have as much holiness as we have of the Spirit. Some believers seek to be holy, but it is much in their own strength. They must see that all they seek comes only from the Spirit.

ANDREW MURRAY

"Has not the Scripture said that the Christ comes from the seed of David and from the town of Bethlehem, where David was?"

John 7:42 NKJV

Faith never finds her wisdom in the thoughts of men or in pretended revelations, but she resorts to the inspired Word of God for her guidance. This is the well from which she drinks, the manna on which she feeds. Faith takes the Lord Jesus to be her wisdom. The knowledge of Christ is to her the most excellent of the sciences.

Jesus Christ is the Alpha and Omega of the Bible. He is the constant theme of its sacred pages; from first to last they testify of Him (see John 5:39). At the creation we at once discern Him as one of the sacred Trinity; we catch a glimpse of Him in the promise of the woman's seed; we see Him typified in the ark of Noah; we walk with Abraham, as He sees Messiah's day; we dwell in the tents of Isaac and Jacob, feeding upon the gracious promise; we hear the venerable Israel talking of Shiloh; and in the numerous types of the Old Testament law, we find the Redeemer abundantly foreshadowed. Prophets and kings, priests and preachers, all look one way—they all stand as the cherubim did over the ark, desiring to look within and to read the mystery of God's great sacrifice for our sin.

Still more manifestly in the New Testament we find our Lord the one pervading subject. It is not a nugget here and there or dust of gold thinly scattered, but here you stand upon a solid floor of gold; for the whole substance of the New Testament is Jesus crucified, and even its closing sentence is jeweled with the Redeemer's name. We should always read Scripture in this light; we should consider the word to be as a mirror into which Christ looks down from heaven; and then we, looking into it, see His face reflected as in a glass darkly, it is true, but still in such a way as to be a blessed preparation for seeing Him as we shall see Him face-to-face.

This volume contains Jesus Christ's letters to us, perfumed by His love. These pages are the garments of our King, and they all smell of myrrh, and aloes, and cassia. Scripture is the royal chariot in which Jesus rides, and it is paved with love for the daughters of Jerusalem. The Scriptures are the swaddling bands of the holy child Jesus; unroll them and you find your Savior. The quintessence of the Word of God is Christ.

CHARLES SPURGEON

Finally the temple guards went back to the chief priests and Pharisees, who asked them, "Why didn't you bring him in?" "No one ever spoke the way this man does," the guards replied.

John 7:45–46

The chief priests and Pharisees sent guards to arrest Christ, lest His preaching completely overthrow their power. Fully armed and completely able to arrest the Preacher, they themselves were arrested by the sincere eloquence of Jesus. They were chained to the spot where they stood, spellbound by the power of His speech. It has always been so. When God sends forth His truth with power, swords and spears are vain in the opposition's hands. We must constantly remember that our appointed weapons, like our Master's, are not of this world, but "have divine power to demolish strongholds" (2 Corinthians 10:4).

Did anyone ever speak as Christ did? Little children gathered around Him and could understand the simplicity of His messages. You never find Him, for the sake of display, careering upon the wings of rhetoric. He never gives dark sayings that His listeners may discover that His learning and thinking are profound. He unveils the mysteries of God. He brings to light the treasures of darkness of the ages past that prophets and kings desired to see, but into which they could not pry. He declared that which is gracious, that which saves the soul and glorifies God. The common people with their common sense heard Him gladly, for even if they could not always grasp the full scope of His teaching, yet upon the surface of His plain speech there glittered lumps of golden ore well worthy to be treasured up. For this quality our Savior remains unrivaled, plain to the understanding yet profound.

His speech also came with an unusual sense of authority, yet He never spoke with proud self-sufficiency. He never pestered you with assumptions of superiority and claims of official dignity. He spoke the word of the Lord with absolute authority. Lowly and gentle of heart, never extolling himself, He was nevertheless the unhesitating minister of righteousness, speaking with power, because the Lord's Spirit had anointed Him. Coming fresh from the bosom of the Father, having looked into the unseen and heard the infallible oracle, He did not debate, but declared the uncompromising truth.

When our Beloved speaks to our heart, how it revives our drooping spirit! It touches our lips as a coal from off the altar (see Isaiah 6:7). It brings healing, consolation, and joy.

Blessed Master, speak to me evermore!

CHARLES SPURGEON

Then they all went home, but Jesus went to the Mount of Olives.

John 7:53–8:1

Perhaps I shall surprise you when I say that Jesus did exactly what His disciples did here. They went to their own houses, and He went to His own house. They sought comfort and counsel, and He did the same. They sought refreshment, and so did He. The Mount of Olives was, to all intents and purposes, Christ's home on earth. It was there that the Man Christ Jesus met with kindred spirits in the Father and the Holy Spirit; it was there that He cast off the cares of the day and unburdened himself as a weary son does in his parent's presence. Jesus came to the Mount of Olives to cry to heaven for wisdom; and it was there that, made strong by fresh contact with His Father, He took on His golden armor to go forth once more fully protected from the arrows of the evil one.

Beloved, that time of prayer upon the Mount of Olives was to Jesus what our going to our houses and to our loved ones is to us. We are saddened that His body was wet with the dew of the night, yet we would gladly have some of those same drops upon our body if we could have communion with Him in spirit. We have sympathy with the members of His physical frame, because they were tried by the cold of the mountain and the loneliness of His night vigil; but we wish that our souls could be braced with something like the same vigor that He received upon the Mount of Olives. Yes, the cold mountain was His home. There, He had a place where He could lay His head and rest, though primarily in a spiritual sense.

How then ought we to live in our own homes? "Be very careful, then, how you live—not as unwise but as wise, making the most of every opportunity, because the days are evil" (Ephesians 5:15–16). Do we, like our Savior, make it a place of prayer and intercession? Do we turn aside from our daily work and cry to God, "Create in me a pure heart, O God, and renew a steadfast spirit within me" (Psalm 51:10)? Prayer to God is more refreshing than sleep, just as the soul is better than the body. The bed gives rest to tired limbs, but the mercy seat gives refreshment to the powers and passions of the spirit. May we never let these slip from our grasp.

CHARLES SPURGEON

The teachers of the law and the Pharisees brought in a woman caught in adultery. They made her stand before the group and said to Jesus, "Teacher, this woman was caught in the act of adultery. In the Law Moses commanded us to stone such women. Now what do you say?"

John 8:3–5

Would we see Jesus in His most fascinating charms? Then we must look at Him as He stands face-to-face with a notorious sinner. That face of His never lightens into such a glory as when it looks upon the darkness of contrite guilt.

Did these teachers of the law and the Pharisees care one ounce for the spirituality and sanctity of the law? When they found this poor unhappy soul, did their hearts bleed with pity, or their eyes dissolve in tenderness, or did they say with true sorrow, "Alas! Our poor sister has fallen to the enemy of mankind, and we must save her from the pit on whose brink she lies"? Not a word of it! Not a tear stained their eyes, not a pang of pity quivered in their steel breasts—their humanity was eaten up by their pompous and zealous bigotry. They looked at her through the medium of the stern law, on the one hand, and on the other regarded her as a practical puzzle for Jesus. They were glad to have a rare example of crime, which they could use as a test of the Messiah's morality. It was an opportunity not to be lost. It was a trap that must be skillfully set. It was an occasion that might lead on to victory.

Let us beware lest we fall into the same pretentious and rotten spirit. Oh, it makes one's heart sore and sad to mark how one child of guilt can eagerly brand another, and send him, amid frantic clapping of unclean hands, to the fellowship of devils. Do we, like the blessed Savior, go forth to seek and save the lost, to lift up the downcast, and turn the wanderer onto the right way? Let us guard against a lifeless and tearless heart that is only interested in exacting judgment. Let us dread the day when we can look upon sin with eyes that glisten only because it exalts our own position. It is entirely possible for the work of the church to fall into mere legalistic formality. Let us remember that it is one thing to be the policemen of the church, bringing in poor prisoners for judgment, and another to be like Him who wept and bled that prisoners might be free. Let us be humbled in our hearts over the brokenness of God because of our sin, and reach out to others in the true Spirit of God.

JOSEPH PARKER

But Jesus bent down and started to write on the ground with his finger. When they kept on questioning him, he straightened up and said to them, "Let any one of you who is without sin be the first to throw a stone at her."

John 8:6–7

Jesus does not nullify the law or set himself in opposition to Moses. The answer He gave withered up the Pharisees' purposes and gave their thoughts a turn that they regarded with supreme loathing. Jesus shows that the law is to be administered by clean hands, the thunders of the law are to be articulated by pure lips, and the stone of judgment is to be thrown with the pity of holiness.

Jesus gives full scope to the faculty of conscience. He did not accuse these men; they accused themselves. He might have arraigned them one by one and passed judgment on each, but He abbreviates the process by making each one judge himself. When He asked the sinless man to step forward, conscience takes the candle into the inmost recesses of our being. Conscience holds up a mirror to the leprous soul. Conscience shows us the cracks in our porcelain respectability and the specks upon our boasted morality. It showed that the difference between them and her was that her sin was discovered, and theirs was not. They wished to pass for respectable men of society, spiritual pillars in the temple, but when conscience, commissioned by divine authority, began to rifle their history, they fled from the sanctuary.

Man saw these teachers of the law in eager haste to honor the law, to brand crime, and to maintain righteousness. But God saw the under-lurking villainy and marked every spring of poison that bubbled in the depraved heart, and told them to look at themselves before looking at and despising others. His eye alights on the interior view, and it is by that view that all His judgments are regulated. Stripping society of its gilded ornaments, God pours the sunlight into the caverns of the heart and shows how the reptiles of iniquity are fattening there. His eye searches the very core and fountain of our being. Where there is most holiness there is most pity. It was God's own holiness that wept itself into the mercy that died and rose again that sinners might leave their life of sin. When we are under the full dominion of that mercy, we shall need but the faintest breeze of appeal to shake the tears of pity from our eyes.

JOSEPH PARKER

Jesus straightened up and asked her, "Woman, where are they? Has no one condemned you?" "No one, sir," she said. "Then neither do I condemn you," Jesus declared. "Go now and leave your life of sin."

John 8:10–11

The good man never ignores the presence of sin. Jesus Christ, with all His gentleness and mercy, did not tell the woman that she was innocent, nor did He treat her as an innocent woman. Christ was ever forward to maintain the broad distinction between right and wrong. I believe that if we follow His example, we shall frown upon sin in all its aspects and tendencies and never cast the faintest smile upon its downward course. We don't treat a thief as an honest man; a liar as though he were truthful; the proud as the humble; the miser as though he were generous. We owe such distinctions to the dignity of virtue, and they must be maintained forever.

At the same time, our lesson is this: never cast the penitent sinner into despair. Jesus said, "Go now and leave your life of sin." Take one more chance in life; turn over a new page; begin again; treat this as a second birthday; go, and make the future better than the past. Thank God for such words of hope! The beams of mercy shoot far across the gloom of guilt; the voice of hope falls on the ear of the remotest wanderer! Christ teaches us the true method of rescuing the sinner—never cast him into doubt.

If you can say one gentle word or give one hopeful glance to the prisoner who is brought before you, I call upon you in the name of God to do it. Would not this poor woman forever feel a kindling love to Him who spoke this word of hope to her? Would she hesitate for a moment on whom to pour the benedictions of her glowing heart? The Pharisees would have stoned her, but the divine Savior spread a new page of life before her and told her to begin again. A word of hope may strike a happy influence through an entire lifetime. Those of us who imagine that we have never sinned do not know the value of such a word. But those of us who have taken our sins into private places and wept over them, and then taken them to Christ's cross and heard His voice of mercy, know how the soul warms and gladdens in reply to the word of liberty and life. "Deal gently with the erring one," Christ says to us. Arrest the harsh word that burns on your tongue. Remember yourself, lest you also be tempted.

JOSEPH PARKER

*When Jesus spoke again to the people, he said, "I am the
light of the world. Whoever follows me will never walk
in darkness, but will have the light of life."*

John 8:12

Ah, my heart, this is indeed good news for you! This is the gospel! If
God is light, what more, what else can I seek than God, the Christ
himself! Away with your doctrines! I am saved—for God is my light!
*My God, I come to you. That you should be yourself is enough for time and
eternity, for my soul and all its endless need.*

Whatever is of darkness I will not believe of my God. If I should mistake
and call what is light darkness, will He not reveal the matter to me, setting
it in the light that lights every man, showing me that I saw but the husk of
the thing, not the kernel? Will He not break open the shell for me, and let the
truth of it, His thought, pour out upon me?

God is light far beyond what we can see. God means for us to be jubilant
in the fact that He is light. If I am not honest enough, if the eye in me is not
single enough, then, Living Light, purge my eyes from their darkness that they
may let the light in, and so I become an inheritor, with your other children,
of that light that is your Godhead and causes your creatures to worship you.
"In your light we see light" (Psalm 36:9).

In proportion as we have the image of Christ mirrored in us we shall know
what is and what is not light. No person, for himself or for another, needs fear
the light of God. All fear of the light comes of the darkness; it will vanish as
we are more and more permeated with the light.

Come to God, then, with all your desires and instincts, all your lofty ideals,
all your longing for purity and unselfishness, all your yearning to love and to
be true, all your aspirations after self-forgetfulness and childlikeness. Come
to Him with all your weaknesses, your shame, your futility; your helplessness
over wayward thoughts; with all your failures, the sense of having missed the
mark. Come to Him with your doubts, fears, dishonesty, meanness, misjudg-
ment, weariness, disappointments, and bitterness. He will surely take you as
you are into the care of His limitless heart!

For He is light and in Him is no darkness at all.

GEORGE MACDONALD

"I am the light of the world."

John 8:12

That Jesus is the light of the world is to be seen in all parts of His blessed history. Look at Him in His cradle. Shines there a star above the place where the young child sleeps. Brighter far than yonder star is He who lies cradled in the manger. He has come, the predictions of whose advent had illumined centuries of darkness. As a babe, devout men hail Him, "A light for revelation to the Gentiles, and the glory of your people Israel" (Luke 2:32). To the eye of faith, what radiance emanates from the newborn! Look, for the like was never looked on before. There God is veiled in human flesh. Behold, God is manifest in our nature; He dwells among us. The light is clear and dazzling.

Well did the angels sing, "Glory to God in the highest heaven, and on earth peace to those on whom his favor rests" (Luke 2:14). Sweet child! You have pierced the thick darkness of earth's sorrow. You have enlightened her scenes of sadness, infusing joy into her gloom. Your coming revealed the love of God, His sweet compassion, and His tender pity toward the guilty sons of men. His baptism throws a wonderful light upon consecration to God; and the fiery temptations that quickly followed, in all of which He foiled the tempter, have thrown a brilliant light on the pathway of believers. As a preacher, He was luminous, expounding the spirituality of the law with a light that penetrated the precept through and through. His light cleared the law of mists and fogs that the rabbinical writers had gathered around it. He shed the light of the glorious gospel of peace, telling of God the Father, who receives His prodigal children back again into His bosom. Eternity dawned on His listeners while He spoke.

His death gave yet more evidence of unfaltering submission to the will of God and unflinching self-sacrifice for the welfare of men. Oh, beloved, the light of Christ comes out brightest upon the cross. This is the lighthouse that throws its beams across the dark waters of human guilt and misery, warning men of the rocks and guiding them to the haven. Behold Him shedding His precious blood to atone for the sins of men. Never did such light gleam on the faith and hope of pure hearts. He has brought life and immortality to light. He before whose eyes Jesus Christ has been set forth crucified has a light that outshines all earthly splendor. Rejoice in His light!

CHARLES SPURGEON

"I am the light of the world. He who follows Me shall not walk in darkness, but have the light of life."

John 8:12 NKJV

Faith is the condition of following Christ; and following is the outcome and test, because it is the operation of faith. He who does not follow does not trust. To follow Christ means to long and strive after His companionship; as the psalmist says, "My soul [my life, my very self] clings to You" (Psalm 63:8 AMP). It means the submission of the will, the effort of the whole nature to reproduce His example, the resolute adoption of His command as my law, His providence as my will, His fellowship as my joy. And the root and beginning of all such following is in coming to Him, conscious of my own darkness, and trustful in His great light. We must rely on a Guide before we accept His directions; and it is absurd to pretend that we trust Him if we do not go as He bids us. So "Follow Me" is the sum of all Christian duty.

Darkness in Scripture is the name for the whole condition of the soul turned away from God. So our Lord here is declaring that to follow Him is the true deliverance from that midnight of the soul. There is a darkness of ignorance, impurity, and sorrow; and in that threefold gloom, thickening to a darkness of death, are those who do not follow the Light. Yet, the feeblest beginnings of trust in Jesus Christ, and the first tottering steps that try to walk in His, bring us into the light. It does not require that we have reached our goal; it is enough that our hearts are turned to it and desire to attain it; then we may be sure that the dominion of the darkness over us is broken. To follow Christ fills our path with increasing brightness, and even though evil and ignorance and sorrow may thrust their blackness upon our day, they are melting in the growing glory.

John tells us that the true Guide of our souls enters in and dwells in us, in all the fullness of life, light, and love. Within us He will primarily prove himself the Guide of our spirits and will not merely cast His beams on the path of our feet, but will fill and flood us with His own brightness. All light of knowledge, of goodness, of gladness will be ours, if Christ is ours. Do we follow Him with loyal obedience, longing love, and humble imitation, since He has become to us the Savior of our souls?

ALEXANDER MACLAREN

"I am not alone, but I am with the Father who sent Me."

John 8:16 NKJV

One cannot but feel the exultant note in Jesus' words. Here is the reality of the perpetual divine presence with Christ and through Him with us. That is the first point: "I am with the Father."

We are not concerned here with that mysterious and divine union between the Father and the Son taught in such words as "I and My Father are one" (John 10:30 NKJV). That belongs to another realm, where thought and language can safely go no further than His declarations lead them.

But our text here refers to the presence of God with Christ's perfect manhood—a presence the same in kind, however different in degree, that is granted to all loving and pure hearts. Take the words, then, as a wonderful utterance of our Lord's own consciousness. That nature, perfect in mind, in will, in heart, was always conscious of an unbroken union with God. The mind was filled with His truth; the will ever consciously bowing to His supreme law; the heart ever at rest in His perfect love and goodness. Like some mirror capable of receiving and giving back in brightness the rays of the sun, the whole Man, Christ Jesus, spread himself beneath the luster of God the Father and was shone upon with the unvarying radiance of His unclouded presence.

And that same union is possible for us through Him. We can come to Him, though our natures be battered and bruised and stained with sin, incapable of catching the light or reflecting it back. We can go to Christ through whom we come near to the Father, and through whom the Father comes near to us; and clinging to Him, we can enter into the wondrous fellowship of the Father God, who will draw near to our minds and hearts and wills and make the fleeting days of our earthly existence noble and happy with the blessedness of His felt presence. "I am with the Father." Is He with you, or has He ever been with you in such a fashion as this? Christ has brought the Father near to us. He is near us in His own gracious presence, and in Him the Father is near. His name is Immanuel—God with us. He who has the Son has the Father also.

ALEXANDER MACLAREN

"And He who sent Me is with Me. The Father has not left Me alone, for I always do those things that please Him."

John 8:29 NKJV

Our Lord Jesus was a solitary champion in the midst of armies of foes; those foes were powerful, cunning, cruel and exceedingly active, yet He was calm, unmoved, faced them without fear, and was victorious all through the campaign of His ministry. Since you also will meet with enemies and difficulties, would you possess the same calm and strength as He? Would you, in fact, live as He lived, and finishing your course, would you enter into His joy? The secret of His power was the presence of His God—"He who sent Me is with Me." And the secret of His comfort was fellowship with His Father—"The Father has not left Me alone." If you would know how you can enjoy the presence and fellowship of the Lord—and all the power and comfort that come thereby, the Savior tells you the secret in the following words: "For I always do those things that please Him." To do the things that please God is the way to secure His presence and consequent power and happiness.

It is the business of every Christian to be able to say, "I always do those things that please Him." In pleasing God there is implied an avoidance of all things that would displease Him. Now, you know what the works of the flesh are, and those, as defiled garments, are to be put off—pride, anger, self-ishness, impure thoughts, malice, bitterness, covetousness, immorality, etc. Pleasing God also means actually doing those things that please Him—to walk in the Spirit and produce the virtues of Christ, such as love, joy, peace, longsuffering, kindness, goodness, faithfulness, gentleness, and self-control. It is to be as Jesus was and is!

Do you wish to do as Jesus did? If you love the Lord, ask Him to search you, and see if there is any evil way in you, and deliver you from it—that you may always do the things that are pleasing in His sight. He will help you, for He works mightily within us. Commit yourself to Him; give yourself up to the purifying power of His Spirit, and He will bear you up to heights of divine grace and glories of character that you never thought you could reach—but which, when you reach them, will not puff you up, for you will feel compelled to cry, "Not to us, not to us, but to your name give praise!"

CHARLES SPURGEON

*Even as he spoke, many believed in him. To the Jews
who had believed him, Jesus said, "If you hold to my
teaching, you are really my disciples."*

John 8:30–31

These Jews who believed simply accepted His word on His claim of
messiahship, yet how shallow and unreliable their devotion to the Lord
was comes out in the course of the next few verses; and by the end of
the chapter they are taking up stones against Him. John shows us that there
is a kind of faith that may be real and may be the basis of something much
better, but which, if it does not grow, will rot away and disappear.

There are three ways in which the New Testament represents the act of
believing in Christ. The beginning of all true Christian faith has in it not
merely the intellectual acceptance of certain propositions as true, but a confidence in the authenticity of Jesus Christ. The least that Christ asks from us
is the entire and unhesitating acceptance of His words as final, conclusive,
and absolutely true. The words of His mouth, and the revelations He made
in the sweetness of His life, are the very unveiling to man of absolute and
certain truth. *Believe Jesus*, but do not stop there.

Believe on Christ. This carries us away from the mere act of acceptance
of His word on His authority to the far more manifestly voluntary, moral,
and personal act of reliance upon Him. Jesus is the basis of our hope, the
guarantee of our security, the foundation of our beliefs, the very ground on
which our whole life rests, the source of our peace. All that I think, feel, desire,
wish, and do should rest upon our dear Lord and be built on Him by simple
faith. Depend on Christ, and it shall not be in vain.

Believe into Christ. True Christian faith is the flight of the soul toward
Christ. Therein is one of the special blessings of the Christian life: it has for
its object and aim infinite and attainable completeness and glory, so that unwearied freshness, inexhaustible buoyancy, and endless progress are given to
every spirit that truly trusts in Christ. By faith, that deep and most real union
of the believing soul with Jesus Christ is effected and may be fitly described
as our entrance into and abiding in Him. To be in Jesus, joined to Him by
the union of will and desire, united to Him in oneness of a life—to be thus
in Christ is the crown and climax of faith and the condition of perfection.
Let us not be as tortoises crawling toward Him, but rather as eagles in our
flight to be near Him.

ALEXANDER MACLAREN

"Then you will know the truth, and the truth will set you free. . . . So if the Son sets you free, you will be free indeed."

John 8:32, 36

Truth must file off the chains of sin, and the Holy Spirit must open our prisons. You may feel that you have a wolf within your heart hungering after sin, which will not be satisfied though it is saturated with evil. Tendencies of inbred corruption may have raged through your soul. You may sit today with your hands fast bound by acts of sin, your heart shackled with corruption, your feet chained fast to the satanic blocks of unbelief, your whole self locked up in the bondage of corruption. He who serves his own passions is the slave of the worst of tyrants. But hear the mighty words of Jesus: Freedom is possible!

You may rivet your shackles by going to the law, to your own good works, to your praying and doing, but you will never be free until you come to Christ. He purchased your freedom at the phenomenal cost of His life. See Him whipped like a common felon in Pilate's hall, scourged like a murderer, and dragged away by hellhounds through the streets, fastened to the cruel cross. See Him yielding up His liberty to the dungeon of death. Dearly did He purchase with His own bondage the liberty that He so freely offers us. Jesus asks nothing of us as a preparation for this liberty. He finds us sitting in darkness, and He brings the true light in His hand, and all without our help, without our merit, and at first without our will. His message is grace, pure grace, undiluted by a single requisition that God might make of man. Just as you are, trust your soul to Christ, and He will give you perfect liberty.

Mark then, if you will come to Christ, you will be free instantly from every sort of bondage. The moment you believe you are free from sin. You may have been chained at a thousand points, but the instant you believe you are free as the bird of the air. Cut the chains, and in an instant you are clear of all, and upward you soar to God. When Christ sets us free, no chains can bind again. Our Savior is mightier than all that comes against us. "The blood of Jesus, his Son, purifies us from all sin" (1 John 1:7). Thank God that nothing can separate us from the love of Christ Jesus, and that we are "more than conquerors through him who loved us" (Romans 8:35, 37).

CHARLES SPURGEON

They answered him, "We are Abraham's descendants and have never been slaves of anyone. How can you say that we shall be set free?" Jesus replied, "Very truly I tell you, everyone who sins is a slave to sin."

John 8:33–34

N ever been slaves of anyone"? Then what about Egypt, Babylon, Persia, and Syria? Was there not a Roman garrison looking down from the castle into the very temple courts where this boastful falsehood was uttered? Is this not an instance of the strange power that we all have and exercise, of ignoring disagreeable facts, and by ingenious manipulation taking the wrinkles out of the photograph? There was a great deal of human nature in these men, who thus put up a screen between them and the penetrating words of our Lord. Were they not doing just what many of us do: ignoring the facts of our own spiritual condition, denying the plain lessons of experience?

Christ follows the vain boast with the calm, profound explanation of what He meant: "Everyone who sins is a slave to sin." This is true in two ways. By the act of sinning, a man shows that he is the slave of an alien power that has captured him; and in the act of sinning, he rivets the chains and increases the tyranny. He is a slave, or he would not obey sin. He is more a slave because he has again obeyed it. I remind each man's conscience that "all have sinned and fall short of the glory of God" (Romans 3:23). This declaration of the universality and reality of the bondage of sin is only turning into plain words the fact that is of universal experience. The truth is that every man, however noble his aspirations may be, however pure and high his convictions, and however much he attempts to do what is right, when he deals honestly with himself, becomes conscious of an influence working upon his heart with the inevitableness and certainty of the law: "Although I want to do good, evil is right there with me" (Romans 7:21).

Jesus teaches us that an alien power has captured and is coercing the wrongdoer. This does not destroy personal responsibility, but it kindles hope. A foreign foe, who has invaded the land, may be driven out and all his prisoners set free, if a stronger than he comes against him. The bondage of sin is real and hard. But the Spirit of the Son of God can conquer it. "Who will rescue me from this body that is subject to death? Thanks be to God, who delivers me through Jesus Christ our Lord!" (Romans 7:24–25).

ALEXANDER MACLAREN

They answered Him, "We are Abraham's descendants and have never been enslaved to anyone. What do You mean by saying, 'You will be set free'?" Jesus answered, "I assure you and most solemnly say to you, everyone who practices sin habitually is a slave of sin."

John 8:33–34 AMP

W e have never been enslaved," they said. We are only too apt to repeat this empty boast, and as they forgot Nebuchadnezzar and Augustus, we forget our failures, our faults, and our sins. We ignore them. Is not that, too, a plain fact of experience? Many believers have never really opened their eyes to the undeniable truth that sin has dominion over them. They go along on the surfaces of things, keeping to the shallows of human life, occupying themselves with various duties and pleasures, and they never know, just because they shut their eyes to the facts, what their real heart condition is in God's sight. Their hearts are "gospel-hardened," and their minds are waterproofed, by repeated application to them, of the truth of Jesus' words.

Let me plead with you. The ignorance of our bondage to sin is characteristic of the tone of mind of this generation. There is a chamber of sin in the deep places of all our hearts. It would be a great deal better that we should go down there and see it than that we should live in this fool's paradise of our own sin. The evils that we do, and that we cherish undone in our hearts, do not change because we choose to ignore them. Sin chokes the conscience; and so the worse a man is, the less he feels himself to be bad. We are ignorant of our sins because we drug and bribe our consciences.

The central thought of the gospel is that Jesus Christ is our Emancipator from sin. "The Spirit of the Lord is on me, because he has anointed me . . . to proclaim freedom for the prisoners" (Luke 4:18). As long as you dwell in the shallows of human experience, a shallow Christianity and a shallow Christ will be enough for you. But when you get to understand the depths of your own need, and the depths of your brother's need, then nothing less than the Christ who died to solve the problem, otherwise insoluble, of how to set free the soul and the world from the tyranny of sin, will be enough for you. Let us run to Christ for the freedom from sin that He wrought for our souls on Calvary's cross. Let us clutch and cling to Him, knowing that only in Jesus are we free, and free indeed.

ALEXANDER MACLAREN

Jesus answered them, "Most assuredly, I say to you, whoever commits sin is a slave of sin. And a slave does not abide in the house forever, but a son abides forever. Therefore if the Son makes you free, you shall be free indeed."

John 8:34–36 NKJV

Not to do wrong may be the mark of a slave's timid obedience. Not to wish to do wrong is the license of a son's free and blessed service. Freedom does not consist in doing what I like—that turns out, in the long run, to be the most abject slavery, under the severest tyrants—but it consists in liking to do what I ought. When my wishes and God's will are absolutely coincident, then, and only then, am I free. That is no prison, out of which we do not wish to go. Not to be confined against our wills, but voluntarily to choose to move only within the sacred, charmed, sweet circle of the discerned will of God is the service and liberty of the sons of God.

Alas! There are a great many believers who know very little about such blessedness. To many of us, religion consists of a number of prohibitions and restrictions and commandments equally unwelcome. "Do not do this," and all the while I would like to do it. "Do that," and all the while I do not want to do it. Pray, because it is your duty; go to church, because you think it is God's will; give money that you would much rather keep in your pocket; abstain from certain things that you desire; do other things that you do not a bit desire to do nor find any pleasure in doing. That is the religion of many people.

They need to ask themselves whether their religion is Christ's religion. Oh, beloved! "My yoke is easy and My burden is light" (Matthew 11:30 NKJV). Not because the things that He bids and forbids are less or lighter than those that a religion requires of its followers, but because, so to speak, the yoke is padded with the velvet of love and inclination coincides in the measure of our true religion with the discerned will of God. This is ever so far ahead of the experience of many believers. There are still great numbers of professing Christians on whose hearts only a very few of the syllables of God's will are written, and these very faintly. But remember that the fundamental idea of a covenant implies two people, and duties and obligations on the part of each. If God is in covenant with you, you are in covenant with God. If He makes a promise, there is something for you to do in order that the promise may be fulfilled to you.

ALEXANDER MACLAREN

"Abraham is our father," they answered. "If you were Abraham's children," said Jesus, "then you would do what Abraham did."

John 8:39

The great law that Christ here lays down is that what is historically true may be morally false. People may be genealogically akin, yet spiritually strangers; natural relation may be forfeited by moral apostasy. These men were ready to produce the record of lineage, but Jesus said the record was not a matter of paper and ink; it was a matter of likeness, spiritual identity, and kindred souls. "Abraham" is not the name of a mere individual. He represents the Abrahamic life, the faith-life; the life that takes his staff at the divine command and goes out not knowing where he is going. If you have not Abraham's faith, Jesus says, then you abuse Abraham's name by using it. In justice to the dead, let sacred names alone, unless in assuming them you fill them with the spirit by which they were first consecrated. The Abrahamic dignity is not superimposed or handed down like an heirloom; every man must support his claim by his spirit and his actions. When the Jews stood upon the Abrahamic pedestal, He swept them off, declaring that they should not stand there, posing as liars.

Let us, then, look at our records and see how we truly stand. Ours may be but respectability on paper; we may have nothing but a written pedigree to show. What Jesus says is fundamental. He leaves nothing untouched with regard to the truth of our profession of faith. Do not boast that you are of God unless you love all that is godly. God is not a mere name. Regarded as a name, it becomes a symbol of all truth, purity, righteousness, goodness, gentleness, love, and redemption. If God is your Father, you are godly. All who are of pure descent from a pure origin are known by their character, sympathy, and fellowship, which no momentary circumstances can conceal. To be of God means to know the truth, love the truth, support the truth, preach the truth, and no one will be able to shut your mouth in the hour of testimony. Test your heart that indeed "you received the Spirit of adoption by whom we cry out, 'Abba, Father.' The Spirit Himself bears witness with our spirit that we are children of God" (Romans 8:15–16 NKJV). He comes upon us like a new sunrise, like a dawn we have never seen before—the Light of eternity.

JOSEPH PARKER

Jesus said to them, "If God were your Father [but He is not], you would love and recognize Me, for I came from God [out of His very presence] and have arrived here."

John 8:42 AMP

To not love the Lord Jesus Christ is a thing so dreadful that those who do love Him can hardly tell you how they tremble at the bare notion of being in such a condition. Sometimes the saints of God have grown so warm concerning what is due Jesus their Lord, and have got to feel such a horror at the sin of not loving Him, that they have pronounced a curse in God's name upon those who do not love Christ. It is the most solemn word of denunciation that could have fallen from apostolic pen: "If anyone does not love the Lord, let that person be cursed. Come, Lord!" (1 Corinthians 16:22), and yet Paul felt that he must write it, even though Paul could not speak of the enemies of Christ's cross without tears.

I beg you to stand by Calvary's cross and see Jesus bleeding and dying, and then say, "He has done all this, and yet I do not love Him." I wish you would go into the garden of Gethsemane and see the drops of blood and sweat fall upon the cold ground, and hear His cries and groans for sinners, and then say, "And yet I do not love Him." Look at Him taken down from the cross with the image of death stamped on His glorious face, a death He endured out of pure love for you, and then could you say, "I will not love Him"? Follow Him in His resurrection and see Him as He breathes peace over His disciples, and then see if you dare say, "I do not love Him." See Him rising as He ascends into glory, and then I would like you to feel as if your heart must burst, while you say, "Yet I do not love Him." I would have you see Him sitting on His throne at the right hand of the Father in all His glory, adored by myriads of angels and saints, with every harp string in heaven trilling out His praise. Amid that splendor, could you stand and begin to strike your chest and say, "Alas, this hard heart does not love Him"?

Nothing is more good, right, true, or beautiful than Jesus Christ the incarnate God. That the heart does not instinctively love Him as soon as it perceives Him is clear proof that it is poisoned at its fountain. Blessed be the grace that has given us power to love our Savior. May it increase more and more.

CHARLES SPURGEON

*"Why is my language not clear to you? Because you are
unable to hear what I say. You belong to your father, the
devil, and you want to carry out your father's desires.
He was a murderer from the beginning, not holding
to the truth, for there is no truth in him. When he lies,
he speaks his native language, for he is a liar and the
father of lies."*

John 8:43–44

There are no words like the words of Jesus. His sayings are unfathomable. How well He maintains His own if this is taken as merely a dramatic dialogue! How calm He is! How clear in statement, how assured in the possession of every qualification that can dominate the history of men! Yet He surprises us by the use of startling language. We speak of the meek and lowly Jesus, but Jesus Christ called the men who were looking at Him fools, hypocrites, liars, murderers, thieves, white sepulchers, devourers, wolves in sheep's clothing, and now children of the devil. Little wonder that He had nowhere to lay His head. Little wonder that He sent a sword upon the earth, dividing whole families, and making relatives strangers and aliens. Jesus was not scolding, merely upbraiding, or trying to exasperate His listeners. He was revealing spirit and character and purpose, and doing it with the calmness of philosophy. We could not call a man a child of the devil without being angry, and our anger would spoil the revelation. It was the solemn, calm, serene manner of the speaker that made the terms so truly awful.

Jesus' speech is delivered from the platform of eternity. How familiarly He speaks of their father, who was a murderer from the beginning! How well He knew ancient history, because there was no history ancient to Him. He knew all there is to know about the devil. He says to the Jews, "You are not yourselves only, for you had fathers, ancestors, and I will show your crest and your motto and your father's image. You want to carry out your father's desire, but you fail to understand who your father is." He speaks calmly of this fate. He does not upbraid the men as if they were to blame; they express a historical moral necessity. Their malice and obstinacy and hatred of truth are in keeping with the family name. They are absolutely consistent to their heritage, and Jesus gives them a chance to see their true hearts.

The words of the meek and lowly Jesus were filled with passion and revelation. May we always be prepared to hear His voice, especially His words of discipline for our soul's good.

JOSEPH PARKER

> *"Whoever belongs to God hears what God says. The reason you do not hear is that you do not belong to God."*
>
> John 8:47

Here is a mystery that cannot be explained, but it is a simple fact. There are some people who cannot be religious from any point that is obvious to their thinking. There are some ministers who cannot pray; they are scholars, they are expositors, they are sincere believers, but they do not know how to pray. "Whoever belongs to God hears what God says"—he who is of music knows music when he hears it; he who is a child of art knows the painter's touch from the daub of the unskilled hand. We are born what we are—musicians, poets, artists, accountants, entrepreneurs, journalists, leaders, heroes—it is birth, not of choice. This may seem to ruin a good deal of hope, but it is meant to do nothing of the kind. Awaken yourself; who can tell what angel sleeps in your dullness? Who knows what bright spirit has taken up its residence in your soul? Arise, awake, and put on your strength! You cannot tell what you are until all the awakening ministries have been brought to bear upon your indifference and obstinacy.

When were deep sayings understandable to corrupt hearts? The Jews did not understand this man's speech. They blundered in every remark they made upon it. They continually took it from the wrong angle, and they so misconstrued the words that they lost all their philosophy and all their music. Blessed be God, therefore, that there are those who teach language. The Beatitudes are mysteries. "Blessed are the pure in heart, for they will see God" (Matthew 5:8). The world heard and passed over it completely, saying that some fanatic who had taken possession of the mountain was raving there, harmlessly but most incoherently. "Blessed are the meek, for they will inherit the earth" (Matthew 5:5). In that one sentence there is a whole library of the deepest, holiest thinking, an infinite philosophy of life. But the people who listened to Jesus knew absolutely nothing of what He was talking about. When He gave away fish and loaves of bread, His followers swelled into the thousands; when He began to give away His own flesh and to hand out in cups of gold His heart's blood, His followers amounted to twelve persons, and even they understood little of His sayings.

Rejoice today that He calls you to know Him and to know His words in the depths of your heart.

JOSEPH PARKER

The Jews answered him, "Aren't we right in saying that you are a Samaritan and demon-possessed?"

John 8:48

The occurrence that gave occasion to these words may be taken as an example of a whole series of facts that underlie this name. Our Lord has just been rebuking the Jews for their sinfulness, denying that they are children of Abraham, asserting that they do not belong to God, telling them to their faces that they are slaves and children of the devil. And they, in their dull brains and malicious hearts, think that no one who was a good Jew at heart could say such unpleasant things about the chosen people. They hear the voice of an enemy in such words, and so they fiercely turn upon Him, "You are a Samaritan and demon-possessed!" They did not recognize the love that underlay the sternness, the throbbing of a heart that desired their good, and therefore warned them of their evil. Nations, like individuals, too often think that the man becomes their enemy who tells them the truth. And these people, misunderstanding the impulse of the words, and feeling keenly their sharp edge, lash out at Him in a desperately cruel manner.

My friend, the same treatment comes to all men who play this same role. Whenever someone stands up to oppose the wild current of popular desires, he may be assured that missiles will be directed at him. Christian men and women must face the same denigrations as your Master had. You, too, must tread in the Master's steps. The church that does not earn the same sort of criticism that attended its Master has probably failed of its duty. The "imitation of Jesus" does not consist merely in the sanctities and secrecies of communion and the blessings of a meek and quiet heart, but includes standing where He stood, in stated and active opposition to widespread evils, and, if need be, in the protesting opposition to popular error. It is good to be called intolerant by the crowd that desires us to be tolerant of immorality and sin; and it is good to be called narrow-minded by those whose only notion of pleasure is exuberant immorality.

Jesus Christ took His full share of such missiles. None of His followers have been called by worse names than was He. Remember that the censure of the crowd is apt to be praise, and its praise blame. The rotten eggs thrown at the godly turn to roses in their flight. The praises of good men and the scoffs of godless ones are equally valuable certificates of character.

ALEXANDER MACLAREN

"I am not possessed by a demon," said Jesus, "but I honor my Father and you dishonor me. I am not seeking glory for myself; but there is one who seeks it, and he is the judge. Very truly I tell you, whoever obeys my word will never see death."

John 8:49–51

The false charge was the occasion of our Lord's uttering another great truth. The Jews rushed on, furious in their rage and denunciations, but He flashed in their faces the light of truth. To put down error, lift up truth. Nothing so baffles the adversaries of the faith as to utter with unshaken confidence the truth of God. The truth stated by Jesus, "Whoever obeys my word will never see death," was full of promise. If they willfully rejected His promise, it became worse to them than a threat. Christ's rejected promises curdle into woes. If the believer shall never see death, the unbeliever shall never see life.

Observe that the one conspicuous characteristic of the man who shall never see death is that he keeps Christ's word. He may have many other characteristics, both great strengths and weaknesses, but they are comparatively unimportant in this respect. This person hears what Jesus says, notes it, clings to it. Making the Lord Jesus his all in all, reverencing His word, he does everything within his power to keep it and obey it. Whatever Jesus has laid down as truth is truth to him. Is it so with you? Some judge the divine revelation itself and claim the right not only to interpret it, but to correct and expand it. They believe a doctrine because the light of the present age confirms it or invents it. Their foundation is in man's own thought. In their opinion, parts of Scripture are exceedingly faulty and need tinkering with scientific hammers. The light of the Holy Spirit is to them a mere glowworm compared with the light of the present age.

But He who is to share the promise stated by Jesus is one who believes the Savior's word because it is His word. To him, the inspiration of the Holy Spirit is the warrant of faith, whether spoken by Christ or by His inspired apostles. This is a very important matter: the foundation of our faith is even more important than the superstructure. Unless you ground your faith upon the fact that the Lord has spoken, your faith lacks that worshipful reverence that God requires. We are to be disciples, not critics. We rest our eternal destiny solely upon the truthfulness of Christ, and He will never disappoint us.

CHARLES SPURGEON

"I assure you and most solemnly say to you, if any-one keeps My word [by living in accordance with My message] he will indeed never, ever see and experience death."

John 8:51 AMP

D eath is a fearsome sight. To *see* is an intense Greek word that Westcott says means "a long steady, exhaustive vision, whereby we become slowly acquainted with the nature of the object to which it is directed." To look at eternal death, which is the threatened punishment of sin, and to stand gazing upon the terror of the wrath to come through a death that never dies, to stand before a gaping cavern that leads to darkness forever, is more haunting and dreadful than anything imaginable.

But there is no death penalty for the believer. When a man receives into his soul the words of Jesus, his spiritual death is over and he begins to see life. It may be at first the breakthrough of a painful life—a life of deep regrets for the past, and dark fears for the future; a life of hungering and thirsting for something, it hardly knows what, but it cannot live without it. This man sees life; and the more he keeps his Savior's word, the more he rejoices in Jesus, the more he rests on His promise, the more he loves Him, the more he serves Him, the more will his new life drive death out of sight. Life now abounds and holds sway, and the old death hides away in holes and corners. Grace frees us from the reign of death as well as from the penalty of death.

But some believers continue to fear their physical death. Why is that? Being in Christ Jesus, we need never fear condemnation. Nothing can separate us from the love of God. Nothing can ever pluck us out of Christ's hand. Yes, we all walk through the valley of the shadow of death, but we need fear no evil. A shadow was cast across my path, but I passed through it and hardly noticed it was there. Why was that? Because I had my eye fixed upon a strong light beyond. Believers so rejoice over the presence of their Lord that they do not observe that they are dying. They rest so sweetly in the embrace of Christ that when they pass from one world into another it is all one kingdom, and one sun shines in both lands. The eternal life that is in the believer glides the stages of growth from glory to glory without a break. In the twinkling of an eye we pass on to heaven, and we never gaze on death. Never fear death, for Jesus says that you need never see it.

CHARLES SPURGEON

At this they exclaimed, "Now we know that you are
demon-possessed! Abraham died and so did the prophets,
yet you say that whoever obeys your word will never taste
death." "Very truly I tell you," Jesus answered, "before
Abraham was born, I am!"

John 8:52, 58

How can you talk to men like these? What can you do with people who think that Abraham is dead? There is nobody dead. They were wrong at the foundation. "'I am the God of Abraham, the God of Isaac, and the God of Jacob'? He is not the God of the dead but of the living" (Matthew 22:32). Who can teach this doctrine properly? Who can feel it in all its heavenliness? Who can find room in the heart for this immortality? To the Jews, Abraham and the prophets were dead—what an empty world they lived in who spoke these words! How hollow their voices sounded in the chambers of the past! What can you teach such people? They think they are the only living people in the world. No man dies. The little child is not dead, but is like a dewdrop that has gone up to the sun to be used in the fashioning of a rainbow. The friend is not dead, but he lives and waits for you from heaven: do not disappoint him.

Jesus said to them these shocking words: "Before Abraham was born, I am!" This is true. His words establish the truth of the declaration. They are not dictionary words, they are not rhetorical terms, they are not sentences and phrases fashioned and carved in a school, and beautifully enameled, and ticketed for sale in the marketplace. These are mysterious words, eternal words. He said, "Your father Abraham rejoiced at the thought of seeing my day; he saw it and was glad" (John 8:56). Then the Jews perfectly reveled in contempt for the man: "You are not yet fifty years old . . . and you have seen Abraham!" (v. 57). Who can reproduce the tone of their bitter speech? Fact seemed to be so dead against this man. Who could bear such talk? Who could bear to have facts so trampled underfoot? Who could have statistics ignored in this reckless way? Little wonder that they took up stones to kill Him.

How marvelous it is to come near this divine Teacher! How He soothes and blesses us, yet how He excites and challenges us! Never stifle His warning voice if you hear it. Beware of those, who like these Jews, bring their false teaching and will never yield to immortal Love.

JOSEPH PARKER

Jesus answered, "It is My Father who honors Me, of whom you say that He is your God. Yet you have not known Him, but I know Him."

John 8:54–55 NKJV

We all know the difference between hearsay and sight. We may have read books of travel that tell of some scene of great natural beauty or historic interest and may think that we understand all about it, but it is always an amazing experience when our own eyes look for the first time at the snowy alps or the Parthenon on its rocky height. We all know the difference between hearsay and experience. We read books of the poets that portray love and sorrow and the other emotions that make up our unpredictable, changing life, but we need to go through the mill ourselves before we understand what the grip of the iron teeth of suffering and misery is; and we need to have had our own hearts opened by a true and blessed affection before we know the sweetness of love. Others may tell us about it, but we have to feel it ourselves before we know.

To come still closer: we all know the difference between hearing about a man and knowing him. We may have been told much about him and be familiar with his character, as we think; but, when we come face-to-face with him, and actually for ourselves experience the magnetism of his presence or come under any of the influences of his character, then we know that what we heard about him was but superficial and a mere shadow.

That is even truer with regard to our knowing God. Job could say, "I have heard of You by the hearing of the ear, but now my eyes see You" (Job 42:5 NKJV). Can you say that? If so, you understand the text: "No more shall every man teach . . . his brother, saying, 'Know the LORD,' for they all shall know Me, from the least to the greatest" (Jeremiah 31:34 NKJV).

There is a great difference between knowing about God and knowing God; the difference there is between beliefs and life, between theology and religion. We may have all the doctrines of the church clear in our understanding, and may owe our possession of them to other people's teaching; we may even, in a sense, believe them—and yet they may be absolutely outside of our lives. And it is only when they pass into the very substance of our being and influence the source of our conduct—it is only then that we know God.

ALEXANDER MACLAREN

Jesus answered, "I tell you the truth, before Abraham was even born, I AM!"

John 8:58 NLT

During the autumn before His death, while in attendance at one of the Jerusalem feasts, the leaders were boasting of their direct descent from Abraham and attacking Jesus. On their part, the quarrel of words got very bitter. For Jesus to say to them, "Your father Abraham rejoiced as he looked forward to my coming. He saw it and was glad" (v. 56), was a tremendous statement, staggering to one who had not yet grasped it.

With a contemptuous curl of the lip, instantly they come back with: "You aren't even fifty years old. How can you say you have seen Abraham?" (v. 57). More quietly than ever, with the calmness of conscious truth, come these magnificent words, emphasized with the strongest phrase He ever used, "I tell you the truth, before Abraham was even born, I AM!" The sharp contrast was made clear. Abraham was born. He came into existence. Jesus says, "I AM!" That "I AM" is meant to mean absolute existence—an eternal now without beginning or ending. Their Jewish ears were instantly caught by that short sentence. Jesus was identifying himself with the One who uttered that same sentence to Moses out of the burning bush! That "I AM" explains the meaning of the expression "my coming." It stretches it out backward beyond Abraham's day. It lengthens it infinitely at both ends.

This is Jesus' point of view, this marvelous Jesus. He is Jehovah in Genesis's first chapters. It is from Him that Adam hid that fateful day, and with Him that Enoch took those long walks. It is His voice and presence in the black-topped, flaming Mount Sinai that awed the Israelite crowd so. His voice it was that won and overwhelmed Moses, who was waiting in the cleft of the rock that early morning, and long after that the other rugged, footsore man, Elijah, standing with his face covered in the mouth of a cave. Isaiah saw His glory that memorable day in the temple. It was He who rode upon the storm before Ezekiel's wondering eyes, and He who reveals to Daniel's opened ears the vision of his people's future. Jehovah—He comes as Jesus. Jesus—He is Jehovah. No sending of messengers for this great work of winning back His people. He comes himself. Jesus is God come down to win man back to himself.

S. D. GORDON

*As [Jesus] went along, he saw a man blind from birth. . . .
Jesus heard that they had thrown him out, and when he
found him, he said, "Do you believe in the Son of Man?"*

John 9:1, 35

Why did Jesus pass that way? Surely He could have gone by another path. But grace has its necessities; love has its predestinations. Jesus Christ always looked for opportunities for doing good, and He made it His business to discover those who needed Him. He even stands at the door and knocks. In a sense, does He not thrust himself upon those who need Him so graciously and quietly that it has no appearance of obtrusiveness or aggression? He makes himself felt by events, by appeals, by sudden recollections, by suggestions from friends, through a church service—yes, in a thousand ways He sends us hints that He is there, and has with Him all the resources that are needed for our redemption, purification, and final coronation in heaven. When you felt inclined to pray, when truth was suddenly made understandable to you, could you trace those gracious influences to the touch, the glance, the blessing of Christ? In this powerful manner, Jesus seeks out the blind man in order to give His healing touch.

Jump ahead in this story and note how Christ completes His own work. When He heard that the blind man had been thrown out, why did He happen to be on that path? For the same reason He was on that path in the first place. He knows all the paths—the crossroad that runs up to the distant farm; the way you walk in the evening to meditate; the back way, the front way. He knows all the roads to human dwellings and human hearts. Jesus finds the man and asks him, "Do you believe in the Son of Man?" He had a right to ask the question. He who heals the body has established the right to ask about the soul. The significance of the first miracle becomes an introduction to the real purpose of Jesus' mission to the man. Was it not enough that the man could see, that he now had a sound body? Jesus Christ always directs himself to the inner man, where the real miracle has yet to take place. It is in our belief in the Son of Man that we see and feel and realize our true life. It is through the opened eye that He leads to an opened soul. Oh, sweetest of words! The man might have known who it was: no other man ever spoke like Jesus. What a voice! What subdued thunder! What tender sympathy! What suggestion! What music! And when the man said, "Lord, I believe," he stood there a completed man!

JOSEPH PARKER

His disciples asked him, "Rabbi, who sinned, this man or his parents, that he was born blind?" "Neither this man nor his parents sinned," said Jesus, "but this happened so that the works of God might be displayed in him. As long as it is day, we must do the works of him who sent me. Night is coming, when no one can work."

John 9:2–4

The blind man sitting by the wayside suggested to the disciples a curious, half-theological, half-metaphysical question, in which rabbinical subtlety delighted. Jesus Christ looked at the same man but did not think about theological cobwebs. What was suggested to Him was to fight against the evil and abolish it. In order to understand how to deal with and get rid of certain problems, discussions of origins are needed. But our first business is not to say, "How did this happen?" but rather to take steps to make it cease to come about. Cure the man first and then argue to your heart's content about what made him blind. And so Jesus Christ taught us that the meaning of the day of life is that we should set ourselves to abolish the works of the devil, and that the work of God is that we should fight against sin and sorrow, and insofar as it is in our power, abolish these in all their forms and advances.

Jesus says to us, "Life is the time for activity, and it must be the more diligent because it is ringed by the darkness of night." The night means a season of compulsory inactivity. Even our Lord was influenced by this common human motive and felt that there was a work to be done that must be crowded into a definite space, because when that space was past, there would be no more opportunity for the work to be done. Indeed, Jesus lets us see that His life was under the solemn compulsion of that great *must* that was so often upon His lips. He knew He was here to do His Father's will, and the pressure of that obligation lay upon Him so that He neither could nor would if He could get rid of it.

It was the Savior's greatest joy to do the will of His Father, yet He called it His *must*. How much more ought you and I to say the same in the same spirit? Jesus teaches us not only diligence, and thus supplies the stimulus, but also determines the direction of our diligence and thus supplies the guidance. We should be wise as to the use of our time and opportunities. Until the kingdoms of this world have become the kingdoms of our God and of His Christ, let us never become weary in the work of God.

CHARLES SPURGEON

Jesus answered, "Neither this man nor his parents sinned, but that the works of God should be revealed in him."

John 9:3 NKJV

Never attribute any special sorrow or difficulty endured by men to some special sin. There is a tendency, for instance, to consider that those on whom the tower in Siloam fell must have been "worse sinners than all other men who dwelt in Jerusalem" (Luke 13:4 NKJV). And if any have met with a very sudden death or illness, some are apt to suppose that they must have been exceedingly guilty—but it is not so. You cannot judge a man's state before God by what happens to him in the course of life. And it is very unkind, heartless, and almost inhuman, to sit down, as the friends of Job did, and suppose that because Job was greatly afflicted, he must, therefore, have been greatly sinful. It was not so. Our Savior bids us to regard illnesses, physical disabilities, and frailties as sent to be an opportunity wherein God may display His power and His grace.

Some believers are very poor, are laid off from their jobs, or lose their businesses. Others are full of aches and pains or are gravely ill, and some die suddenly as a result. Perhaps all this suffering is permitted that the work of God may be manifest in their afflictions by their patience, submission to the divine will, and persevering holiness amid all their loss and trials. All this is sent that God's grace may be seen in them. Will you look at your afflictions in that light and believe that they are not sent as a punishment, but as a platform upon which God may stand and display His free grace in you?

The same is true of your weaknesses. None of us are perfect, but we may also have various weaknesses and disabilities. Now believe, if you are sent to preach the gospel, or to teach children, or in any way to advance the kingdom of God, that you would not be any better fitted for your work if you had all the eloquence of a Cicero and all the learning of a Newton! You, as you are, can serve the Lord and can fill a certain place, better, with all your drawbacks, than you could without those drawbacks. A sensible Christian will make use of his weaknesses for God's glory.

So it will be with all the oppositions with which we meet. If we serve the Lord, we shall be sure to meet with difficulties and oppositions—but they are only more opportunities for the works of God to be seen in us.

CHARLES SPURGEON

"As long as it is day, we must do the works of him who sent me. Night is coming, when no one can work. While I am in the world, I am the light of the world."

John 9:4–5

I n this miracle we see Jesus Christ working from the clear consciousness of His own authority. "While I am in the world, I am the light of the world." That is not the word of a weak man; that is not the word of a man who is going to fail in a miracle. Men should be very careful how they address themselves to great events, because they may fail in the very middle of the process, and their boasting increase the completeness of their humiliation. But omniscience need not calculate, for it knows all things; omnipotence need not pause, for it can do all things. Jesus speaks himself as God.

He has already said that "we must do the works of him who sent me," as if there were cooperation, fellowship, in these processes that lie around us as indicative of our sphere of work. As the light of the world, Jesus says, "All blind men are my parishioners. They are the souls that I must look after. If any say they can see, I have nothing to do with them. I have come to call not the righteous, but sinners to repentance. All the hungry souls are mine—make them sit down, the feast shall be spread; this miracle shall surely be wrought. All the ignorant are mine—enlarge the school; bring the most backward scholars in, for they belong to me." It is our ignorance that gives us our right to pray; it is our sin, rightly comprehended, that is our letter of introduction to the cross.

How the face of Jesus flushes with a consciousness of power when He is face-to-face with a case of indisputable necessity! He is a warrior who sees the victory before the battle is begun. This is precisely what the church should do and ought to say. There is a plurality of action in this divine beneficence: "We must do the works of him who sent me." If we are called to partnership with Christ, we should say, "This is my program. Wherever there is a blind man, I claim him; a hungry man, he is mine; a poor child, that child belongs to me; a poor, lost wandering one, that creature, homeless, destitute, friendless, is mine." If the church could speak this way, there would be nobody to speak against it. Let the church do good and claim the poor, the lost, the suffering, the hungry, and insist upon having them, and treat them as nobody else can treat them. Then the church becomes inexplicably profound to a world of skeptics.

JOSEPH PARKER

After saying this, he spit on the ground, made some
mud with the saliva, and put it on the man's eyes. "Go,"
he told him, "wash in the Pool of Siloam" (this word
means "Sent"). So the man went and washed, and came
home seeing.

John 9:6–7

There is only one other instance in the Gospels where a miracle is wrought in a similar manner (see Mark 7:33–35). The variety of methods in our Lord's miracles serves important purposes, teaching us that the methods are nothing, and that He moved freely among them all, the real cause in every case being one and the same, the bare putting forth of His will. It also teaches us that in each specific case there were reasons in the moral and spiritual condition of the persons operated upon for the adoption of the specific means employed, which we of course have no means of discovering. There is here, first then, healing by material means. The clay has no power of healing; the water of Siloam had no power of healing. What healed them was Christ's will, but He uses these externals to help the poor blind man to believe that he is going to be healed. He condescends to drape and veil His power in order that the dim eye, unaccustomed to the light, may look upon that shadowed representation of it when it could not gaze upon the pure brightness.

This healing by material means in order to accommodate himself to the weak faith that He seeks to evoke and to strengthen thereby is parallel, in principle, to His appointment of external rites and ceremonies. Baptism, the Lord's Supper, a visible church, outward means of worship, and so on, all these come under that same category. There is no life or power in them except His will works through them, but they are helps for a weak and sense-bound faith to climb to the knowing of the spiritual reality. It is not the clay, not the water, not the church, the ordinances, the form of prayer, the sacrament—it is none of these things that have the healing and grace in them. They are only ladders by which we may ascend to Him. Let us neither presumptuously predate the time when we shall be able to do without them, nor superstitiously elevate them to a place of importance and of power in the Christian life that Christ never meant them to fill. He heals through material means; the true source of healing is His own loving will.

ALEXANDER MACLAREN

Some of the Pharisees said, "This man is not from God,
for he does not keep the Sabbath."

John 9:16

The miracle has been wrought, and Jesus Christ immediately comes face-to-face with criticism. The transformation of the man was so great that even His own neighbors were unsure of his identity. Some said he was, others said he was a look-alike. But he himself insisted, "I am the man" (v. 9). Thus we have the criticism of the world to deal with. We cannot have an honest judgment pronounced, because of infinite and unmanageable prejudices. We do not like to confess the supernatural, for the supernatural demands a personal response from us. So we cast about upon the identity of the man, upon the reality of the work, upon the accuracy of the report, preparing to explain it away upon another basis. We prefer this to simply and directly accepting the miracle and blessing God for His intervention in life.

The Pharisees proceeded upon another line. They began by taking away the character of the man who had done the miracle. They start their argument with the theological point that Jesus is not from God because He breaks the Sabbath rules. Why not start on the charitable side and say, "This man must be of God, because He heals blind men"? Some minds cannot get beyond the metaphysical center. They could pass by all the healed blind men in creation for seven days a week and never speak to one of them, yet keep quoting their doctrine. The Pharisees were so filled with pride that they had to deny Jesus' power. They could not believe concerning the man that he had been born blind and had received his sight. Not only did they take away the character of the Healer, they took away the character of the healed, and practically called the man a false witness. Not believing the man or his parents, the Pharisees said, "Give glory to God by telling the truth. We know this man is a sinner" (v. 24). Translated, this meant: "Confess, speak the truth to God; admit you have been telling lies, and be faithful to God."

If you have been genuinely converted to Christ, you are a walking miracle of God the Holy Spirit. Those around you, like the Pharisees, will abuse you. It is the same trick all time, the unchangeable ingenuity of moral insanity. If they cannot persuade you against the gospel, cannot answer the questions that your changed life brings, they will abuse you. Never fear, my friend. Jesus is still with you. No man can take away from you the testimony of your own heart.

JOSEPH PARKER

His parents answered them and said, "By what means he now sees we do not know, or who opened his eyes we do not know. He is of age; ask him. He will speak for himself."

John 9:20–21 NKJV

Believers, however reserved their natural disposition may be, are often compelled to speak out when they are very much pressed, even when loved ones turn the cold shoulder to them and show no sympathy with their faith. These Pharisees took this man and put questions to him by way of examination and cross-examination. "What did He do to you? How did He open your eyes?" And so on. He does not appear to have been disconcerted by the questions. He acquitted himself grandly. Self-contained, quiet, shrewd, immovable, his mind was made up, and with a thorough mastery of the situation he was ready for them. He did not hesitate.

Well now, I trust if ever you and I are questioned as to our faith, even though it is with intent to entangle us, we shall never be ashamed to acknowledge our Lord or to defend His cause. When others revile and slander our Lord Jesus, it becomes imperative on us to commend and extol Him. Shall we hear the cause of Christ denounced in society and for fear of feeble men refrain our tongue or smooth over the matter? When my dearest Friend is thus abused, I must and will proclaim the honors of His name.

It is well to cultivate a general habit of openheartedness and boldness. We have no need to intrude and push ourselves into people's way and so become a nuisance to them. Far from it, but let us walk through the world as those who have nothing to conceal, conscious of the integrity of our own motives and the rightness of our heart before God, not needing to wear armor and sleep in it like the knights of old, knowing rather that the truth unarmed is the best apparel. Let us show that we have nothing to cloak or cover, nothing to disguise or hide—that the gospel has worked in us such honesty and frankness of spirit that nothing can make us blush, no foe can cause us fear. Let us tell what we believe as true because we can vouch for its truthfulness. Let us renounce those who quarrel at these things, not so much by our combat as by our character. Let us prove to them that we have a solid reason for our simple protest, that we have actually received the grace in which we earnestly believe. Our words will have weight when they see that the fruit of our faith accords with the flower of our profession. There is great power in this manner of answering the adversary.

CHARLES SPURGEON

A second time they summoned the man who had been blind. "Give glory to God by telling the truth," they said. "We know this man is a sinner." He replied, "Whether he is a sinner or not, I don't know. One thing I do know. I was blind but now I see!"

John 9:24–25

In this marvelous story, we find two contrasted classes. The blind man stands for an example of honest ignorance, knowing himself ignorant, and not to be cajoled or frightened or in any way provoked to pretending to knowledge that he does not possess. He firmly holds to what he does know, and because he is conscious of his little knowledge, he is therefore waiting for light and willing to be led. He is humble and sturdy, meek and independent, ready to listen to any voice that can really teach, and formidably quick to prick with wholesome sarcasm the inflated claims of mere official pretenders.

The Pharisees, on the other hand, are sure that they know everything that can be known about anything in the fields of religion and morality, absolutely confident of their absolute possession of the truth. Theirs was a complete incapacity to discern the glory of a miracle that broke religious proprieties and conventionalities. Their contempt for the supposed ignorant, their cruel taunt directed against the man's calamity, and their swift resort to the weapon of excommunication (v. 34) are but too plain a type of character that is as ready to corrupt the teachers of the church as of the synagogue.

The beauty of the story is that through the process of the argument, the man is getting more and more light at each step. He begins with "the man they call Jesus" (v. 11). Then he gets to "a prophet" (v. 17), then he comes to "the godly person who does [God's] will" (v. 31). Then he comes to "if this man were not from God, he could do nothing" (v. 33). These are his own reflections, the working out of the impression made by the facts on an honest mind. Because he had so used the light that he had, Jesus could give him more light by asking him, "Do you believe in the Son of Man?" (v. 35). To the man's open heart was given the full revelation of the person of Jesus, and he hears the words that the Pharisees were not worthy to hear: "He is the one speaking with you" (v. 37).

God's method has not wavered. If you have honesty in your soul, no matter how ignorant you feel, Jesus Christ will open the eyes of your understanding into the illumination of perfect vision.

ALEXANDER MACLAREN

"One thing I know: that though I was blind, now I see."

John 9:25 NKJV

Every now and then, you and I are called into a debate regarding faith. There are legitimate questions that people have, and we need to go into these debates well-armed with the true gospel of God. Never be afraid of a debate, and at least take with you the powerful weapon that this man used: "Though I was blind, now I see."

The testimony is powerful because it is a personal argument. The personal factor of the argument gives it power. Lifted up from sin, delivered from bondage, from doubt, from fear, from despair, from any agony intolerable—lifted up to joys unspeakable and into the family of God—we can rightly say, "I bear my personal witness to the truth of Christ's gospel in my case." The psalmist said, "I believed, therefore I spoke" (Psalm 116:10 NKJV), which is an argument that cannot be disputed. That man will never move the world who lets the world move him, but the man who stands firm and says, "I *know* such-and-such a thing because it was burned into my own inner life"—such a man's very appearance becomes an argument to convince others.

Moreover, this man's argument was a forcible appeal to other men's senses. "You saw that I was blind, but now you see that I can see." He appealed to their senses, and so should we through living holy lives. The change that the gospel works in men must be the gospel's best argument against all opposers. If our religion does no more in the world than any other, well then, despise it. If men can receive the gospel of Christ and yet live as they did before and be none the better for it, then our gospel is understandably not sought. But that is not the case. Just state the difference that the gospel made in you. This supernatural work in your own innermost spirit will overthrow a thousand other arguments.

Some of you have grace in your heart but have not the courage to confess it. If Jesus has given you eyes, as He did the blind man, I am sure you should do what the blind man did and give Him your tongue. If He has taught you to see things in the light of the gospel, you ought not to be unwilling to confess Him before others. You cannot tell how much good you might do to others. Your taking the decisive stand might be just the last grain cast onto the scale that leads others to decide to follow Jesus.

CHARLES SPURGEON

17

Jesus heard that they had thrown him out, and when he found him, he said, "Do you believe in the Son of Man?" "Who is he, sir?" the man asked. "Tell me so that I may believe in him." Jesus said, "You have now seen him; in fact, he is the one speaking with you." Then the man said, "Lord, I believe," and he worshiped him.

John 9:35–38

"Fᴏʀ it is by grace you are saved" is the unchanging purpose of heaven. And it is further decreed that this grace shall be received by men through the channel of faith, and by that channel only. God will save only those who trust in His Son. Jesus Christ came into this world and took upon himself our humanity, and being found in human likeness, He took the sinner's place. The transgressions of His people were numbered upon Him, imputed to Him, charged to His account, and He suffered for them as if they had been His own sins. He was scourged, tormented, crucified, and slain. The stripes He bore were the chastisements due to human sin, and the death He endured was the death threatened to sinners. Whoever will trust in Jesus shall participate in the result of all the Redeemer's substitutionary agonies, and the case shall stand thus—the sufferings of Christ shall be instead of the believer's suffering, and the merits of Christ shall be instead of the obedience that man should have rendered.

Faith in Jesus makes us righteous through the righteousness of another; it causes us to be accepted in the beloved, perfect in Christ Jesus. Let it be understood that believing in Jesus is not a mysterious and complex action. It does not require a week to explain what faith is. Faith believes what God has revealed concerning Christ, and it therefore trusts in Christ as the divine Savior. I believe that Jesus was God's Son, that the Father sent Him into the world to save sinners, that to do so He became a substitute for justice for all who trust Him. As I trust Jesus, I know that I am clear before God. God's justice cannot put me to eternal death for which Jesus my substitute has died. God's truth cannot demand a second time the debt that has been fully paid on my behalf. Whatever a person's character may have been, the moment he believes in Christ he receives new life, and God will give to him all the graces and excellence of character that will adorn his faith, and his faith shall save him. To believe in the Son of God is the point, and nothing else.

Cʜᴀʀʟᴇꜱ Sᴘᴜʀɢᴇᴏɴ

*Jesus said, "For judgment I have come into this world,
so that the blind will see and those who see will become
blind."*

John 9:39

A s the man who was born blind went upward in his faith, so steadily and tragically downward went the others. For they had light and they would not look at it; and it blasted and blinded them. They had the manifestation of Christ, and they scoffed and jeered at it, and turned their backs upon it. The light of the world became a curse to them, falling not like dew but like reproach upon their spirits, blistering, not refreshing.

Therefore Christ pronounced their fate. The purpose of His coming is not to judge, but to save. But if men will not let Him save, the effect of His coming will be to harm. Therefore, His coming will separate men as a magnet draws all the iron filings out of a heap and leaves the brass. He comes not to judge, but His coming judges. "This child is destined to cause the falling and rising of many in Israel . . . so that the thoughts of many hearts will be revealed" (Luke 2:34–35).

Light has a twofold effect. It is torture to the diseased eye; it is pleasing to the sound one. Christ is the light of the world, as He is also both the power of seeing and the thing seen. He has come to show us God, to be the light by which we see God, and to strengthen and restore our faculty of seeing Him. If you welcome Him, and take Him into your heart, He will be at once light and eyes to you. But if you turn away from Him, He will be blindness and darkness to you. He comes to pour eyesight on the blind, but He comes also to make still blinder those who refuse Him.

Those who see themselves as blind, who know themselves to be ignorant, the lowly who recognize their sinfulness and misery and helplessness, and turn in their need to Christ, will be led by paths of growing knowledge and blessedness to the perfect day where their strengthened vision will be able to see the blaze of glory. Those who say, "I see," and know not that they are blind, nor hearken to His counsel to buy "salve [for] your eyes, so you can see" (Revelation 3:18), will have yet another film drawn over their eyes by the shining light they reject. Jesus Christ is for us light and vision. Trust in Him, and your eyes will be blessed because they see God.

ALEXANDER MACLAREN

"When he has brought out all his own, he goes on ahead of them, and his sheep follow him because they know his voice."

John 10:4

What gives the alpine climber confidence in wild, lonely, difficult passes or ascents? It is that his guide has been there before, and that in every present step over unknown and possibly treacherous ice or snow, his guide goes before (see Isaiah 45:2). It is to Christ's sheep that His promise applies; simply those who believe and hear His voice. It is when He brings them out that it comes true; not when they put themselves forth, or when they let a stranger lure them out, or such traitors as self-cowardice or impatience drive them forth.

Sometimes it is a literal bringing us forth. We have been in a sheltered nook of the fold, and we are sent to live where it is windier and wilder. He brings us out into less hospitable surroundings, to live with different people or in a different position. But Jesus "goes on ahead." He prepares the earthly as well as the heavenly places for us. He will be there when we get to the new place. He "went ahead of you on your journey . . . to search out places for you to camp" (Deuteronomy 1:33), but let us remember that the Israelites were in tents and not palaces. If we willfully persisted in staying where we are when He says, "Get up, go away! For this is not your resting place" (Micah 2:10), we shall find that His presence is gone and that we can no longer find rest. He is not sending us away from Him, but only leads us forth with His own gentle hand.

Sometimes it is a bringing forth into service. We had such a nice little quiet shady corner in the vineyard, and then the Master comes and puts us into a part of the field where we never thought of going and where we feel totally insufficient for these things (see 2 Corinthians 2:16). But would we really go back? He would not be in the old shady corner with us now; for when He brought us forth, He went before us, and it is only by close following that we can abide with Him.

Sometimes it is a bringing forth into rough places of suffering, whether from temptation, pain, or adversity. Sooner or later, perhaps again and again, He puts forth His own sheep into a position of greater separation from the world—from an outer into an inner circle, always nearer and nearer to the great Center. Let us watch very sensitively for such leading. Every hesitation to yield to His gentle separation from the world results in heart separation from Him.

FRANCES RIDLEY HAVERGAL

"Very truly I tell you, I am the gate for the sheep. . . . I am the good shepherd; I know my sheep and my sheep know me . . . I lay down my life for the sheep."

John 10:7, 14–15

The parable of the first five verses of this chapter—what could be more beautiful? This is the very beginning of poetry. What could be sweeter, lovelier? Jesus was making new clouds, and showing those clouds in new lights. They were beautiful clouds, but they seemed to have no direct relation to human life. Jesus was rewarded therefore with the applause of silence. The people simply didn't understand Him.

So Christ changed His approach and brought words full of direct personal application and claim. Now the tone of the crowd will change. The original parable passed by as a gilded cloud in the soft wind, but when the dreamy, poetical fanatic becomes the claimant of deity, a point of hostility breaks out. There is nothing so much dreaded as a personal sermon, but what love of poetry there is! When a milestone is reached with a shout of joy, how beautiful it is! Clouds in infinite number and variety—how charming the upward look! But let a man attack the false weights and false measures of his day, the false philosophies and hypocrisies that are to be found in places of custom, and see where it gets him. Congregations have an infinite hunger for beautiful parables; they can eat up endless parables at a meal, but applications are not popular. They say, "Sing some lullaby, O Son of Man. Rock us to sleep by the splash of your liquid music. Send no sword, no fire, and no controversy. Your applications bring a cross, and that is what it shall cost you."

Let any man stand up today in the marketplace and say about himself, "I am a Christian. I am a Christ-man. My badge is the cross of Calvary," and he will have a hard time of it from that hour. Let a man say, "I lay down my life for the sheep," and he will be avoided as a leper or an extremist. Yet this is what every Christian is called upon to do in his own degree and in his own way by means of service, devotion, and consecration. Let him say, "For me to live is Christ" and no one will want to see him. If he could speak parables without applications, he would be invited evening after evening to delight the minds that never think. Expect the same reaction from the world that the Master received. Christianity, even in the most indifferent hands, always gives some indication of its anti-worldliness, anti-selfishness, its love of truth and fairness and justice and honor and progress.

JOSEPH PARKER

"I am the door. If anyone enters by Me, he will be saved, and will go in and out and find pasture."

John 10:9 NKJV

Here is the house of mercy and, inside there is forgiveness for one's sins, healing for the sick, food for the hungry, clothing for the naked. Suppose there was no door to the house—what use would it have been to us? Blessed be God, see how Jesus, the great I AM, is the door into the true church and the way of access to God himself. And He gives to the man who comes to God by Him four choice privileges:

He shall be saved. The fugitive manslayer passed the gate of the city of refuge and was safe (see Numbers 35:25). None can be lost who take Jesus as the door of faith to their souls. Entrance through Jesus into peace is the guarantee of entrance by the same door into heaven. Jesus is the only door, an open door, a wide door, a safe door; and blessed is he who rests all his hope of admission to glory upon the crucified Redeemer.

He shall go in. He shall be privileged to go in among the divine family, sharing the children's bread and participating in all their honors and enjoyments. He shall go into the chambers of communion, to the banquets of love, to the treasures of the covenant, to the storehouses of the promises. He shall go in to the King of kings in the power of the Holy Spirit, and the secret of the Lord shall be with him.

He shall go out. This blessing is often forgotten. We go out into the world to labor and suffer, but what a mercy to go in the name and power of Jesus! We are called to bear witness to the truth, to cheer the hurting, to warn the careless, to win souls, and to glorify God; and as the angel said to Gideon, "Go in this might of yours" (Judges 6:14 NKJV), even thus the Lord would have us proceed as His messengers in His name and strength.

He shall find pasture. He who knows Jesus shall never want. Whatever his heart needs to live upon, to fill it, to sustain it, to comfort it, to make it grow, to develop it, to perfect it, he shall find it all in Christ Jesus his Lord and Savior! Going in and out shall alike be helpful to him: in fellowship with God he shall grow, and in watering others he shall be watered. Having made Jesus his all, he shall find all in Jesus. His soul shall be as a watered garden, and as a well of water whose waters fail not.

CHARLES SPURGEON

"I am the gate; whoever enters through me will be saved. They will come in and go out, and find pasture."

John 10:9

One does not know whether the width or the depth of this marvelous promise is the more noteworthy. Jesus Christ presents himself before the whole human race and declares himself able to deal with the needs of every individual in the tremendous whole. *Whoever*—no matter who, where, or when. To any and every soul, no matter how ringed about with danger, no matter how hampered and hindered with work, no matter how barren of all supply earth may be, He will give the tremendous provision of the Christian life.

Step by step, conflict by conflict, in passing danger after danger, external and internal, Jesus Christ, through our union with Him, will keep us safe, and at the last we shall reach eternal and everlasting salvation. He will keep us safe by the continual protecting power into His eternal kingdom. Only as we take shelter in the strong love and mighty Hand will we pass through life without real harm. In our union with Christ, by simple faith in Him and loyal submission and obedience, we receive an impenetrable defense against true evils and the only things worth calling dangers. For the only real evil is the peril that we shall lose our confidence and be untrue to our best selves and depart from the living God. Nothing is evil except that which tempts, and succeeds in tempting, us away from Him. And in regard to all such danger, to hold on to Christ, to realize His presence, to think of Him, to wear His name as a shield on our hearts, to put the thought of Him between us and temptation as a filter through which the poisonous air shall pass and be deprived of its virus is the one secret of safety and victory.

There is power in the name of Jesus to slay every wicked thought. And the things that tempt us most, that appeal most directly to our ambition, our pride, our distrust, our self-will, all these lose their power upon us and are discovered in their emptiness and insignificance when Jesus Christ is seen as our defense. Keep Christ between you and the storm. Keep on the sheltering side of the Rock of Ages. Keep behind the breakwater, for there is a wild sea running outside that will swamp your little boat. Keep within the fold, for wolves and lions lie in every bush. Live moment by moment in the realizing of Christ's presence, power, and grace. So, and only so, shall you be safe.

ALEXANDER MACLAREN

JUNE
23

"I am the door. If anyone enters by Me, he will be saved, and will go in and out and find pasture."

John 10:9 NKJV

J esus' metaphor of going out and coming in is partly explained by the image of the flock, which passes into the fold for peaceful rest, and out again, without danger, for exercise and food; and is partly explained by the frequent use in the Old Testament as the designation of the two-sided activity of human life. The one side is the contemplative life of interior union with God by faith and love; the other, the active life of practical obedience in the field of work that God provides us. These two are both capable of being raised to their highest power and of being carried out with the most unrestricted and joyous activity, on condition of our keeping close to Christ and living by faith in Him.

"He will go in." This comes first. As we enter by the Door, there must be very frequent and deep inward acts of contemplation, faith, hope, and desire. You must go into the depths of God through Christ. You must go into the depths of your own souls through Him. You must become accustomed to withdraw yourself from spreading yourself out over the distractions of any external activity, however urgent, charitable, or necessary, and live alone with Christ. It is through Him that we draw near to the depths of deity. It is through Him that we learn the length and breadth and height and depth of the largest, loftiest, and noblest truths that concern the spirit. It is through Him that we become familiar with the inmost secrets of our own selves. Only those who habitually live this hidden life of solitary and secret communion will ever do much in the field of outward work.

If we commune with Christ, there will follow an enlargement of opportunity and power for outward service such as nothing but emancipation by faith in Him can ever bring. The truth is that the greatest hindrance to our Christian service never lies without, but within; and it is only to be overcome by that plunging into the depths of fellowship with Christ. If we carry the sweet presence of Christ with us into all places where we go to labor, we shall find that external labor, drawing its pattern, its motive, its law, and the power of its carrying out, from communion with Him, is no more work but joy.

ALEXANDER MACLAREN

"The thief comes only to steal and kill and destroy; I have come that they may have life, and have it to the full."

John 10:10

L ife is a matter of degrees. Some have life, but it flickers like a dying candle. Others are full of life, bright and passionate, like the fire upon the blacksmith's forge when the bellows are in full blast. Christ has come that His people may have spiritual life in all its fullness.

Our Lord Jesus desires to have us in total spiritual health. He has for that end become the Great Physician of our souls. He heals all our diseases and is the health of our countenance. We grow in grace, advance in knowledge, in experience, in confidence, and in conformity to His image. From babes in Christ we advance to young men, and from young men we become fathers in the church. Mark well that if the Son of God shall make you free, you shall be free indeed, and in that freedom find life sparkling, flashing, and overflowing like the streams of a fountain. He comes to make us capable of demanding service and powerful action. He would have us walk without weariness and run without fainting.

None of us know what we may be, we are but in our infancy yet. Christ has come to give us fuller life than we have yet attained. Look at the apostles before Pentecost and after. I ask, what happened to these men? Beloved, you pray; yet, if God gives you more life, you will pray as readily as Elijah. Even now you seek after holiness; but if you have life more abundantly, you will walk before the Lord in glorious uprightness as Abraham did. I know that you praise the Lord; but if He gives you more abundant life, you will rival the angels in their songs. Gladly would I fire you with holy aspiration. Pray to Jesus to make you all you can be. Say to Him, *Use me to the fullness of my capability. Touch my silent tongue, equip my idle hands, and open my frostbitten wallet. Send a full stream of life upon me that all my soul may wake up, and all that is within me may adore you. Get out of me all that can possibly come out of such a poor thing as I am. Let your Spirit work in me to the praise of the glory of your grace.* Oh, for men and women who are alive from head to foot, whose entire existence is full of consecration to Jesus and zeal for the divine glory; these have life "to the full."

CHARLES SPURGEON

"I came that they may have and enjoy life, and have it in abundance [to the full, till it overflows]."

John 10:10 AMP

Many people have great spiritual capacities, but they lie still for lack of intensity of purpose. The Lord Jesus has furnished us with a purpose that is sure to stimulate us to life in abundance, "for Christ's love compels us" (2 Corinthians 5:14). He has given us a motive and an impulse that we cannot resist, and we are in covenant with Him that we will glorify His name as long as we have our being. This gives intensity to life that increases its abundance by arousing it. Our divine Master has aroused the flame of our life by inspiring us with the glorious passion of love for Him. This provides us with stimulus and motivation. A heart that is wholly surrendered to the love of Jesus is capable of thoughts and deeds to which colder souls must forever be strangers. Energetic, forceful, triumphant life belongs to souls enamored of the cross and wedded in love to the heavenly Bridegroom.

Because of the power of the divine Spirit, it is not possible for us to tell how potent for good anyone among us may become. However feeble sin may have made him, so that man possessed by the Holy Spirit becomes supernaturally strong and refuses to be the captive of sin or Satan. Look at Martin Luther. Who would have believed that one poor monk could shake the world? Look at other people through the church's history whom God has raised up for a special purpose; what abundant life their holy passion gave them! They were like Samson of old. The Spirit is on the man, and he works wonderfully. If the Holy Spirit shall come upon you, He will make you do greater things than these and achieve loftier victories.

Believers have such abundant life in Christ that their circumstances should not be able to overcome them. In poverty they are rich, in sickness they are in spiritual health, in contempt they are full of triumph, and in death full of glory. Christ has given us a supreme life; it cannot be destroyed and nothing can separate us from Him. What I desire beyond everything is to have this life so full that it may be supreme over my entire being. Our life has dashed death and holds it beneath its feet, but tremendous is the struggle of death to rise again and get control. We must not allow sin to have dominion over us, but life more abundant must, through grace, triumph over every inward weakness.

CHARLES SPURGEON

"I am the good shepherd."

John 10:11

Perhaps even Christ never spoke more fruitful words than these. Just think how many solitary, wearied hearts they have cheered, and what a wealth of encouragement and comfort there has been in them for all generations. Christ is my guide, my defense and guardian, my companion, my provider—all responsibility is laid upon His broad shoulders and on all the tenderness of His deep heart. The good Shepherd exercises care, which means that my only duty is simple obedience, meek following, and quiet trust.

Note that Christ says He is "the *good* shepherd." That word *good* is interpreted in a kind of sentimental, poetic way, as expressing our Lord's tender loving care, but that is not the full meaning. There is a special significance attached to the original Greek word that is lost in our Bible. I do not know that it could have been preserved; but the expression here is the one that is generally rendered "fair," "lovely," or "beautiful." It was a word used for moral purity, considered as being lovely, the highest goodness, and the serenest beauty. And so here the thought is that the Shepherd stands before us, the realization of all that the name means, set forth in such a fashion as to be infinitely lovely and perfectly fair, and to draw the admiration of any man who can appreciate that which is beautiful.

Our Lord not only declares that He is the flawless, perfect Shepherd, but that He alone is the reality. "I am the good Shepherd; in me and in me alone is that which men need." And that leads me to another point: We shall not reach the full meaning of these great words without taking into account the history of the metaphor in the Old Testament. "The Lord is my shepherd, I lack nothing" (Psalm 23:1) is but one example of a series of utterances in the old revelation in which Jehovah himself is the shepherd of mankind. So sweet, so gracious are the words that we lose the sense of the grandeur of them and need to think before we are able to understand how great and immense the claim that is made here upon our faith. This Man stands before us and lays claim to himself the divine prerogative witnessed from of old by psalmist and prophet, and says that for Him were meant the prophecies of ancient times that spoke of a human shepherd, and asserts that all the sustenance, care, authority, and command that the emblem suggests meet in Him in perfect measure.

ALEXANDER MACLAREN

"I am the good shepherd; I know my sheep and my sheep know me—just as the Father knows me and I know the Father—and I lay down my life for the sheep."

John 10:14–15

Of all our Lord's words, the sweetest ones are those when He speaks about himself. After all, who can speak of Jesus but himself? He masters all our eloquence. His perfection exceeds our understanding; the light of His excellence is too bright for us, it blinds our eyes. Our Beloved must be His own mirror. None but Jesus can reveal Jesus. We are most glad that in His tenderness to us He sets himself forth by many choice metaphors and symbols, which let us know a measure of that love that passes knowledge. With His own hand He fills a golden cup out of the river of His infinity and hands it to us that we may drink and be refreshed.

When Jesus tells us that He is the good shepherd, He fills out all possible meanings for the words, and then there is overflow. Metaphors to set Him forth may be multiplied as the dew of the morning, but the whole multitude will fail to reflect all His brightness. Human thought is too contracted to set Him forth to the full. The Eastern shepherd is the owner of the flock. He remembers when and where each of the sheep was born, where he has led them, and what trails he had in connection with them. His wealth consists in them. He is also the constant caretaker for all the needs of the sheep. He provides for them and leads them wherever they go. He is the defender of the flock from wild beasts of prey, willing to risk his own life for their safety. There is goodness, tenderness, willingness, and powerfulness in all that Jesus does that makes Him to be the best possible shepherd that can be. Every good thing that you can imagine to be, or that should be, in a shepherd, you find in the Lord Jesus.

If Jesus is so pleased to be my shepherd, let me be equally pleased to be His sheep. Let me avail myself of all the privileges that are wrapped up in His being my shepherd, and in my being His sheep. I see that my needs will cause Him no perplexity. I see that He will not be going out of His way to tend to my weakness and trouble. He invites me to come and bring my wants and woes to Him, and then look up to Him and be fed by Him. Therefore, I will do it.

CHARLES SPURGEON

"Therefore My Father loves Me, because I lay down My life that I may take it again. No one takes it from Me, but I lay it down of Myself. I have power to lay it down, and I have power to take it again. This command I have received from My Father."

John 10:17–18 NKJV

The suffering and solitude of Christ were voluntarily endured, and that for us. All man's sorrow He experienced. Every ingredient that adds bitterness to our cup was familiar to His taste, and He tasted them, as He tasted death, "for every man," that His experience of them might make them less hard for us to bear, and that the touch of His lips lingering on the cup might sweeten the drink for us.

His endurance of this, as of all the sorrows of human life, was at every moment a fresh act of willing surrender of himself for us. He wore our manhood and He bore manhood's griefs, not because He must, but because He would. He willed to be born. He willed to abide in the flesh. He willed, pang by pang, to bear our sorrows. He could have ended it all, but His love held Him here. So all that dreary solitude in which He groped for a hand to grasp and found none was voluntarily borne and was as truly a part of His bearing the consequences of man's sin as when He bowed His head to death to redeem us.

These thoughts may encourage us all to bear the necessary isolation of life, and in a special manner may strengthen some of us whom God in His providence has called upon to live outwardly lonely lives. But after all companionship, we have to live alone. Each man has to live his own life. We come singly into the world; and though God sets the solitary in families, and there are manifold blessings of love and companionship for most of us, yet alone we live in the depths of our hearts; alone we have to face joy and sorrow. "The heart knows its own bitterness" (Proverbs 14:10 NKJV). For some of us, solitary days are appointed. We may think of Christ and see the prints of His footsteps before us on the loneliest road. If any of us are called to know the pain of unsatisfied longings for earthly companions, let us stretch out our hands to lay hold on the hand of that solitary Man who knew this sorrow as He knows all. He felt all the bitterness of having to stand alone, with no arm to lean upon and no heart to trust. If we are left alone, let us make Christ our companion. We shall not be utterly solitary if He is with us. Perhaps God takes away earthly props that our love and desires may reach higher and reach the throne where Christ sits.

ALEXANDER MACLAREN

JUNE

29

Then the Jews surrounded Him and said to Him, "How long do You keep us in doubt? If You are the Christ, tell us plainly."

John 10:24 NKJV

What is "plainly"? There are people who think that all human conversation is divisible into *yes* and *no*. If the question were "Are you going east or west?" there would be no difficulty in replying plainly. But the questions that gather around the name of Christ, which are summed up in His marvelous character, are not questions that admit of easy, plain, and superficial answers. We must live with Christ to know Him; we must love Him to understand anything He says. To have said plainly, "I am the Christ," would have been to trifle with the infinity of His personality, His sovereignty, and His claim. Great subjects cannot be dealt with in this particular way, each in single sentences and evaluated in plain words. You cannot snap off an inch or two of infinity and say, "This is a sample of it." Infinity has no samples. As soon might you take one little stone out of a palace and say, "This will give you an idea of the royal residence."

The mystery of Christianity is in its infinity. It is because it is so great that it cannot be reduced to the comprehension of men who have no heart for its study. Hence Jesus told the people that they could not understand Him because they were not of His sheep—"I told you, and you do not believe" (v. 25). They had a plain answer and did not understand it to be plain. They kept it outside of them, and therefore they could not comprehend it. These are the people who say they will come to Christ when they understand all about Him, when they can meet Him on equal terms and say they completely comprehend all His meaning, at which point they will admit Him to their society. That is not the way of salvation.

Similarly, many people say they will believe the Bible when they know every fact about its authors, dates, and manuscripts—then they will come in, but that is not the way. There are two ways of coming to the Book or of coming to Jesus Christ: one, the outside way that will do nothing until certain long lists of questions are answered one by one; and the other by coming into the offered light and the offered blessing, and beginning where we can, and going on little by little, until we feel the inspiration of the book, until we get in touch with the heart of Christ, and thus become enabled to say, when He asks us, "Who am I?" "You are the Christ of God."

JOSEPH PARKER

"My sheep hear My voice, and I know them, and they follow Me."

John 10:27 NKJV

The distinctive mark of those who are Christ's is that they hear His voice. Sometimes it thrills forth from the Word of God, which is often grossly neglected; sometimes it truly sounds in a sermon or a book; sometimes His voice comes in the night watches or when we are in the street. Silent as to vocal utterance, but like familiar tones that sometimes greet us in our dreams, the voice of Christ is distinctly audible to the soul. It will come to you in sweet or in bitter providences. Yes, there is such a thing as hearing Christ's voice in the sounds of nature.

We should follow our Lord as unhesitatingly as sheep follow their shepherd, for He has a right to lead us wherever He pleases. We are not our own, we are bought with a price—let us recognize the rights of the redeeming blood. We are not true to our profession of being Christians if we question the bidding of our good Shepherd. Submission is our duty; objecting is our folly.

Often might our Lord say to us as to Peter, "What is that to you? You follow Me" (John 21:22 NKJV). Wherever Jesus may lead us, He goes before us. If we know not where we go, we know with whom we go. With such a companion, who will dread the perils of the road? The journey may be long, but His everlasting arms will carry us to the end. The presence of Jesus is the assurance of eternal salvation; because He lives, we shall live also. We should follow Christ in simplicity and faith, because the paths in which He leads us all end in glory and immortality. It is true they may not be smooth paths—they may be covered with intense, relentless trials, but they lead to the "city which hath foundations, whose builder and maker is God" (Hebrews 11:10 NKJV). "All the paths of the LORD are mercy and truth, to such as keep His covenant" (Psalm 25:10 NKJV).

Let us put full trust in our Shepherd, since we know that, come prosperity or adversity, sickness or health, popularity or contempt, His purpose shall be worked out, and that purpose shall be pure, unmingled good to every heir of mercy. We shall find it sweet to go up the bleak side of the hill with Christ; and when rain and snow blow into our faces, His dear love will make us far more blessed than those who sit at home and warm their hands at the world's fire.

Precious Jesus, draw us, and we will run after you.

CHARLES SPURGEON

JULY

1

*"And I give them eternal life, and they shall never perish;
neither shall anyone snatch them out of My hand."*

John 10:28 NKJV

If God has given you eternal life, that comprehends all the future. Beneath the wings of the Almighty God, night with its pestilence cannot strike you, and day with its cares cannot destroy you. Life with all its whirl of business shall be navigated in safety. Your spiritual existence will flourish when empires and kingdoms decay. Your life will live on when the heart of this great world shall grow cold, when the pulse of the great sea shall cease to beat, when the eye of the bright sun shall grow dim with age! You possess eternal life. You have an existence that will run parallel with the existence of the Deity. Eternal life! Oh, what an avenue of glory is opened by those words—*eternal life*! "Because I live," said Christ, "you will live also" (John 14:19 NKJV).

We have a position guaranteed—"in Christ's hand." It is to be in a place of honor; we are the ring He wears on His finger. It is a place of love: "I have inscribed you upon the palms of My hands" (Isaiah 49:16 NKJV). It is a place of power—His right hand encloses all His people. It is a place of property—Christ holds His people; "All His saints are in Your hand" (Deuteronomy 33:3 NKJV). It is a place of discretion—we are yielded up to Christ, and Christ wields a discretionary government over us. It is a place of guidance, a place of protection—as sheep are said to be in the hand of the shepherd, so are we in the hand of Christ.

We shall be in His hand forever, we shall be in His heart forever, we shall be in His very self forever—one with Him—and no one shall snatch us out of His hand. Happy is the man who can lay claim to such a promise as this! We shall never cease to exist in perpetual blessedness! We shall never cease to be like God in our natures, never! Think about your having been in heaven a thousand years—can you imagine it? A thousand years' blessed communion with the Lord Jesus! A thousand years with the sight of Him to ravish your spirit! Well, but you will have just as long to be there as if you had never begun, for you shall never, never, *never* perish! What an eternity of glory, what unspeakable delight is wrapped up in this promise—"They shall never perish!"

CHARLES SPURGEON

Therefore they sought again to seize Him, but He escaped out of their hand.

John 10:39 NKJV

Because our Savior's reasoning to the Jews was unanswerable, "therefore they sought again to seize Him." When men are convinced against their wills, when the heart struggles against the head, it usually happens that they turn persecutors. If they cannot answer holy arguments with fair reasoning, they can give hard answers with stones. If they cannot destroy the reasoning, they may, perhaps, destroy the reasoner, and this naturally suggests itself to the heart that is rendered cruel by obstinate unbelief. He who hates truth soon hates its advocate.

Jesus must have been wounded when the inhabitants of Jerusalem again and again took up stones to stone Him. But when He found that all He said and did only provoked more furious opposition, He escaped out of their hand and turned away from them to more hopeful spirits. He knew when to speak, and when to refrain. Divinely guided, no sooner does He cross the river than we read that "many believed in Him there" (v. 42 NKJV). So great a difference may we find in a few miles and a few hours. This was to be an oasis of comfort for our Lord before He traversed the burning desert of His passion and death. Before He was called by His last bitter agony to finish the work that the Father had given Him to do, He was to be refreshed by many hearts putting their trust in Him.

Opposition is no sign of defeat, but the contrary. When the devil roars, it is because his kingdom is being shaken, or he is afraid that it will be shaken. You must not consider yourself to have been unsuccessful in your evidences of faith when your opponent gets angry at them; perhaps it is your success that has startled his conscience and rendered it necessary for him to become malicious to retain his obstinacy. It should not depress us when we see a bitter spirit awakened, nor should it lead us to abstain from spreading the gospel. In the name of God expect victory. The unresponsive indifference of a thoughtless age is hard to deal with, but there is hope for people who resist you. Take courage from the blackening darkness, and hope that very soon you will see the dawn of a better day. If today men take up stones to stone the Christ, tomorrow hearts of stone may be turned to flesh, and we may hear that "many believed in Him there."

CHARLES SPURGEON

Now a certain man was sick, Lazarus of Bethany, the town of Mary and her sister Martha. . . . Therefore the sisters sent to Him, saying, "Lord, behold, he whom You love is sick."

John 11:1, 3 NKJV

We can sometimes better understand Jesus Christ's character and spirit when they are brought to bear upon a comparatively small space than when they are so enlarged as to embrace the universe. Let us, then, study His relationship with this family at Bethany. The family is in distress and sends for Jesus, the one Healer and eternal Friend. It is no stranger's name that is spoken to Jesus Christ. Lazarus was deeply loved by Jesus and lies now at the very gate of death.

Some would say that surely this one who was loved by Jesus should be in the fullness of health and vitality, that surely Lazarus should have been spared from sickness and suffering. One can imagine someone pointing out the case with a finger of suspicion and scorn and saying, "See, the one beloved by Christ suffers and dies just like an unbeliever. I know many Christians who have had many bad things happen to them. A believer's faith makes no difference in this life." Those who look at the outside only have a very short way to take in order to get at such conclusions.

If we lived altogether upon the space of a fingernail, some of those conclusions might be right enough. When, however, we come to look at circumferences rather than at mere points, to put today and tomorrow and the next day together, and to consider divine movement and divine purpose, we come to change those conclusions. To time we must add eternity, to man add God, and wait, for the time of drawing conclusions is not yet. It may be that weakness will turn out to be the highest strength, and some kinds of poverty may prove to be the only enduring wealth. God's way with men is "No discipline seems pleasant at the time, but painful. Later on, however, it produces a harvest of righteousness and peace for those who have been trained by it" (Hebrews 12:11). I only ask for a pause; I only beg that men be not rash. We shall have time, by and by, to say how things have been managed. The people in Christ's day, who waited and saw His works and kept themselves in restraint until those works were completed, said in a shout, in a song, at last, "He has done all things well" (Mark 7:37 NKJV). It shall be so with those who keep a strong and loving faith constantly in exercise in the Son of God.

JOSEPH PARKER

When Jesus heard that, He said, "This sickness is not unto death, but for the glory of God, that the Son of God may be glorified through it."

John 11:4 NKJV

s it not truly beautiful to find that Jesus Christ knows the purpose of every event in our individual and family life? Many a messenger of providence comes to our door, and we are at a loss to see what that messenger signifies. Is it not a comfort to the heart to believe that there is One who knows why our door was opened, that the oftentimes unwelcome visitor might be admitted? Jesus knew exactly why the sickness had fallen upon Lazarus. It is not that death may finish the process that sin began in the history of mankind. But you will see that in this case, circumstances shall so conspire that the result of the whole will be an additional glory given to the Lord of Hosts and to His Son Jesus. The earth and the heavens work together. Things below and things above come into strange union and combinations, and sometimes things have to be broken down that they may be lifted up.

Oftentimes, indeed, God comes to us along a path that is strewn with wrecks, with blasted hopes, with ruined towers. And we say when the wind rages very highly, and when things are toppled over into confusion, "Behold, this is death!"—not knowing that in this way, strange though it may appear beyond all other mystery, God is working a way upon which His own foot shall pass. Is there not joy, peculiar and oftentimes intense, in the companionship of the One who can tell you what your dream means, what your pains signify, and what that great loss, which has so discouraged you, was intended to speak to your heart? He is the One who can whisper to us amid all suffering and all loss, "The meaning of this is that God intends to work out in your life a higher refinement and a nobler strength, a more dignified patience, and to perfect you by trial severe as fire." This is what Jesus Christ does for us. He interprets things; He gives them their right meanings. He stops us from imperfect, and especially godless, conclusions. In this way He enriches our life continually.

It is a great thing, amid misinterpretations, and prayerlessness, and worldliness, to have Jesus bring to our understanding and heart such a sense of the rightness of things as has comforted us and lifted up our soul from the midst of the lions that had assailed it and the darkness that was gathered around it.

JOSEPH PARKER

*So, when He heard that [Lazarus] was sick, He stayed
two more days in the place where He was.*

John 11:6 NKJV

This is an aspect of the divine government that we have great difficulty in understanding. Would not the sentence have read much better had He instantaneously left His work and sped to Bethany? There, we should have said, is the outworking of love; that is precisely how affection shows its genuineness and its depth. Yet Jesus Christ delayed. God does appear sometimes to be slow in His movements. Our impatience cries for Him, as He sits still, as if we were but noisy children, not knowing what we were talking about. We say, "Speak to us, Lord, or it will be too late," because we measure time by our standard. But God takes His times from something higher than our standards. We now and again wonder that God does not make more haste than He appears to do. At such times there comes in this solemn, majestic sound, "With the Lord a day is like a thousand years, and a thousand years are like a day. The Lord is not slow in keeping his promise, as some understand slowness" (2 Peter 3:8–9). God does not measure himself or His movements by our idea of time. He takes the beat of His step from another standard altogether.

Is God delaying? With whom is He delaying? "He is delaying with me!" says some poor, fainting heart. Do I doubt it? Far from it. Has He not delayed with me many a time? Do I not want Him now, instantaneously, to come down to my relief? I do. Yet He sits away on that great resplendent throne, and my prayers seem unable to hasten Him in any one movement. What then? Wherever I have been privileged to see anything of the meaning of His delay, I have always found that He has been delaying not for His benefit but for mine; and that when He does come, He will bring with Him some greater blessing than I had ventured either to hope or expect. Let God be the Judge. There can be but one Lord.

There are many mysteries about this side of the divine government. There are mysteries about every side of the divine administration, and we glory in this mystery. Tomorrow is the mystery of today; night is the mystery of noontide; immortality is the mystery of death; heaven is the mystery of earth. I would not care to live if all mystery were taken away. It is in the exercise of a deep, tender, loving faith in the Unseen and the Unlimited that I find joy that animates my suffering and wounded heart!

JOSEPH PARKER

*The disciples said to Him, "Rabbi, lately the Jews sought
to stone You, and are You going there again?"*

John 11:8 NKJV

That the Jews sought to kill Jesus would be, for certain natures, a sufficient reason for not venturing into their presence. Christ teaches us one
divine lesson by this act of fortitude—to go wherever there is work to
be done. In Judea there was a sleeper who could be awakened by His power
alone; hence He returned to Judea, in spite of the danger. Christ was called,
by the sympathy of His own heart, to remove the sorrow that threatened to
engulf two bereaved sisters, and to prove His divinity by a miraculous exertion
of His power. He knew that in Judea there were those who were ready to put
Him to death; yet His own convictions outweighed the fury of His enemies
and brought Him to the graveside of His beloved Lazarus.

Christianity develops true courage. There is a bravery that results from instinctive passion, and there is a courage that arises from ambition, pride, and
love of applause; but these must be distinguished from Christian heroism. The
valor of a Christian is the result of a reigning conviction: he is heroic because
he is right; he fights to prove his loyalty to divine principles. Can your faith
bear stoning? Dare you venture into Judea? These are test questions. It is but a
lean, shivering, miserable faith that dreads any form of censure or punishment.

Getting other people's attention is not necessary to the exhibition of true
fortitude. Some people cannot fight without acquainting others to their battles.
Christ was often silent in His sufferings; He had not always the relief that speech
or complaint often insures: "He was oppressed and He was afflicted, yet He
opened not His mouth" (Isaiah 53:7 NKJV). His was true endurance; His deepest
sufferings secretly exhausted themselves. Christ endured many stonings of which
history is ignorant. The severest trials of fortitude are not necessarily visible: the
deadliest blows are aimed in the sacred hours when eye and pen are excluded.

The church that fears stoning is useless for practical purposes; it may be
ornamental, but its beauty is perishable. It will make no vital impact on a
neighborhood; it is a delicate hothouse plant that cannot bear the climate of
an unsympathetic and ruthless world. Christ in a church will lift that church
above the fear of stoning, for Christ transforms the churches into His own
nature. The fellowship of believers must be entirely filled by the spirit of Him
who never flinched in the presence of danger or blushed in the enunciation
of the principles on which His life was founded.

JOSEPH PARKER

These things He said, and after that He said to them,
"Our friend Lazarus sleeps, but I go that I may wake
him up."

John 11:11 NKJV

It is to Jesus primarily that the New Testament writers owe their use of this gracious emblem of *sleep*. For the word was twice upon our Lord's lips: once when, over the twelve-year-old maid, from whom life had barely ebbed away, he said, "She is not dead, but sleeping" (Luke 8:52 NKJV); and once in regard to Lazarus. But Jesus was not the originator of the expression. You find it in the Old Testament, where the prophet Daniel, speaking of the end of the days and the bodily resurrection, designates those who share in it as "those who sleep in the dust of the earth shall awake" (Daniel 12:2 NKJV). And the Old Testament was not the sole origin of the phrase. For it is too natural, too much in accordance with the visibilities of death, not to have been shrined in many tongues. Many ancient Greek and Roman inscriptions speak sadly of death under this figure. But almost always it is with the added, deepened note of despair; that it is a sleep that knows no waking, but lasts through eternal night.

Now, the Christian thought associated with this emblem is the precise opposite. The Gentile heart shrank from the ugly thing because it was so ugly. So dark and deep a dread coiled round the man as he contemplated it that he sought to drape the grimness in some kind of thin transparent veil and to put the buffer of a word between him and its ugliness. But the Christian's motive for the use of the word is the precise opposite. He uses the gentler expression because the thing has become gentler.

You find one class of representations in the New Testament that speak of death as "to depart and be with Christ," where it is softened down to be merely a change of environment, a change of locality (Philippians 1:23 NKJV). Then another class of representations speak of it as when "the earthly tent we live in is destroyed, we have a building from God" (2 Corinthians 5:1)—where there is a broad, firm line of demarcation drawn between the inhabitant and the habitation, and the thing is softened down to be a mere change of dwelling. Again, another class of expressions speak of it as being an "offering," where the main idea is that of a voluntary surrender and my life poured out upon the altar of God (see 2 Timothy 4:6). Such is the passing of the believer from this life to eternity!

ALEXANDER MACLAREN

*Now Martha said to Jesus, "Lord, if You had been here,
my brother would not have died."*

John 11:21 NKJV

I f You had been here . . ." This was an expression on the part of Martha
as well as Mary (v. 32) that arose from great love, great trust, but void of a
true understanding of the meaning of Christ's presence. Is there a tone of
reproach in that statement? Does it mean, "If you had not delayed, our brother
would still have been with us"? Or does it say, "Lord, where you are, no death
can be"? Probably the meaning was exhausted by the first view, namely, that if
Jesus had come earlier and been in the house, death dare not have come in at
the front door. This is a beautiful "if," without doubt. It is employed for the
purpose of increasing emphasis, deepening and enlarging spiritual certitude:
"Lord, though death stood at his bedside ready to leap upon him, you would
have kept him back and our brother would be alive today."

Yet this declaration is marked by ignorance. For death is the servant of
God. Why do we think of death as something wholly apart from God? As
an enemy that has taken advantage of God's absence from the household of
creation? Yes, Death—old, old Death—thriving these countless ages upon
man and overthrowing him—this monster is a servant of the court of heaven.
The Lord reigns! Has not the Lord a right to send for those whom He will, for
those who are ready, for those whose time upon earth must come to an end?
Death is a necessity. Death is servant, not master. And there is a final great day
coming when "Death is swallowed up in victory" (1 Corinthians 15:54 NKJV).

Yet, it is a beautiful thought that where Jesus is, there can be no death.
Jesus assured Martha, "I am the resurrection and the life. He who believes
in Me, though he may die, he shall live. And whoever lives and believes in
Me shall never die" (John 11:25–26 NKJV). Men do not die when Christ is in
the house; they ascend. Christians must be liberated, must accept the word
of emancipation and receive the crown of freedom. With Jesus in the house
there can be no death; the little child will not die, but go up like a dewdrop,
called for by the warm sun. In the house of the saint, mourning itself becomes
a sacrament. Death does but enlarge the horizon and show the greater width
of the universe.

JOSEPH PARKER

*Jesus said to her, "I am the resurrection and the life. He
who believes in Me, though he may die, he shall live."*

John 11:25 NKJV

By the grave of Lazarus, to that weeping sister, Jesus spoke these precious
words of calm assurance that have brought hope to millions around
the world ever since. One cannot but note the difference between His
attitude in the presence of the great mystery of death and life and that of all
other teachers. How calmly, certainly, and confidently He speaks!

Mark that Jesus, even at that hour of agony, turns Martha's thoughts to
himself. He is, in His person, the all-important thing for her to know. If she
understands Him, "the resurrection and the life," then life and death will
have no insoluble problems or any hopelessness for her. Jesus lays a sovereign
hand on resurrection and life and discloses that both are inherent in Him, and
from Him flow to all who shall possess them. He claims to have in himself
the fountain of life, in all possible senses of the word.

Further, He tells Martha that by faith in Him, any and all may possess that
life. And then He majestically goes on to declare that the life that He gives
is immune from, and untouched by, death. The believer shall live though he
dies. It is clear that to die is used in two different meanings, referring in the
former case to the physical fact, and in the latter carrying a heavier weight
of significance, namely the expectant sense that it usually has in this gospel,
of separation from God. Physical death is not the termination of human life.
The grim fact touches only the surface life and has nothing to do with the
essential, personal being. He who believes in Jesus truly lives, and his union
with Jesus secures his possession of that eternal life, which victoriously persists
through the apparent, superficial change that men call "death." For a believer
to die is to live more fully, more triumphantly, more blessedly.

He will show Martha the great truth that His being the "life" necessarily
involved His being also the "resurrection," for His life-communicating work
could not be accomplished till His life had flowed over into not only the
spirit that believes but its humble companion, the soul, and its yet humbler,
the body. A bodily life is essential to perfect existence, and Jesus will not stay
His hand till every believer is perfect in body, soul, and spirit, after the image
of Him who redeemed Him.

ALEXANDER MACLAREN

*"Where have you laid him?" he asked. "Come and see,
Lord," they replied. Jesus wept. Then the Jews said,
"See how he loved him!"*

John 11:34–36

Our Lord loved all men whether they loved Him or not, but there were some men whom He loved with a special love. And Lazarus was one of the most eminent of those men. In a household where Martha and Mary took most of the Master's attention, Lazarus brought a silent love, a worshiping love. But his love could not elude the eyes of Jesus, who knows what is in a man without man expressing what is in him. And He so loved Lazarus back again, and more so as He returned to Bethany to accomplish one last grand miracle for the awakening of Jerusalem at such a cost to Lazarus.

Despite the glory of God about to be revealed, Jesus clearly foresaw that it would not change the final outcome. Caiaphas, Pilate, Herod, and the people of Jerusalem would finally reject Him, and at such a price to Lazarus. Jesus wept. Yes, and if you saw a friend of yours in glory, and then saw also that he was called to lay aside his glory and to return and be a savor of death to many of your fellow citizens, you could not but weep also. Even if you knew it was God's will, you could not but weep. And our Lord wept because Lazarus, who had been but four days in glory, was to be called to lay aside his glory and return to this world of sin and death, on an errand that would lead to a final hardness of heart to His enemies. Martha and Mary gained by it, as did His disciples, but Lazarus must depart glory on an errand that would cost him much.

The great demands that God sometimes makes on His great saints is the great lesson that Lazarus teaches us. The demand on Lazarus made his divine Friend mourn and weep for him. And God's work in this world demands this same meekness, humbleness, self-emptiness, and laying aside of our own glory from some believers among us every day. Some surrender, some humiliation, as of heaven itself in exchange for earth, may be demanded of you as your contribution to the glory of God. Something that will make your best friends groan and weep for you. He asked it of His own Son and of Lazarus. Are you willing to be made able and ready? Let your answer be the same as that of Jesus: "I have come to do your will, my God" (Hebrews 10:7).

ALEXANDER WHYTE

Jesus wept.

John 11:35

A great storm was stirring the mind of Jesus. When He saw Mary weeping, we see that "He was deeply moved in spirit [to the point of anger at the sorrow caused by death] and was troubled" (v. 33 AMP). What was this holy indignation He felt? Jesus now stood face-to-face with the last enemy to be destroyed, death (see 1 Corinthians 15:26). He saw what sin had done in destroying life and in corrupting the fair handiwork of God in the human body, and some translations say, "He troubled himself." Between anger at the powers of evil, grief for the family who had been bereaved by death, sorrow over those who stood by in unbelief, and a distressing realization of the effects of sin, the Lord's heart was evidently in a great storm. Yet the result of the storm was not a word of terror or a glance of judgment but simply a blessed shower of tears.

Jesus was not ashamed to acknowledge the affliction that sin caused to His holy soul or the gash that the sight of death made in His heart. He saw in that one death the representation of what sin has done on so enormous a scale that it is impossible to compute the devastation, and therefore He wept. What have you not done, O Sin! You have slain all these, O Death! What a field of blood has Satan made this earth! The Savior could not stand unmoved in the presence of the destroyer or approach the gate of death's palace without deep emotion. Of this He was by no means ashamed. Holy emotion is not a weakness. If at any time in the midst of the world's wickedness and celebration you weep, do not hide those tears.

We should weep, for Jesus wept. Jesus wept for others. I do not know that He ever wept for himself. His were sympathetic tears. He embodied the command "Weep with those who weep" (Romans 12:15 NKJV). He has a narrow soul who can hold it all within the compass of his ribs. A true soul, a Christlike soul, lives in other men's souls and bodies as well as his own. A perfectly Christlike soul finds all the world too narrow for its own abode, for it lives and loves; it lives by loving, and loves because it lives. Think of other weepers and have pity upon the children of grief. Grieve on their account and stand ready to help them to the best of your ability.

CHARLES SPURGEON

Then the Jews said, "See how He loved him!"

John 11:36 NKJV

A t the grave of Lazarus Jesus wept, and His grief was so manifest to the onlookers that they said, "See how He loved him!" Those of us who have a share in the special love of Jesus see evidences of that love not only in His tears but also in the precious blood that He so freely shed for us. We should marvel even more than these onlookers did at the love of Jesus and see further into His heart than they ever did.

Think how the Lord dealt with us before we came to Him. He called us again and again, but we would not go to Him; and the more lovingly He called us, the more resolutely we refused to accept His gracious invitation. This refusal may have lasted for years, and we wonder now that the Lord waited for us so long. Jesus refused to take our no for an answer but called and called until at last we yielded to His open arms. Do you remember when He first came to you with His sweet grace and how you received pardon, justification, adoption, and the indwelling of the Spirit? Surely your heart glows in grateful remembrance of Christ's mercy, and you cannot help but say, "See how He loved me!"

To this day, has Christ's love for you cooled in the slightest degree? We have all tried that love by our wandering and waywardness, but its fire still burns just as hot as at the first. We have sometimes fallen so low that our hearts have been like stones, yet Jesus has loved us all the while and softened our hearts as the glorious sun melts the icebergs of the ocean. Though our hearts may not have sought it, our hearts were refreshed by His love. Our Lord has indeed proven how He loves us by the gracious way in which He has borne with our many provocations and sins. And think, too, with what gifts He has enriched us, with what comforts He has sustained us, with what divine energy He has renewed our failing strength, and with what blessed guidance He has led and is still leading us!

Try to set down in words the total indebtedness of your heart to His love: where will you begin, when you have begun, and where will you finish? If you were to record only one out of a million of His gifts of love, would the whole world be able to contain the books that might be written concerning them? "See how He loved us!"

CHARLES SPURGEON

"Take away the stone," he said. "But, Lord," said Martha, the sister of the dead man, "by this time there is a bad odor, for he has been there four days."

John 11:39

The Bethany story is one of the tenderest of all. It touches the heights. It's a hilltop story, both in its setting amid the Bethany blue hills where it grew up and in the height of faith it records. It has personal friendship and love of Jesus and implicit trust in Him as its starting point. And from this it reaches up to levels unknown before. Faith touches high water here. It rises to flood, a flood that sweeps mightily through the valleys of doubt and questionings all around it.

At the beginning there is faith in Jesus of the tender, personal sort. At the close there is faith that He will actually meet the need of your life and circumstance without limit. The highest faith is this: connecting Jesus' power and love with the actual need of your life. Abraham believed God with full sincerity that covenant-making night under the dark sky. But he didn't connect his faith in God with his need and danger among the Philistines (see Genesis 15:6; 20:11). Peter believed in Jesus fully, but his faith and his action failed to connect when the trials came that night in Gethsemane.

The Bethany pitch of faith makes connections. It ties our God and our need and our action into one knot. This is the heart of this whole story. Jesus' one effort in His tactful, patient wooing is to get Martha up to the point of ordering that stone aside. He got her faith in touch with the gravestone of her need. Her faith and her action connected. That spoke of her expectancy. Beliefs are best understood when they are acted out. Moving the stone was her confession of faith. Not that Jesus was the Son of God. That was settled long before.

No, it meant that the Son of God was now actually going to act as the Son of God to meet her need. Under His touch her dead brother was going to live. The deadness that broke her heart would give way under Jesus' touch. The Bethany faith doesn't believe that God *can* do what you need, merely. It believes that He *will* do it. And so the stone is taken away that He may do it. God has our active consent. Are we up to the Bethany level? Has God our active consent to do all He would? Is our faith being lived, acted out?

S. D. GORDON

*Then Jesus said, "Did I not tell you that if you believe,
you will see the glory of God?"*

John 11:40

Like Lazarus who had been dead for four days, you may actually feel buried. Satan has told you that there is no hope for someone who is as corrupt in soul as you are. Your fears that God will leave you buried out of His sight seem to prove true. Turn your thoughts to the truth: If you believe in Jesus, you will see the glory of God.

Trust Jesus Christ alone to utterly save you. Sink or swim, throw yourself into the sea of Jesus' love. You shall see the glory of God in your pardon, in your new creation, in your being sustained under temptation, in your being kept in the hours of life and in the night of death, in your being lifted up at the day of judgment to receive an acquittal and being pronounced faultless before His presence with exceeding great joy (see Jude 24)! I have known myself as defiled, corrupt, unworthy, but I see the day coming when I shall be wearing a crown, waving a palm branch, bowing before the eternal throne, having neither spot nor wrinkle nor any such thing. My soul has leapt at the very thought that I shall walk the streets of gold, pass through the gates of pearl, see His face, and bow before Him! I, who was once filled with sin and corruption, filled to the brim with the vision of God. You and I will meet there, and what a wonder it will be that we should have gotten there! It is no wonder that in heaven they strike up that grand old song that will always be new: "To him who loves us and has freed us from our sins by his blood, and has made us to be a kingdom and priests to serve his God and Father—to him be glory and power for ever and ever!" (Revelation 1:5–6). I am of the same mind as the good old soul who said that if Jesus Christ ever took her to heaven, He would never hear the last of it. And He never shall!

Come forth from the grave! Come forth! Jesus calls you to come and trust Him! Not only will He make you a new creature, but He promises to take you one day to where the angels dwell, above all, where He dwells. What a glorious sight that will be!

CHARLES SPURGEON

And he who had died came out bound hand and foot with graveclothes, and his face was wrapped with a cloth. Jesus said to them, "Loose him, and let him go."

John 11:44 NKJV

The death of Lazarus, his burial, and his corruption are a figure and picture of the spiritual condition of every soul by nature. The voice of Jesus, crying, "Lazarus, come forth!" is the emblem of the voice of Jesus, by His Spirit that brings new life to our soul. And the fact that Lazarus, even when alive, wore his graveclothes for a little while, until they were taken from him, is extremely significant. If we allegorize it, it teaches us that many of us, though we are alive in Christ, still have our graveclothes.

What do I mean by that? Many believers still are not quite free from trusting in works. They have not yet come to believe that salvation is by grace alone, and will have some works mixed up with it. These believers are constantly trying to do enough to feel they've pleased God, but always feel they're falling short, and some fear that they may fall so short that they lose their salvation. To them, I hear Jesus Christ saying, "Loose him, and let him go."

Most of us carry around some remaining graveclothes. Even though we have become a child of God, we sometimes find old habits clinging to us. We may find that we have indulged in vices and sins, whether it be an anger issue, a drug or alcohol addiction, or seeking others' approval, and whenever an opportunity presents itself, there is the old feeling getting up and saying, "Let me do it; let me have it. I must have it." And we have strived to keep it down, but we have hardly been strong enough. The graveclothes have been torn to shreds by divine grace, but the shreds hang about us still.

Those graveclothes will remain on very tightly until the habit is completely broken off. Look at the apostle Paul; who could have been a more holy man than he? Yet he cried, "O wretched man that I am! Who will deliver me from this body of death?" (Romans 7:24 NKJV). Let this comfort and cheer you who are striving against your own corruption. If you feel your sins to be graveclothes and are anxious to get rid of them, though you cannot conquer all your sins and corruptions, be not dismayed. Trust in Christ, trust His mercy and His grace, for by and by Jesus Christ will say, "Loose him, and let him go." We are loosed from one bad habit and then another.

CHARLES SPURGEON

Then the chief priests and the Pharisees gathered a council and said, "What shall we do? For this Man works many signs. If we let Him alone like this, everyone will believe in Him."

John 11:47–48 NKJV

There are some people who must do mischief, who must circulate malicious reports, who must pass narrow criticisms, who must write stinging articles in journals that have small enough circulation to take them in, in the hope that they may sell an extra copy. There are people who must run down other people, depreciate them, and find a way to eliminate them in order to retain their position and prominence in other people's eyes.

So the Pharisees get into a council. There are some people who are never strong except when they are on a committee. Meet such people one by one, and they are deferential; let them get together on a committee, a council, or a board of directors, and perhaps a finer set of cowards could hardly be met. They assist public deliberations by crying, "Vote, vote!" "Hear, hear!" That is the sum total of their contribution to the illumination and advancement of great questions. The Pharisees must get into council. One will speak and another will say, "Hear, hear!" and the rest will applaud, and nobody can tell exactly who said it. When did a Pharisee boldly and frankly come up to Jesus Christ and face Him as man faces man in singularity? Oh, when the pack of hounds met, how the hounds barked!

Some men have been killed by councils, killed by committees, killed by numbers of persons who have absorbed their own personality in the troubled existence of other and indescribable lives. This matter is a personal one. We cannot be saved by councils nor ought we to fear being condemned by them. We cannot be saved by committees; why should we wait for them as if they had it in their power to pervert our judgment or trouble our conscience? Be right, and go on; be sure of your ground, and then stand still, and advance, pray, and consider as the circumstances that come and go may determine.

JOSEPH PARKER

And one of them, Caiaphas, being high priest that year, said to them, "You know nothing at all, nor do you consider that it is expedient for us that one man should die for the people, and not that the whole nation should perish."

John 11:49–50 NKJV

While the Jewish council was wavering with how to deal with Jesus, Caiaphas, the high priest, has the advantage of a perfectly clear and single purpose, and no restraint of conscience keeps him from speaking it out. He takes one point of view only in regard to the mightiest spiritual revelation that the world ever saw—its bearing upon his own miserable personal interests and the interests of the order to which he belongs. And so, "Never mind about His miracles, His teaching, or the beauty of His character. His life is a perpetual danger to our prerogatives. This man must die!" The head and crown of the national religion, with centuries of illustrious traditions embodied in his person, set by his very office to tend the sacred flame of their messianic hopes, is as blind as a mole to the beauty of Christ's character and the greatness of His words, utterly unspiritual, undisguisedly selfish, cruel as a cutthroat, and having reached that supreme height of wickedness in which he can dress his ugliest thought in the plainest words and send them into the world unabashed.

The lessons of this speech and character are for us all. The selfish consideration of our own interests will make us as blind as bats to the most radiant beauty of truth, and to Christ himself, if the recognition of Him and of His message seems to threaten any of these. Men who are always living in the dark holes of their own selfishly absorbed natures lose their spiritual sight; and the fairest, loftiest, truest, and most radiant visions pass before their eyes, and they see them not. If ever there comes into the selfish man's mind a truth, or an aspect of Christ's mission that may seem to cut against some of his interests, how blind he is to it!

We have all of us to fight against the developed selfishness that takes the form of this, that, and the other sin; and we have all of us, if we are wise, to fight against the undeveloped sin that lies in all selfishness. Remember that if you begin with laying down as the canon of your conduct, "It is expedient for me," you place yourself upon an inclined plane that tilts at a very sharp angle, is very sufficiently greased, and ends away down yonder in the depths of darkness, and it is only a question of time how far and how fast, how deep and irrevocable, will be your descent.

ALEXANDER MACLAREN

Lazarus was one of those who sat at the table with Him.

John 12:2 NKJV

Lazarus is to be envied. It was well to be Martha and serve, but better to be Lazarus and commune. There are times for each purpose, and each is fitting in its season, but none of the trees of the garden yield such clusters as the vine of fellowship. To sit with Jesus, to hear His words, to mark His acts, and receive His smiles was such a favor as must have made Lazarus as happy as the angels. When it has been our happy lot to feast with our Beloved in His banqueting hall, we would not have given half a sigh for all the kingdoms of the world if so much breath could have bought them.

It would have been a strange thing if Lazarus had not been at the table where Jesus was, for the people had come together particularly to see Lazarus who had been raised from the dead. For him to sit there and to show himself was to do the best thing to convince onlookers that he was, indeed, alive! For the risen one to be absent when the Lord who gave him life was at his house would have been ungrateful indeed. Lazarus eating and drinking was a testimony for Jesus, and I would that we all knew how even to eat and drink to the glory of God! There are some believers who cannot do much or say much, but their godly lives, their patient suffering, their quiet holiness are witnesses to Jesus.

Lazarus is to be imitated. We, too, were once dead, yes, and like Lazarus in the grave of sin. Jesus raised us, and by His life we live—can we be content to live at a distance from Him? Do we omit to remember Him at His table, where He consents to feast with His brethren? Oh, this is cruel! It befits us to repent and do as He has bidden us, for His least wish should be law to us. To have lived without constant communication with one of whom the Jews said, "See how He loved him!" (John 11:36 NKJV) would have been disgraceful to Lazarus; is it excusable in us whom Jesus has loved with an everlasting love? To have been cold to Him who wept over his lifeless corpse would have demonstrated great callousness in Lazarus. What does it argue in us over whom the Savior has not only wept, but bled? Come, let us return unto our heavenly Bridegroom, and ask for His Spirit that we may be on terms of closer intimacy with Him, and henceforth sit at the table with Him.

CHARLES SPURGEON

Then Mary took a pound of very costly oil of spike-nard, anointed the feet of Jesus, and wiped His feet with her hair. And the house was filled with the fragrance of the oil.

John 12:3 NKJV

As Mary looked at her resurrected brother sitting there beside Jesus, she wondered how she could show the love that welled up in her heart. She had one costly possession, the pound of perfume. So, without thinking of anything but the great burden of love that she blessedly bore, she "anointed the feet of Jesus, and wiped His feet with her hair." True love is profuse, not to say extravagant. It knows no better use for its best than to lavish it on the beloved, and can have no higher joy than that. It does not wait to calculate utility as seen by colder eyes, such as Judas's. A basin of water and a towel would have served the same purpose, but not for relieving Mary's full heart. Do we know anything of that omnipotent yearning?

After Judas's criticism of Mary's extravagance, Jesus said, "Let her alone; she has kept this for the day of My burial. For the poor you have with you always, but Me you do not have always" (vv. 7–8 NKJV). That Jesus should see in the anointing a reference to His burial touchingly indicates how that vision of the cross occupied His thoughts, yet it did not so absorb Him as to make Him indifferent to Mary's love. He accepts every offering that love brings and, in accepting, gives it significance beyond the offerer's thought. We know not what use He may make of our poor service, but we may be sure that if that which we can see to is right—namely, its motive—He will take care of what we cannot see to—namely, its effect—and will find noble use for the sacrifices that unloving critics pronounce as useless waste.

Opportunities for the exercise of human liberality are ever present, and therefore the obligation to it is constant. But these duties do not preclude the opportunities for such special forms of expressing love to Jesus as Mary showed, and as must soon end. The fact of His being about to leave them warranted extraordinary tokens of love, as all loving hearts know only too well. Besides the customary duties of generous giving laid on us by the presence of ordinary poverty and distress, there is room in the Christian experience for extraordinary outflow from the heart filled with love for Christ. The world may mock what it sees as useless extravagance, but Jesus sees what is done for Him, and therefore accepts it and breathes meaning into it.

ALEXANDER MACLAREN

The next day a great multitude that had come to the feast, when they heard that Jesus was coming to Jerusalem, took branches of palm trees and went out to meet Him, and cried out: "Hosanna! 'Blessed is He who comes in the name of the Lord!' The King of Israel!"

John 12:12–13 NKJV

T o understand the events of that day we must try to realize how rapidly and, as the rulers thought, dangerously, excitement was rising among the crowds who had come up for the Passover and had heard of the raising of Lazarus. The Passover was always a time when national feeling was high and any spark might light the fire. It looked as if Lazarus would be the match, and so the rulers had made up their minds to have both him and Jesus put to death. It might have been expected that Jesus would have escaped into privacy (as He had done previously) or discouraged the offered praise of a crowd whose messianic ideal was so different from His.

The meaning of the popular demonstration was plain, both from the palm branches, signs of victory and rejoicing, and from the chant that is in part taken from Psalm 118. The messianic application of that quotation is unmistakable. Little did the shouting crowd understand what sort of Savior He was. Deliverance from Rome was what was on their minds.

We must remember what distorted notions of the Messiah they had, and we can understand how unlike His past conduct His present action was. He had shrunk from crowds and their misplaced enthusiasm; He had slipped away into solitude when they wished to come by force to make Him a king, and had in every possible way sought to avoid publicity and the rousing of popular excitement. Now He deliberately sets himself to intensify it. His choice of a young donkey on which to ride into Jerusalem was, and would be seen by many to be, a plain appropriation to himself of a very distinct messianic prophecy and must have raised the heat of the crowd by many degrees. One can imagine the roar of acclaim that hailed Him when He met the chanting multitude.

Why did He now court the enthusiasm that He had previously dampened? Because He knew that His hour had come and that the cross was at hand, and He desired to bring it forth as speedily as possible and to finish the work He was eager to complete. The urgency, almost impatience, that had marked Him on that last journey had reached its height, and would indicate His human longing to get the dark hour over with, even His fixed willingness to die for all humanity.

ALEXANDER MACLAREN

Then Jesus, when He had found a young donkey, sat on it; as it is written: "Fear not, daughter of Zion; behold, your King is coming, sitting on a donkey's colt."

John 12:14–15 NKJV

As was shown in yesterday's reading, Jesus accepted the acclamations of the large Passover crowd in Jerusalem and deliberately set himself to stir up enthusiasm, yet He sought to purify the tainted ideas of the crowd. What more striking way could He have chosen to declare that all the turbulent passion and eagerness for insurrection against Rome were alien to His purposes and to the true messianic ideal than choosing a meek donkey colt to bear Him? A conquering king would have made his triumphal entry in a chariot or on a battle horse. Jesus is enthroned on a donkey. It was not only for a verbal fulfilment of the prophecy but also for a demonstration of the essential nature of His kingdom that He thus entered the city.

John characteristically takes note of the effects of the entry on two classes: the disciples and the rulers. At the resurrection, the disciples remembered with a sudden flash of enlightenment the meaning of the entry. The rulers were made more determined to take vigorous measures to stop the madness of the mob when the popular feelings ran high.

Jesus brought into prominence the true nature of His rule by His choosing the donkey to carry Him, so declaring that His dominion rested not on conquest but on meekness. He also revealed a yet deeper aspect of His work, teaching that His influence over men is won by utter self-sacrifice, and that His subjects must tread the same path of losing their lives in order to reveal His glory. The world's war cries today are two: "Get!" and "Enjoy!" Christ's command is "Renounce!" And in renouncing, we shall realize both of these other aims, which they who pursue them only, never attain.

Christ's servant must be Christ's follower: indeed, service is following. The cross has in it an aspect that must be reproduced in every disciple. And he who takes it for the ground of his trust only, and not as the pattern of his life, must ask himself whether his trust in it is genuine or worth anything. Of course, those who follow a leader will arrive where the leader has gone, and though our feet are feeble and our progress winding and slow, we have here His promise that we shall be sustained by Him, will reach His side, and at last be where He is.

ALEXANDER MACLAREN

*Now there were some Greeks among those who went
up to worship at the festival. They came to Philip, who
was from Bethsaida in Galilee, with a request. "Sir,"
they said, "we would like to see Jesus."*

John 12:20–21

I t is most striking to realize that Jesus was recognized by men of all nations, and how His love was understood and yielded to by men of all sorts.
The intense Jew, the despised Samaritan, the forceful Roman, the cultured
Greek—these made up the world. The waves of His personal influence were
from Jerusalem to Judea, through Samaria, and out into the uttermost parts
of the earth.

And all sorts of men understood. Jesus wiped out social differences and
distinctions in the crowds that gently jostled one another in His presence. The
wealthy such as Joseph of Arimathea, and the beggar such as the man born
blind, the pure in heart such as Mary of Bethany, and the publicly shamed
sinner such as the accused woman of Jerusalem all felt alike that this Jesus
belonged to them, and they to Him.

And the centuries have not changed this. Time finds the human heart is the
same, and so is Jesus. I was greatly struck with this in my travels among the
nations. Some people say there is no point of contact between the East and
the West. But I have seen people in every culture catch a glimpse of Jesus—their
eyes light, their faces glow, their hearts leap in response. Jesus is the point of
contact. One touch of Jesus reveals the kinship that is there between Him and
men, and between all men. Wherever the knowledge of Jesus has been carried,
He is recognized and claimed as their own regardless of national and social lines.

The truth is that Jesus had a heart of all racial color. He had a Jewish
heart, a Roman, a Greek, a Samaritan heart. Yes, He had a world heart, He
had a human heart. And He has. There's a Man on the throne of glory, bone
of our bone, heart of our heart.

Since Jesus went to heaven, human experience has been taken up into the
heart of God. Jesus belongs to us, and we to Him. The human heart has
recognized its Kinsman wherever He has been able to get to them, and it has
gladly yielded to the plea of His love. Jerusalem might make a cross for Him,
but the world would weave its heartfelt devotion into a crown of love for Him,
adorned with the dewy tears of its gratitude, sparkling like diamonds in the
light of His face.

S. D. GORDON

But Jesus answered them, saying, "The hour has come that the Son of Man should be glorified."

John 12:23 NKJV

How constantly our Master used the title *the Son of Man*. If He had chosen, He might always have spoken of himself as the Son of God, the Everlasting Father, the Wonderful Counselor, the Prince of Peace; but behold the lowliness of Jesus! He prefers to call himself the Son of Man. Let us learn a lesson of humility from our Savior; let us never court great titles or proud degrees. There is here, however, a far sweeter thought. Jesus loved manhood so much that He delighted to honor it. And since it is a high honor and, indeed, the greatest dignity of manhood that Jesus is the Son of Man, it is His custom to display this name that He may as it were hang royal stars upon the breast of manhood and show forth the love of God to Abraham's seed.

Son of Man—whenever He said that word, He shed a halo round the head of Adam's children. Yet there is perhaps a more precious thought still. Jesus Christ called himself the Son of Man to express His oneness and sympathy with His people. Without a murmur, Christ, as man, was glorified by enduring bravely, patiently, and to the end, what no other man has ever borne. He thus reminds us that He is the one whom we may approach without fear. As a man, we may take to Him all our griefs and troubles, for He knows them by experience; in that He himself has suffered as the Son of Man, He is able to relieve and comfort us.

All hail, blessed Jesus! Inasmuch as you are evermore using the sweet name that acknowledges that you are a brother, it is to us a dear token of your grace, your humility, and your love.

Oh, see how Jesus trusts himself
Unto our childish love,
As though by His free ways with us
Our earnestness to prove!
His sacred name a common word
On earth He loves to hear;
There is no majesty in Him
That love may not come near.

CHARLES SPURGEON

*"If anyone serves Me, let him follow Me; and where I
am, there My servant will be also."*

John 12:26 NKJV

From the beginning, Christ's disciples did not look upon Him as a rabbi's
disciples did, as being simply a teacher, but recognized Him as the Messiah, the Son of God. So that they were called upon by His commands
to accept His teaching in a very special way, not merely as the Jewish rabbis
asked their disciples to accept theirs. Do you do that? Do you take Him as your
final authority in all matters of truth and of practical wisdom? Is His declaration of God your theology? Is His affirmation of His own person your living
creed? Is His teaching that the Son of Man comes to give His life a ransom
for many the ground of your hope? Do you follow Him in your belief, and
in doing so, do you accept Him as the Savior of your soul, by His death and
passion? That is the first step, to follow Him, to trust Him wholly for who
He is, the incarnate Son of God, the sacrifice for the sins of the whole world,
and therefore for yours and mine. This is a call to faith.

It is also a call to obedience. "Follow Me!" means to carefully plant your
feet in His firm footsteps; where you see His track going across the bog, be
not afraid to walk after Him, though it may seem to lead you into the deepest and the blackest of it. Follow Him, and you will be right; follow Him,
and you will be blessed. Do as Christ did, or as according to the best of your
judgment it seems to you that Christ would have done if He had been in
your circumstances; and you will not go far wrong. The imitation of Christ
is the sum of all practical Christianity. "Follow Me!" makes discipleship to
be something better than intellectual acceptance of His teaching, something
more than even reliance for my salvation upon His work. It makes discipleship to be, springing out of these two, the acceptance of His teaching and the
consequent reliance, by faith, upon His word—to be a practical reproduction
of His character and conduct in mine.

It is a call to communion. If a man follows Christ, he will walk close behind
Him and near enough to Him to hear Him speak. He will be separated from
other people and from other things. In these four things—*faith, obedience,
imitation, communion*—lies the essence of being a follower of Jesus.

ALEXANDER MACLAREN

"Now My soul is troubled, and what shall I say? 'Father, save Me from this hour'? But for this purpose I came to this hour."

John 12:27 NKJV

I shall not be too bold if I say that Gethsemane was rehearsed in public upon the occasion before us. He felt a sort of foreshadowing of that midnight among the olives, in which His soul was "exceedingly sorrowful, even to death" (Matthew 26:38 NKJV). And as the mind of Christ perceived the dark shadow of human guilt that must pass over His soul and the iniquity of us all placed upon His spirit, He was deeply troubled. It was the culminating point, the climax, and the conquest of a great mental battle in the Savior's heart.

He who could still the sea and bid the storms retreat was tempest-tossed in His own soul. He who could send a legion of demons into the deep was nevertheless troubled in spirit and cried, "What shall I say?" Master of all worlds, supreme over the angels, and adored at His Father's right hand, yet He confesses, "Now My soul is troubled." Lord of all, yet He learned obedience by the things that He suffered. How human! How near akin it makes Him to us!

Have you not cried out in anguish, "Now my soul is troubled"? Then remember that your Lord used the same words. Are you tossed to and fro in your thoughts? Do you ever ask, "What shall I say?" Jesus also understands by empathy what it is you mean. Have you ever felt you didn't know what to do and so prayed, "Father, save me from this hour"? In all this you may see your Savior's footprints. You are not upon a new and strange track. He leads you through no darker rooms than He went through before. There is nothing in them novel or surprising to His sympathetic heart.

I feel so glad to think our Lord spoke out His feelings when He was passing through this inward conflict. He did not endeavor to conceal His emotions from others. It may be that by this He intended to teach us wisdom. He would show us by His own example that it is well for us not to be too much shut up within ourselves. Smother not your sorrow, tell it out, or it may gather ungovernable heat. It is the worst of grief that cannot weep or mourn. Give vent to pent-up feelings. Anything is better than banking up the fires and concentrating all the heat within the soul. Act not the stoic's part. Be not ashamed to let it be known that you are human and can grieve and be troubled even as others.

CHARLES SPURGEON

"Father, glorify Your name."

John 12:28 NKJV

I will say no more about the trouble of our Redeemer that was the focus of yesterday's reading. I would now ask you to fix your thoughts upon the firm resolve that today's text sets forth. The surface of Jesus' mind was ruffled, but deep in His heart the current of the Redeemer's soul flowed on irresistibly in the ordained channel. Shall there be no cross, no resurrection, no gates of heaven set wide open for coming souls? Jesus answers the question with the resolute words, "Father, glorify Your name. For this purpose I came to redeem the sons of men. Cost me what it may, I will endure the cross and despise the shame, to honor you, my Father."

The glory of God was the chief end and object of our Savior's life and death. It is that the Father's name may be illustrious that Jesus would have souls redeemed. And how completely He has glorified Jehovah's name! Upon the cross we see the divine justice in the streaming wounds of the great Substitute, for the Son of God must die when sin is laid on Him. There also you behold infinite wisdom, for what but infallible wisdom could have devised the way whereby God might be just and yet the justifier of him who believes (see Romans 3:26). There, too, is love—rich, free, boundless love—never so conspicuous as in the death of man's Redeemer. That the Father might be glorified, Jesus pushed on to the end that He has set before Him.

Have you ever prayed this prayer? "Father, glorify your name"? When we find ourselves in conditions where we do not know which way to turn, in times of distress of mind, we cry, "What shall I do? What shall I say? Where can I look? I am overwhelmed and oppressed!" In those times, if you pray, "Father, glorify your name," there is no more question about "what shall I say?" You have said the right thing and there let it end.

I wish you great happiness, but our Lord made it clear that troubles will come in this life. The comforts that surround us today may take themselves wings tomorrow. What shall we do? We shall breath this prayer, "Father, glorify your name." That is to say, if I must lose my property, glorify your name in my loss; if I must be bereaved, glorify your name in my sorrows; if I must die, glorify your name in my departure. When you pray in that fashion, your conflict is over, no outward fright or inward fear remains.

CHARLES SPURGEON

"Now is the judgment of this world; now the ruler of this world will be cast out."

John 12:31 NKJV

It was the love for men in Jesus' own heart that drew Him down here and drove Him along even to the Calvary hill. He died *for* us, in our place, on our behalf. This was His one thought. Through this our bondage to sin and to Satan would be broken and we would be set free. And we would be drawn; our hearts would be utterly melted and broken by His love for us. The influence would reach out until all the race would feel its power and respond.

The devil was a real personality to Jesus. This whole terrific struggle ending at the cross was a direct spirit battle with the spirit prince. So Jesus understood it. All the bitter enmity to himself traces straight back to that source. That enmity found its worst expression in Jesus' death. The pitched spirit battle was there. But that prince was judged, condemned, utterly defeated, and cast out in that battle, and his hold upon men broken.

And so this was the greatest victory of all. It was greatest in its intensity of meaning *to the Father*. It revealed His unbending, unflinching ideals of right, and the great strength and tenderness of His love for men. He would even give His Son. It was greatest in its intensity of meaning *to the Son*. It meant the utmost of suffering ever endured, the utmost of love underneath ever revealed; and it would mean the race-wide sweep of His gracious power.

It was greatest in its intensity of meaning *to Satan*, the hater of God and man. It told his utter defeat and loss of power over man. So it broke our bonds and made us free to yield to the pursuit of God to win us. And it was greatest in its intensity of meaning *to us*. For it showed to our confused eyes the one ideal of right standing clear and full. It set us free from the fetters of our bondage, gave us the tremendous incentive of love to reach up to the ideal of right, and more, immensely more, gave us *power* to reach it.

It was the greatest reaching out of its influence, for all men of all the earth would be touched. And it was greatest in the in-reach to all the life of each one who came under its blessed influence. It would mean newness of life in body, in mind, in social nature, in spirit, and in the eternal quality of life lived here, and to be lived without ending.

S. D. GORDON

"Now is the time for judgment on this world; now the prince of this world will be driven out."

John 12:31

When the Lord Jesus came to earth, Satan knew His purpose and stirred the spirit of Herod to slay Him. And subsequent to that failure, Satan tried to end the life of Christ many times. At last, after Judas took the thirty pieces of silver, the court of hell rang their bells with delight to see the Savior stand in Pilate's court. When it was said, "Let Him be crucified," the devil's joy knew no bounds. And when they saw Him on the cross, there stood the exulting fiend, declaring to himself, "Ah! I have the King of glory in my dominion. I have the power of death, and I have power over Him."

How short-lived was the hellish victory! How brief was the satanic triumph! Jesus died, and "It is finished!" shook the gates of hell. Down from the cross the Conqueror leapt, pursued the fiend with thunderbolts of wrath; swift to the shades of hell the fiend did fly, and swift descending went the Conqueror after him. And seize him He did—chained him to His chariot wheel, dragged him up the steeps of glory, angels shouting all the while, "He led captivity captive, and gave gifts to men" (Ephesians 4:8 NKJV).

"That through death He might destroy him who had the power of death, that is, the devil" (Hebrews 2:14 NKJV). Death was the devil's primary entrenchment. When Jesus took death from him and dismantled that once impregnable fortress, He took away from him not only death but also every other advantage that the devil had over the saint. And now Satan is a conquered foe, not only in the hour of death but also in every other hour and every other place. He is an enemy both cruel and mighty; but he is a foe who quakes and quails when a Christian gets into the ring with him, for he knows that though the fight may waver for a little while in the scale, the balance of victory must fall on the side of the saint, because Christ by His death destroyed the devil's power.

The devil may hurl his darts by tempting you to indulge in the lusts of the flesh or in the pride of life, but you have the shield of faith, Christ and His cross, to extinguish them. Let his insinuations be ever so dire, the death of Christ has destroyed the devil's power to tempt or to destroy. The death of Christ has destroyed him.

CHARLES SPURGEON

"And I, if I am lifted up from the earth, will draw all peoples to Myself."

John 12:32 NKJV

Remember that our Lord Jesus died by a most shameful death. The cross to the ancients was a repulsive instrument of death for felons. It was regarded as the death penalty of a slave. It was not only painful but also disgraceful.

But herein is a wonderful thing. The Lord Jesus lost no influence by having been hanged upon the tree. Rather, it is because of His shameful death that He is able to draw all men to himself. His glory rises from His humiliation; His honorable conquest from His ignominious death. When He "became obedient to the point of death, even the death of the cross" (Philippians 2:8 NKJV), shame cast no shame upon His cause but gilded it with glory. Christ's death of weakness threw no weakness into Christianity, but rather it is the right arm of her power. By a love that is as strong as death, she has always been victorious and must forever remain so. When she has not been ashamed to put the cross in the forefront, she has never had to be ashamed, for God has been with her, and Jesus has drawn all men to himself. The crucified Christ has irresistible attraction. When He stoops to the utmost suffering and scorn, even the heartless must relent. Men may love a living Savior, but a crucified Savior they *must* love. If they perceive that He loved them and gave himself for them, their hearts are stolen away. The city of Mansoul is captured before the siege begins, when the Prince Immanuel uncovers the beauties of His dying love before the eyes of the rebellious ones.

Christ is drawing all peoples to himself by the power of His love. The only crime that ever could be laid to Jesus' charge was that of loving beyond all reason and beyond all bounds—loving as none ever loved before. If all the rivers of human love did run together, they could not fill such an ocean of love as was in the heart of Jesus the Savior. This it is—the unique, unrivaled love—that draws men to Jesus. The pierced heart of Christ is a magnet to draw all other hearts.

Always keep a dying Christ to the forefront. The cross without Christ is no cross at all. That is the eternal God; bind with that truth the fact that He was nailed to a Roman cross. It is on the cross that He triumphed over Satan, and it is by the cross that He must triumph over the world.

CHARLES SPURGEON

Then Jesus said to them, "A little while longer the light is with you. Walk while you have the light, lest darkness overtake you; he who walks in darkness does not know where he is going."

John 12:35 NKJV

This word *while* is full of significance. Christ used it more than once. It indicates opportunity, chance, occasion. It is as if to say, "Now is the time: be no longer slow and dull of heart; arise, know the light, and receive it with thankfulness. You have me today, make the most of me; tomorrow I shall be gone." There is only one time for the Christian, and that is today. We do not realize this with sufficient clearness. Tomorrow may come and bring with it darkness.

"Lest darkness overtake you": This darkness is not that of the darkness that comes quietly, inoffensively as at twilight. It is rather the picture of being pulled down, attacked, and humiliated. This is what can happen to us in life. We are not dealing with trivial issues. It is the imagery of a man traveling along a road frequented by robbers or ravenous beasts; it is altogether a dangerous road. Then the warning is "Up! The danger is least while the light is brightest. Be well on your road by noon, lest the tiger spring upon you and bring you to the dust, lest the robber lay his hands upon you and violently assail you. Make haste!"

There is darkness yet to overtake all of us and take us down if we have not made a right use of the light. There is the darkness of suffering and sorrow. That will try anyone. We are in reality what we are in our deepest affliction or poignant agony. Pain gets at our faith. Do not hand me some written statement of belief made in a time of health and wealth and prosperity; that creed is only so much paper and ink. Tell me what you said when the teeth of the enemy closed upon your heart; tell me what you said when the night of grief and loss was very dark. Had you made any preparation for that darkness? We should know there will come a time when we will be sprung upon, torn, and overpowered, if we have not the strength to overpower. It comes to one of two things: we will be overpowered, or we will overpower the assailant. In order to overpower the assailant, what shall we do? Walk while we have the light. We cannot carry the light into midnight. Midnight and midday each has its own place. Know this: the light is for a time, and that time is *now*.

JOSEPH PARKER

31

Then Jesus said to them . . . "While you have the light,
believe in the light, that you may become sons of light."

John 12:35–36 NKJV

Jesus said, "Walk while you have the light, lest darkness overtake you."
What darkness can come upon us? All our life is exposed to this overpowering darkness—the darkness, for example, of the loss of one's
health, wealth, loved ones and friends, memory, career, etc. How can we be
prepared? Only by having and believing in Christ, the Light of the World.
Walking while we have Christ—an opportunity of studying Christ; an opportunity of receiving Christ into the heart; an opportunity of serving Christ
in this world.

Walk in the light, receive the light, store up the light. Christ tells us that if
we walk in the light, we may be children of the light; that is to say, not having
the light outside of us but within us. That is the test of spiritual progress.
Christ is here that He may be within us. He does not want to stand in front
of us historically, the finest spectacle on the landscape. He wants to come to
us and take up His abode with us, and be part of us, and live with us, and
never go away from us. Oh, while He remains, be up and doing! Let me seize
the moment of His presence that I may receive Him into my heart. I do not
want to make an external study of Him; He is not a forest to be painted, a
landscape to be sketched, a lamp to be gazed upon. No, He is Life, Light to
be received within, that He may shine forth from my heart. Herein is that
saying true, "You are the light of the world" (Matthew 5:14). Walk with the
light, that you may become light; walk with Christ, that you may become
Christ's; so company with the Savior that others shall say of you, "As He is,
so are [you] in this world" (1 John 4:17 NKJV).

A sweet, gracious possibility is set before us. While you have light, believe
in the light of God, that you may be the children of light, that you may be
fountains of glory, centers of splendor, out of your life going forth an irra-
diating illumination that shall make your families and neighborhoods glad
with your brightness. Perhaps you thought that the light was always to be
outside of you; it is to be an internal or spiritual light. This is what the Savior
is himself, and what He is He would have His sons and daughters be. Walk
while you have the light.

JOSEPH PARKER

Nevertheless even among the rulers many believed in Him, but because of the Pharisees they did not confess Him, lest they should be put out of the synagogue; for they loved the praise of men more than the praise of God.

John 12:42–43 NKJV

This is a fatal calamity. They were believers, not confessors of Christ, and for this pitiful, humiliating reason: "they loved the praise of men more than the praise of God." Is this the reason why many do not confess Jesus today? Is there a good deal of secret belief, unspoken wonder difficult to distinguish from faith? Do some hearts go to Jesus covertly and look on until they burn? And does the glow become so intense that the tongue almost speaks? How we are conquered by immediate circumstances! The larger future can have but little effect upon men who are thrust down by that which is present, immediate, and overshadowing. Ought not the praise of others be overshadowed by the praise of God? One would have thought that what God approved, man would instantly accept, and that he would be ashamed to put his opinion in opposition to the judgment of heaven.

Men applaud that which is immediate, momentary, an advantage that can be realized *now*. But the praise of men will bear no stress upon it. If you rely and live upon human praise, those who praise you will leave you the moment they feel the sting of fire; they can turn their once beaming faces into the uttermost blank; they will pass you on the street without a word, lest some man should mistake it as a sign of friendship. The praise of men is a flying wind, a kindly breeze when the sun shines upon it; but it can soon cease, or fly away, or deepen into a groan, or heighten into a storm under change of circumstances.

Not only is living in the praise of men shortsighted—it is servile. See man looking out to see what his brother is going to do before he himself will take a definite position. Moreover, he does not remember that his brother is at this moment watching him to see what he will do. This is what we call servility, walking softly where we should walk straightly; peeping where we should look squarely and directly; muttering where we ought to speak like thunder.

We want the loud voice. If one father could with modest boldness say that he is a Christian, with humility and integrity, he might turn a whole household round and finally be blessed for a most sacred influence. And out of that declaration might come additional numbers and influence—all coming through the influence of the one man who dared to say, "As for others, whatever they do, I will serve the Lord."

JOSEPH PARKER

AUGUST

2

"For I have not spoken on My own authority; but the Father who sent Me gave Me a command, what I should say and what I should speak."

John 12:49 NKJV

t is a sweet thought that Jesus Christ did not come forth without His Father's permission, authority, consent, and assistance. He was sent by the Father as our Father's messenger, with a message for each of us—pardon for sin, restoration from the fall, acceptance in the Beloved, and eternal life and glory. Oh, when He comes from the Father, comes for the Father, and comes with a message meant to lead us to the Father, we who are the children of God must love Him for all these reasons. When we live only to serve self, our love begins to dry up for lack of secret springs, but when we perceive that Jesus Christ did not come of himself but was sent of the Father—that His aims and objectives were not for himself in any degree, but entirely for the Father and for us—our heart must go out toward Him.

We are too apt, though, to forget that while there are distinctions as to the persons in the Trinity, there are no distinctions of honor. We too frequently ascribe the honor of our salvation more to Jesus Christ than to the Father. This is a very great mistake. What if Jesus came? Did not His Father send Him? If He spoke wondrously, did not His Father pour grace into His lips, that He might be an able minister of the new covenant? He who knows the Father and the Son and the Holy Spirit as he should know them never sets one before another in his love; he sees them at Bethlehem, at Gethsemane, and on Calvary, all equally engaged in the work of salvation.

Have you put your sole confidence in the Man Christ Jesus? And are you united with Him? Then believe that you are united with the God of heaven. Since to the Man Christ Jesus you are brother and hold closest fellowship, you are linked thereby with God the Eternal as your Father and your friend. Did you ever consider the depth of love in the heart of Jehovah, when God the Father equipped His Son for the great enterprise of mercy? If not, let this be your day's meditation. The Father sent Him! Meditate on this great sending. Think how Jesus works what the Father wills. In the wounds of the dying Savior see the love of the great I AM. Let every thought of Jesus be also connected with the Eternal, ever-blessed God, self-revealed through Jesus in the fullness of grace and truth.

CHARLES SPURGEON

*Now before the Feast of the Passover, when Jesus knew
that His hour had come that He should depart from this
world to the Father, having loved His own who were in
the world, He loved them to the end.*

John 13:1 NKJV

The latter half of John's Gospel, which begins with these words, is the holy of holies of the New Testament. Nowhere else do the blended lights of our Lord's superhuman dignity and human tenderness shine with such radiance. Nowhere else is His speech at once so simple and so deep. Nowhere else have we the heart of God so unveiled to us. On no other page, even of the Bible, have so many eyes, glistening with tears, looked and had the tears dried. The immortal words that Christ spoke in that upper chamber are His highest self-revelation in speech, even as the cross to which they led is His most perfect self-revelation in act.

Many commentators prefer to read, "He loved them to the uttermost," rather than "to the end"—so expressing the depth and degree rather than the permanence and perpetuity of our Lord's love. And that seems to me to be the worthier meaning. It is important to know that the emotions of these last moments did not change Christ's love. In fact, in some sense they perfected it, giving a greater vitality to its tenderness, a more precious sweetness to its manifestation. So understood, the words explain for us why it was that in the sanctity of the upper chamber there ensued the marvelous act of the foot washing, the marvelous discourses that follow, and, the climax of all, the High Priestly Prayer. They give utterance to a love that Christ's consciousness at that solemn hour tended to sharpen and to deepen.

"Jesus knew that His hour had come." All His life was passed under the consciousness of a divine necessity laid upon Him, to which He lovingly and cheerfully yielded himself. On His lips there are no words more significant, and few more frequent, than that divine "I must!" It befits the Son of Man to do this, that, and the other—yielding to the necessity imposed by the Father's will and sealed by His own loving resolve to be the Savior of the world. And, in like manner, all through His life He declares himself conscious of the hours that mark the several crises and stages of His mission. They come to Him and He discerns them. No external power can coerce Him to any act till the hour comes. No external power can hinder Him from the act when it comes. When the hour strikes, He hears and obeys. And thus, at the last and supreme moment, to Him it dawned unquestionable and irrevocable.

ALEXANDER MACLAREN

AUGUST

4

And supper being ended, the devil having already put it into the heart of Judas Iscariot, Simon's son, to betray Him . . .

John 13:2 NKJV

It is the Passover evening. They have met, the Twelve and their Master, by appointment, in the home of one of Jesus' faithful unnamed friends. In a large upper room they are shut in, gathered about the supper board. As they eat, Jesus is quietly but intently thinking. Four trains of thought pass through His mind side by side. The Father had entrusted all into His hands. He had come down from the Father on an errand and would return when the errand was done.

And now the hour was come. The turn in the road was reached, the sharp turn down leading to the sharp turn up and then back. It had seemed slow in coming, that hour. Dreaded things seem to linger even while they hasten, dreaded longed-for things, dreaded in the experience of pain to be borne, eagerly longed for in the blessed result, as with an expectant mother. Now the hour is here.

In chapter 13, another door opens. The inner door into Jesus' heart is being opened by Him. And the inner door into the disciples' heart is being knocked at that it may open. It is the betrayal night. Jesus is alone with the inner circle. They have received Him. Now He will receive them into closer intimacy than ever before. They have opened their hearts to His love. Now He opens His heart to show more of the love that is there. Love that is accepted is free to reveal itself. And love revealing its warmth and tenderness and depth calls out quickly a deeper, tenderer love.

And across the board sits the man so faithfully loved and called, yet dead set in his inner heart on a dark purpose, more evil in its outcome than he realizes. There must be more and tenderer loving. He shall have yet another full opportunity. And under all is the heartthrob of love for these who are His own, being birthed into a new life by the giving of His very own life these months past. He loves His own and will to the uttermost in the time left Him before the great event. These are the thoughts passing quietly, clearly, intensely, through Jesus' mind as they sit at supper.

S. D. GORDON

Jesus, knowing that the Father had given all things into His hands, and that He had come from God and was going to God, rose from supper and laid aside His garments, took a towel and girded Himself.

John 13:3–4 NKJV

The washing of the disciples' feet is made the more beautiful by certain features of surpassing grandeur that are found in immediate connection with it. There seems, indeed, at first an inequality between the majesty of the mountain and the value of the frail flower that blooms on its sunny height. We are startled by the difference between the great thunderings of the introduction and the gentle, quiet progress of the narrative. Jesus knows the fullness of the mystery set forth in His incarnation; He sees the beginning in the light of the end; He has come within sight of the end; all the fragments of His life are gathering themselves together and taking wondrous shape—what will He do now? We wait almost breathlessly for the next sentence to tell us that He then called a dazzling host of angels to bring the crown He had left in heaven. This is our notion of greatness. Rather, when the whole thing, in all the brightness of its glory, showed itself to His inmost heart, He stooped to wash the feet of the men who had followed Him!

This was how Jesus Christ turned to practical account His highest consciousness of sonship. Sublime consciousness was thus turned into condescending service; high spiritual dominion and joy found expression in a deed of humility without which even the greatest revelation of majesty, the revelation of the Son of God, would have been incomplete. The deed was simultaneous with the consciousness. Jesus did not wait until the keenness of His joy had abated a little. In the very fullness and glory of His power, He washed the disciples' feet.

Do not let that picture pass away from your mind. If that picture will not melt men and make them solemn, it can do them no good. It was in the highest moment of His consciousness that He did this. We are to do even little things when we are at the highest stretch of our strength. All the work of life should be done under inspiration. Not only the greatest things; not only the fine carving, but the cement mixing; not only the fighting of splendid battles, but the searching for stray lambs and caring for widows. So, if we catch the meaning of Christ, the elevation of our consciousness is to express itself in the beauty of social charity and service. It is not to consume itself in saintly solitude and sentimental contemplation; rather it is to prove itself divine by embodiment in visible and useful service.

JOSEPH PARKER

Jesus knew that the Father had put all things under his power, and that he had come from God and was returning to God; so he got up from the meal, took off his outer clothing, and wrapped a towel around his waist. After that, he poured water into a basin and began to wash his disciples' feet.

John 13:3–5

Quietly Jesus rises from the meal, picks up a towel, and fastens its end in His waistband for convenience to use, after the servant's usual fashion. Then He pours water into a basin and, turning, stoops over the feet of the disciple nearest Him. And before they can recover from their wide-eyed astonishment, He begins bathing his feet and then carefully wiping them with the towel. And so around the circle. Peter, of course, protests, and so calls out a little of the explanation. And then with tender passion he asks for the washing to take in head and hands as well as feet. How their hearts must have felt the touch upon their feet!

Then follows a bit of explanation. But the chief thing had already been done. The acting was more than the speech. The teaching about humility lies on the surface, within easy reach. It was sorely needed then, and is still today. In it was the key to Jesus' great victory within the twenty-four hours following, and would have been for the disciples had they used it. Humility is the foundation of all strength and victory. Only the strong stoop. It takes the strongest to stoop the lowest. He who so stoops is revealing strength.

Humility is not thinking low thoughts about yourself. It is merely getting into correct personal relation with God, and so with men. It is our true normal attitude, as dependent creatures, as those who have sinned, as those who have been bought with blood. Everything we have is from Another, originally and continuously; we are utterly dependent. All rights have been forfeited by our willful conduct; we retain nothing in our own right. And all we have now has been secured for us at the cost of blood; we are being carried at enormous cost. Not much room for self-satisfaction is there.

Humility is simply recognizing our utter dependence upon Another and living it. And this controls our touch with others. In this lies the secret of all strength—mental keenness and vigor, sympathetic touch with others, and power of action in life and in service. All this touches the weakest spot in these men, and in us.

S. D. GORDON

After that, he poured water into a basin and began to wash his disciples' feet.

John 13:5

How little this Scripture is understood in the church! The notion of rank in the world is like a pyramid; the higher you go up, the fewer there are above you whom you must serve, and the more you are served by those beneath you. When you come to the apex, there stands someone who has to do no service, but whom all the others have to serve.

In the kingdom of heaven, however, the figure is exactly reversed. The pyramid is upside-down. The Son of God lies at the inverted apex of the pyramid. He upholds, serves, and ministers to all, and they who would be high in His kingdom must go near Him at the bottom. There is no other law of rank and position in God's kingdom. And that is the only kingdom.

There are some who, when just beginning to learn this, look about in a blind kind of way and say, "I wish I could serve God. But I don't know what to do or where to begin!" Looking about for something grand, something, no doubt, also recognized by men, they ignore the service God has already put right in front of them. And He can give them nothing more to do until they do that.

Service begins where it began with Jesus, who was, and still is, a servant. Service is obedience, or it is nothing. We obey God by serving our neighbor—just as Jesus did—by getting underneath the pyramid rather than seeking to climb to the top of it. Our Lord came to give His life and to minister to all in obedience to His Father's will. He did not give the commands; He obeyed them. Obedience is the grandest thing in the world to begin with. Yes, and we shall end with it too.

Do you want to know how to minister, how to be a servant like Jesus was a servant? Begin by obeying! Obey everyone who has a right to command you. But above all, look to what our Lord has said, and find out what He wants you to do out of what He left behind. Obedience to that will make you part of the grand scheme and way of God in this world. Take your place in God's kingdom by so doing. Let us go forth and do this service of God in ministering to our fellow man.

GEORGE MACDONALD

*After that, He poured water into a basin and began to
wash the disciples' feet, and to wipe them with the towel
with which He was girded.*

John 13:5 NKJV

The Lord Jesus loves His people so much that every day He is still doing for
them much that is analogous to washing their soiled feet. Their poorest
actions He accepts; their deepest sorrow He feels; their slenderest wish
He hears, and their every sin and greatest sin He forgives. He is still their
Servant as well as their Friend and Master. He not only performs majestic
deeds for them, such as wearing the crown on His brow and the precious
jewels glittering on His breastplate and standing up to plead for them in the
courts of heaven, but humbly, patiently, He yet goes about among His people
with the basin and the towel. He does this when He puts away from us day by
day our constant weaknesses and sins. Even when you have fallen again into
the selfsame foolishness and sin from which grace delivered you long ago, yet
Jesus will have great patience with you. He will hear your confession of sin
and say, "I am willing; be cleansed" (Mark 1:41 NKJV); He will again apply the
blood of sprinkling, speak peace to your conscience, and remove every spot.

It is a great act of eternal love when Christ once for all forgives the sinner
and puts him into the family of God; but what condescending patience there
is when the Savior with much long-suffering bears the oft recurring follies
of His wayward disciple; day by day, and hour by hour, washing away the
multiplied sins of His erring but beloved child! To dry up a flood of rebellion is something marvelous, but to endure the constant dripping of repeated
offenses—to bear with a perpetual trying of patience, this is divine indeed!
While we find comfort and peace in our Lord's daily cleansing, its legitimate
influence upon us will be to increase our watchfulness and hasten our desire
for holiness. Is it not so?

He whom the angels worship takes a towel and girds himself. Listen to the
song, "Holy, holy, holy, Lord God Almighty! Early in the morning our song
shall rise to Thee." Then, "Lord, are you washing my feet?" Oh, think of
this; think till your heart melts with love! No one else could cleanse us. The
infinite God must take away the infinite blackness and filth of His people's
sins! What a stoop is here! Let us lift up our eyes and wonder; let us lift up
our voices and praise His name, that He should ever wash our feet!

CHARLES SPURGEON

And Peter said to Him, "Lord, are You washing my feet?"
Jesus answered and said to him, "What I am doing you
do not understand now, but you will know after this."

John 13:6–7 NKJV

Peter saw nothing beyond the mere fact of washing the disciples' feet; it was not a parable full of divine meaning to him because he did not look at it in a spiritual light. Now, in Jesus' answer to Peter we find the other half of the gracious truth that divine consciousness is to express itself in service. We see that, as consciousness sometimes precedes service and dictates it, as was the case with Jesus (v. 3), so occasionally facts prepare the way for consciousness. There is a kind of reciprocal action. Some men work best from consciousness—from the intuitive, the internal, the spiritual. Other men must see something, handle something, and work their way from the visible to the unseen. It was so in the case of Peter: hence Jesus said, "What I am doing you do not understand now, but you will know after this." We are not always to work from the point of knowledge and understanding. There are occasions in life when our highest powers of reasoning are to be set aside and we are to become little children. Those who are blind are invited to put their hands into the great hand of God. It is as if Christ had said, "Peter, just do what I wish. Do the will, and afterward you will know the teaching—that external thing that seems a mere waste on my part shall in due time be seen to have deep meaning and an inspiring example."

Sometimes things are to be done, and the explanation is to come after the fact. Our first question must always be, "Is this the will of God?" If so, we shall find the explanation of the mystery in God's way and God's time. The little seed planted in the dark ground may question why it is kept from the bright sunshine, but eventually the flower comes forth beautiful in form and exquisite in color. It is even so with children whose minds and memories are stored with the truths of God's Word. At first they know only the words. For long years those words may lie dormant in the heart; but in some season of trouble and sore distress, it may arise and bring deliverance and lead the soul into the very presence of God. Believe, then, in the mysteries of life; believe in facts, ordinances, and means. The intent and purpose of each do not lie upon the surface. Whatever God may ask of us, let us hasten to obey, for there we shall find His blessing.

JOSEPH PARKER

"For I have given you an example, that you should do as I have done to you."

John 13:15 NKJV

Herein lies the unfathomable simplicity of Christ—the thing that appears to be so understandable, and yet that carries with it all philosophies, theologies, and possibilities of thinking worthy of reference. Where is there a man who does not instantly see the whole meaning of an incident of this kind? And yet the simplicity of Christ is the profundity of God. God is love; love lives to serve. God is always stooping and washing men's feet.

The eternal meaning of the text is: Humility is to be the hallmark of the Christian. Humility is silent; humility keeps no mirror; humility knows not that its face, having been turned toward God in long fellowship, burns with the reflected glory of the image it has gazed upon. Humility has to be an active power in life. The more we know ourselves, the humbler will be the service we shall render, without knowing that it is a service of humiliation—not self-display. There is a way of washing feet that says, "Look how I am serving others!" Humble service can only be done in Christ's spirit; but being done in that spirit, it is no longer the service of humiliation because it is balanced by the consciousness that was its first inspiration. And thus while we are on earth we are in heaven, and being in heaven we stoop to take up the earth to cleanse it and lift it back up to its Maker's smile.

This is Christianity—not outward performance, not eye service, but the unconscious doing of works of humiliation through the higher consciousness that there is nothing small that is done for Christ's sake. When this spirit is in us, we shall have no refined dislike for certain kinds of service. We do not pick and choose what we think is worthy of our doing. We do service in the Spirit of Christ—by that I mean service that shall have in it the true quality of Christian sacrifice and offering on the one altar of the cross. There is but one great man in all creation—he who does not know he is great, but who is swallowed up in the love of God and the consequent desire to cleanse the lives of men. In what spirit are we working? Is our Christianity "Lord, what will you have me to do?" Do we covet the honors, but leave others to do the drudgery? Or is the drudgery the honor, the deeper the higher, the lower the diviner? Do you follow Jesus' example? No man then shall take your crown.

JOSEPH PARKER

"If you know these things, blessed are you if you do them."

John 13:17 NKJV

The blessing of God's Word is only to be known and enjoyed by obeying it: "If you love Me, keep My commandments" (John 14:15 NKJV). Keeping His Word is the only proof of a genuine saving knowledge of God, of not being self-deceived in our faith, of God's love being experientially known and not merely imagined. Those who obey His commands live in Him, and He in them. Keeping the commandments is the secret of confidence toward God and intimate fellowship with Him.

Our profession of love is worthless until it is proven true by the keeping of His commandments in the power of a life born in God. Knowing God, being born of Him, having the love of God perfected in us, having boldness in God, and abiding in Him—all these depend on one thing: our keeping the commandments.

When we realize the prominence Christ and Scripture give to this truth, we will desire to give it the same prominence in our life. It will become one of the keys to successful Bible study. The person who reads his Bible with longing and determination to learn and to obey every commandment of God is on the right path to receiving all the blessing the Word is meant to bring. He will learn two things in particular: the need to wait for the Holy Spirit to lead him to do God's will, and the blessedness of performing daily responsibilities not only because they are right but also because they are the will of God.

Make a determined effort to grasp what this life of full obedience means. Embrace Christ's clearest commands. "Love one another as I have loved you" (John 15:12 NKJV); "Wash one another's feet" (John 13:14 NKJV); "Do as I have done to you" (John 13:15 NKJV), and practice Christlike love and humility as the law of the supernatural life you are called to live.

ANDREW MURRAY

After he had said this, Jesus was troubled in spirit and testified, "Very truly I tell you, one of you is going to betray me."

John 13:21

Jesus had just washed Judas's feet, as He had the other disciples'. There is the love touch. Jesus was giving them all the tenderest touch yet of His love, to hold them. The personal touch is the tenderest. Man yearns for the personal touch—of presence, of lips, and of hands. Something seems to go through the personal touch from heart to heart. The spirit-currents find their connection so. Jesus gave the tender, personal touch that evening, the closest yet. His hands touched their feet, but He was not thinking most about their feet. He was reaching past their feet for their hearts.

And they felt it so. Their hearts understood, if their heads didn't yet. Judas felt those hands reaching to touch his heart. And he had to set himself afresh to resist that touch. John felt it and remained steady. Peter felt it and came back with tears. The fleeing nine felt that touch and yielded to it as they penitently returned. Love won. That personal touch did it.

But Jesus feels Judas's heart hardening as He touches his feet, and the gentle word already spoken did not avail (see John 13:18). Now His great heart is deeply troubled for Judas. He tries once again to reach his heart and stop his wayward feet. Quietly, but with tactful indirectness, Jesus lets Judas know that He knows. He says, "One of you is going to betray me."

The men stare at one another in questioning astonishment. Peter touches John's arm and with eye and word quietly asks him to find out. John asks Jesus the question in undertones and as quietly, Jesus makes His reply. Then the last appeal is made to Judas in the final delicate touch of special personal attention. Judas's unchanged spirit is his wordless answer. The hardening of purpose is a further opening of the downward door, and that door is quickly used by the evil one.

Judas arises abruptly with jaw set and eye tense, and goes out into the blackest night the clouds had ever shut in. So the first tremendous part of the evening's drama is now done. The wooing of Judas has been intense and tender right up to the last moment, and resisted. The extremes have parted. One man has gone out. Eleven stay in, and in staying come closer to the heart of Jesus.

S. D. GORDON

*His disciples stared at one another, at a loss to know
which of them he meant.*

John 13:22

E very man is a mystery to himself as to his fellows. With reverence, we
may say of one another as we say of God: "Clouds and thick darkness surround Him" (Psalm 97:2). After all the manifestations of a
life, we remain riddles to one another, mysteries to ourselves; for no man is
fixed, but a growing personality, with dormant possibilities of good and evil
lying within, which up to the last moment of life may flame up in unexpected
developments. We all must feel that after self-examination there lie possibilities within us that we have not fathomed; and after all our knowledge of one
another, we yet do see but the surface; each soul dwells alone.

There is in every heart a dark chamber. There are very few of us who dare
tell all our thoughts and show our inmost selves to the dearest ones. The
most silvery lake that lies sleeping amid beauty, itself the very fairest spot
of all, when drained shows ugly ooze and mud and all manner of creeping
abominations. I wonder what we should see if our hearts were, so to speak,
drained and the very bottom layer of everything brought into the light? Do
you think you would like it? Do you think you could stand it?

Well, then, go to God and ask Him to keep you from unconscious sins. Go
to Him and ask Him to root out of you the mischiefs that you do not know
are there, and live humbly and self-distrustfully, and feel that your only hope
is "Search me, O God, and know my heart" (Psalm 139:23 NKJV).

Trust Christ! And so your soul shall no longer be like "the sea that cannot
rest," full of turbulent wishes, full of passionate desires that come to nothing, full of endless moanings, like the restless ocean that is ever working and
never flings up any product of its work but foam and weeds. Rather, your
heart shall become translucent and still, like some landlocked lake, where no
winds rage nor tempests ruffle; and on its calm surface there shall be mirrored the clear shining of the unclouded blue and the perpetual light of the
sun that never goes down.

ALEXANDER MACLAREN

Now there was leaning on Jesus' bosom one of His disciples, whom Jesus loved.

John 13:23 NKJV

There are some believers, such as John, who know Jesus' love more than others, live in it more than others, drink of it more than others, reflect it more than others, and become more conformed to it and saturated with it and perfumed with it, than others are. John was full of tenderness, and therefore, his Master at once selected him to be His dearest friend. You know the way, then, to the heart of Christ—let your own heart be full of love, and you will know His love. For the special manifestation of that love, for your personal enjoyment of it, to fit you for such enjoyment, you must have much love to Him. You greatly need, not a great head, but a great heart. You must have not more knowledge, but more affection. Less of self and more of Jesus, and then you shall enjoy more of His love.

This being the case, that John had this loving spirit, it led to the fact that John was the recipient of privileges from Christ that others did not have. This special love brings us into the privilege of nearness and endearment and intimacy with Christ. There was a gracious confidence and great liberty given to John in thus leaning where no head of king or emperor might aspire to rise. He was the most honored of all human beings, for the Lord himself gave him access with boldness. Great love has privileges that make her boldest advances no intrusion. Love has the key to all the rooms of the Father's house. Love may read the very heart of God. If His love is with you, you shall know what prophets and kings desired to know and what angels desire to look into.

Jesus seeks to reach our hearts. Let us pluck up courage to draw near to Him, to lean on the bosom of the Christ of God who loves us and has given himself for us. Believe me, at this moment we can have such intimate enjoyment of the love of Jesus, that even if He were here and we could lean our heads upon His bosom, the endearment could not be more certain, more sweet, or more ravishing to our delighted souls. There is an intimate communion that is one of the private privileges of those whom Jesus loves much. I hope you know this choice blessing of living in the immediate enjoyment of your Savior's love. May you never lose it!

CHARLES SPURGEON

"A new command I give you: Love one another. As I have loved you, so you must love one another."

John 13:34

The Lord Jesus told His disciples that as the Father had loved Him, even so He loved them. And now, following His example, we must love one another with the same love. "By this everyone will know that you are my disciples, if you love one another" (John 13:35). He had prayed: "that all of them may be one, Father, just as you are in me and I am in you" (John 17:21). If we exhibit the love that was in God toward Christ, and in Christ to us, the world will be obliged to confess that our Christianity is genuine and from above.

This is what actually happened. The Greeks and Romans, Jews and Gentiles, hated one another. Among all the nations of the world there was hardly a thought of love to one another. The very idea of self-sacrifice was a strange one. When the heathen saw that Christians from different nations, under the powerful workings of the Holy Spirit, became one and loved one another, even to the point of self-sacrifice in time of plague or illness, they were amazed and said, "Behold how these people love one another."

Among professing believers there is a certain oneness of belief and feeling of brotherhood, but Christ's heavenly love is often lacking, and we fail to bear one another's burdens or to love others from the heart.

Pray that you may love your fellow believers with the same love with which Christ has loved you. If we abide in Christ's love, and let that love fill our hearts, supernatural power will be given us to take all God's children into our hearts in love. As close as is the bond of love between the Father and the Son, between Christ and His followers, so close must the bond of love be between all of God's children.

ANDREW MURRAY

"By this everyone will know that you are my disciples, if you love one another."

John 13:35

We are taught in most of our creeds that the true church is to be found where God's Word is rightly preached and the holy sacraments dispensed as instituted by Christ. Christ himself took a much broader view. Not merely what the church teaches through her ministers was, to Him, the distinguishing mark of His followers, but a life lived in love for our brothers and sisters.

It is most important that we should understand this. In God, love reaches its highest point and is the culmination of His glory. In the man Christ Jesus on the cross, love is at its highest. We owe everything to this love. Love is the power that moved Christ to die for us. In love, God highly exalted Him as Lord and Christ. Love is the power that broke our hearts, and love is the power that heals them. Love is the power through which Christ dwells in us and works in us. Love can change my whole nature and enable me to surrender all to God. It gives me strength to live a holy, joyous life, full of blessing to others. Every believer should show forth, as in a mirror, the love of God.

Alas, how seldom do Christians realize this! They seek to love Christ and the brethren in the power of human love. And then they fail. They are sure it is impossible to lead such a life, and they do not even greatly desire it or pray for it. They do not understand that we may and can love with God's own love, which is poured into our hearts by the Holy Spirit.

Oh, that this great truth might possess us: "God's love has been poured out into our hearts through the Holy Spirit, who has been given to us" (Romans 5:5). If we fully believe that the Holy Spirit, dwelling within us, will maintain this heavenly love from hour to hour, we shall be able to understand the word of Christ: "Everything is possible for one who believes" (Mark 9:23), and to love God and Christ with all our hearts; and, what is even harder, to love our brothers and sisters, and even our enemies, while love flows from us as a stream of living water through the Holy Spirit.

ANDREW MURRAY

Simon Peter said to Him, "Lord, where are You going?"
Jesus answered him, "Where I am going you cannot
follow Me now, but you shall follow Me afterward."

John 13:36 NKJV

This is the second time in this chapter that Jesus has said the same thing
to the impatient Simon Peter. So Peter was constantly told to wait till the
hour when he should have the keener vision and understanding mind.
Peter was a man who wanted everything done the moment the desire was
expressed. The Lord, knowing this, always said to him, "Not now," that most
vexing reply. We want it *now*; we want to know *why* now; it seems to us the
very time to have it; and He quietly says, "Not now." He speaks sovereignly
as from a throne; there is no uncertainty in His tone. This is a grand doctrine;
who can receive it? It has to be drilled into us; patience of this kind is not
born in us. Blessed be God, we can be humbled to receive the doctrine that
afterward is greater than *now*, and that not to have an afterward is to be
imprisoned and impoverished.

There cannot be an afterward of revelation without a now of obedience.
To obey in the darkness is a test of growth in grace. Who then has grown in
grace? The man who says, "Though he slay me, yet will I trust Him" (Job
13:15 NKJV). That is faith. I want to be able to say, "Though the fig tree may
not blossom, nor fruit be on the vines . . . yet I will rejoice in the LORD"
(Habakkuk 3:17–18 NKJV). That is maturity in the life divine, and that is the
lesson that we learn now; the afterward is not in that particular lesson: it
is the agony, the stinging fire of the immediate moment. This growth is the
miracle of God; this is the ideal attainment. We are bound to keep it steadily
before our dazzling eyes; we count not ourselves to have attained; far from
it, but this one thing we do—we press toward the mark.

Obedience now is revelation afterward. We shall know, if we follow on to
know. Obedience prepares the mind for revelation, takes from that revelation
the light that dazzles the spirit's vision and prepares the heart to receive wider
demonstrations of the grace of God. There is marvelous grace in a gradual
revelation. If "the path of the just is like the shining sun, that shines ever
brighter unto the perfect day" (Proverbs 4:18 NKJV), it is because our spiritual
education is so priceless.

JOSEPH PARKER

Peter said to Him, "Lord . . . I will lay down my life for Your sake."

John 13:37 NKJV

Peter meant it, every word of it. But the moments of intense enthusiasm and the calls to martyrdom do not always coincide. In the upper room, with its sacred atmosphere, it was easy to feel and would have been easy to do, nobly. But it was not so easy huddled up by the fire at the lower end of the hall in the gray morning, when his energy was at its lowest. The sincere but impulsive utterance lifted Peter for a moment, but we forget that however high, noble, or divinely inspired an utterance may be, the nature of our emotions is transient. Feelings can be a substitute for action. Is it not so remarkable that the word *benevolence*—"kindly feeling"—has come to take on the meaning belonging to *beneficence*—"kindly doing." The emotional believer blinds himself by thinking that his lofty enthusiasm is the same as, or as good as, action.

God forbid that I should seem to deprecate spiritual emotion! It is the thing we need to see more of in our churches, not less. We should see stronger impulses, swifter, more spontaneous worship. Let us be compelled by these and not merely by the reluctant recognition that such and such a sacrifice or effort is a debt that we are obliged to pay. Our service will be glad service, only when it is moved by love and devotion. A Christian whose life is not influenced by the deepest and most fervent emotion of love to the great Love who died for him is a contradiction.

The lesson to be taken from this incident is not the danger of emotion, but rather the necessity of it, but with two provisions. First, it shall be emotion based upon a clear recognition of the great truth that He has laid down His life for me; and second, that it shall be emotion harnessed to work and not wasted in words. Do not be afraid of emotion; you will make little of your Christianity unless you have it. But be sure that it is under the guidance of a clear perception of the truth that arouses it. Emotion is a good servant, but a bad master. Convert impulses and emotions into steadfast principle, warmed by and borne on impulse.

ALEXANDER MACLAREN

Jesus answered him, "Will you lay down your life for
My sake? Most assuredly, I say to you, the rooster shall
not crow till you have denied Me three times."

John 13:38 NKJV

We cannot say that Peter's fall was at all an uncommon thing. He did exactly what a great many of us are doing. Though he draws a sword for Jesus at the time of the arrest, he could not stand being ridiculed by a servant girl. We all find ourselves with people and in situations in which to be recognized as a Christian will be equated with bigotry, intolerance, or being backward, and all of us have sometimes to gather our courage and not be afraid to declare whose we are. No doubt life is a better witness than words, but no doubt life is also not so good a witness as it might be, unless it sometimes has the commentary of words as well. Thus, to confess Christ means two things: to say—in the face of a smile of scorn or something far more serious—"I am His," and to live Christ and to say by our conduct "I am His." Live Jesus, and, when advisable, preach Jesus.

But Peter's fall, which is typical of what we are all tempted to do, has in it a gracious message; for it proclaims the possibility of recovery from any depth of descent and of coming back again from any distance of wandering. He never forgot his denial, and it remained with him as the expression of all that is wrong in one's relationship to Jesus Christ. And I suppose not only was it burned upon his memory, but it burned out all his *self*-confidence.

And do you not think that his fall drew him closer to Jesus Christ than ever he had been before, as he learned more of His pardoning love and mercy? Was he not nearer the Lord on that morning when the two together, alone, talked after the resurrection? Was he not nearer Him when he struggled to his feet from the boat on the lake, on that morning when he was received back into his office as Christ's apostle (see John 21)? Did he ever forget how he had sinned? Did he ever forget how Christ had pardoned him? Did he ever forget how Christ loved him and would keep him? Of course not! The rope that is broken is strongest where it is spliced, not because it was broken, but because a cunning hand has strengthened it. We may be the stronger for our sins, not because sin strengthens, for it weakens, but because God restores us. It is possible that we may turn every field of defeat into a field of victory.

ALEXANDER MACLAREN

"Let not your heart be troubled; you believe in God, believe also in Me."

John 14:1 NKJV

We cannot understand the opening of the fourteenth chapter unless we read it in immediate connection with the close of the thirteenth. Peter had declared that he did not understand where Jesus was going, and Jesus had just told Peter that he would deny Him. "Let"—notwithstanding all cowardice and uncertainty—"not your heart be troubled; you believe in God, believe also in Me," and wait with sweet prayerful patience until the dawn; when the light comes, all things will be seen as they are.

Jesus says the Christian heart is not to be troubled because "in My Father's house are many mansions . . . I go to prepare a place for you. And if I go and prepare a place for you, I will come again and receive you to Myself; that where I am, there you may be also" (vv. 2–3 NKJV). The plain meaning of that is never-ending fellowship in permanent residence together. Not only are believers the constant objects of Jesus Christ's most zealous and tender care, but they are to be eternally His joy and delight.

Seeing that believers shall be forever with the Lord, they are entitled to look at the present through the medium of the future. The more we can bring the power of His eternal love to bear upon the passing moments, we can look into the things that are seen and at the things that are not seen with peace in our hearts. We lay the hands of our expectant love on the golden bars of heaven and draw ourselves forward thereby. With visions of God's eternity and Christ's blessed immortality, we step onward through all the care and sorrow and bitterness and unrest of time by loving, intelligent anticipation of eternity.

Yes, Jesus is waiting for us. He will open the door presently, and we shall go straight in. And the prepared place will be worthy of himself. Jesus Christ says, "I have made worlds, stars, and planets. Now I am going to get a place ready for those whom I have bought with my blood." What kind of place will He get ready for us, who has all things at His command—when He can speak light and command worlds to fashion themselves and shine upon His children? If He has loved us with unutterable love, He will enrich us with inconceivable glory. "Eye has not seen, nor ear heard, nor have entered into the heart of man the things which God has prepared for those who love Him" (1 Corinthians 2:9 NKJV)!

JOSEPH PARKER

*"In My Father's house are many mansions; if it were
not so, I would have told you. I go to prepare a place
for you."*

John 14:2 NKJV

L et us thankfully consider how, in the profound language of Scripture,
in some mysterious manner of which we can but dimly conceive, Christ
in His complete humanity has entered into the highest heavens and is
preparing a place for us. As if, without His presence there, there could be no
entrance for human nature within that state, and no power in a human foot
to tread upon the crystal pavements of the Celestial City; but as if, where He
is, there the path is wide open and the place a true home to all who love and
trust Him.

Stand, therefore, with His disciples, as they gazed upon their ascended Savior, and looking upward as the cloud receives Him out of our sight (see Acts
1:9), our faith follows Him, still our Brother, still clothed with humanity, still
wearing a bodily frame; and we say, as we lose Him from our vision, "What
is man?" He is capable of being lifted to the most intimate participation in
the glories of divinity, and though he be poor and weak and sinful here, he is
capable of union and assimilation with the Majesty that is on high. For what
Christ's body is, the bodies of them who love and serve Him shall surely be,
and He, the Forerunner, is entered there for us, that we, too, in our turn, may
pass into the light and walk in the full blaze of the divine glory, as of old the
children in the furnace were unconsumed, because they were together with
the One who "is like the Son of God" (Daniel 3:25 NKJV).

The exalted Christ, sitting at the right hand of God, is the pattern of what
is possible for humanity, and the promise of what will be actual for all who
love Him and bear the image of Him upon earth that they may be conformed
to the image of His glory and be with Him where He is (see 1 John 3:2). What
firmness, what reality, what solidity this thought of the bodily exalted Christ
gives to the otherwise dim and vague conception of a heaven beyond the stars
and beyond our present experience! I believe that no doctrine of a future
life has strength and substance enough to survive the agonies of our hearts
when we part from our dear ones, the fears of our spirits when we look into
the unknown future for ourselves, except this: heaven is Christ and Christ is
heaven. "Where He is, there also shall His servants be."

ALEXANDER MACLAREN

Jesus said to him, "I am the way, the truth, and the life.
No one comes to the Father except through Me."

John 14:6 NKJV

The main idea in these three profound words is the first "I am the way," which is made certain because the last words dwell only upon the metaphor of the "way"—"No one comes to the Father except through Me." We are to regard the "truth" and the "life" as explanatory of the "way." He is saying, "I am the way to the Father because I am the truth and the life."

Note, then, as belonging to all three of these clauses that remarkable "I am." We show a way; Christ is it. We speak truth; Christ is it. We receive life; Christ is it. He separates himself from all men by the representation that He is not merely the communicator or the teacher or the guide, but that He himself is, in His own personal Being, the way, the truth, and the life.

And then note, further, that He sets forth His unique relation to the truth as being one ground on which He is the way to God. He is the truth in reference to the divine nature. It is not only His speech that teaches truth, but His whole life and character are the truest and highest representation within human conditions of the invisible God that men can ever have. In Him alone, men find foundational truths of a moral, ethical, and spiritual sort.

Further, He is the way because He is the life. Christ taught that men apart from Him are dead, and the only life they can have is the divine life that is in Him. The only way He could give His life to us was by giving up His physical life for us. Because He communicates life to our spirits by which we are knit to God, He is the only way to the Father.

Dear friend, see that you seek the Father by Him alone. He is truth; clasp Him to your heart and by patient meditation and continual faithfulness, enrich yourself with all the treasures you have already received from Him. He is your life; cleave to Him, that the life-giving Spirit may make you victors over death, temporal and eternal. Know Him as a Friend, not as a mere historical person or with mere head knowledge, for to know a friend is something far deeper than to know a truth.

ALEXANDER MACLAREN

Jesus said to him, "Have I been with you so long, and yet you have not known Me, Philip? He who has seen Me has seen the Father."

John 14:9 NKJV

In these words we have a glimpse into the pained and loving heart of our Lord. We seldom hear Him speak about His own feelings; and when He does, it is always in some such incidental way as this. So that these glimpses, like little windows opening out upon some great vista, are the more precious to us.

We shall not misunderstand the tone of this question to Philip if we see in it wonder, pained love, and tender complaint. "Have I been with you so long . . . ?" In another place we read, "He marveled because of their unbelief" (Mark 6:6 NKJV). And here there is almost surprise that He should have been so long with them and so near, and yet their eyes should have seen so little.

But there is more than that—there is the pain of vainly endeavoring to teach, to help, and to love. And there are few pains like that. All who have tried to help and bless their fellow men have known what it is to have their compassion and their efforts rejected. There are few sorrows heavier to carry than a heart that would pour its love into another if that one would only let it, but is repelled. If ever you have had a child or a friend or a dear one whom you have tried to get to receive your love, and who has thrown it back in your face, you may know in some faint measure what was at least one of the elements that made Him the "Man of sorrows and acquainted with grief" (Isaiah 53:3 NKJV).

But there is not only the pain caused by slow apprehension and unrequited love, but also the depth and patience of a love that is not turned away by the pain. How tenderly the name *Philip* comes with a whole world of feeling and appeal. We may think of that patient love of His that will not be soured by any slowness or lack of response. Held back by our sullen rejection, it still flows on, seeking to conquer by long-suffering. Refused, it still lingers at the closed door of the heart and knocks for entrance. Misunderstood, it still meekly manifests itself. The same feelings of pain and patient love are in the heart of the enthroned Christ today. Mystery and paradox as it may be, I suppose there passes over even His victorious and serene repose in the heavens some shadow of pain and sorrow when you and I turn away from Him.

ALEXANDER MACLAREN

"Anyone who has seen me has seen the Father."

John 14:9

What has Christ done for men that men could not have done for themselves? He has revealed the Father. Clearly, as far as human conditions made it possible, He visibly embodied the Father. He also made the Father universally understandable: "My teaching is not my own. It comes from the one who sent me" (John 7:16). And Jesus made the Father universally accessible: "For through him we both have access to the Father by one Spirit" (Ephesians 2:18). The first revelation carries with it the remaining two, for if Christ made the Father visible, it follows from the necessity of the terms that He also made the Father understandable and accessible in exactly the degree in which He himself could be understood and approached. We are not to insist on a literal visibleness, for that is impossible, but on a manifestation so distinct and unique as to justify the declaration, "Anyone who has seen me has seen the Father."

I propose a new use of these words, as illustrative of the whole life of Christ: "Anyone who has seen me healing the sick and feeding the hungry has seen the Father doing these things. The invisible care of God has been exercised from the beginning, but now you see it in this action of mine. What you now see is but a revelation of that which God in secret has never ceased to do! Anyone who has seen me teaching the crowds and offering the weary rest has seen the Father doing these very things. From His habitation in eternity He has been doing so ever since He made man to possess the earth. This, therefore, is no new act, no new love, no changed affection; it is the invisible revealed to your eyes! Anyone who has seen me seeking and saving the lost, receiving sinners and forgiving sins, has seen the Father so doing; and anyone who has seen me sorrowful unto death, surrendering my own will, taking upon myself the form of a servant and becoming obedient unto death, even the death of the cross, has seen what the Father has been and has done through all time!"

The things of the Father that had been hidden from eternity, and which had been the secret and mystery of the universe, have thus been revealed in Christ's earthly ministry. So "do not let your hearts be troubled. You believe in God; believe also in me" (John 14:1).

JOSEPH PARKER

"Believe Me that I am in the Father and the Father in Me."

John 14:11 NKJV

The disciples did believe in God. They should believe in Jesus just as implicitly. This is the warp into which is woven the whole fabric of that evening's talk in the upper room. The whole talk is a plea for their trusting and loving acceptance of himself as fully God. The word *believe* changes shape three times during that evening, but it's always the same underneath. Note that Jesus brings out the word *believe* four times in verses 10–12.

Then by a subtle turn He changes the word, though not the thing, to help them understand better: "If you love Me" (v. 15). That puts the thing at once upon the *heart* level. Believing is a thing of the heart. Their heads were bothered and confused. He said in effect, "All your head questions will be answered in good time, but this thing is higher than that. It's a matter of your heart." And so the word *believe* becomes *love*, its second shape. And with that is quickly coupled *obey*, the third shape He gives the word *believe* that night: "Keep My commandments" (v. 15).

It is all the same thing underneath. *Love* is the heart side of *believe*, the inner side. *Obey* is the life side of *believe*, the outer, the action side. Love looks out the window of life and then comes out and walks down the street on an errand. Love doesn't simply love: it loves *someone*. Love that simply loves isn't love. Love comes to life only in the personal touch.

And love keeps in perfect rhythm of action with the one loved. That is another way of saying *obey*. Obedience is the music of two wills acting together. "*Believe* Me, *love* Me, *obey* Me"—this is the three-noted music of the upper room; three notes but one music.

In the verses that follow, Jesus says in effect, "I go to the Father. We, the Father and I, will send the Holy Spirit to you. He will come in through this opened door of obedience. He will abide in you, come in to stay. He will be everything and do everything that you need in every sort of circumstance. Keep in closest touch with Him: this is to be your one rule. Your part is simple. *Believe*; that means *love*; that means *obey*."

S. D. GORDON

"And whatever you ask in My name, that I will do, that the Father may be glorified in the Son."

John 14:13 NKJV

A name calls to mind the whole being and nature of a person or thing. When I speak of a lamb or a lion, the name at once suggests the nature peculiar to each. The name of God is meant to express His divine nature and glory. So also the name of Christ means His nature, His person and work, His disposition and Spirit. To ask in the name of Christ is to pray in union with Him.

As Christ's prayer nature lives in us, His prayer power becomes ours as well. The measure of our attainment or experience is not the ground of our confidence; it is the wholeheartedness of our surrender to all that Christ seeks to be in us. If we abide in Him, He says, we can ask whatever we desire.

As we live in Him, we receive the spiritual power to avail ourselves of His name. As the branch wholly surrendered to the life and service of the vine can count upon its sap and strength for its fruit, so the believer who in faith has accepted the fullness of the Spirit to possess his whole life, benefits from the power of Christ's name.

Christ came to earth as a man to reveal what true prayer is. To pray in the name of Christ, we must pray as He prayed. He taught us to pray in union with Him. Let us in love, and faith, accept Him as our example, our teacher, and our intercessor.

As Christ did, we must make it our primary effort to receive from the Father. No time or trouble will be too great to serve others by prayer and intercession.

Be of good courage as servants of Christ and children of God. Let no weakness or lack cause you to fear—simply ask in the name of Christ. His name has all the power of Christ himself. His promise stands: "If you ask anything in My name, I will do it" (John 14:14 NKJV).

ANDREW MURRAY

"And I will ask the Father, and He will give you another
Helper (Comforter, Advocate, Intercessor—Counselor,
Strengthener, Standby), to be with you forever."

John 14:16 AMP

The unspeakable gift of the Son of God was followed up by the equally priceless gift of the Holy Spirit. Unfortunately, most of us think far less of the Holy Spirit than we should. While we often exalt the Savior and make Him the subject of our thoughts, we give the Holy Spirit a very disproportionate place. I fear that we may even grieve the Spirit by our neglect of Him.

All that Jesus was, the Spirit of God is now to the church. If there is any power in the church of today, it is because the Holy Spirit is in the midst of the church. If the church is able to work any spiritual miracles, if there is any light in her instruction, if there is any glory given to God, if there is any good accomplished among the sons of men, it is entirely because the Holy Spirit is still with her. We shall do well to treat the Holy Spirit as we would have treated Christ were He yet among us.

Let the Spirit of God reveal God to you as the everlasting Father who loved you before the world was, as the unchanging God who can never turn His heart from you; and can you do otherwise than rejoice with exceedingly great joy? Let the Spirit of God reveal to you the pierced hands and feet of Jesus, let Him enable you to put your finger into the prints of the nails and touch the wounds of His feet and lay your heart to His heart. If you still have no peace, you are a melancholy miracle of perverse despondency. But you must have rest when you have Jesus Christ, and such a rest that Jesus calls it "my peace," the very peace that is in the heart of Christ, the unruffled serenity of the conquering Savior, who has finished forever the work that God gave Him to do. What rich comfort is this that the Counselor brings to us!

If there is not a miraculous spiritual power in the church of God today, the church is an impostor. At this moment, the only vindication of our existence is the presence and work of the Spirit among us. By her fruits shall the church be proven to be a tree of life to the nations.

CHARLES SPURGEON

"The Spirit of truth. The world cannot accept him, because it neither sees him nor knows him. But you know him, for he lives with you and will be in you."

John 14:17

The Spirit of truth is the teacher of truth—pure truth, practical, divinely effective truth. He never teaches anything but the truth. He takes the things of Christ and shows them to us. He is the very Spirit and soul of truth, the essence, life, and power of it. Divine truth, when merely heard, has no effect upon the mind until the Spirit of God gives it life, and then it becomes a quickening force. He makes the truth itself to enter the soul and affect the heart, making the truth to be truth to us in the assurance of our inmost souls.

He is the Spirit of truth in this sense, too, that He works truthfulness in His people. "There is no guile" in those with whom the Holy Spirit works effectually; they are open-minded, honest, sincere, and true; they have an intense affection and passion for the truth. He works true conversion, sincere repentance, and saving faith, such as no sun of persecution can dry up and wither. He works a deep conviction of sin and simple faith in Jesus, and these abide in the heart. He produces real sanctification—not the pretense of perfection, but the reality of holiness. Everything the Spirit of God does is substance and not shadow. Much of what excites the church is only the work of man, but the eternal, abiding, everlasting work of grace is wrought by the Spirit of truth alone.

The divine communications of the Spirit are the precious heritage of true saints, but they are a peculiar voice to their own souls. If you know these divine workings, then through His operations you are made to know the Holy Spirit. That deep calm, that peace that only He can give, that exhilaration, that superlative joy as of heaven begun below that only the Lord can work, that steadfast courage, that holy patience, that fixedness of heart, that gentleness of manner and firmness of purpose, which only come from above—these all introduce you to the wonder-working Spirit who delights to work upon the minds of the heirs of eternal glory.

CHARLES SPURGEON

"But you know Him, for He dwells with you and will be in you."

John 14:17 NKJV

Divine strength has its seat in, and is intended to influence the whole of, the inner life. We are to be "strengthened with might through His Spirit in the inner man" (Ephesians 3:16 NKJV) or in "the hidden person of the heart" (1 Peter 3:4 NKJV). This only refers to the distinction that we all draw between the outward, visible, material frame, and the unseen self that gives it life. It is this inner self, then, in which the Spirit of God is to dwell and into which He is to breathe strength.

And the point to note is that the whole inward region that makes up the true person is the field upon which the divine Spirit is to work. It is not a corner of your inward life that is to be made holy; it is not any one aspect of it that is to be strengthened—but it is the whole intellect, affections, desires, tastes, powers of attention, memory, and will. The whole inner man in all its fullness is to be filled and to come under the influence of this power.

So for this divine Indweller there is no part of my life that is not welcome to His entrance. There are no rooms of the house of my spirit into which He is not to go. Let Him come with the master key in His hand into all the dark chambers of your feeble nature; and as life is light in the eye, and color in the cheek, and strength in the arm, and pulsation in the heart, so He will come and strengthen your understandings and make you able for loftier tasks of intellect and of reason than you can face in your unaided strength. He will dwell in your affections and make them strong to lay hold upon the holy things that are above their natural inclinations. And He will come into that feeble, vacillating, wayward will of yours, that is obstinate in its devotion to what is low and wrong; He will lift your will and make it fix upon the good and hate the evil, and through the whole being He will pour a great tide of strength that shall cover all the weakness. As some plant, drooping beneath the hot rays of the sun, when it has received a soaking splash of cool, clean water, will, in all its being, energize itself and stand up, so this divine Spirit will search every corner of the inner man, illuminating and invigorating all.

ALEXANDER MACLAREN

"Because I live, you will live also."
John 14:19 NKJV

Time forbids me to dwell upon that majestic proclamation of His own absolute and divine life, from lips that were so soon to be paled with death. Mark the grand "I live"—the timeless present tense, which expresses unbroken, underived, undying, and, as I believe, divine life. The depth and sweep of its meaning are given to us in this apostle's Apocalypse, where Christ is called "He who lives, and was dead, and behold, I am alive forevermore" (Revelation 1:18 NKJV). And this Christ, coming to all His friends, possessor of the fullness of life in himself is Life-giver to all who love Him and trust Him.

We live because He lives. In all senses of the word *life*, the life of men is derived from the Christ who is the Agent of creation, the channel from whom life passes from the Godhead into the creatures, and who is also the one means by whom any of us can ever hope to live the better life that consists in fellowship with God and union to Him.

We shall live as long as He lives, and His being is the pledge and the guarantee of the immortal being of all who love Him. The great promise of our text assures us that the worshiper is to live as long as does He whom He adores. We shall live as He lives, nor ever cease the appropriation of His being until all His life we know, and all its fullness has expanded our natures—and that will be never. Therefore we shall not die.

Without Jesus Christ, we are orphans in a fatherless world. Without Him, our wearied and yet unsatisfied eyes have only trifles and trials and trash to look at. Without Him, we are dead while we live. He and He only can give us back a Father and renew in us the spirit of sons. He and only He can satisfy our eyes with the sight that is purity and restfulness and joy. He and He only can breathe life into our death. Oh, let Him do it for you! He comes to us with all these gifts in His hands, for He comes to give us himself, and in himself are all that lonely hearts and wearied eyes and dead souls can ever need. All are yours, if you are Christ's. All are yours, if He is yours. And He is yours, if by faith and love you make yourself His and Him your own.

ALEXANDER MACLAREN

"Whoever [really] loves Me will be loved by My Father, and I will love him and reveal Myself to him [I will make Myself real to him]."

John 14:21 AMP

The Lord Jesus gives special revelations of himself to His people, and there are many children of God who testify the truth of it from their own experience. They have had manifestations of Jesus Christ in a peculiar manner, such as no mere reading or hearing could afford. In the biographies of many saints, you will find numerous instances recorded in which Jesus has been pleased, in a very special manner, to speak to their souls and to unfold the wonders of His person. Yes, some have had their souls so permeated in happiness that they have thought themselves to be in heaven—for when Jesus manifests himself to His people, it is heaven on earth. Yes, and it shall be the consummation of that bliss when Jesus Christ shall perfectly unveil himself to the admiring eyes of all His people, and they shall be like Him and shall see Him as He is!

How does the Father reveal Jesus to us? Some of you may have seen Jesus with the eyes of faith quite as plainly as if you had seen Him with your natural eyes. You could see your Savior hanging on the cross. You heard His cry. You beheld the nails. You could have wrapped Him up in linen and spices and carried His body and washed it with tears and anointed it with precious ointment. At other times, you may have seen that mighty sacrifice He offered and the justifying righteousness He has put upon you.

These special manifestations of Christ exercise a holy influence on the believer's heart. One effect will be humility. If a man says, "Because I have had such-and-such spiritual communications, I am a great man," he has never had any communion with Jesus at all; for God "regards the lowly; but the proud He knows from afar" (Psalm 138:6 NKJV). He will never give them any visits of love. Another effect will be happiness; for in God's presence, there are pleasures forevermore. Holiness will be sure to follow. A man who has not holiness has never had this manifestation. Some men profess a great deal, but we must not believe anyone unless we see that his deeds answer to what he says. "Do not be deceived, God is not mocked" (Galatians 6:7 NKJV). He will not bestow His favors upon the wicked: for while He will not cast away a perfect man, neither will He respect an evildoer. Thus there will be three effects of nearness to Jesus—humility, happiness, and holiness. May God give them to you!

CHARLES SPURGEON

"And he who loves Me will be loved by My Father, and I will love him and manifest Myself to him. . . . If anyone loves Me, he will keep My word; and My Father will love him, and We will come to him and make Our home with him."

John 14:21, 23 NKJV

Here is a promise of divine manifestation to the human mind and of divine indwelling in the human heart. So, then, God may be in the heart as a gracious Father; His presence need not be as a coldly glittering star away in the inaccessible heights, but as a summer working in the life all the delights of intermingling colors and covering the soul with abundant fruitfulness. Thus we have distinctly set before us the highest possibility in spiritual life—the possibility of being temples of the Holy Spirit, of having fellowship with the Father and with His Son Jesus Christ, and of being made partakers of the divine nature. When the spirit of holiness is in a man, his whole life will be made holy thereby; the spirit of holiness that is in him will lead him into truth, into purity, into the very holiness of the all-holy God. This thought should silence the clamor of all earthly appeal to our affections and give us the true idea of our potential character as children of God. We can do the daily business of life, yet through it all can have shining upon us the most holy and transfiguring image of the Son of Man. Our feet may be in the dust, but we may carry with us Him whose name is Wonderful Counselor, the Mighty God.

"If anyone loves Me, he will keep My word." We must begin with love, the love that comes of earnest desire to know that which is heavenly, and then, in due time, will come a still tenderer affection. We must get to the point of love. All our self-sufficiency, all our high notions and mighty imaginings, must be cast away as things unclean and unsatisfying, and then we shall see the Father. "Blessed are the pure in heart, for they shall see God" (Matthew 5:8 NKJV). Love is the brightest purity. Purity is the divinest love. I cannot tell you how wondrously God reveals himself to love! He can never do enough for it. It moves Him to lavish upon us unsearchable riches. Nor is love on our part a fixed quantity; we may grow in love forever, constantly going out after God, never exhausting His grace, yet ever increasing in capacity to receive it. Blessed is our life—blessed is our peace—blessed is our hope. Daily we draw ourselves through the discipline of earth by the inspiring expectation of heaven, and by the sweetness of grace we overcome the bitterness of sin.

JOSEPH PARKER

*"But the Advocate, the Holy Spirit, whom the Father
will send in my name, will teach you all things and will
remind you of everything I have said to you."*

John 14:26

The personality of the Holy Spirit is seen in the many actions ascribed to the Spirit that are actions only a person can do. Paul tells the Corinthians that the Spirit is far more than a mere illumination to our minds concerning truth, He is a person who "searches all things, even the deep things of God" and "has revealed to us by his Spirit" the things that He discovers (1 Corinthians 2:10).

"In the same way, the Spirit helps us in our weakness. We do not know what we ought to pray for, but the Spirit himself intercedes for us through wordless groans" (Romans 8:26). Here the Holy Spirit is represented as doing what only a person can do, that is, praying. He is not merely an influence that comes upon us and urges us to pray, nor is He a mere guidance to us in offering our prayers. No, the Holy Spirit is praying for us and through us down here on earth.

"But the Advocate, the Holy Spirit, whom the Father will send in my name, will teach you all things and will remind you of everything I have said to you" (John 14:26). Here the Holy Spirit is represented as doing what only a person can do, namely, teaching. We have the same thought in John 16:12–14: "I have much more to say to you, more than you can now bear. But when he, the Spirit of truth, comes, he will guide you into all the truth. He will not speak on his own; he will speak only what he hears, and he will tell you what is yet to come. He will glorify me because it is from me that he will receive what he will make known to you." Again, the Holy Spirit is represented as a living, personal teacher to us.

Every time we study our Bible it is possible to have this divine person, the author of the Book, to interpret it to us, and to teach us its real and innermost meaning. It is a precious thought. How often have we thought that if only we could hear some great human teacher, we could make some progress in our spiritual life; but listen, we can have a teacher every day more competent by far than the greatest human teacher who ever spoke on earth, for that peerless teacher is the Holy Spirit.

R. A. TORREY

"But the Comforter (Counselor, Helper, Intercessor, Advocate, Strengthener, Standby), the Holy Spirit, Whom the Father will send in My name [in My place, to represent Me and act on My behalf], He will teach you all things."

John 14:26 AMP-CE

This age is peculiarly the dispensation of the Holy Spirit, in which Jesus cheers us, not by His personal presence, as He shall do by and by, but by the indwelling and constant abiding of the Holy Spirit, who is evermore the loving Comforter of the church. Do you know how much the Holy Spirit loves you? Can you measure the love of the Spirit toward you? Go, take the ocean's water and count each drop. Go count the sand upon the seashore—and when you have accomplished this, you can tell how much He loves you! He has loved you long, He has loved you well. He loved you always and He still shall love you. Surely He is the person to comfort you, because He loves you. Admit Him, then, to your heart, that He may comfort you in your troubles!

It is His office to console the hearts of God's people. He convinces of sin; He illuminates and instructs; but still the main part of His work lies in making glad the hearts of the renewed, in strengthening the weak, and lifting up all those who are bowed down. He does this by revealing Jesus to them. The Holy Spirit consoles, but Christ is the consolation. If we may use the figure, the Holy Spirit is the Physician, but Jesus is the medicine. He heals the wound, but it is by applying the holy ointment of Christ's name and grace. He takes not of His own things, but of the things of Christ.

So if we give to the Holy Spirit the Greek name of *Paraclete*, then our heart confers on our blessed Lord Jesus the title of *Paraclesis*. If the one is the Comforter, the other is the Comfort. Now, with such rich provision for our need, why should we be downhearted? The Holy Spirit has graciously engaged to be our Comforter: do we imagine that He will be negligent of His sacred trust? Can you suppose that He has undertaken what He cannot or will not perform? If it is His special work to strengthen and comfort you, do you suppose He will fail in the loving office that He sustains toward you? No, think not so hardly of the tender and blessed Spirit whose name is the Comforter. He delights to give the oil of joy for mourning and the garment of praise for the spirit of heaviness. Trust in Him, and He will surely comfort you till the house of mourning is closed forever and the marriage feast has begun.

CHARLES SPURGEON

"Peace I leave with you; my peace I give you."

John 14:27

Peace I leave with you" is much. "My peace I give you" is more. The added word tells the fathomless marvel of the gift—"my peace." Not merely "peace with God" (Romans 5:1); Christ has made it His peace by "making peace through his blood, shed on the cross" (Colossians 1:20), and being justified by faith we have it through Him. But after we are reconciled to God, the enmity and the separation having ended, Jesus has a gift for us from His own treasures; and this is its special and wonderful value, that it is His very own (see Ephesians 4:8). How we value a gift that was the giver's own possession! What a special token of intimate friendship we feel it to be! To others we give what we have made or purchased. It is only to very near and dear ones that we give what has been our own personal enjoyment or use. And so Jesus gives us not only peace made and peace purchased, but a share in His very own peace—divine, eternal, incomprehensible peace—that dwells in His own heart as God, and which shone in splendor of calmness through His life as man. No wonder it "transcends all understanding" (Philippians 4:7).

But how? Why does the sap flow from the vine to the branch? Simply because the branch is joined to the vine (see John 15:5). Then the sap flows into it by the very law of its nature. So, being joined to our Lord Jesus by faith, that which is His becomes ours and flows into us by the very law of our spiritual life. If there were no hindrance, our peace would indeed flow as a river (see Isaiah 48:18). Then how sincerely we should seek to have every barrier removed to the inflowing of such a gift! Let it be our prayer that He would clear the way for it, that He would take away all the unbelief, all the self, all the hidden cloggings of the channel.

Then He will give a sevenfold blessing: "my peace," "my joy," "my love," at once and always, now and forever; "my grace" and "my strength" for all the needs of our pilgrimage; "my rest" and "my glory" for all the grand sweet home life of eternity with Him.

FRANCES RIDLEY HAVERGAL

5

"Peace I leave with you, My peace I give to you; not as the world gives do I give to you."

John 14:27 NKJV

Jesus said that the disciples had to receive "the Spirit of truth, whom the world cannot receive, because it neither sees Him nor knows Him; but you know Him, for He dwells with you and will be in you. I will not leave you orphans; I will come to you" (vv. 17–18 NKJV). They were to become new men, the subjects of new desires; they were to be under new dominion, and yet to be set free; to have an increased liberty, and yet an ennobled discipline. Jesus promised them that He would not leave them as orphans or fatherless, but that He and His Father would come and dwell with them.

So Christ proceeds to speak to the heart, quietly, sympathetically, culminating in this benediction, "Peace I leave with you, My peace I give to you; not as the world gives do I give to you"—an expression that is rarely properly understood. "Not as the world gives" is not a reflection upon the manner in which the world gives, but a characteristic of the kind of things the world gives. "Not as the world gives"—gold and silver, horses and chariots, estates and social status. Jesus is saying, "I will not operate as the world operates. I give what the world cannot give—rest for your heart, the balm of tranquility, the jewel of peace." Thus He always separates himself from the world, and from all rivalry, and all attempt to approach Him along His own line.

Whenever men think they are going to do what Christ does, He steps away to the invisible height and leaves them cringing in the valley of darkness below. He will have no rivalry; He will not pluralize himself and be like other redeemers and gods; He is Christ by virtue of His uniqueness; "only begotten" marks Him off from all the tribes and families of men, but never prevents His coming down to them with fruit plucked from heaven's trees and water drawn from the river of God. When, therefore, we read about His not giving as the world gives, He is speaking not of manner but of quality, not of limitation but of contrast: the world can give gold, but not wisdom; the world can give estate, but not peace. Thus the world can never be a substitute for Christ; and the things the world gives can never make up for the things that Christ gives. The worldling and the Christian live in different universes.

JOSEPH PARKER

"I will no longer talk much with you, for the ruler of this world is coming, and he has nothing in Me."

John 14:30 NKJV

Note how the Master, with that clear eye that saw to the depths as well as the heights, and before which men and things were but, as it were, transparent media through which unseen spiritual powers worked, sees here—beneath Judas's treachery, the Pharisees' and priests' envy, and the people's indifference—the workings of a personal source and center of all. The "ruler of this world," who rules men and things when they are severed from God, "is coming." Christ's sensitive nature apprehends the approach of the evil thing, as meteorologists can tell when a thunderstorm is about to burst. His divine omniscience, working as it did, even within the limits of humanity, knows not only when the storm is about to burst upon Him, but knows who it is that has raised the tempest.

But more important, note that tremendous and unique consciousness of absolute invulnerability against the assault. "He has nothing in Me." In other words, "He is the ruler of the world, but he has no rule or authority in my life. His dominion is not recognized within that sacred realm." Was there ever a man who could say that? Are there any of us, the purest and the noblest, who, standing in front of the power of evil, dare to profess that there is not a thing in us on which he can lay his dark claw and say, "That is mine"? Is there nothing inflammable within us that the fiery darts of the wicked can kindle? Are there any of us who bar our doors so tightly that we can say that none of his seductions will find their way therein, and that nothing there will respond to them?

Christ sets himself here against the whole embodied power of evil when He calmly declares, "He has nothing in Me." It is an assertion of His absolute freedom from sin, and it involves the other assertion—that He is not subject to the consequence of sin, which is death. Thus, Jesus stands waiting for the enemy's charge, knowing that all its forces will be broken against His immaculate purity, and that He will come from the dreadful encounter triumphant forevermore.

But do not let us suppose that because there was not even a spot on Christ's heel into which the arrow could go, therefore the conflict was an unreal or shadowy one. It was a true fight, and it was a real struggle that He was anticipating, thus calmly in these solemn words, as knowing himself the coming Victor, He entered on the dreadful field.

ALEXANDER MACLAREN

"But that the world may know that I love the Father, and as the Father gave Me commandment, so I do. Arise, let us go from here."

John 14:31 NKJV

With His awareness that the enemy was approaching, Christ evidently rose to His feet while the disciples were still reclined around the table and bid them, "Arise, let us go from here." But there is more in the words than the mere close of a conversation and a summons to change of place. They indicate a kind of divine impatience to be in the fight and to have it over, the resolute advance to the conflict. The same emotion is plainly revealed in the whole of the latter days of our Lord's life. You remember how His disciples followed astonished as He strode up the road from Jericho, hastening to His cross (see Mark 10:32). You remember His deliberate purpose to draw upon himself public notice during that dangerous and explosive week before the Passover, as shown in the publicity of His entry into Jerusalem, His sharp rebukes of the rulers in the temple, and in every other incident of those days. You remember His words to the betrayer: "What you do, do quickly" (John 13:27 NKJV). These latter hours of the Lord were strongly marked by the emotion to which He gave utterance in His earlier words: "I have a baptism to be baptized with, and how distressed I am till it is accomplished!" (Luke 12:50 NKJV).

There is the resolved determination to carry out the Father's purpose for the world's salvation, which was Christ's own purpose, and was nonetheless His though He knew all the suffering that it involved. Let us adore the steadfast will that never faltered, though the natural human weakness was there, too, and which, as compelled by some strong spring, kept persistently pressing toward the cross that on it He might die, the world's Redeemer.

And do not let us forget that He summoned His disciples to follow Him on the road. "Let us go from here." It is ours to take up our cross daily and follow the Master, to do with persistent resolve our duty, whether it be welcome or unwelcome, and to see to it that we plant no faltering and reluctant foot in our Master's footsteps. For us, too, if we have learned to flee to the cross for our redemption and salvation, the resolve of our Redeemer and the very passion of the Savior become the pattern and law of our lives. We, too, have to cast ourselves into the fight and take up our cross, that the world may know that we love the Father, and as the Father gave us commandment.

ALEXANDER MACLAREN

"I am the true vine, and My Father is the vinedresser."

John 15:1 NKJV

Now they're walking down the street, the Master in the lead, with John and Peter close-by. Now they see the temple, the moonlight falling full upon it. And the great brass grapevine with which it had been beautified by Herod at his building of it shines with wondrous beauty in the enchantment of moonlight.

The Master is speaking again. Very quietly the words come as they still gaze at the beauty of the brass vine. Listen to Him: "I am the true vine, and My Father the vinedresser." Here is the illustration that exactly pictures what He had been saying in the upper room. It supplies the fourth word, the fourth shape that word *believe* takes on in chapter 14: *believe*, that is—*love*, that is—*obey*, that is—*abide*.

Look at the vine and you have the whole story pictured, simple, clear, and full. Each of these four words grows out of the other as fruit out of blossom, and blossom out of the new branch and that out of the old stock of the vine: *believe, love, obey, abide*. The fruit grows out of the vine; yet it is the very life of the vine. *Abiding* grows out of *believing*, yet it is the very heart and inner life of believing.

So He goes on ringing the changes back and forth, now here, now there. *Pruning*—that insures fruit, more and better. *Praying*—that *is* the fruit, some of it, that naturally grows out of the abiding. *My words*—that is part of the abiding, the life-juice of the vine coming into branch and blossom and fruit. *Joy*—that is the rich, red juice of the grape in your mouth. *Friends*—that is another word for abide. That's what abiding makes and reveals. *Abiding*—that is what friends do: that's what friendship is, the real thing. *Obey*—that is the swing of our step with our great Friend as we go along the road together. So these clusters of rich, ripe fruit hang thick on the vine of this simple teaching-talk as they walk along in the moonlight.

And now they're passing through some of the narrower streets as they make their way east toward the city gate. And these narrow streets are shadowed. And you feel the shadows creeping into His talk. The world will *hate* them. Of course. This is a natural result of the abiding. The outer crowd can no more put up with the Jesus-swayed man than with Jesus himself. But if they would clearly understand what to expect ahead it would help them keep their feet when the worst storm came.

S. D. GORDON

"Every branch in Me that does not bear fruit He takes away; and every branch that bears fruit He prunes, that it may bear more fruit."

John 15:2 NKJV

In the whole plant world there is not a tree to be found that so suits the image of man in his relationship to God as the vine. No other plant has fruit and juice that are so full of spirit, so alive and stimulating. But there is also none that has such a natural tendency toward evil, growth that loves to run into wood that is utterly worthless except for the fire. Of all plants, the vine most needs the pruning knife to be used unsparingly and unceasingly. But even with all these problems, no other plant yields a richer reward for the vinedresser.

In His wonderful parable, the Savior refers to this need of pruning the vine, and the blessing it brings. In this dark world, often full of suffering and sorrow for believers, we can take comfort in His words about pruning, knowing that He means it for our good. Abide in Christ! This is the Father's object in sending the trial. In a storm the tree puts down deeper roots into the soil; through suffering the Father leads us to enter more deeply into the love of Christ.

Our hearts are continually prone to wander from Him; prosperity and enjoyment all too easily satisfy us, dull our spiritual perception, and make us unfit for communion with God. It is an unspeakable mercy that the Father comes with His affliction and makes the world around us dark and unattractive. This leads us to feel more deeply our sinfulness, and for a time we lose our joy in what was becoming so threatening to our spiritual life. He does this in the hope that when we have found our rest in Christ in time of trouble we will learn to choose abiding in Him as our best option. Then when the affliction is removed, His hope for us is that we will have grown firmly in Him, so that in prosperity He will still be our joy.

ANDREW MURRAY

"He cuts off every branch in me that bears no fruit, while every branch that does bear fruit he prunes so that it will be even more fruitful."

John 15:2

To no apprentice hand is committed the culture of the true Vine; the great Father himself undertakes this alone. Speaking of Christ's people as a flock, under shepherds are found; but as a branch, each believer is directly united to the true Vine, which receives all things needful through the care of the great Gardener himself. This is very blessed; over pruning or under pruning is impossible. He will train and sustain every individual branch; the needs of each are known to Him and He will supply sunshine or shade, darkness or light, fair weather or shower, as seems best to Him. The branch may abide satisfied without care or worry.

We learn from these solemn words that it is possible to be in Christ and yet to bear no fruit. These words do not refer to those who have professed a faith in Christ merely by word and who are not really in Christ at all. The subject of this chapter in not salvation but fruitfulness. The unfruitful branch taken away does not mean a soul lost, but a life lost. Men may be "saved, yet so as through fire" (1 Corinthians 3:15 NKJV), saved as Lot was saved out of Sodom—property gone, wife gone; saved, with a loss the extent of which eternity alone will reveal. The Lord keeps His people from loving the world or the things of the world.

Not only does the great Gardener remove the fruitless branches, but He prunes the fruitful ones, that they may bring forth more fruit. The word rendered *prune* is the verbal form of that rendered *clean* in the next verse. The methods of the divine Gardener are not necessarily severe. He cleanses by the application of the Word; and where the gentle voice of the Spirit through the Word is listened to, severe and painful discipline may be unneeded. How much of restraint as well as of constraint we might be spared, did the Word of God dwell in us more richly and were the leadings of the Spirit more implicitly obeyed!

HUDSON TAYLOR

"Remain in me, as I also remain in you. No branch can bear fruit by itself; it must remain in the vine. Neither can you bear fruit unless you remain in me."

John 15:4

What our Lord taught in John 14, of the union with Him in the likeness of His being in the Father, He seeks to reinforce by the wonderful parable of the branch and the vine. And all for the sake of bringing home to every believer the absolute necessity of a life lived daily in full communion with Him. "Remain in me."

On the one hand, Jesus points to himself and to the Father and says in effect: "Just as truly and fully as I am in the Father, so you are in me." Then, pointing to the vine, He says, "Just as truly as the branch is in the vine, you are in me. And now, just as the Father abides in me, and works in me, and I work out what He works in me; and just as truly as the branch abides in the vine, and the vine gives its life and strength to the branch, and the branch receives it and puts it forth in fruit—even so do you remain in me and receive my strength. I will work with an almighty power in you and through you. Abide in me!"

Dear child of God, do you not feel how much there is still to learn if you are to have Christ's almighty power working in you as He would wish you to have? The great need is to take time in waiting on the Lord Jesus in the power of His Spirit until the two great truths get the complete mastery of your being. As Christ is in God—this is the testimony from heaven; as the branch is in the vine—this is the testimony of all nature: the law of heaven and the law of earth combine in calling to us: "Abide in Christ." "If you remain in me and I in you, you will bear much fruit" (John 15:5). Fruit, more fruit, much fruit, is what Christ seeks, is what He works, and is what He will assuredly give to the soul who trusts Him.

To the weakest of God's children Christ says: "You are in me. Abide in me. You shall bear much fruit." To the strongest of His messengers He still has the word, there can be nothing higher: "Abide in me, and you will bear much fruit." To one and all the message comes: daily, continuous, unbroken abiding in Christ Jesus is the one condition of a life of power and of blessing. Take time and let the Holy Spirit so renew in you the secret of abiding in Him that leads to the fullness of joy.

ANDREW MURRAY

*"Abide in Me, and I in you. As the branch cannot bear
fruit of itself, unless it abides in the vine, neither can
you, unless you abide in Me."*

John 15:4 NKJV

We need not enlarge upon the importance that Jesus gives to abiding in Him. If we do not remain in Him, it is not that we bear less fruit or inferior fruit, but apart from Him we can do nothing. It is either fruit and abiding, or no fruit at all, nothing but mere works. The distinction between fruit and works is important. Works do not show the character of the worker, but only his skill: a corrupt person may build a good chair. Works, it is true, may be good and useful, but they do not propagate themselves. Fruit, on the contrary, reveals the character of the fruit bearer and has its seed in itself—is productive.

What is the meaning of the words "Abide in Me, and I in you"? The two words, *I am*, are the key to this chapter. The question is not what you are, not what you can do. "I am the true vine," and further, "my Father is the gardener." Jesus turns our thoughts away from self altogether and practically says, "Believe in God, believe also in me."

"I am the vine." He is not just any part of the vine, but the whole vine. The vine is the whole tree—root, trunk, branches, twigs, leaves, flowers, fruit. Some of us, failing to see this, have read the passage as though it were written, "I am the root; you are the branches," and we have said, "Ah! There is sap enough in the root, but how am I to get its riches into my poor, puny branch?" The branch gets nothing out of the vine, it enjoys all in the vine. So are we in Christ.

The little word *in* requires more than a passing notice. It is not in the sense of within, as when the less is contained within the greater. As used in the text, *in* implies union with, identification. The branch is vitally and organically one with the vine, as the eye or ear is in the body. And the word *abide* conveys the idea of rest rather than of labor or motion, of enjoyment attained, not of seeking and striving.

The twofold expression indicates a mutual indwelling. Recognize both truths, not sometimes, but at all times.

HUDSON TAYLOR

"I am the vine, you are the branches. He who abides in Me, and I in him, bears much fruit; for without Me you can do nothing."

John 15:5 NKJV

It is really a simple thing to be a branch of tree or a vine. The branch grows out of the vine or the tree, and in due time bears fruit. It has no responsibility except to receive its nourishment from the root and stem through the sap. Similarly, if by the Holy Spirit we understood our relationship to Jesus Christ, our work would be transformed into an effectual influence. Instead of being an exhausting experience, our work would be new and fresh, linking us to Jesus as never before.

Of course, the vine does the vital work. It sends its roots down into the soil underground—the roots often far-reaching—and finds the necessary nourishment and moisture. If fertilizer is added to the soil, the vine naturally sends its roots toward it; then the roots turn the moisture and fertilizer into a sap that energizes the growth of the rich fruit to be borne. I have heard of a particular vine that has borne more than two thousand clusters of grapes in one season. People were understandably astonished at such extraordinary production. It was discovered that the vine stretched its roots hundreds of yards underground to the River Thames. There in the rich soil of the riverbed it found abundant nourishment and moisture, and the roots drew the sap that incredible distance into the vine, resulting in an abundant harvest.

Whether I preach a sermon, teach a Bible class, or visit the sick of my congregation, all the responsibility of the work is on God, who supplies the strength.

The flow of power to the branches is not intermittent. It is a vital relationship that is ongoing and healthy. The branch abiding in the Vine is our position as a servant. Every day I must be conscious of my part to abide in Him, to rest and trust and know that without the Vine I am nothing.

ANDREW MURRAY

"If you remain in me and my words remain in you, ask whatever you wish, and it will be done for you."

John 15:7

Prayer comes spontaneously from those who abide in Jesus. Prayer is the natural outpouring of a soul in communion with Jesus. As the leaf and fruit come out of the vine branch without any conscious effort and simply because of its living union with the stem, so prayer buds and blossoms and fruits come out of souls abiding in Jesus. As stars shine, so do abiders pray. They do not say to themselves, "It is time for us to get to our task and pray." No, they pray as wise men eat—namely, when the desire for it is upon them. They do not cry out as under bondage, "We ought to be in prayer, but I do not feel like it. What a weariness it is!" They have a glad errand at the mercy seat and rejoice to go there. Hearts abiding in Christ send forth prayers as fires send out flames and sparks. Souls abiding in Jesus open the day with prayer; prayer surrounds them as an atmosphere all day long; at night they fall asleep in prayer. They are able joyfully to say, "When I awake, I am still with you" (Psalm 139:18). Consistent asking comes out of abiding in Christ.

The fruit of our abiding also includes liberty in prayer. Have you not been on your knees at times without the power to pray? Have you not felt that you could not pray as you desired? You wanted to pray, but the waters were frozen and would not flow. The will was present, but not the freedom to present that will in prayer. Do you, then, desire liberty in prayer so that you may speak with God as a man speaks with his friend? Here is the way: "If you remain in me and my words remain in you, ask whatever you wish." I do not mean that you will gain liberty as to a mere fluency of words, for that is a very inferior gift. Fluency is a questionable endowment, especially when it is not accompanied with the weight of thought and depth of feeling. Some believers pray by the yard, but true prayer is measured by weight, not by length. A single groan before God may have more fullness of prayer in it than a fine oration of great length.

CHARLES SPURGEON

15

"If you remain in Me and My words remain in you [that is, if we are vitally united and My message lives in your heart], ask whatever you wish and it will be done for you."

John 15:7 AMP

There is no experience more common in these days than this, nothing more constantly said to me by professing believers: "Well, I have prayed a long time for certain things, but I don't seem to get any answers to my prayers." I often wonder why these people don't give up praying altogether. This is a very God-dishonoring experience, and there must be something wrong either with the person praying or the Giver.

The fact is that there are conditions that God has given to answering prayer. We may pray ourselves blue in the face, if we do not comply with God's conditions. Until then, God will never move an inch to meet us and never fulfill the promises of our experience.

The first condition of answered prayer is to be living in fellowship with God. Having been brought into living fellowship by a living faith, the promises are made to those people who maintain that union, who walk in it, who live in it, and who avail themselves of the opportunities and privileges that Jesus has bestowed upon them by virtue of that union.

It is not enough that you were once in union with Jesus, in order to get answers to your prayers. There are thousands who have let go of the grasp of faith and are not abiding in Christ. They are abiding out of Him, and, yet, they are constantly praying and wondering why God does not answer their prayers. They fail to see that there is no possible way to approach the Father but through the Son. All prayers that are not offered to Him through His Son and in His Son are an abomination to God. They may say the words "In the name of Jesus," but they don't mean it. They are not in union, and, therefore, their prayers never rise any higher than the room in which they are offered.

Never drop out of living in union with Jesus. Keep in it—hold it fast—walk in it and you will get answers to your prayers every day. You will be as sure of it as if you saw God doing what you ask and heard Him speaking to you. You will be able to say, "I know that you hear me always." Bless His name! Those who abide in Him can say those words in their full measure.

CATHERINE BOOTH

"As the Father has loved me, so have I loved you. Now remain in my love."

John 15:9

In a relationship between friends, everything depends on their love to each other. Of what value is an abundance of wealth if love is lacking between husband and wife, or parents and children? And in our faith, of what value is all the knowledge and zeal in God's work without the knowledge and experience of Christ's love (see 1 Corinthians 13:1–3)? O believer, the only thing needful in the inner chamber is to know by experience how much Christ loves you and to learn how you may abide and continue in that love.

Think of what Christ says: "As the Father has loved me"—what a divine, everlasting, wonderful love—"so have I loved you." It was the same love with which He loved the Father and that He always bore in His heart that He now gave into the hearts of His disciples. He yearns that this everlasting love should rest upon us and work within us that we may abide in it day by day. What a blessed life! Christ desires every disciple to live in the power of the self-same love of God that He himself experienced. Do you realize that in your fellowship with Christ in private and in public, you are surrounded by and kept in this heavenly love? Let your desire reach out to this everlasting love. The Christ with whom you desire fellowship longs unspeakably to fill you with His love.

Read from time to time what God's Word says about the love of Christ. Meditate on the words and let them sink into your heart. Sooner or later you will begin to realize: the greatest happiness in my life is that I am beloved of the Lord Jesus. I may live in fellowship with Him all the day long.

Let your heart continually say: His love to me is unspeakable. He will keep me abiding in His love.

ANDREW MURRAY

"As the Father loved Me, I also have loved you; abide in My love."

John 15:9 NKJV

A s the Father loves the Son, in the same manner Jesus loves His people. What is that divine method? He loved Him without beginning, and thus Jesus loves His people. "Yes, I have loved you with an everlasting love; therefore with lovingkindness I have drawn you" (Jeremiah 31:3 NKJV). You can easily trace the beginning of your love to Christ, but His love to us is a stream whose source is hidden in eternity. God the Father loves Jesus without any change. Take this for your comfort, that there is no change in Jesus Christ's love to those who rest in Him.

Communion with Christ is a certain cure for every trouble. Whether it is the bitterness of grief or the excess of earthly pleasure, close fellowship with the Lord Jesus will take bitterness from the one and overindulgence from the other. Live near to Jesus, and it is a matter of secondary importance whether you live on the mountain of honor or in the valley of humiliation. Living near to Jesus, you are covered with the wings of God and underneath you are "the everlasting arms" (Deuteronomy 33:27 NKJV). Let nothing keep you from that sacred abiding in Jesus Christ. Be not content with a conversation now and then, but seek always to retain His company, for only in His presence have you either comfort or safety.

You have a difficult road before you: See, oh, traveler to heaven, that you go not without your guide. You must pass through the fiery furnace; do not enter it unless, like Shadrach, Meshach, and Abednego, you have the Son of God as your companion (see Daniel 3:15–27). You must storm the Jericho of your own corruptions: attempt not the warfare until, like Joshua, you have seen the "Commander of the army of the LORD," with His sword drawn in His hand (Joshua 5:13–15). You are to meet the Esau of your many temptations: do not meet him until at Jabbok's brook you have laid hold upon the angel and prevailed (see Genesis 32:2–30). In every case, in every condition, you will need Jesus; but most of all, when the iron gates of death shall open to you. Keep close to your Savior, and you shall be found of Him at the last, without spot, or wrinkle, or any such thing. Seeing you have lived with Him, and lived in Him here, you shall abide with Him forever.

CHARLES SPURGEON

"If you keep My commandments, you will abide in My love, just as I have kept My Father's commandments and abide in His love."

John 15:10 NKJV

That vine is still hanging out in fine view, all softly ablaze with the clear beautifying light of Christ, in His face, His life, His words. That vine becomes for all time to every heart the pictured meaning of *abide*. And that word *abide* gives the whole of the *true life*.

We say *Christian* life, and rightly so. I like to say also, the *true life*. Any other is abnormal, unnatural, and untrue. I might speak of "the higher Christian life," but I still prefer to say true life. Higher means that there is a lower life. And that this lower is deemed Christian too. That is the bother, the cheapening of things; we call a thing Christian that is less than the thing it is called.

Some of us need to sit down in the lower classes where spelling is taught. We can spell *believe* in the common way with seven letters. We must learn to spell it with four letters—*love*. We need to learn to spell *love* with four other letters—*obey*. We need to learn to spell *obey* with five letters *abide*. We need to find that *abide* is spelled best with four letters *obey*.

We need to learn this simplified spelling, then *all* will become simplified: living, loving, witnessing, praying, winning, singing with joy over the results of our new spelling in the syllables of daily life. *Blessed Master, we would come to your school today. Please let us start down in the spelling class, and you teach us.*

But the vine—let us make that the central picture on the wall, with the Master in the picture pointing to the vine. And under the picture the one word *abide*. Then the whole story is in easy shape to help, pictured before our eyes. *Abide*—that is Jesus walking around in your shoes, looking out through your eyes, touching by your hand, speaking through your lips and your presence. He is free to do so; that's *your* side of it. He's unhindered. He does it; that's *His* side of it.

Look up at the picture on the wall. The whole vine is in the fruit, is it not? The whole of the fruit is in the vine, is it not? That's abiding. The whole of Jesus will be in you as you go about your daily common task, singing. The whole of you is in Jesus as everything, simple and great, is done to please Him, singing as you do it. The proper word is *service*. But it is so much more than the word ever seems to mean.

S. D. GORDON

"I have told you this so that my joy may be in you and that your joy may be complete."

John 15:11

When we have once known anything of joy in the Lord, why do we ask, "But will it last?" And why has the question been so often the very beginning of its not lasting? I think it is because we have either asked it of ourselves or of others rather than the Lord alone. His own answers to this question are so different from the cautious, chilling ones that His children so often give. They are absolute, full, and reiterated. We little realize how unscriptural we are when we meet His good gift of joy with a doubtful, faithless "If it lasts."

His word is clear. So long as you believe your Lord's word about it, so long it will last (see Isaiah 7:9). As soon as you ask of other counselors and believe their word instead, it will fail. Jesus meets your difficulty explicitly. He has provided against it by giving the very reason why He spoke the gracious words "that my joy may be in you." Is not this exactly what we were afraid to hope, what seemed too good to be true, that it might remain? And lest we think that this abiding joy only meant some moderate measure of qualified joy, He adds, "and that your joy may be complete," repeating and intensifying it in the next chapter (see John 16:24). And lest we might think this was said with reference only to an exceptional case, He inspired His beloved disciple to add: "We write this to make our joy complete" (1 John 1:4).

Never in His Word are we told anything contradicting or to explain away this precious promise. Throughout we are pointed not merely to hope of permanence but to increase. There are mingled promises and commands as to growth and increase in grace, knowledge, love, strength, and peace, and does not increase in these imply and ensure joy (see 2 Peter 3:18; Colossians 1:10; 1 Thessalonians 3:12; 4:10; Isaiah 40:29; Galatians 5:22–23)? Is joy to be the only fruit of the Spirit of which it may not be said that it "grew and produced a crop, some multiplying thirty, some sixty, some a hundred times" (Mark 4:8)?

Always remember that "the joy of the LORD is your strength" (Nehemiah 8:10). Perhaps in the word *of* lies the whole secret of lasting joy, for it is His own joy flowing into the soul that is joined to Jesus. Let us seek not the stream, but the fountain; not primarily the joy, but that real and living union with Jesus by which His joy becomes ours.

FRANCES RIDLEY HAVERGAL

"This is My commandment, that you love one another as I have loved you."

John 15:12 NKJV

We know that God is love and that Christ came to reveal this not as a doctrine but as a life. His life, in its wonderful self-abasement and self-sacrifice, was above everything the embodiment of divine love that showed humankind in a new way they could understand, how God loves. In His love to the unworthy and the ungrateful and to enemies, in humbling himself to walk among men as a servant, in giving himself up to death, He lived and acted out the life of divine love that was in the heart of God. He lived and died to show us the love of the Father.

And now, just as Christ was to show forth God's love, believers are to show forth to the world the love of Christ. They are to prove to others that Christ loves them, and in loving, fill them with a love that is not of this earth. By living and by loving just as He did, they are to be perpetual witnesses to the love that gave itself over to death. Christians are to love so that men are compelled to say, "See how Christians love one another."

In their daily interactions with one another, believers are "made a spectacle to the world, both to angels and to men" (1 Corinthians 4:9 NKJV); and in the Christlikeness of their love to one another they are to prove what manner of spirit they are. In all the diversity of character, creed, language, or status in life, Christians are to prove that love has made them members of one body and of one another and has taught them each to forget and to sacrifice self for the sake of the other. Their life of love is the primary evidence of Christianity, the proof to the world that God sent Christ and that He has shed abroad in them the same love with which He loved Him. Of all the evidences of Christianity, this is the most powerful and the most convincing.

ANDREW MURRAY

"Greater love has no one than this, than to lay down one's life for his friends."

John 15:13 NKJV

Christ sets himself forward to the disciples as being the realized Ideal of them all. The Son receives and transmits the Father's love for Him to the disciple, and the disciple is to love his fellow man, in some deep and august sense. The most divine thing in God, and that in which men can be like God, is love. In all our other attitudes to Him we receive rather than copy. For instance, my emptiness *receives* His fullness, my faith *receives* God's grace, but my love is *like* God's love. "Therefore be imitators of God as dear children," and having received that love into your hearts, "walk in love, as Christ also has loved us" (Ephesians 5:1–2 NKJV).

Our Lord here sets forth the very central point of His work, even His voluntary death upon the cross for us, for the good of those whom He loved; and He tells us that—and nothing else—is the true pattern and model toward which all our love is bound to tend and to aspire. That is to say, the heart of the love that He commands is self-sacrifice. And no man loves as Christ would have him love who does not bear in his heart affection that has so conquered selfishness that, if need be, he is ready to die.

The expression of Christian life is not to be found in honeyed words or the do-nothing excess of compassionate sentiments, but in self-sacrifice, modeled after that of Christ's sacrificial death, which is imitable by us. This is a solemn obligation that may well make us tremble. Calvary was less than twenty-four hours off, and He says to us, "*That* is your pattern." Contrast our love at its height with His—a poor little flickering candle held up beside the sun. My love, at its best, has so far conquered my selfishness that now and then I am ready to suffer a little inconvenience, to sacrifice a little spare time, to give away a little money, to spend a little dribble of sympathy upon the people who are its objects. Christ's love led Him down from the throne, nailed Him to the cross, and shut for a time the gates of the glory behind Him. And He says, "That is your pattern!"

Oh, let us bow down and confess how His word, which commands us, puts us to shame, when we think of how miserably we have obeyed. Christ's death is the pattern for our lives as well as the only hope of our hearts.

ALEXANDER MACLAREN

"I no longer call you servants, because a servant does not know his master's business. Instead, I have called you friends, for everything that I learned from my Father I have made known to you."

John 15:15

I t is a blessed thing to be Christ's servant; His redeemed ones delight to call themselves His slaves. Christ had often spoken of the disciples as His servants, as ones who were to obey without being consulted or admitted into the secret of all His master's plans. But now in His great love, with the coming of the Holy Spirit ushering in a new era, He tells His disciples, "Instead, I have called you friends, for everything that I learned from my Father I have made known to you." Christ's friends share with Him in all the secrets the Father has entrusted to Him.

The highest proof of true friendship, and one great source of its blessedness, is the intimacy that holds nothing back and admits the friend to share our inmost secrets. And this now is the blessedness of being Christ's friends: we do not as servants do His will without much spiritual insight into its meaning and aim, but are admitted into the inner circle, into some knowledge of God's more secret thoughts. From the day of Pentecost on, by the Holy Spirit, Christ was to lead His disciples into the spiritual comprehension of the mysteries of the kingdom, of which He had previously spoken only by parables.

Friendship delights in fellowship. Friends trust to each other what they would not have others know. What is it that gives a Christian access to this holy intimacy with Jesus? What gives us the spiritual capacity for receiving from Christ what the Father has shown Him? "You are my friends if you do what I command" (v. 14). It is loving obedience that purifies the soul. It refers not only to the commandments of the Word but also to that blessed application of the Word to our daily lives, which none but our Lord himself can give. As this knowledge is waited for in dependence and humility, and faithfully obeyed, the soul becomes tailored for ever closer fellowship, and the daily walk may become a continual experience: "I have called you friends; for everything that I learned from my Father I have made known to you."

"I have called you friends." What an unspeakable honor! What a heavenly privilege!

O Savior, speak your Word with power into my soul: "I have called you my friend, whom I love, whom I trust, to whom I make known all that passes between my Father and me."

ANDREW MURRAY

SEPTEMBER

23

"You did not choose Me, but I chose you and appointed you that you should go and bear fruit, and that your fruit should remain, that whatever you ask the Father in My name He may give you."

John 15:16 NKJV

There is a world around us with millions who are perishing without Christ. The work of intercession is its only hope. Much of our expressions of love and work in ministry are comparably vain because there is so little real intercession connected with it. Millions live as though there never were such a one as the Son of God who died for them. Millions pass into eternity without hope year after year. Of the millions who bear the name of Christ, the great majority live in utter ignorance or indifference.

Every soul is worth more than the world and nothing less than the price paid for it by Christ's blood. Each is within reach of the power that can be tapped through intercession. We have no concept of the magnitude of the work to be done by God's intercessors or we would cry out to God for an outpouring of the Spirit of intercession.

When God called His people out of Egypt, He separated the priestly tribe to draw near to Him, stand before Him, and bless the people in His name. From time to time He sought, found, and especially honored intercessors, for whose sake He spared or blessed His people.

We may praise God that in our day, too, there is an ever-increasing number who are beginning to see and prove that in the church and in missions, in large organizations as well as small groups and individual efforts, intercession is being acknowledged as the primary power by which God moves and opens heaven.

Because there is a lack of intercession, there is lack of blessing. Oh, that we would turn our eyes and hearts from everything else and fix them upon God who hears our prayers until the magnificence of His promises and His power and His purpose of love overwhelms us!

ANDREW MURRAY

"If they persecuted Me, they will also persecute you. If they kept My word, they will keep yours also."

John 15:20 NKJV

We may legitimately infer that in the reception a disciple of Christ may expect from the world, we have one of the points in which the likeness of a true disciple to the Master will be brought out. "If they have called the master of the house Beelzebub," they will not grace us with fine names of admiration and respect (Matthew 10:25 NKJV). If they do "not receive My words," they will turn a deaf ear to yours (John 12:48 NKJV). "If you were of the world, the world would love its own" (John 15:19 NKJV).

Now, let me say a clear word about this matter. The *world*—meaning today's society or modern culture—had been largely tempered by Christian principles and opinions in years past, but that has eroded and continues to change. And while it is true that in lands such as ours we do not need to be afraid of the violent forms of the world's enmity that the early church faced, this law has not ceased to operate, nor will it, until either the church has become wholly worldly—which, thank God, it never will do—or until the world has become wholly Christ's. There are many evidences around us that it still remains true that an out-and-out consistency of Christian conduct shall be unwelcome to the mass of society. You have only to look at the bitter antagonism to evangelical Christianity that is manifested in much of our media to see that. They used to openly persecute us; they only threaten and condemn and sneer at us nowadays; but the sentiment is pretty much the same.

If your commitment to living the Christian life touches the social sins of this generation, you will see the claws come out fast enough and scratch deep enough, for all the velvet skin and the purring that sometimes is heard. Let a man live the life and shape himself after Christ's example, and he will not miss having to bear his share of the treatment given to his Master. If we take Him for our pattern and try to be like Him, we have to make up our minds to "go forth to Him, outside the camp, bearing His reproach," and to live a godly life amidst ungodly people (Hebrews 13:13 NKJV); and that will never be done without some experience of the deep-seated antagonism between the true disciple and the world.

ALEXANDER MACLAREN

"They hated Me without a cause."

John 15:25 NKJV

No person was ever lovelier than the Savior. It would seem almost impossible not to have loved Him. And yet, altogether lovely as He was, no one has ever been met with such hatred and endured such continual persecution as He did! There was nothing in Christ's person, teaching, or actions that had a natural tendency to make any person hate Him—He was pure goodness in every way. There was nothing in Him but holiness—and any person with half an eye can see that the thing men hated was simply that Christ was perfect. And thus you see the abominable, detestable evil of the human heart—that man naturally hates goodness simply because it is such! Sinful man cannot but detest holiness and goodness because it shines a light on their sin!

If your Master was hated without a cause, do not expect to get off very easily in the world. If your Master was subject to contempt and pain, do you suppose you will always ride through this world in a chariot? If you do, you will be marvelously mistaken! As your Master was persecuted, you must expect to be the same. Some people pity us when we are scorned and despised, but they should save their pity for those of whom the world speaks well! "Woe to you when all men speak well of you" (Luke 6:26 NKJV). No, in all these things, we rejoice and "glory in tribulations, knowing that tribulation produces perseverance" (Romans 5:3 NKJV). We count it all joy, for we rejoice that thus the name of Christ is known and His kingdom extended!

The other lesson is, take care—if the world does hate you—that it hates you without a cause. If the world is to oppose you, it is of no use making the world oppose you! This world is bitter enough without my adding vinegar to it. Some people seem to fancy the world will persecute them—therefore they put themselves into a fighting posture. Do not make other people dislike you. Really, the opposition some people meet with is not for righteousness' sake, but for their own sin's sake, or their own nasty attitudes! Christ has nothing to do with the persecutions you bring on yourself.

They hated Christ without a cause. Then fear not to be hated. They hated Christ without a cause. Then seek not to be hated and give the world no cause for it.

CHARLES SPURGEON

"When the Advocate comes, whom I will send to you from the Father—the Spirit of truth who goes out from the Father—he will testify about me. And you also must testify, for you have been with me from the beginning."

John 15:26–27

I t is the work of the Holy Spirit to testify about Jesus Christ. All the work of the Holy Spirit centers in Jesus Christ. It is His work to magnify Christ to us, to glorify Christ by taking of the things of Christ and declaring them to us.

It is only through the direct testimony of the Holy Spirit in the individual heart that any man ever comes to a true and saving knowledge of Jesus Christ (see 1 Corinthians 12:3). No amount of listening to the testimony of men regarding Jesus Christ, and no amount even of studying what the Scriptures say about Christ, will ever lead anyone to the knowledge of Jesus Christ unless the Holy Spirit, the living Spirit of God, takes the message of men or the testimony of the written Word and interprets it directly to our hearts.

It is true that the Holy Spirit's testimony regarding Jesus Christ is found in the Bible. In fact, that is exactly what the whole Bible is, the Holy Spirit's testimony to Jesus Christ. But the Holy Spirit must take His own testimony as it is found in the Word of God and interpret it directly to the heart of the individual and make it a living thing in his heart, or he will not come to a saving knowledge of Jesus Christ.

If you wish men to get such a true view of Jesus Christ that they will believe in Him, you must seek for them the testimony of the Holy Spirit, and you must put yourself in such a relationship to God that the Holy Spirit can bear His testimony through you. No amount of argument and persuasion will ever bring anyone to know Jesus Christ.

And if you wish to have a true knowledge of Jesus Christ yourself, it is not enough that you study the Word and what the Spirit of God has said about Jesus Christ in the Word: you must seek for yourself the testimony of the Spirit of God directly to your own heart through His Word.

R. A. TORREY

"These things I have spoken to you, that you should not be made to stumble."

John 16:1 NKJV

Look at the loving reason that Christ here suggests for His present speech—"that you should not be made to stumble." The stumbling block for these first Jewish converts, in the attitude of the whole mass of the nation toward Christ and His claims, is one of such a magnitude of persecution as we cannot, by any exercise of our imagination, realize. But that does not in the slightest degree destroy the fact that it also has a bearing upon every one of us. For if you and I are trying to live like our Master, and to do as He would have us do, we will often have to stand in a very small minority and be surrounded by people who take such an entirely opposite view of duty and of truth that we may be disposed to give up and falter in the clearness of our utterance and think, *Well, perhaps it is better for me to hold my tongue.*

Jesus Christ does not try to enlist recruits by rosy pictures of the blessings and joys of serving Him. It is far better to tell us frankly and fully of the difficulties and dangers we may face than to coax us by dwelling on the pleasures and ease. Jesus Christ will have no service on false pretenses, but lets us know at the beginning that we must make up our minds about the hardships and antagonism that otherwise we may escape, and about more than an ordinary share of sorrow, suffering, and pain.

And the way by which all these troubles and cares can best be faced and overcome is precisely by this thought: *The Master has told us before.* Sorrows anticipated are more easily met. It is when the ship is caught with all its sails set that it is almost sure to go down or to be badly damaged in the tempest. To be forewarned is to be forearmed. Since we know that it is coming, when it does come, it is only a passing darkness. Sorrow anticipated is sorrow half overcome; and when it falls on us, the bewilderment will be escaped when we can remember that the Master has told us it all beforehand. Sorrow foretold gives us confidence in our Guide. He *has* told us *this*; if there had been anything worse than this, He would have told us *that*. "If it were not so, I would have told you," our Guide has assured us (John 14:2 NKJV).

ALEXANDER MACLAREN

"But these things I have told you, that when the time comes, you may remember that I told you of them. And these things I did not say to you at the beginning, because I was with you."

John 16:4 NKJV

There had been in Christ's early ministry hints, and very plain references, to persecutions and trials, but He reserved most of it for these last moments. If He had spoken more plainly in those early days, they probably would have forgotten or misunderstood it, as they did His death and resurrection. There needs to be an adaptation between the hearing ear and the spoken word, in order that the word spoken should be of use, and there are great tracts of Scripture dealing with the sorrows of life that lie perfectly dark to us until experience vitalizes them.

It is merciful that there should be a gradual unveiling of what is to come to us. Did you never say to yourself, "If I had known all this before, I don't think I could have faced it"? And did you not feel how kind and loving it was, that in the revelation there had been concealment, and that the specific form of sorrow and trial had not been foreseen by us until we came close to it? Thank God for the loving restraint, and for the loving eloquence of His speech and of His silence, with regard to sorrow.

And take this further lesson, that there ought to be in all our lives times of close and blessed communion with the Master, when the sense of His presence with us makes all thought of sorrows and trials in the future needlessly disturbing. When He was near the disciples, there was something better for them to do than to be concerned about the future—namely, to grow into His life, to drink in the sweetness of His presence and spirit, to be molded into the likeness of His character, and to understand Him better. And for us all there are times—and it is our own fault if these are not frequent—when thus, in such an hour of sweet communion with the present Christ, the future will be all radiant and calm, if we look into it, or, better, the present will be so blessed that there will be no need to think of the future. These men in the upper chamber, if they had drunk in His spirit while He was with them, would not have slept in Gethsemane and run away like frightened sheep from the cross. And you and I, if we sit at His table and keep our hearts near Him, eating and drinking of His presence, shall go forth in the strength of that blessing.

ALEXANDER MACLAREN

"But now I go away to Him who sent Me."

John 16:5 NKJV

It must have been an extremely distressing trial for this small band of disciples to lose the presence of the visible, personal Jesus Christ. Surely the very thought of the loss of their beloved Lord and Master left them disorientated and in dread. Try to realize their circumstances, if you would get really into the spirit of the text.

However, His words must be regarded as revealing part of a plan—"I go away; I am not sent away; I am not going away against my will; I am moving according to a plan." There are no unexpected thoughts in the mind of God. The changes that are strange and startling to us are links in the chain of God's own fashioning. Lay hold of this and you escape the atheism of chance and come into the peaceful region of familiar trust. Therefore, in proportion as I think of God's government as a plan am I at rest. In proportion as I take it to pieces and discuss it in detail am I troubled, confounded, even disappointed.

Now, here is one of the instances of unexpected blessing, of unexpected movements, of movements that escape all calculation and set aside all that the heart would have predicted. Jesus said to His troubled disciples, "It is to your advantage that I go away" (v. 7 NKJV). We cannot see that. Let us, therefore, be fair and candid with the spirit of the text. It looks to us exactly the contrary of that; and we should therefore say it is to our disadvantage that Christ should go away. It is the blackest and direst calamity that can befall us that Christ should go away. Here, then, is an upset of our ordinary notions.

Let us be gently reminded that God is working out a plan—that there is nothing fragmentary and detached and isolated in God's movement. Where we see confusion, He sees a plan and is working it out. We shall have a poor notion of life if we regard it as being a blessing only in proportion as it is a succession of sunny scenes. No great life is made up of all sunshine; we get strong by discipline, we grow by strife. The great storm rocks us into rugged power, and by this power of endurance we come into the grace of gentleness. Great sorrows make tender hearts. We are softened and refreshed by the dew of tears. When we are weak, then are we strong. Disciples are made great and reliable through the school of a thousand disappointments.

JOSEPH PARKER

"But very truly I tell you, it is for your good that I am going away. Unless I go away, the Advocate will not come to you; but if I go, I will send him to you."

John 16:7

How precious Christ was to His disciples can be told only by those who loved Him much. Love always desires to be in the company of the one beloved, and absence causes grief. Jesus had become the joy of the disciples' eyes, the sun of their days, the star of their nights. They were as little children, and now that their Lord and Master was going, they felt like orphans. So much love, so much sorrow, when the object of love is withdrawn.

Yet the presence of the Holy Spirit is shown to be superlatively valuable. We may gather this from the effects that were seen upon the day of Pentecost. On that day the Holy Spirit sounded the alarm of war. The soldiers were hardly prepared for it; they were a frail group, content to sit and wait until power was given to them. That mighty sound was heard across Jerusalem and filled the place where they were sitting. Here was a prediction of what the Spirit of God was to be to the church.

The Holy Spirit is to come mysteriously upon the church according to the sovereign will of God. But when He comes like the wind, it is to purge the moral atmosphere and to quicken the pulse of all who breathe spiritually. I would that this rushing mighty wind would come upon His church with an irresistible force that should carry everything before it—the force of truth, but of more than truth, the force of God driving truth home upon the heart and conscience of men. I would that you and I could breathe this wind and receive its invigorating influence that we might be made champions of God and of His truth. Oh, that it would drive away our mists of doubt and clouds of error.

Come, sacred wind, our nation needs you—the whole world requires you. The foul odors that brood over this deadly calm would flee if your divine lightnings enlightened the world and set the moral atmosphere in commotion. Come, Holy Spirit, come. We can do nothing without you, but if we have your wind, we spread our sail and speed on toward glory.

CHARLES SPURGEON

"But I tell you the truth, it is to your advantage that I go away; for if I do not go away, the Helper (Comforter, Advocate, Intercessor—Counselor, Strengthener, Standby) will not come to you; but if I go, I will send Him (the Holy Spirit) to you [to be in close fellowship with you]."

John 16:7 AMP

One aspect of the personality of the Holy Spirit is that an office is predicated of the Holy Spirit that could only be centered in a person. Look at today's verse. Here the Holy Spirit is represented as the Helper, Advocate, Intercessor, Counselor, Strengthener, and Standby who is coming to take the place of our Lord Jesus. Up to this time our Lord Jesus had been the friend always at hand to help the disciples in every emergency that arose. But now He is going, and He tells them that though He is going, a Helper is coming to take His place. Can you for a moment imagine our Lord Jesus saying this if the other who is coming to take His place were a mere impersonal influence or power? No! No! What our Lord said was that He, one divine person, was going, but that another person, just as divine as He, was coming to take His place.

I take this as one of the most precious promises in the Word of God: that another person just as divine as Jesus, just as loving and tender and strong to help, is by my side always, yes, dwells in my heart every moment to commune with me and to help me in every emergency that can possibly arise. The Greek word for *Helper* or *Counselor* is *Parakletos*, which means "one called to stand alongside another," one called to take his part and help him in every emergency that arises. Just like Jesus, the Holy Spirit is with us wherever we go, every hour of the day or night, always at our side.

What a precious and wondrous thought. If this thought gets into your heart and stays there, you will never have another moment of fear as long as you live. How can we fear under any circumstances if we really believe that He is by our side? How can loneliness or a broken heart remain? Do you know this Friend, the Holy Spirit?

R. A. TORREY

"And when He has come, He will convict the world of sin, and of righteousness, and of judgment."

John 16:8 NKJV

The Holy Spirit convicts the world of guilt by bringing the law of God to bear on the past life, showing the sinner the awful condemnation resting on him because of his past sins, and also by revealing the innate alienation and rebellion of his heart. The Holy Spirit turns, so to speak, His light on the sinner's soul and exposes the depravity and impurity within. God's way is always in keeping with the laws of man's nature; and we are so constituted that before we can be persuaded to change our course, we must be convinced that our present one is wrong. Yet the great aim of many sinners is to assure themselves that they are all right, or, if wrong at all, not very wrong. God sees that there is no possibility of salvation until men see that they are all wrong, and therefore He strives with them—labors to make them realize that they are guilty.

God does not answer a sinner's objections, but thunders in his conscience, "Guilty! And in danger of everlasting death!" Alas, instead of yielding to these strivings, men quench them by stifling their convictions; and they do this by hiding them, refusing to give them expression in tears and prayers. They keep silence; and none, but they who feel it, know what a hell is thus created in the soul. David said, "When I kept silent, my bones wasted away through my groaning all day long" (Psalm 32:3). This stifling of conviction is done to a much greater extent than any of us imagine. Many people think it is a sign of weakness to confess their sins. They are ashamed to confess what all heaven would be interested in hearing. If you yield to these strivings, give expression to your shame, sorrow, and remorse for your past sins, your heart will melt and gush out in tender repentance toward God and man. Beware lest you dam up these feelings, silence your conscience, and thus resist the work of the Spirit on your heart. The Spirit is continually working if we allow Him. Let us never quench the Spirit!

CATHERINE BOOTH

OCTOBER
3

"When he comes, he will prove the world to be in the wrong about sin and righteousness and judgment."

John 16:8

God's special agency in the conviction of sin is by His Holy Spirit. Having direct access to the mind, and knowing infinitely well every person, the Holy Spirit employs the truth that is best adapted to each particular case, and then sends it home with divine power. He gives it such a vividness, strength, and power, that the person surrenders, throws down his weapons of rebellion, and turns to the Lord. Under His influence, the truth burns and cuts its way like fire. He makes the truth stand out in such aspects that it crushes the proudest man down with the weight of a mountain. If men were inclined to obey God, the truth is given with sufficient clearness in the Bible that they could learn all that is necessary to know. But because they are wholly predisposed to disobey it, God clears it up before their minds and pours in a blaze of convincing light upon their souls, which they cannot withstand, and they yield to it.

In the same way, because we do not know what we should pray for as we should, the Holy Spirit makes intercession for believers (see Romans 8:26). He does not do it by praying for us while we do nothing. He prays for us by stirring our own faculties. Not that He suggests to us words or guides our language. But He enlightens our minds and makes the truth take hold of our souls. He leads us to consider the state of the church and the condition of sinners around us. The manner in which He brings the truth before the mind and keeps it there till it produces its effect, we cannot tell. But we can know this much—that He leads us to a deep consideration of the state of things; and the result of this, the natural and philosophical result, is deep feeling. That is, by turning away a man's thoughts and leading him to think of other things. When the Holy Spirit brings a subject into contact with his heart, it is just as impossible that he would not feel it as that his hand would not feel a fire.

CHARLES FINNEY

*"And He, when He comes, will convict the world about
[the guilt of] sin [and the need for a Savior], and about
righteousness, and about judgment."*

John 16:8 AMP

I t is the work of the Holy Spirit to convict people of sin in such a way as
to produce a deep sense of personal sinfulness. This is where the work of
salvation begins in most people: they are brought to realize that they are
sinners and that they need a Savior, and then they are ready without much
urging to accept Jesus Christ as their Savior, when He is presented to them
as the all-sufficient Savior they so profoundly need.

One of the great needs of the present day is conviction of sin. Men and
women have no realization of the awfulness of sin or of their standing before
God. We are very sharp-sighted with regard to the sins and shortcomings of
others, but very blind to our own. "The heart is deceitful above all things
and beyond cure" (Jeremiah 17:9). And the world is so blind to its sinfulness
that no one but the Holy Spirit can ever convince the world of sin, bringing
men to see how sinful they are. Neither you nor I can convince any man of
sin, even with the most persuasive reasoning and powerful stories. We may
get men to cry by a moving story, but mere shedding of tears over emotional
stories and touching songs is not conviction of sin. Real conviction of sin can
only be produced by the Holy Spirit.

But while it is utterly impossible for us to convince men of sin, the Holy
Spirit can do it. And, if we put ourselves at the disposal of the Holy Spirit
for Him to use us as He will, and if we would look to the Holy Spirit to convince men of sin through us, and if we would be more careful to be in such
relationship with God that the Holy Spirit can work through us, we would
see far more conviction of sin than we do.

The Holy Spirit can convict men as powerfully today as He did on the day
of Pentecost when three thousand men and women "were cut to the heart"
(Acts 2:37). If Peter had preached the same sermon the day before the Holy
Spirit came, there would have been no such results. Oh, we need to believe in
the Holy Spirit's power to convict men of sin, and we need to trust Him to
do His glorious work through us.

R. A. TORREY

"[The Holy Spirit] will prove the world to be in the wrong . . . about sin, because people do not believe in me; about righteousness, because I am going to the Father, where you can see me no longer; and about judgment, because the prince of this world now stands condemned."

John 16:8–11

The sin of which the Holy Spirit convicts men and women is the sin of unbelief in Jesus Christ, not in the endless list of others sins. This was the sin of which the Holy Spirit convicted the three thousand on the day of Pentecost (see Acts 2:36–37). When they realized they had rejected the Lord and Christ, they were cut to their hearts. This awful sin is the very sin of which it is most difficult to convince proud and arrogant men. But when the Spirit of God comes to a man, he does not look upon unbelief in Jesus Christ as a mark of intellectual superiority or excuse it behind an inherent inability to believe. While he may bitterly regret his dishonesty or his impurity or whatever other sins he may be guilty of, he sees and feels that the most awful of his sins is the sin of rejecting the glorious Son of God.

The Holy Spirit also convicts the world of righteousness; not of our righteousness, for we have none, but of Jesus Christ's righteousness, attested by His resurrection from the dead and by His ascension to the Father. The convicted sinner needs to see the righteousness that God has provided for him in Christ, and only the Holy Spirit can bring this to him.

The third thing that the Holy Spirit convicts men about is judgment, attested by the judgment of the prince of this world, the devil. There has perhaps never been a day in the whole history of the church when the world needed more to be convinced of judgment than today. The average man has almost no knowledge of a future judgment, and the church has largely lost all realization of future judgment and of a future awful hell. Only the Holy Spirit can bring this revelation of the infinite majesty and glory of Jesus Christ, and such a revelation of the awfulness of sin and the future eternal destiny of those who would not accept Jesus Christ.

R. A. TORREY

"I have much more to say to you, more than you can now bear. But when he, the Spirit of truth, comes, he will guide you into all the truth."

John 16:12–13

D o you count it a great faith to believe what God has said? It seems to me a little faith. What should I think of my child if I found that he limited his faith in me and hope from me to the few promises he had heard me utter? The faith that limits itself to the promises of God seems to me of a trivial character. To believe what God has not said is faith indeed! For that comes of believing in Him!

Let us not be unbelieving children. Let us keep in mind that the Lord blesses those who have not seen and yet have believed. It is dull-hearted, unchildlike people who are always reminding God of His promises. Those promises are good to reveal what God is. But if they think them good as binding God, let them have it so for the hardness of their hearts. They prefer the Word to the Spirit.

But let us dare to look beyond, to the "uncovenanted mercies of God." Those are the mercies beyond our height, beyond our depth, beyond our reach. We know whom we have believed, and we look for that which has not entered into the heart of man to conceive. Shall God's thoughts be surpassed by man's thoughts? God's creation by man's imagination?

No. Let us climb to the height of our alpine hopes. Let us leave them behind and ascend the spear-pointed Himalayas of our aspirations. Still we find the depth of God's sapphire above us. Still we shall find the heavens higher than the earth, and His thoughts and His ways higher than our thoughts and ways.

Ah, Lord! We dare not think that some things are beyond your beholding, some questions not to be asked of you. For are we not yours—utterly yours? Our very passions we hold up to you and say, "Behold, Lord! Think about us for you have made us." We would not escape from our history by fleeing into the wilderness, by hiding our heads in the sands of forgetfulness, or the repentance that comes of pain, or the lethargy of hopelessness. We take it, as our very life in our hand, and flee with it to you. Triumphant is the answer that you hold for every doubt. Our God, we will trust you.

GEORGE MacDONALD

"He will glorify me because it is from me that he will receive what he will make known to you."

John 16:14

Our Lord, on the last night that He was with His disciples, promised to send the Holy Spirit as a Comforter and Advocate. Although His bodily presence was removed, they would realize His presence in them and with them in a wonderful way. The Holy Spirit as God would so reveal Christ in their hearts that they would experience His presence with them continually. The Spirit would glorify Christ, and would glorify Christ in heavenly love and power.

How little do believers understand and believe and experience this glorious truth. We should fail in our Christian duty if we encourage believers to love the Lord Jesus without at the same time warning them that it is not a duty they can perform in their own strength. No, that is impossible. It is God, the Holy Spirit alone, who will shed abroad His love in our hearts and teach us to love Him fervently. Through the Holy Spirit we may experience the love and abiding presence of the Lord Jesus all the day.

But let us remember the Spirit as God must have entire possession of us. He claims our whole heart and life. He will strengthen us with might in the inner man, so that we have fellowship with Christ and keep His commandments and abide in His love.

When once we have grasped this truth, we will begin to feel our deep dependence on the Holy Spirit, and will pray the Father send Him in power into our hearts. The Spirit will teach us to love the Word, to meditate on it and to keep it. He will reveal the love of Christ to us, that we may love Him with a pure heart fervently. Then we shall begin to see that a life in the love of Christ in the midst of our daily life and distractions is a glorious possibility and a blessed reality.

ANDREW MURRAY

"He will glorify me because it is from me that he will receive what he will make known to you. All that belongs to the Father is mine. That is why I said the Spirit will receive from me what he will make known to you."

John 16:14–15

I can understand the Holy Spirit's taking the things of Christ and rejoicing in them, but the marvel is that the Holy Spirit should glorify Christ by coming and showing these things to us. And yet, it is among us that Christ is to receive His glory. Our eyes must see Him. An unseen Christ is little glorious; and the things of Christ unknown, the things of Christ untasted and unloved, seem to have lost their brilliance to a high degree. The Holy Spirit, therefore, feeling that to show a sinner the salvation of Christ glorifies Him, spends His time, and has been spending these centuries, in taking the things of Christ and showing them to us. Ah, it is a great condescension on His part to show them to us, but it is a miracle too! If it were reported that suddenly stones had life and hills had eyes and trees had ears, it would be a strange thing; but for us who were dead and blind and deaf in an awful spiritual sense, and for the Holy Spirit to be able to show the things of Christ to us, is to His honor. But He does do it.

I am never sure which act of condescension I admire more—the incarnation of Christ or the indwelling of the Holy Spirit. Christ's incarnation is marvelous—that He should dwell in human nature. But observe, the Holy Spirit dwells in human nature in its sinfulness, not in perfect human nature but in imperfect human nature. And He continues to dwell, not in one body, which was fashioned mysteriously for himself, and was pure and without stain, but He dwells in our bodies. These bodies are the temples of the Holy Spirit, bodies that were defiled by sin and in which a measure of corruption remains, despite His indwelling. And this He has done for centuries, not in one instance or in thousands of instances only but in a number that no man can number. Not to the angels or to the seraphim does He show the things of Christ, but He shows them to us.

Charles Spurgeon

"All things that the Father has are Mine."

John 16:15 NKJV

We think so often of Jesus Christ as meek and lowly that we are apt to forget His majesty. We often speak of the union between Christ and His disciples, as if these terms were mutually equivalent. We must not get into that easy way of thinking that Jesus Christ and His people are practically one, in any sense that denotes equality as between them; as if a Christian were a Christ and as if Christ were but a Christian, differing in some sense in degree, but identical in quality. All that line of thought needs guarding lest we lose reverence, loyalty, and sense of what is due in worship, trust, and sacrifice. Jesus Christ was very condescending, but in His condescension there was a majesty, unequalled and uncomprehended. We should therefore dwell frequently upon the difference, which is incalculable in degree and in quality, between the Son of God and those whom He has saved by the shedding of His blood.

Hear the words of our Lord: "All things that the Father has are Mine." Who can claim to hold in His hands what God holds? Who dare say that He is part-proprietor of the universe? Who could say, "Most assuredly, I say to you, whatever you ask the Father in My name He will give you" (v. 23 NKJV)? In these words Jesus pledges the Father. He is saying, "I pledge His existence, His honor, and His throne." This is not the language of a mere man. Yet the language fits Him like a robe; there is no discrepancy between the word and the thing, the symbol and the substance. In every aspect of His life there is an outshining of glory that justifies the use of language so sublime. Jesus Christ guarantees the answer. He speaks as the inhabitant of eternity, as the custodian of the riches of the universe, as one who lays His hand familiarly upon everything and says in effect, "Ask for it, and the Father, through me, will give it. I will take it up with my own hand and pass it down until it reaches your hand."

Let us never forget His majesty. Our place is to glory in Christ and say, "Christ is mine, and I am His, and because of the union between us, all that He has I have. I have no confidence in myself, but Christ lives in me; and the life that I now live in the flesh, I live by the faith of the Son of God. I can do all things through His strength."

JOSEPH PARKER

"All that belongs to the Father is mine. That is why I said the Spirit will receive from me what he will make known to you."

John 16:15

There are times when all the promises of the Bible are of no avail, unless a gracious hand shall apply them to us. We are thirsty, but too faint to crawl to the water brook. When a soldier is wounded in battle, it is of little use for him to know that there is a hospital nearby: what he needs is to be carried there and to have the remedies applied. It is thus with our souls, and to meet this need the Spirit of truth takes of the things of Jesus and applies them to us. Think not that Christ has placed His joys on heavenly shelves that we may climb up to them for ourselves, but He draws near and sheds His peace abroad in our hearts.

If you are laboring under deep distresses, your Father does not give you promises and then leave you to draw them up from the Word like buckets from a well, but the promises He has written in the Word He will write anew on your heart. He will manifest His love to you, and by His blessed Spirit, dispel your cares and troubles. The Good Samaritan did not say, "Here is the wine, and here is the oil for you"; he actually poured on the oil and the wine (see Luke 10:34). So Jesus not only gives you the sweet wine of the promise, but holds the golden chalice to your lips and pours the lifeblood into your mouth. The exhausted pilgrim is not merely strengthened to walk, but he is borne on eagles' wings.

Beloved, the Holy Spirit favors you by taking what is Christ's, namely His love, and showing that to you. We have seen it sometimes more vividly than at other times. But if the full blaze of the Holy Spirit were to be concentrated upon the love of Christ—and our eyesight enlarged to its utmost capacity—it would be such a vision that heaven could not excel it! Oh, to see the love of Christ in the light of the Holy Spirit! When the essence of the love of Christ is revealed to us—that love without beginning, without change, without limit, without end—what tongue can tell? Oh, it is a ravishing sight!

Glorious gospel! That provides everything for the helpless, that draws nigh to us when we cannot reach after it—brings us grace before we seek for grace! Here is as much glory in the giving as in the gift. Happy are the people who have the Holy Spirit to bring Jesus to them.

CHARLES SPURGEON

*"Most assuredly, I say to you, whatever you ask the
Father in My name He will give you."*

John 16:23 NKJV

This is the definition of Christian prayer, but what does it mean? Is a prayer
that from beginning to end is reeking with self-will, answered because
we say, as a kind of charm at the end, "In Jesus' name"? Is *that* praying in Christ's name? Surely not! What is the "name" of Christ? His whole
revealed character. So these disciples could not pray in His name before this,
because His character was not fully revealed. Therefore, to pray in His name
is to pray, recognizing who He is, as revealed in His life and death and resurrection and ascension, and to base all our dependence of acceptance of our
prayers upon that revealed character.

Is that all? Are any kinds of wishes, which are presented in dependence
upon Christ, certain to be fulfilled? Certainly not! To pray "in My name"
means not only to pray in dependence upon Christ as God's only channel of
blessing, but it means exactly what the same phrase means when it is applied
to us. If I say that I am doing something in your name it means on your behalf,
as your representative, and to express your mind and will. And if we pray in
Christ's name, that implies, not only our dependence upon His merit and
work, but also the harmony of our wills with His will, and that our requests
are not merely the products of our own selfishness, but are the calm issues of
communion with Him. Christian prayer is the submissive effort to make my
wish what God wills, and that is to pray in Christ's name.

Is that how we pray? Do we try to bring our desires into harmony with
Him before we venture to express them? Do we go to His throne to pour
out wishes after questionable and possible good, or do we wait until He fills
our spirits with longings after what it must be His desire to give, and then
breathe out those desires caught from His own heart and echoing His own
will? Ah! The discipline that is wanted to make men pray in Christ's name is
little understood today.

But notice how certain such prayer is of being answered. Of course, if it
is in harmony with the will of God, it is sure not to be offered in vain. God's
gifts come down through the same channel through which our prayer goes up.
We ask in the name of Christ, and receive our answers in the name of Christ.

ALEXANDER MACLAREN

"Until now you have not asked for anything in my name.
Ask and you will receive, and your joy will be complete."

John 16:24

During Christ's life upon earth, the disciples had learned very little of the power of prayer. In Gethsemane, Peter and the others had utterly failed. They had no concept of what it was to ask in the name of Jesus and to receive. The Lord promised them that there was a day coming when they would be able to pray with such a power in His name, that they might ask what they would, and it would be given to them.

"Until now you have not asked for anything." "In that day you will ask in my name" (John 16:26). These two conditions are still found in the church. With the great majority of Christians there is such a lack of knowledge of their oneness with Christ Jesus, and of the Holy Spirit as the Spirit of prayer, that they do not even attempt to claim the wonderful promises Christ spoke so specifically about here. But where God's children know what it is to abide in Christ and in vital union with Him, and to yield to the Holy Spirit's teaching, they begin to learn that their intercession avails much, and that God will give the power of His Spirit in answer to their prayer.

It is faith in the power of Jesus' name, and in our right to use it, that will give us the courage to follow on where God invites us to the holy office of intercessors. When our Lord Jesus, in His farewell discourse, gave His unlimited prayer promise, He sent the disciples out into the world with this consciousness: "He who sits upon the throne, and who lives in my heart, has promised that what I ask in His name I shall receive. He will do it."

Oh, if believers only knew what it is to yield themselves wholly and absolutely to Jesus Christ and His service, how their eyes would be opened to see that intense and unceasing prayerfulness is the essential mark of the healthy spiritual life; and that the power of all-prevailing intercession will indeed be the portion of those who live only in and for their Lord!

ANDREW MURRAY

*"Until now you have not asked [the Father] for anything
in My name; but now ask and keep on asking and you
will receive, so that your joy may be full and complete."*

John 16:24 AMP

Who is there that does not wish his joy filled full and complete?
Well, Jesus states simply and beautifully that the way to have it
filled full is by praying in the name of Jesus. We all know people
whose joy is filled full; indeed, it is running over, it is shining from their eyes,
bubbling out of their lips, and running off their fingertips when they shake
hands with you. Coming in contact with them is like coming in contact with
an electrical outlet charged with gladness. Now, people of that sort are always
people who spend much time in prayer.

Why is it that prayer in the name of Christ brings such fullness of joy? In
part, because we receive what we ask. But that is not the only reason, nor the
greatest. It makes God real. When we ask something definite of God, and
He gives it, how real God becomes! He is right there! It is blessed to have a
God who is real, and not merely an idea. I remember how once I was taken
suddenly and seriously sick all alone in my study. I dropped upon my knees
and cried to God for help. Instantly, all pain left me—I was perfectly well. It
seemed as if God stood right there and had put out His hand and touched
me. The joy of the healing was not as great as the joy of meeting God.

There is no greater joy on earth or in heaven than communion with God,
and prayer in the name of Jesus brings us into communion with Him. The
psalmist was surely not speaking only of future blessedness, but also of present
blessedness when he said, "In Your presence is fullness of joy" (Psalm 16:11
NKJV). O the unutterable joy of those moments when in our prayers we really
press into the presence of God!

If you say, "I have never known any such joy as that in prayer," I would ask,
"Do you take enough time for prayer to actually get into God's presence? Do
you really give yourself up to prayer in the time which you do take?"

R. A. TORREY

"A time is coming and in fact has come when you will be scattered, each to your own home. You will leave me all alone."

John 16:32

Few had fellowship with the sorrows of Gethsemane. The disciples were not sufficiently advanced in grace to truly behold the mysteries of "the agony." To eleven only was the privilege given to enter Gethsemane and see "this great sight." Out of the eleven, eight were left at a distance; they had fellowship, but not of that intimate sort to which men greatly beloved are admitted. Only three highly favored ones could approach the veil of our Lord's mysterious sorrow: within that veil even these must not intrude; a stone's throw distance must be left between. None could enter into the inner circle of His sufferings. In the bloody sweat and the agony of Gethsemane, the Savior must tread the winepress alone.

From the time when He bowed in agony amid the deep shades of the Mount of Olives, till the moment when He entered the thicker darkness of the valley of the shadow of death, He was left to suffer alone. It was a condition of His sufferings that He should be forsaken. Desertion was a necessary ingredient in that cup of suffering that He had covenanted to drink for us. We deserved to be forsaken and, therefore, He must be. Since our sins against man, as well as our sins against God, deserved that we should be forsaken of men, He, bearing our sins against God and man, is forsaken.

Peter and the two sons of Zebedee represent the few eminent, experienced saints, who may be written down as "Fathers"; these having done business on great waters, can in some degree measure the huge Atlantic waves of their Redeemer's passion. To some selected spirits it is given, for the good of others, and to strengthen them for the future, special, and tremendous conflict, to enter the inner circle and hear the pleadings of the suffering High Priest—they have fellowship with Him in His sufferings and are made conformable unto His death. Yet even these cannot penetrate the secret places of the Savior's woe. "Thine unknown sufferings" is the remarkable expression of the Greek liturgy: there was an inner chamber in our Master's grief, shut out from human knowledge and fellowship. There Jesus is "left alone." Here Jesus was more than ever an "unspeakable gift"!

Is not hymn writer Isaac Watts right when he sings, "It cost Him death to save our lives; to buy our souls it cost His own; and all the unknown joys He gives, were bought with agonies unknown"?

CHARLES SPURGEON

"Indeed the hour is coming, yes, has now come, that you will be scattered, each to his own, and will leave Me alone. And yet I am not alone, because the Father is with Me."

John 16:32 NKJV

I think attention has been too exclusively directed to the physical sufferings of our Lord's passion and to the mysterious element in His mental passion that made it unique and atoning. We have too much forgotten the sorrows that pressed upon Him as upon us, the same in kind, only infinitely deeper in degree, and hence we have lost some of the sense of reality of our Lord's sufferings of these sorrows. I do not know that any is sharper than the solitude in which He lived and yet more dreadful solitude in which He died. While He shared the love and outward companionship of His disciples, there was not a single human being who truly understood or believed Him or with whom He could share His confidences. His life's purpose was shrouded in mystery. "He came to His own, and His own did not receive Him" (John 1:11 NKJV). And so, He traveled on, bearing a great burden of love that none would accept. Jesus Christ was the loneliest man who ever lived.

All great spirits are solitary; the men who lead the world have to go before the world, and often have to go by themselves. Starlings fly in flocks; the eagle soars singly. And so the pages of the biographies of the great teachers, religious reformers, thinkers, and path breakers generally tell us of the pains of uncomprehended aims, of the misery of living apart from one's kind, of the agony of hungering for sympathy, for understanding, for acceptance of a truth that dooms its possessors to isolation. But all that men have experienced in that kind is as nothing as compared with the blackness of darkness that the loneliness of Jesus Christ assumed as it settled down upon Him.

Let me remind you what it was that condemned Him to this absolute loneliness. It was the very purity and sinlessness of His nature that necessarily made Him separate from sinners. He read men as no other eye read them: He saw not only the clockface, but the springs. He looked upon the flesh and behind the spirit, its inmost essence, its destiny and end. Before His human eye there stood plainly manifested the pale kingdoms of the dead, and all that vision separated Him from men. It made His life an absolute solitude; and when He spoke what He knew, and testified what He had seen, no man received His testimony. Hence came a deeper loneliness . . . borne for us.

ALEXANDER MACLAREN

"In the world you will have tribulation; but be of good cheer, I have overcome the world."

John 16:33 NKJV

Our Lord states emphatically that in the world you will have tribulation. If anybody else has it, you shall, and if nobody else has it, yet you will have it. You will have it, perhaps, when you least wish it or anticipate it. Are you asking the reason of this? Look upward to your heavenly Father and behold Him pure and holy. Do you know that you are one day to be like Him? Will you easily be conformed to His image? Will you not require much refining in the furnace of affliction to purify you? Will it be an easy thing to make you "perfect, just as your Father in heaven is perfect" (Matthew 5:48 NKJV)?

Next, turn your eye downward. Do you know what foes you have beneath your feet? You were once a servant of Satan, and no king will willingly lose his subjects. Do you think that Satan will leave you alone? No, he will be always after you, for he "walks about like a roaring lion, seeking whom he may devour" (1 Peter 5:8 NKJV). Expect trouble, therefore, when you look beneath you.

Then look around you. Where are you? You are in an enemy's country, a stranger and a pilgrim. The world is a foe to grace, and not a friend to it or to you. If the world is your friend, you are not God's friend, for he who is the friend of the world is the enemy of God. Be assured that you shall find adversaries everywhere. When you sleep, remember that you are resting on the battlefield; when you walk, suspect an ambush around every corner. You are in Christ, and the Savior saves you from your sins, but He has not promised to screen you from any of the common trials and tribulations of mankind.

Lastly, look within you, into your own heart and observe what is there. Sin and self are still within. Ah! if you had no devil to tempt you, no enemies to fight you, and no world to ensnare you, you would still find in yourself evil enough to be a sore trouble to you, for "the heart is deceitful above all things, and desperately wicked; who can know it?" (Jeremiah 17:9 NKJV).

Expect trouble then, but Jesus also said in effect, "Be of good cheer, I have overcome the world. My overcoming of the world belongs to you. I have conquered the adversaries that you have now to fight with, and thus I have virtually won the battle before you begin it."

CHARLES SPURGEON

After Jesus said this, he looked toward heaven and prayed: "Father, the hour has come. Glorify your Son, that your Son may glorify you."

John 17:1

It was a marvelous wooing of the love of Christ for His disciples. Here Christ takes them into His innermost heart for a brief moment. It must have reminded John afterward of that mountaintop experience when Jesus drew aside the drapery of His humanity and let a little of the inner glory shine out (see Matthew 17:2). Here He takes them with Him into His own inner life with His Father.

Let no one think that Jesus was simply letting them hear Him pray so that they might learn. He was taking them into the sacred privacy of His own innermost life. That was a bit of the wooing, under the desperate happenings just ahead. But now as He takes them in, He quite forgets them, though He knows they are there. He is absorbed with the Father. He isn't thinking now of the effect of all this on them. That is past. He is alone in spirit with the Father, freely talking aloud as though actually alone.

We are in the innermost holy of holies here. The heart of the world's life is its literature. The heart of all literature is this sacred Book of God. The heart of this Book is the Gospels. The heart of these four gospels is John's. The heart of John's is the exquisite chapters, thirteen to seventeen. And there's yet an inner heart here. It is this seventeenth chapter, where the inner side of Jesus' prayer life lies open to us. And we shall find an innermost heart yet again here.

They're out in the open, down near the Kidron Brook. Jesus stops and looks up toward the blue, the Father's open door, and quietly talks out of His heart into His Father's heart, "Father, the hour has come"; talked of long before this errand was started upon, brooded over these human years, felt in His inner being as it ticked itself nearer in the tremendous passing events. Now it is come. The clock is striking the hour, striking on earth and echoed distinctly in the Father's ear.

The simplicity of speech here catches the heart. The holy intimacy of contact with God hushes the spirit. The certainty of the Father's presence awes the heart greatly. The unquestioning confidence in the outcome is to one's faith like a glass of kingdom wine fresh from the King's own hand. The tenseness and yet exquisite quietness holds one's being still with a great stillness. Both shoes and hat go off instinctively, and we stand with head bowed low and heart hushed, for this is holy ground.

S. D. GORDON

"And this is the way to have eternal life—to know you, the only true God, and Jesus Christ, the one you sent to earth."

John 17:3 NLT

It is the great wonder of human history that after two thousand years the world knows so little of Jesus Christ. The leaders who profess to guide the thoughts of this generation, how little they know about this Master! What profound misconceptions of Christianity, and of Him who is Christianity, we see among those who pay Him conventional respect as well as among those who reject Him and His mission! How little, too, the majority of people know about Him! It is enough to break one's heart to think that He has been so long a time with the world and this is all that has come of it.

Light has been shining for two thousand years, and yet the mist is so little cleared away and the ice is so little melted. The great proof that the world is evil is that it does not believe in Jesus Christ the Son of God, and that He has stood before it for all these centuries now, and so few have been led to turn to Him with the adoring cry, "My Lord and my God!" But let us narrow our thoughts to ourselves. Many of us have known about Jesus Christ all our lives, and yet in a real, deep sense, do we know Him at this moment? For the knowledge of which I speak is the knowledge of acquaintance with a person rather than the knowledge one may have from a book. And it is the knowledge of experience. Do we have that? Do we know Christ as a man knows his friend, or do we know Him as we know about a neighbor who lives across the street to whom we may smile but have never actually gotten to know? If so, it is no knowledge at all. "I have heard of You by the hearing of the ear" (Job 42:5 NKJV) describes all the acquaintance that a great many of us have with Him.

Oh, the very fact that He has been so long with us may be the reason why we know so little about Him. People may have lived all their lives within the sound of Niagara Falls and never gone to look at the rush of the waters. Is that what you do with Jesus Christ? Are you so accustomed to hearing about Him that you do not know Him; having so long heard of Him that you never came to see Him?

ALEXANDER MACLAREN

"Now this is eternal life: that they know you, the only true God, and Jesus Christ, whom you have sent."

John 17:3

The knowledge of God is absolutely necessary for the spiritual life. It is life eternal. Not the intellectual knowledge we receive from others or through our own power of thought, but the living, experiential knowledge in which God makes himself known to the soul. Just as the rays of the sun on a cold winter's day warm the body, imparting its heat to us, so the living God sheds the life-giving rays of His holiness and love into the heart that waits on Him.

How is it we so seldom experience this life-giving power of the true knowledge of God? Because we do not give God time enough to reveal himself to us. When we pray, we think we know how to speak to God. And we forget that one of the very first things in prayer is to be silent before God, that He may reveal himself. By His hidden but mighty power, God will manifest His presence, resting on us and working in us. To know God in the personal experience of His presence and love is life indeed.

You may have heard of Brother Lawrence. He had a great longing to know God, and for this purpose went into a monastery. His spiritual advisors gave him prayer books to use, but he put them aside. It helps little to pray, he said, if I do not know the God to whom I pray. And he believed that God would reveal himself. He remained a long time in silent adoration, in order to come under the full impression of the presence of this great and holy Being. He continued in this practice until later he lived consciously and constantly in God's presence and experienced His blessed nearness and keeping power. As the sun rising each morning is the pledge of light through the day, so the quiet time waiting upon God, to yield ourselves for Him to shine on us, will be the pledge of His presence and His power resting with us all the day. See that you be sure the sun has risen upon your soul.

Learn this great lesson: as the sun on a cold day shines on us and imparts its warmth, believe that the living God will work in you with His love and His almighty power. God will reveal himself as life and light and joy and strength to the soul that waits upon Him.

ANDREW MURRAY

"I pray for them. I do not pray for the world but for those whom You have given Me, for they are Yours."

John 17:9 NKJV

Here Jesus assumes the great office of Intercessor. "I pray for them" is not so much prayer as it is His solemn presentation of himself before the Father as the High Priest of His people. It marks an epoch in His work. The task of bringing God to man is substantially complete. That of bringing men by prayer to God is now to begin. It is the revelation of the permanent office of the departed Lord. There is no limitation to the sweep of His redeeming purpose or the desires of His compassionate heart for us.

The reasons for His intercession follow through verse 11. The disciples are the Father's, and continue so even when "given" to Christ, in accordance with the community of possession, which oneness of nature and perfectness of love establish between the Father and the Son. God cannot but care for those who are His. The Son cannot but pray for those who are His. Their having recognized Him for what He is binds Him to pray for them. He is glorified in His disciples, and if we show forth His character, He will be our Advocate.

In the petition itself (v. 11), observe the "Holy Father" with special reference to the prayer for preservation from the corruption of the world. God's holiness is the pledge that He will make us holy, since He is "Father" as well. Observe the substance of the request that the disciples should be kept, as in a fortress, within the enclosing circle of the name that God has given to Jesus. The name is the manifestation of the divine nature. And observe the issue of this keeping; namely, the unity of believers. The pattern of the true unity of believers is the indescribable union of Father and Son, which is oneness of will and nature, along with distinctness of persons; and therefore this purpose goes far deeper than outward unity of organization.

Then the flow of the prayer recurs to former thoughts. Going away so soon, He yearned to leave them sharers of His own emotions in the prospect of His departure to the Father, and therefore He had admitted them—and us—to hear this sacred outpouring of His desires. If we laid to heart the blessed revelation of this disclosure of Christ's heart, and followed Him with faithful gaze as He ascends to the Father, and realized our share in that triumph, our empty vessels would be filled by some of that same joy that was His. Earthly joy can never be full; Christian joy should never be anything less than full.

ALEXANDER MACLAREN

*"Holy Father, keep through Your name those whom
You have given Me, that they may be one as We are."*

John 17:11 NKJV

Many a heart has echoed my little song: "Take my life, and let it be consecrated, Lord, to Thee!" Consecration is not a religiously selfish thing. If it sinks into that, it ceases to be consecration. We want our lives kept by God, not that we may feel happy and be saved the distress that follows our wandering away from Him, but to get the power with God and man, and all the other privileges linked with it. We shall have all this, because the lower is included in the higher; but our true aim, if the love of Christ constrains us, will be far beyond this. Not for "me" at all, but "for Jesus"; not for my safety, but for His glory; not for my comfort, but for His joy; not that I may find rest, but that He may see the travail of His soul and be satisfied! Yes, for *Him* I want to be kept. Kept for His sake; kept for His use; kept to be His witness; kept for His joy! Kept for Him, that in me He may show forth some tiny sparkle of His light and beauty; kept to do His will and His work in His own way; kept, it may be, to suffer for His sake; kept for Him, that He may do just what seems good to Him for me; kept, so that no other lord shall have any more dominion over me, but that Jesus shall have all there is to have—little enough, indeed, but not divided or diminished by any other claim. You who love the Lord, is this not worth living for, worth asking for, worth trusting for?

This is consecration, and I cannot tell you the blessedness of it. The Lord Jesus does take the life that is offered to Him, and He does keep the life for himself that is entrusted to Him; but until the life is offered, we cannot know the taking, and until the life is entrusted, we cannot know or understand the keeping. All we can do is to say, "O taste and see!" and bear witness to the reality of Jesus Christ, and set to our seal that we have found Him true to His every word, and that we have proved Him able even to do exceeding abundantly above all we asked or thought. Why should we not, then, glorify His grace by acknowledging that we have found Him so wonderfully and tenderly gracious and faithful in both taking and keeping as we never supposed or imagined?

FRANCES RIDLEY HAVERGAL

"But now I come to You, and these things I speak in the world, that they may have My joy fulfilled in themselves."

John 17:13 NKJV

Jesus has revealed the Father to them, and they have believed and followed. Now He prays for them, that they may be kept; not taken out of the world; kept in it, giving their witness to it, yet never of its spirit, always controlled by another Spirit. They were being sent into the world for witness even as He had been.

And a great word breaks out like the bursting of a flood of sunlight out of dark clouds—*joy*. He had used it that evening before in the upper room, and again along the road. Now it flashes out again. This reveals the meaning of that *good cheer* and *overcome* with which the roadway talk closed (John 16:33 NKJV). With the clouds of hate at their blackest, and the storm just about to break in uncontrolled fury, He speaks of "My *joy*." He is singing. In the thick of hatred and plotting here's the bit of music, in the major key, rippling out. Such a spirit cannot be defeated. Joy is faith singing in the storm because it sees already the clearing light beyond.

And so He prays on, touching the same keys of the musical instrument of His heart, back and forth, yet ever advancing in the theme. Now He broadens out, in clear vision, beyond the gathering storm, to those, through all the earth, and down the centuries, who would believe through these men who are listening. What a sweep of faith. That singing cleared His vision.

And then He sees them all, of many races and languages and radical differences, all blended into one body of earnest loving believers drawn by the one vision of himself back in the glory of the Father's presence, where they will all gather. And then love ties the knot on the end. A personal love ties together Father and Son—and us, who humbly give the glad homage of our hearts.

What must it have meant to these men to stand there quietly awed as they listen to Him praying that prayer. How it reveals the deep consciousness of the intimacy of relation between Father and Son. How it must have touched and stirred them to the very depths to hear Jesus telling the Father so simply about *their* faith in Him, and *their* obedience, *their* break with their national allegiance to follow Him. And that word *joy*—did they wonder about it? And wonder more later that night and the days after? But the keynote of the music stuck, and soon they were singing the same tune, and in the same pitch.

S. D. GORDON

"I do not pray that You should take them out of the world, but that You should keep them from the evil one."

John 17:15 NKJV

We have, running through these precious discourses recorded by John, many allusions to the separation that was to follow, and to His leaving His followers in peril, defenseless and solitary. "Now I am no longer in the world, but these are in the world, and I come to You. Holy Father, keep through Your name those whom You have given Me" (v. 11). The same contrast between the certain security of the Shepherd and the troubled perils of the scattered flock seems to be in the words just quoted and suggests a blessed reason for the special tenderness with which He looked upon them. Christ here is represented as conscious of an accession even to the tender longings of His heart when He thought of the loneliness and the dangers to which His followers were to be exposed.

Ah! It seems a strange contrast between the ascended Christ sitting at the Father's right hand and the poor disciples contending in the stormy sea of life. But the contrast is only superficial—for you and me, if we love and trust Him, are with Him in the heavenly places even while we toil here; and He is with us, working with us, even while He sits at the right hand of God (see Ephesians 1:19–21).

We may be sure of this, that His love ever increases its manifestations according to our deepening necessities. The darker the night the more lustrous the stars. The deeper, the narrower, the wilder the alpine gorge, usually the fuller and swifter the stream that runs through it. And the more enemies and fears gather round about us, the sweeter will be the accents of our Comforter's voice, and the fuller will be the gifts of tenderness and grace with which He draws near to us. Our sorrows, dangers, and necessities are doors through which His love can come near.

So we have had the experience of sweet and transient human love; we have had the experience of changeful and ineffectual love. Turn away from them all to this immortal deep heart of Christ's, welling over with a love that no change can affect, which no separation can diminish, which becomes greater and tenderer as our necessities increase; and ask Him to fill your hearts so that you "may be able to comprehend with all the saints what is the width and length and depth and height—to know the love of Christ which passes knowledge; that you may be filled with all the fullness of God" (Ephesians 3:18–19 NKJV).

ALEXANDER MACLAREN

"Sanctify them by Your truth. Your word is truth."

John 17:17 NKJV

O ur text is the heart of the Lord's Prayer, the holy of holies where the Son of God speaks with the Father in closest fellowship of love. Here we look into the heart of Jesus as He sets out in order His desire and requests before His Father on our behalf. How invaluable must the blessing of sanctification be when our Lord, in the highest reach of His intercession, cries, "Sanctify them!"

The word *sanctify* is one of considerable range of meaning. It means, first, "dedicate them to Your service," as is reflected in Jesus' words, "and for their sakes I sanctify Myself" (v. 19 NKJV). In the Lord's case, it cannot mean purification from sin, because He was unblemished by sin. Our Lord's sanctification was His consecration to the fulfillment of the divine purpose: "Behold, I have come to do Your will, O God" (Hebrews 10:9 NKJV). This same consecration of service to God is seen in multiple ways throughout the Old Testament, with people, places, and things being reserved for holy purposes, and any other use of them was strictly forbidden.

Our Lord would have each of us be consecrated to Him, designated and ordained for divine purposes. We are not the world's or Satan's or our own. We are bought with a price. We belong to Jesus, and He presents us to His Father and asks Him to accept us and sanctify us to His own purposes. Do we not most heartily concur in this dedication?

In addition to this, we are set apart and separated from others. Again, this is seen throughout the Old Testament and into the life of the church: "Come out from among them and be separate, says the Lord. Do not touch what is unclean" (2 Corinthians 6:17 NKJV). Believers are not to be conformed to this world. They are strangers and pilgrims upon the earth. The heart that should be given to Christ and purity must not wander forth wantonly to woo the defiled and polluted things of this present evil world. Separation from the world is Christ's prayer for us.

Sanctification is a higher word than purification, for it includes that word and vastly more. It is not sufficient to be negatively clean. We need to be adorned with all the virtues. This is our prayer:

Lord, spiritualize us. Elevate us to dwell in communion with you. May we exhibit your love and be filled with zeal for your glory. May your Spirit write across our lives, "Holy to the Lord."

CHARLES SPURGEON

"Sanctify them by the truth; your word is truth."

John 17:17

The primary means of sanctification that God uses is His Word. And yet how much there is of reading and studying, of teaching and preaching the Word, that has almost no effect in making men holy. It is not the Word that sanctifies; it is God himself who alone can sanctify. Nor is it simply through the Word that God does it, but through the truth that is in the Word. As a means, the Word is of unspeakable value as the vessel that contains the truth, if God uses it; as a means, it is of no value, if God does not use it. Let us strive to connect God's Word with the Holy God. God sanctifies in the truth through His Word.

Jesus had just said, "I gave them the words you gave me and they accepted them" (John 17:8). Think of that great transaction in eternity: the Infinite One, whom we call God, *giving His words* to His Son; through His words opening up His heart, communicating His mind and will, revealing himself and all His purposes and love. In a divine power and reality passing all conception, God gave Christ His words. In the same living power, Christ gave them to His disciples, all full of a divine life and energy to work in their hearts, as they were able to receive them. And just as in the words of a man on earth we expect to find all the wisdom or all the goodness there is in him, so the Word of the Holy One is alive with the holiness of God (see Isaiah 6:3). All the holy fire, alike of His burning zeal and love, dwells in His words.

And yet men handle these words, and study them, and speak them, and remain entire strangers to their holiness or their power to make holy. It is God himself who must make men holy through the Word. It is only where there is a heart in harmony with God's holiness, longing for it, yielding itself to it, that the Word will make it holy. It is the heart that is not content with the Word, but seeks the Holy One in the Word, to which He will reveal the truth, and in it himself. It is the Word given to us by Christ as God gave it to Him, and received by us as it was by Him to rule and fill our life that has power to make it holy.

ANDREW MURRAY

"For them I sanctify myself, that they too may be truly sanctified."

John 17:19

n His prayer on His way to Gethsemane and Calvary, Jesus spoke to the Father: "I sanctify myself." This self-sanctifying of our Lord was seen through His whole life, but culminates in His crucifixion. This is made clear by the writer of Hebrews: "Then he said, 'Here I am, I have come to do your will. . . .' And by that will, we have been made holy through the sacrifice of the body of Jesus Christ once for all. . . . For by one sacrifice he has made perfect forever those who are being made holy" (10:9–10, 14). It was the offering of the body of Christ that was the will of God: in doing that will, He sanctified us. The giving up of His will to God's will in the agony of Gethsemane, and then the doing of that will in the obedience unto death was Christ's sanctifying himself.

To accomplish His redemptive work on earth, amid the trials and temptations of a human life, Jesus held fast to doing the will of the Father. In Gethsemane, the conflict between the human will and the divine will reaches its height: it manifests itself in language that almost makes us tremble for His sinlessness, as He speaks of His will in antithesis to God's. But the struggle is a victory, because in the presence of the clearest consciousness of what it means to have His own will, He gives it up and says, "Your will be done." To enter into the will of God, He gives up His very life. In His crucifixion He reveals the law of sanctification. Holiness is the full entrance of our will into God's will. Or rather, holiness is the entrance of God's will to be the death of our will. The only end of our will and deliverance from it is death to it under the righteous judgment of God. Through the cross Christ sanctified himself, and sanctified us, that we also might be sanctified in truth.

And now, we have to appropriate it to ourselves. In no other way than crucifixion could Christ realize the sanctification He had from the Father. And in no other way can we realize the sanctification we have in Him. In Christ we see that the path to perfect holiness is perfect obedience, and it is an obedience that leads to death on the cross. We cannot enter into holiness except as we die. Crucifixion is the path of sanctification.

ANDREW MURRAY

"And for their sakes I sanctify Myself, that they also may be sanctified by the truth."

John 17:19 NKJV

The first human ears these wonderful words ever fell on were the ears of the Eleven. Their Master had chosen the Eleven to be the future preachers of the gospel and pastors of the flock. They heard all their Lord's words, both of counsel and of comfort and of prayer that night; only, they did not understand what they heard. But after their Master's crucifixion and resurrection, all these things came back to their understanding and their remembrance. And, as time went on, there was nothing in that great prayer the apostles remembered more in their daily ministry than this: "For their sakes I sanctify Myself." They remembered these words every day, and they saw something of the unfathomable and inexhaustible depth of these words as they worked out their own salvation in a daily life of increasing holiness and intercessory prayer.

The apostle John said, "As [Jesus] is, so are we in this world" (1 John 4:17 NKJV). We are to be God's remembrancers on the earth. We are to be people of prayer, and especially of intercessory prayer. We are to be, for a time, in this world, that which our Lord is everlastingly in heaven. We are to be kings and priests unto God the Father by the blood of the Lamb. As He was sanctified, as He sanctified himself, for their sakes, so is it to be with us. As He was in His life of holiness, and consequent intercession, so are we to be in this world. We must sanctify ourselves for the sake of others. We must *first* sanctify ourselves, and *then* pray, first for ourselves, and then for others.

In particular, let every father and mother see to it that they make this blessed Scripture the law and the rule of their family life. Let all fathers, and all mothers, look upon their families every day and say together before God: "For their sakes we sanctify ourselves." Every father and mother makes daily intercession before God on behalf of their children. But if they would succeed in that, they must do more than that. They must add sanctification to intercession. They must learn of Christ the true secret of His intercessory and prevailing prayer. They must take this text to heart: "For their sakes I sanctify Myself."

ALEXANDER WHYTE

*"I do not pray for these alone, but also for those who will
believe in Me through their word; that they all may be one,
as You, Father, are in Me, and I in You; that they also may
be one in Us, that the world may believe that You sent Me."*

John 17:20–21 NKJV

What is Christian unity? Is it an affair of regulation, compromise, concession, and tolerance for the sake of so-called oneness? That view of Christian unity certainly receives no support from the Lord's intercessory prayer. The deepest meaning of Christian unity is union with Christ, oneness with the Son of God, identification with Christ in spirit, purpose, and effort; and coming out of that, as a cause and an inspiration, union of Christians, genuine brotherly love and trust, a love that sees the Christian in the man and that sees Christ in the Christian. Christian unity is living in sympathy with Christ; it is being so like Christ as to be almost himself; it is to be under the sweet dominion of passionate devotion to the blessed and all-blessing cross of Christ.

By what authority do some say, "This is the church, and there is none other"? That we are at liberty to organize ourselves into denominations and fellowships for mutual edification, instruction, and comfort, is a necessity of grace, the gracious compulsion of sympathy and love. But having so gathered ourselves into companies of believers who agree substantially, what right have we to say that we take in the whole universe of truth and that there is nothing hidden from us in all the counsel of God? We should hold a very different view. Our communion should be thankful for the truth that it believes itself to hold and should always be on the lookout for more light and grasp of treasure until then unpossessed. What if it takes all Christian communions to constitute the church? Who expects that we can all see everything in the same light and terms and can declare ourselves sufficiently and finally in one form of expression? There is no such uniformity in God's kingdom. Our idea of union, if founded upon doctrinal standards and denominational standards, prevents union.

Our spiritual union in Christ is so large, so dynamic, and so divine that it can permit the widest divergences—so wide as to amount to contradictions. If we had more of the spirit of Christ we might even rejoice in the differences that abound among us. All denominations are right in the proportion in which they love and serve the Son of God. Why may not our creed be substantially reduced to one line—"I believe in Christ Jesus, the Son of God"? After that we might welcome differences, we might be pleased to hear diversity of speech and accent; and things previously called deviations and divisions might be brought within the great astronomic action and made parts of the redeemed universe.

JOSEPH PARKER

"That they all may be one, as You, Father, are in Me, and I in You; that they also may be one in Us, that the world may believe that You sent Me."

John 17:21 NKJV

t is significant, beloved, that the Savior should in His last moments with His disciples pray for the unity of His people. He was not satisfied that they should be saved as a result of His death. He must have His people fashioned into a glorious body. Unity lying so very near the Savior's heart at such a time of overwhelming trial must have been held by Him to be priceless.

The unity that Christ so anxiously desired was to be composed of the people who are here called "they"—read through this entire prayer and you see that "they" are the people who have put their faith in and are united to Jesus. It is not "churches" that He prays for but the believers in all denominations of Christians. Christ's body is not made up of denominations or of presbyteries or of societies. It is made up of believers who are redeemed by the blood of Jesus, called by His Spirit, and made one with Jesus.

Being one with Christ, we are one with His people. Our unity is not written in church memberships but written on hearts and consciences and souls. If you look for a union in form or in every teaching, you will not find it. Look for a spiritual union and you will find it. Spiritual men, look for spiritual unity by first asking whether you are spiritual yourself. Are you alive by the life of Christ? Does God dwell in you, and do you dwell in Him? Then give me your hand. Never mind about a thousand differences. If you are in Christ and I am in Christ, we cannot be two; we must be one.

Let us love one another with a pure heart fervently. Let us live on earth as those who are to live together a long eternity in heaven. Let us help one another's spiritual growth. Let us aid one another as far as possible in every holy, spiritual enterprise that is for the promotion of the kingdom of the Lord. Let us chase out of our hearts everything that would break the unity that God has established. Let us cast from us every false doctrine, every false thought of pride, enmity, envy, and bitterness, that we whom God has made one may be one before men as well as before the eye of the heart-searching God. May the Lord bless us, dear friend, as His body, make us one, and keep us so.

CHARLES SPURGEON

"And the glory which You gave Me I have given them, that they may be one just as We are one."

John 17:22 NKJV

The matchless Man of Nazareth had this glory—that He was one with God. The objectives and aims and thoughts of God were His objectives and aims and thoughts. His life ran parallel with the path of the Most High. This man was accepted of God—the love of God ever rested upon Him—He had access to God; He could speak with the Father when He would, and answers out of the excellent glory were given to Him. He was powerful with God, for His prayers brought down (and still do) countless blessings upon the sons of men. He was the Son of God, and He overcame the world in the power of His sonship. Now this glory that the Father gave Him, He has given us, that we too may be accepted, that we too may have access, that we too might prevail in prayer; that we may have the Spirit of adoption, and that we may trample upon sin and overcome the hosts of darkness. This is the glory that rests upon all the faithful.

Behold the superlative liberality of the Lord Jesus, for He has given us His all. Although a tenth of His possessions would have made a universe of angels rich beyond all thought, yet was He not content until He had given us all that He had. It would have been a surprising grace if He had allowed us to eat the crumbs of His bounty, but He makes us sit with Him and share the feast. Had He given us some small pension from His royal treasuries, we should have had cause to love Him eternally; but no, He will have His bride as rich as himself, and He will not have a glory or a grace in which she shall not share. He has not been content with less than making us joint heirs with himself. He gives them full liberty to take all that He has to be their own; He loves them to take freely from His treasure and appropriate as much as they can possibly carry. The boundless fullness of His all-sufficiency is as free to the believer as the air he breathes. Christ has put the container of His love and grace to the believer's lips and invited him drink forever; for could he drain it, he is welcome to do so, and as he cannot exhaust it, he is invited to drink abundantly, for it is all his own. What truer proof of fellowship can heaven or earth afford?

CHARLES SPURGEON

"I in them, and You in Me . . ."
John 17:23 NKJV

If such a union exists between our souls and the person of our Lord, how deep and broad is the channel of our communion! This is no narrow pipe through which a tiny stream may wind its way; it is a channel of amazing depth and breadth, along whose glorious length a strong volume of living water may roll its floods. Behold, He has set before us an open door of welcome; let us not be slow to enter. If there were but one small loophole through which to talk with Jesus, it would be a high privilege to speak a word of fellowship; how much we are blessed in having so large an entrance! Had the Lord Jesus been far away from us, with many a stormy sea between, we should have longed to send a messenger to Him to carry Him our love and bring us tidings from His Father's house. But see, He has taken lodging with us and dwells in our humble hearts, so that He may have perpetual fellowship with us. Oh, how foolish must we be if we do not live in consistent communion with Him. When the road is long and dangerous, we need not wonder that friends seldom meet one another; but when they live together, shall Jonathan forget his David? Why, believer, do you not sit at His banquet of wine? Seek your Lord, for He is near; embrace Him, for He is your Brother. Hold Him fast and press Him to your heart, for He is of your own flesh.

Christ lives in us and we are so to act, in the power of the Holy Spirit, that onlookers shall say, "Surely Christ lives again in that man, for he acts as Jesus did. Did you notice how he bore the insult? Did you notice how he gave himself to help and serve? Do you see how his presence is soon felt by the pleasure that he spreads, the confidence that he inspires?" He is everyone's friend; when he is needed—the servant of all, the example of all. It is a glory to be the sweetener of life at home, the self-forgetting friend of all around. The world before long confesses that Christ is in such a man. The true Christian is Jesus come to life. Is it so? Is the love of Jesus, the generosity of Jesus, the zeal of Jesus, the gentleness of Jesus, the consecration of Jesus to be seen in us? If so, the glory of Jesus rests on us through "I in them."

CHARLES SPURGEON

*"Father, I will that they also, whom thou hast given me,
be with me where I am; that they may behold my glory,
which thou hast given me: for thou lovedst me before
the foundation of the world."*

John 17:24 KJV

The prayer of the Savior rises as it proceeds. Now He reaches His crowning point—that they may be with Him where He is and behold His glory. Like a ladder, this prayer rises round by round until it loses itself in heaven. He here ascends, not from one blessing to another of higher degree, but He mounts right away from all that is of this present state into that which is reserved for the eternal future. He quits the highest peak of grace, and at a single stride, His prayer sets its foot in glory.

"Father!" Why, it is the bell that rings us home. He who has the spirit of adoption feels that the Father draws him home, and he would gladly run after Him. How intensely did Jesus turn to the Father! He cannot speak of the glory wherein He is to be without coupling His Father with it. This is the consummation that the Firstborn looks for and to which all of us who are like Him are aspiring also, namely, that God may be all in all, that the great Father may be held in honor and may be worshiped in every place. Such is the glory that Christ desires us to share in.

The force that draws us home lies in the words *I will*. Jesus Christ, our most true God, veiled in human form, bows His knee and prays, throwing His divine energy into the prayer for the bringing home of His redeemed. This one irresistible, everlastingly almighty prayer carries everything before it; the "I will" is the centripetal force that is drawing all the family of God toward its one home.

How shall the chosen get home to the Father? Chariots are provided. Here are the chariots of fire and horses of fire in this prayer. "I will," says Jesus, "that they be with me"; and with Him they must be. There are difficulties in the way—long nights and darkness between, and hills of guilt and forests of trouble and bands of fierce temptations. Yet the pilgrims shall surely reach their journey's end, for the Lord's "I will" shall be a wall of fire round about them. Here I see the eagles' wings on which they shall mount up till they enter within the golden gates. Jesus says, "I will," and who is he who shall hinder the homecoming of the chosen? He may as well hope to arrest the marches of the stars of heaven.

CHARLES SPURGEON

"I have made you known to them, and will continue to make you known in order that the love you have for me may be in them and that I myself may be in them."

John 17:26

We are made with hearts that need to rest upon an absolute love. We are made with understandings that need to grasp a pure, a perfect, and a personal Truth. We are made with wills that crave for an absolute authoritative command. We are made with a moral nature that needs a perfect holiness. And we need all that love, truth, authority, and purity to be gathered into one; for the misery of the world is that when we set out to look for treasures, we have to go into many lands and to many merchants to buy many goodly pearls. But we need One of great price, in which all our wealth may be invested (see Matthew 13:46). We need that One to be an undying and perpetual possession.

There is One to whom our love can ever hold fast and never fear the sorrows or imperfections that make earthward-turned love a rose with many a thorn, One who is plainly the only worthy recipient of the whole love and self-surrender of the heart. And that One is God, revealed and brought near to us in Jesus Christ. In that great Savior we have a love at once divine and human; we have the great transcendent instance of love leading to sacrifice. On that love and sacrifice for us Christ builds His claim on us for our hearts, and our all. Life alone can communicate life; it is only love that can kindle love; it is only sacrifice that can inspire sacrifice. And so He comes to us and asks that we should love Him back again as He has loved us. He first yields up His own life for us, and then asks us to give ourselves wholly to Him. The object, the true object, for all this depth of love that lies slumbering in our hearts is God in Christ, the Christ who died for us.

God's love is Christ's love; Christ's love is God's love, and the good news is that the love of God is deeper than all our sins. "But . . . because of [God's] great love with which He loved us, even when we were dead in trespasses, made us alive together with Christ" (Ephesians 2:4–5 NKJV). Sin is but the cloud behind which the light of the love of Christ will yet pierce through, with its merciful shafts bringing healing in their beams, dispersing all the pitch darkness of our sins, and at last restoring our hearts to knowing the One who is our undying and perpetual possession.

ALEXANDER MACLAREN

When Jesus had spoken these words, He went out with His disciples over the Brook Kidron, where there was a garden, which He and His disciples entered.

John 18:1 NKJV

At the top of the mountain is the peak. The peak is the range at its highest reach. The peak grows out of the range and rests upon it and upon the earth under all. The whole of the long mountain range and of the earth lies under the peak. The peak tells the story of the whole range—at the last the highest and utmost. All the rest is for this capstone.

The great thing in Jesus' life is His death. The death crowns the life. The whole of the life lies under and comes to its full in the death. The highest point is touched when death is allowed to lay Him lowest. It was the life that died that gives the distinctive meaning to the death. Let us take off hat and shoes as we come to this peak event.

There's a change in John's story here. The evening has gone, the quiet evening of communion. The night has set in, the dark night of hate. The intimacies of love give place to the intrigues of hate. The joy of communion is quickly followed by the jostling of the crowd, out of the secret place of prayer, into the turmoil of passion. And the Master's sensitive spirit feels the change. Yet with quiet resolution He steps out to face it. It is part of "this hour" (John 12:27), part of His great task, the greatest part.

For the holy task of winning hearts to himself is not changed. It still is pursuing, but there's a difference now. There's a shifting. The pursuit goes from closer to wider, from the disciples to the outer crowd, from the direct reaching out to the national leaders by personal plea to the indirect by action, tremendously personal action.

It moves out into a yet wider sweep. It goes from the pursuit of a nation to the pursuit of a race, from Jew distinctively to Roman representatively, from Annas standing in God's floodlight rejected to Pilate in nature's lesser light obscured, from God's truant messenger nation to the world's mighty ruling nation.

In the epochal event just at hand Jesus begins His great pursuing of a race. And that pursuit has gone on ever since, wherever He has been able to get through the human channels to the crowd. He was lifted up and at once men began coming, running broken in heart by the sight. He is being lifted up, and men of the entire race are coming as fast as the news gets to them.

S. D. GORDON

Jesus therefore, knowing all things that would come upon Him, went forward and said to them, "Whom are you seeking?"

John 18:4 NKJV

Now the mob of hate comes seeking with torch and lantern, soldiers and officers, chief priests and rulers, the ever present rabble, and in the lead the shameless traitor. They are pushing their quest now, seeking Jesus in the hiding whence He had gone days before led by the man who knew His accustomed haunts.

But there's no need for seeking now. Jesus is full ready. He decides the action that follows. He is masterful even in His purposeful yielding. Quietly He walks out from the cover of the trees to meet them. And as their torches turn full upon His advancing figure again, that marvelous power not only of restraint but decidedly more is felt by them. "Now when He said to them, 'I am He,' they drew back and fell to the ground" (v. 6). And the whole company—traitor, soldiers, rulers, rabble—overpowered in spirit, fall back and then drop to the ground utterly overawed and cowed by the lone man they are seeking.

Does Judas expect this? Will this power they are unable to resist not open the eyes of these rulers! But there's no stupidity equal to that which goes with stubbornness. In a moment Jesus reveals His purpose in this, to shield His disciples. Now the power of restraint is withdrawn and He yields to their desires. They shall have full sway in using their freedom of action as they will.

John had significantly stated, "Jesus therefore, knowing all things that would come upon Him, went forward." With masterly forethought and self-control and deliberation He would do the thing He had set himself to do. Never was yielding so masterful. Strong, thoughtful, self-controlled, anticipating every move, He was using all the strength of His great will in yielding. Never was a great plan carried out so fully through the set purpose of one's enemies. His every action bears out the word He had spoken, "Therefore My Father loves Me, because I lay down My life that I may take it again. No one takes it from Me, but I lay it down of Myself. I have power to lay it down, and I have power to take it again. This command I have received from My Father" (John 10:17–18 NKJV).

Jesus died deliberately. This is quite clear. It was done of love aforethought. It was His own act fitted into the circumstances surrounding Him. This makes His death mean just what He meant it to mean.

S. D. GORDON

*Now when He said to them, "I am He," they drew back
and fell to the ground.*

John 18:6 NKJV

I am He!" When the soldiers and officers were thus doubly assured by the traitor's kiss and by Jesus' own confession, why did they not immediately lay hands upon Him? There He stood in the midst of them, alone, defenseless; there was nothing to hinder their binding Him on the spot. Instead of that they recoil and fall in a huddled heap before Him. Some strange awe and terror, of which they themselves could have given no account, was upon their spirits. How did it come about?

The impression appears to be that there was something more than human in Christ's look and tone. Might it not be that here we see, perhaps apart from Christ's will altogether, rising up for one moment to the surface, the indwelling majesty that was always there? We do not know the laws that regulated the dwelling of the Godhead, bodily, within that human frame, but we do know that at one other time there came upon His features a transfiguration and His clothes became as white as light that was not thrown upon them from without, but rose up from within (see Matthew 17:2). And I am inclined to think that here, as there, though under such widely different circumstances and to such various issues, there was for a moment a little rending of the veil of His flesh and an emission of some flash of the brightness that always dwelt within Him. And that one stray beam of manifest divinity shot through for an instant and was enough to prostrate with a strange awe even those hardened men.

The incident brings out very strikingly the elevation and dignity of Christ, and the powerful impressions made by His personality, even at such a time of humiliation. The apostle John is always careful to bring out the glory of Christ, especially when that glory lies side by side with His lowliness. This strange blending of opposites—the glory in the lowliness, and the abasement in the glory—is the keynote of this singular event. He will be delivered into the hands of men, yes, but before He is delivered He pauses for an instant, and in that instant comes a flash of the hidden glory.

Do not forget that we may well look upon that incident as a prophecy of what shall be. What will He do coming to reign, when He did this coming to die? And what will His manifestation be as a Judge when this was the effect of the manifestation as He went to be judged?

ALEXANDER MACLAREN

Jesus answered, "I have told you that I am He. Therefore, if you seek Me, let these go their way."

John 18:8 NKJV

Mark, my soul, the care that Jesus manifested even in His hour of trial toward the sheep of His hand! The ruling passion is strong in death. He yields himself to the enemy, but He interposes a word of power to set His disciples free. As to himself, like a sheep before her shearers He opened not His mouth, but for His disciples' sake He speaks with almighty energy. Herein is love, constant, self-forgetting, faithful love.

But is there not far more here than is to be found upon the surface? Have we not the very soul and spirit of the atonement in these words? The Good Shepherd lays down His life for the sheep and pleads that they must therefore go free. The Surety is bound, and justice demands that those for whom He stands a substitute should be free to go on their way. In the midst of Egypt's bondage, that voice rings out as a word of power: "Let these go their way." Out of the slavery of sin and Satan the redeemed must come. In every cell of the dungeons of Despair, the sound is echoed, "Let these go their way," and forth come Despondency and Much-Afraid. Satan hears the well-known voice and lifts his foot from the neck of the fallen; and Death hears it, and the grave opens her gates to let the dead arise. Their way is one of progress, holiness, triumph, glory, and none shall dare to restrain them from it. No lion shall be on their way, neither shall any ravenous beast go up thereon. The trophy buck has drawn the cruel hunters upon himself, and now the most timid does and bucks of the field may graze in perfect peace among the lilies of His love. The thundercloud has burst over the cross of Calvary, and the pilgrims of Zion shall never be smitten by the bolts of vengeance.

O child of God, take this with you for your safe conduct everywhere! Take this command, and when unbelief stops you, draw it out, and say, "He has said, 'Let these go their way.'" And when Satan stops you, hold out to him this divine mandate: "Let these go their way." And when Death shall stop you, take out this sweet permit from your Master: "Let these go their way." Come, rejoice in the immunity that your Redeemer has secured for you, and bless His name all the day and every day.

CHARLES SPURGEON

Now the servants and officers who had made a fire of coals stood there, for it was cold, and they warmed themselves. And Peter stood with them and warmed himself.

John 18:18 NKJV

J esus Christ was being tried. One does not wonder at the high priest's servants standing to warm their hands at a fire of coals, for they knew but little, comparatively, of Christ. They had never tasted of His love, had not been asked to watch with Him in the garden of Gethsemane, had never heard Him say, "Blessed are you, Simon Bar-Jonah, for flesh and blood has not revealed this to you" (Matthew 16:17 NKJV). The marvel is that Peter should stand there among them, acting as they did, so as to escape suspicion. What can be more inconsistent than the disciple warming his hands while the Master endures such hostility from sinners against himself?

A few coals in a fire suffice to warm Peter's hands, but even the infinite love of Jesus did not, just then, warm his heart. The scene at the end of the hall was enough to set all hearts aglow. It was the Son of God struck on the mouth and vilely slandered—and yet bearing it all for love of us! Oh, there was a furnace at the other end of the hall—a furnace of divine love! If Peter had but looked at his Master's face, marred with agony, surely, had his heart been right, it would have burned within him! If Peter had only been true to that true heart of his, he would have braved the malice of the throng, placed himself side by side with his Lord, and said, "Do to me whatever you do to Him." But alas, the sight of his betrayed Lord did not warm Peter's heart.

Dear one, every time we refrain to speak out for Jesus because it would involve us in censure, every time we retreat from a labor because we desire ease, every time we pull back from the suffering that the cross involves, every time we seek honor where He was put to shame and comfort where He endured an ignominious death—we are warming our hands at the fire of coals! It was when the Holy Spirit used the glance of Jesus as a special means of grace that Peter's heart was thawed and his eyes dropped with tears of repentance! (See Luke 22:62.)

O Lord and Master, if your blessed Spirit will come upon us, we shall see you by faith, and the sight will make our hearts burn within us! Come, sacred Spirit, shed abroad the love of Jesus in our souls and so shall our love be kindled and burn fervently!

CHARLES SPURGEON

Then Annas sent Him bound to Caiaphas the high priest.

John 18:24 NKJV

There was no need to put any bands upon one so gentle as Jesus was. Out of spiteful malice, they must have done it, that they might express their hatred and scorn by every conceivable method, both in the little details and in the great end at which they were aiming all the while—namely, to put Him to a most painful death. How shamefully was our blessed Master treated in this inhospitable world!

Our Lord Jesus Christ was bound, and there flows from that fact its opposite—then His people are all free. When Christ was made a curse for us, He became a blessing to us. When Christ was made sin for us, we were made the righteousness of God in Him. When He died, we lived. And so, as He was bound, we were set free.

Do you think, dear friend, we use our liberty as we should? Do we not sometimes pray to God as if we were tongue-tied, the bonds upon our tongue? Do we not go to the great treasuries full of grace and, instead of helping ourselves as we have the right to do, we stand there as if our hands were bound and we could not take a single pennyworth of the abundant fullness that is laid up there for us? O believer, why do you stand like one who is still in bonds? Your freedom is sure, and it is a righteous freedom. Christ, the great Emancipator, has made you free and you are "free indeed." Enjoy your liberty! Enjoy access to God! Enjoy the privilege of claiming the promises that God has given to you! Enjoy the exercise of the power with which God has endowed you! Enjoy the holy anointing with which the Lord has prepared you for His service!

Do not sit and mope like a bird in a cage when you are free to soar away! Away with you, sweet songster! The green fields and the blue sky are all your own. Stretch your wings and soar away above the clouds—and sing the carol of your freedom as though you would make it reach the ears of the angels! So let it be with your spirit, beloved! Christ has set us free! Therefore let us not go back into bondage, or sit still as though we were in prison—let us rejoice in our liberty this very hour and let us do so all our days!

CHARLES SPURGEON

*One of the servants of the high priest, a relative of
him whose ear Peter cut off, said, "Did I not see you
in the garden with Him?" Peter then denied again; and
immediately a rooster crowed.*

John 18:26–27 NKJV

Peter was on dangerous ground. We read of the high priest's servants,
that they warmed themselves, and "Peter stood with them and warmed
himself" (v. 18 NKJV). He was in bad company, and he remained there,
which was worse still (see v. 25). First the maid, then several men, and last of
all this relative of the man whom he had wounded put questions to Peter that
led him to deny that he ever was a disciple of the Prophet of Galilee. Peter,
who might at first have acknowledged his Master, did not do it, but denied
Him; having once denied Him, it was almost inevitable that he should do the
same again. And so he added lie to lie and said, "I know not the man." As
the weakness increases and the sin gains force, the fault deepens in blackness
and there is no hope for the deserter.

The lesson of this: flee from the place of temptation as speedily as possible.
Any man may inadvertently stumble into a place where temptation abounds,
but if he is wise, he will leave immediately. Take heed of abiding in the place
of danger, toying with danger and courting destruction! While you remain on
dangerous ground, your weakness increases. The longer you stop in an evil place,
the more numerous will your temptations become. Temptations are like flies—
they come one or two at the first, but eventually they buzz about you in swarms.

There are some who are in positions of life and associations and relationships that they ought to give up—that are sinful and cannot be held by persons
who are honest, truthful, and virtuous. It is of no use to try to fight the battle
of the cross where some people are—they are harnessed to the chariot of the
devil and they must come out of it or be driven to destruction. If they are
engaged in a business or in associations and relationships that are distinctly
sinful, they must break loose from these and not pretend to be Christians.
Yet many try to keep in with the world and keep in with Christ, and they will
never do it—but will make a terrible fall of it before long.

Get right into Christ, and let the Lord Jesus, by the power of His Holy Spirit,
carry you away from the unclean place. May the Lord grant you divine grace
to leap into the gospel chariot and leave all sinful company and doubtful ways
behind, so that you may acknowledge the Lord Jesus and be His true disciple!

CHARLES SPURGEON

Then Pilate said to them, "You take Him and judge Him according to your law." Therefore the Jews said to him, "It is not lawful for us to put anyone to death."

John 18:31 NKJV

The Jewish council had condemned Jesus to death, and the next thing was to get the Roman authority to carry out the sentence. The necessity of this appeal was a bitter pill, but it had to be swallowed, for the right of capital punishment had been withdrawn by the Romans.

Pilate was probably not pleased at being roused so early or at having to comply with their appeal that was so obviously unjust, and through all his bearing to the council a certain irritation shows itself with some flashes of sarcasm. His first question as to the charge they brought against Jesus was embarrassing to them. Why did they not wish to formulate a charge? Partly from pride. They hugged the delusion that their court was competent to condemn and wanted to shut their eyes to a plain fact, as if ignoring it annihilated it. Partly because the charge on which they had condemned Jesus—that of blasphemy in calling himself "the Son of God"—was not a crime known to Roman law, and to allege it would probably have ended in the whole matter being scornfully dismissed. So they stood on their dignity and tried to bluster. "He is an evildoer; that is enough."

Pilate saw an opening to get rid of the whole matter, and with just a faint flavor of irony suggests that, as they had their own law, they had better go by it and punish as well as condemn. That sarcastic proposal compelled them to acknowledge their subjection. Pilate had given the reins the least touch, but enough to make them feel the bit; and though it went sore against the grain, they will own their master rather than lose their victim. So their reluctant lips say, "It is not lawful for us." Pilate has brought them on their knees at last, and they forget their dignity and own the truth. Malicious hatred will eat any amount of dirt and humiliation to gain its ends, especially if it calls itself religious zeal.

John sees in the issue of this first round in the duel between Pilate and the rulers the sequence of events that brought about the fulfilment of our Lord's prediction of His crucifixion, since that was not a Jewish method of execution. This encounter of keen wits becomes tragic and awful when we remember who it was that these men were wrangling about.

ALEXANDER MACLAREN

Then Pilate entered the Praetorium again, called Jesus,
and said to Him, "Are You the King of the Jews?"

John 18:33 NKJV

Now comes the great Pilate phase. It was the intense malignity of the Jewish leaders that made them bother with Pilate. They could easily have killed Jesus, and Pilate would never have concerned himself about it. But they couldn't have put Him to such exquisite suffering and such shameful indignity before the crowds as by the Roman form of death by crucifixion.

Clearly there is hate at work *behind* theirs. Their hate is distinctly *inhuman*. Is *all* hate? There's an unseen satanic power in action here set on spilling out the utmost that malignant hate can upon the person of Jesus. But these men are cheerful tools.

This is Pilate's opportunity, and he seems to sense it. And a struggle begins between conscience and cowardice, between right action with an ugly fight for it, and yielding to wrong with an easy time of it. Clearly he feels the purity and the personal power of this unusual prisoner. The motive of envy and hate under their action is as plain to his trained eyes.

Twice the two men, Pilate and Jesus, are alone together. Did ever man have such an opportunity, personally and historically? With rare touch and loving care Jesus reaches out to Pilate. And Pilate feels it to the marrow under all his rough speech. His repeated attempts with the leaders make that clear. But cowardice gripped him hard. It's a way cowardice has.

The name of Caesar conjures up fears—loss of position, of wealth, of reputation, maybe of life itself. Pilate surrenders. Conscience is slain on the judgment seat. Cowardice laughs and wins. A sharp cry of allegiance to Caesar from their reluctant throats, as their hatred wins the day. Jesus strikes them back an ugly blow as He surrenders. That reluctant Caesar cry told the intensity of their hatred. They hated Caesar much, but they hated Jesus immeasurably more. They gulp down Caesar to be able to vent their anger upon Jesus.

And so they crucified Him. The hate burning within finds its full vent. Its hateful worst is done, and horribly well done. And they stand about the cross with unconcealed gloating. Their part of the story is done, and they exit history's stage and are gone.

But Jesus' part—ah! That was just begun! With flooded eyes and broken hearts, bending wills and changed lives, men of all races bow gratefully at the feet of Jesus, our Savior and Lord and coming King.

S. D. GORDON

Jesus replied, "My kingdom is not of this world. . . . If My kingdom were of this world, My servants would be fighting [hard] to keep Me from being handed over to the Jews; but as it is, My kingdom is not of this world."

John 18:36 AMP

Undoubtedly the peacefulness of Christ and His disciples confounded His contemporaries, forasmuch as the sword has ever been called into requisition by the founders of empires, and yet here is one who attempts to establish a kingdom without shedding the blood of a single foe! Christ's answer could hardly be understood and appreciated by Pilate, who only knew worldly thrones, crown, and scepters.

What, then, is the Savior's meaning? His kingdom is a purely spiritual constitution—He came not to found a physical empire but to establish the sovereignty of great and holy principles. His mission was not to contend with earthly governors for their thrones, but to lay the foundation of a kingdom whose royalty will survive the splendor of material pomp. He unsheathed no sword but the "sword of the Spirit." He marshaled no army except the army of divine doctrines and precepts. He breathed no inflammatory speeches against governments, as such. When He sought the overthrow of a sovereign, it was the prince of the power of the air whose throne He shook. When, therefore, Christ declares that His "kingdom is not of this world," we are to infer the pure spirituality of the Christian church.

And what does that kingdom look like in the life of the believer? The believer regards the world as a means rather than as an end. The watchword of the Christian is "Here we have no continuing city, but we seek the one to come" (Hebrews 13:14 NKJV). He uses this world as the builder uses scaffolding, merely for temporary purposes. He never looks upon this world as a final resting place and thus does not lay up for himself treasures on earth. If he has wealth, it is to him a means of usefulness; if he has influence, he employs it in the promotion of the highest good. He is too wise to expect satisfaction in the merely temporal—things are great to him just in proportion as they rightly affect his eternal well-being. His highest ambition is to fulfill his master's mission to seek and save the lost. Under this kingdom he finds freedom from the strong attachment to the charms of this world that bind the hearts of those who are earthbound. And he takes as his final goal the day when he walks in "the city which has foundations, whose builder and maker is God," and breathes its untainted air, and sings, "Worthy is the Lamb who was slain to receive power and riches and wisdom, and strength and honor and glory and blessing!" (Hebrews 11:10; Revelation 5:12 NKJV).

JOSEPH PARKER

Pilate therefore said to Him, "Are You a king then?"
Jesus answered, "You say rightly that I am a king. For
this cause I was born, and for this cause I have come
into the world, that I should bear witness to the truth.
Everyone who is of the truth hears My voice."

John 18:37 NKJV

Do not forget that our Savior was a prisoner in bonds, on trial for His life. He appeared to be absolutely in the power of a man who cared nothing about what means he employed so long as he could attain his own evil ends. And the judge contemptuously says to Him, "Are You a king then?" And He answers, most decidedly and undoubtedly, "You say rightly that I am a king." I think I see Pilate's lip curl with supreme contempt as he looked upon the victim before him—yet Jesus avowed the truth of God!

He boldly declared that His life purpose was to bear witness to the truth—why should He conceal it? He who seeks to bear witness to the truth of God should be true enough to declare what the objective of his witness is. And the Savior did so, before Pilate, and wherever He was! All His life He was a witness to the truth—He was the truest man who ever lived! His teaching is delivered straight on as from a mountaintop and men may stand and gaze upon the Truth He is and speaks! As a truthful man, He was a fit witness to bear testimony to the truth of God.

He went on to say to Pilate, "Everyone who is of the truth hears My voice." Do you hear that declaration, Pilate? You are a very great man, and this poor prisoner tells you plainly that everyone who is of the truth hears His voice. Then, Pilate, if you are of the truth, you will have to listen to His words and learn of Him! I can well conceive what Pilate thought as he contemptuously asked, "What is truth?" He had heard quite enough of such talk as that.

But therein lies the glory of the Master, that He is not content with merely teaching truth of God, but He presses it home even upon His judge! If His teaching is true, that which is opposed to God and His truth is not from Him and cannot stand on the same footing with that which is divinely revealed. It takes a good deal of courage to say that, nowadays. If you go into society, you will get three cheers if you declare there is no absolute truth. And so Christ divides and separates between the precious and the vile. So must you and I do, dear friend, if we are faithful followers of the faithful Witness to the truth.

CHARLES SPURGEON

14

*"You are a king, then!" said Pilate. Jesus answered, "You
say that I am a king. In fact, the reason I was born and
came into the world is to testify to the truth. Everyone
on the side of truth listens to me."*

John 18:37

J esus answers Pilate that He is a king indeed, but shows him how His
kingdom is a very different kind from what is called a kingdom in this
world. Jesus could have called twelve legions of angels to destroy the
Romans and reigned over the world from Jerusalem as the just monarch that
was the dream of the Jews. But the Lord would rather wash the feet of His
weary brothers than to be the singular perfect monarch who ever ruled in the
world. That was an empire He rejected when He ordered Satan behind Him
in the wilderness temptation.

The kingdom over which the Lord cares to reign is a kingdom of kings,
where every man is a king. A king must rule over his own kind. Jesus is a king
in virtue of no conquest or inheritance, but in right of essential being; and
He cares for no subjects but such as are of His own kind, in their very nature
and essence kings. To understand His answer to Pilate, see what manifestation
of His essential being gives Him a claim to be king. He says, "I am a king. In
fact, the reason I was born and came into the world is to testify to the truth.
Everyone on the side of truth listens to me." In effect, "He is a king like me
and belongs as one of my subjects." Pilate thereupon—as would most Christians nowadays, instead of setting about to be true—requests a definition of
truth. Neither Pilate nor they ask the one true question, "How am I to be a
true man? How am I to become a man worth being a man?" The Lord is a
king because His life, the life of His thoughts, of His imagination, of His
will, of His smallest action, is true—true first to God in that He is altogether
His, true to himself in that He forgets himself altogether, and true to His
fellow men in that He will endure anything they do to Him and never stop
declaring himself the Son of God. They will kill Him, but it matters not: the
truth is as He says!

We see, then, that the true king is the man who stands up a true man and
speaks the truth no matter the cost. The truth is God; the witness to the truth
is Jesus. The kingdom of the truth is the hearts of men, your heart and my
heart. The man who responds to this with his whole being is of the truth.

GEORGE MACDONALD

So then Pilate took Jesus and scourged Him.

John 19:1 NKJV

We read about that Roman punishment in the ancient books, but men do not understand what they read so much as what they feel. The victim was tied by the hands to a post and compelled to assume a stooping position; the knotted whip was in the hands of a Roman executioner, and he administered the punishment largely according to his own will. The Jewish law was that "forty stripes minus one" should be administered (2 Corinthians 11:24 NKJV). There was no corresponding reservation in the Roman law; the executioner might administer punishment according to personal disposition; there was no restraint as to the number of the stripes.

"Scourged Him" who spoke the Beatitudes. It is impossible! Surely a mistake has been made in the writing. The man who is now bent and on whose bared back the whip falls, said, "Blessed are the poor in spirit, for theirs is the kingdom of heaven" (Matthew 5:3 NKJV). "Scourged Him" who took little children in His arms and blessed them. To have been in those arms—what a heaven was that! A caress that only a child could feel: and this was the Man. "Scourged Him" who had fed the hungry multitude and spoke such marvelous parables of the prodigal son and good Samaritan and lost sheep and a pearl of great price. "Scourged Him" who healed the lepers and the blind and raised the dead!

Yet all this was foretold. The fifty-third chapter of Isaiah would make an excellent introduction to these closing chapters of the evangelic story. The same Jesus, in the Old Testament, "was wounded for our transgressions . . . bruised for our iniquities . . . yet He opened not His mouth; He was led as a lamb to the slaughter" (vv. 5–7). But who has eyes to see eternity? "And by His stripes"—a still larger scourging—"we are healed" (v. 5 NKJV). What do these words mean? We cannot tell. Whoever took the sun into his own house to examine it and tell what it was made of? We can only say that the sun gives light, and we can only say that Jesus makes us see, gives us life and hope and immortality, and has so worked in our lives so that we can say to death, "Where is your sting? O Hades"—black, grim, grave—"where is your victory?" (1 Corinthians 15:55 NKJV). Any Man who has wrought this miracle in us is worthy of all the crowns that make heaven royal. We stand to say that Jesus has done this for us.

JOSEPH PARKER

NOVEMBER

16

Then they said, "Hail, King of the Jews!" And they struck Him with their hands.

John 19:3 NKJV

Let us beware lest we focus all our sentiments on Christ's historical humiliation. It is not enough to weep because this Man was scourged and beaten twenty-one centuries ago. Pilate is dead, as are the soldiers, but the process of scourging still goes on. How so? Certainly, they scourge Jesus who nominally profess to serve Him but do not serve Him with all their mind, heart, soul, and strength. They scourge Him today when they use Him as a mere decoration, when His cross is worn as an ornament and not felt as a burden to be lived. They scourge Christ who are silent when hostile attacks are made upon Him. He feels our silence more than He feels the attack. His flesh wounds were but for a moment; He now feels everything upon His naked heart.

Who has not stood back and heard Jesus attacked and reviled and dishonored, and never spoken a word for his Friend? In that case what did Jesus Christ feel? Not the attack at all; but how His eyes reddened with tears when He marked the silence! "What?" said He. "Have you nothing to say? Does no tender association enlarge your love and stimulate your courage with a noble inspiration?" Our relation to Christ is nothing if it is not one of love. It is simplicity, submissiveness, felt necessity, rising love, answering sympathy. Jesus feels it, therefore, when anyone who has been redeemed by Him dare not say to hissing and mocking Pharisees, "Whether He is a sinner or not I do not know. One thing I know: that though I was blind, now I see" (John 9:25 NKJV). If every believer would speak there would be eloquence enough.

They scourge Jesus who use His name for unworthy purposes, as a social key, as a means to giving the appearance of goodness and integrity. The same ones pay less attention to their Christianity than others pay attention to their atheism. They crown Jesus who obey Him. Do not let us imagine that by singing about crowning Jesus that we are going to do some wonderful work in coronation. We could crown Him now. We speak of that great future day when we will cast our crowns before Him, being lost in wonder, love, and praise. That is perfectly right; there is a holy meaning attached to such sacred words. But all who would crown Jesus now may do so by saying, and meaning, "Lord, what will you have me to do now?"

JOSEPH PARKER

And Pilate said to them, "Behold the Man!"

John 19:5 NKJV

I f there is one place where our Lord Jesus most fully becomes the joy and comfort of His people, it is where He plunged deepest into the depths of woe. Come near and behold the Man of Sorrows in the garden of Gethsemane; behold His heart so brimming with love that He cannot hold it in—so full of sorrow that it must find a vent. Behold the bloody sweat as it distills from every pore of His body and falls upon the ground. Behold the Man as they drive the nails into His hands and feet. Look up and see the sorrowful image of your suffering Lord. Mark Him, as the crimson drops stand out on the crown of thorns and adorn with priceless gems the diadem of the King of Misery. Behold the Man when all His bones are out of joint, and He is poured out like water and brought into the dust of death; God has forsaken Him, and hell compasses Him about. Behold and see, was there ever sorrow like unto His sorrow?

All you who pass by draw near and look upon this spectacle of grief, unique, unparalleled, a wonder to men and angels, a prodigy unmatched. Behold the Emperor of Woe who had no equal or rival in His agonies! "He is despised and rejected by men" (Isaiah 53:3 NKJV), even He who was and is the King of kings, the Lord of lords! For the innocent Christ to be made sin for us—for the wrath of God to roll over Him instead of us—must have caused within His spirit a depth of anguish that the tenderest heart cannot fathom! Gaze upon Him, for if there is not consolation in a crucified Christ, there is no joy in earth or heaven. If in the ransom price of His blood there is not hope, oh, harps of heaven, there is no joy in you, and the right hand of God shall know no pleasures forevermore.

We have only to sit more continually at the foot of the cross to be less troubled with our doubts and woes. We have but to see His sorrows, and our sorrows we shall be ashamed to mention; we have but to gaze into His wounds and heal our own. If we would live correctly, it must be by the contemplation of His death; if we would rise to dignity, it must be by considering His humiliation and His sorrow. "Behold the Man!"

CHARLES SPURGEON

18

But Jesus gave him no answer.

John 19:9 NKJV

Jesus had never been slow of speech when He could bless the sons of men, but He would not say a single word for himself. "No man ever spoke like this Man!" the officers of the chief priest and Pharisees had reported (John 7:46 NKJV), and never was a man silent like Him. His adversaries slandered Him, but He replied not. False witnesses arose, but He answered them not. Here He is silent before Pilate. The hill of the cross might have become a volcano's mouth to swallow up the whole multitude that stood there jeering at Him. But no, He kept back the natural indignation that must have come over His spirit against the injustice, the lies, the shameful malice of His foes. He held it all back and was patient, meek, silent to the end.

Was this singular silence the index of His perfect self-sacrifice? Did it show that He would not utter a word to stay the execution of His sacred person, which He had dedicated as an offering for us? Had He so entirely surrendered himself that He would not interfere on His own behalf, even in the minutest degree, but be bound and slain an unstruggling, uncomplaining victim? Was this silence a type of the defenselessness of sin? Nothing can be said to reduce or excuse human guilt; and, therefore, He who bore its whole weight stood speechless before His judge.

Is not patient silence the best reply to a naysaying world? Calm endurance answers some questions infinitely more conclusively than the loftiest eloquence. The best apologists for Christianity in the early days were its martyrs. The anvil breaks a host of hammers by quietly bearing their blows. Did not the silent Lamb of God furnish us with a grand example of wisdom? The ambiguous and the false, the unworthy and mean, will eventually overthrow and confute themselves, and therefore the true can afford to be quiet and finds silence to be its wisdom.

Evidently our Lord, by His silence, furnished a remarkable fulfillment of prophecy. A long defense of himself would have been contrary to Isaiah's prediction. "He was led as a lamb to the slaughter, and as a sheep before its shearers is silent, so He opened not His mouth" (Isaiah 53:7 NKJV). By His quiet He conclusively proved himself to be the true Lamb of God. As such, we salute Him.

Be with us, Jesus, and in the silence of our heart, let us hear the voice of your love.

CHARLES SPURGEON

From then on Pilate sought to release Him, but the Jews cried out, saying, "If you let this Man go, you are not Caesar's friend. Whoever makes himself a king speaks against Caesar."

John 19:12 NKJV

Probably there is not, in the whole compass of history, a more vivid illustration of hesitancy and instability than that afforded by the conduct of Pilate immediately prior to the crucifixion. At the outset, Pilate was reluctant to undertake the judgment of the case, but the people pressed upon him, insisting that such and such a course be taken, driving him to his wit's end, not allowing him to hesitate more than a moment, bearing away all his protestation in a storm of anger. Finally the mob made the omnipotent appeal to Pilate's allegiance to Caesar. That did it. Being destitute of strong conviction, he capitulated in the presence of a determined opposition.

Such are life circumstances. Is any position more unenviable than when we must stand for right in the face of passionate wrong? Only strong convictions will deliver us from the tyranny of pleasing people. A man of strong conviction in such a position will abide in perfect calm until the storm cries itself to sleep; then will he ascend the throne and show that right has patience to wait and power to conquer.

Strong convictions also enable men to sacrifice the highest human patronage. To be "Caesar's friend" is an object in whose allegiance the sublimest principles are often trodden in the dust. There are men who can see no higher than Caesar. Their feeble vision is so dazzled by the light of earthly pomp and prestige that they cannot see the palace where reigns the King Eternal, whose garment is light and whose throne is built of the riches of the universe. Beholding the Majesty of heaven, one scorns the patronage of any Caesar for which he must pay his blood or mortgage his eternity!

And strong convictions enable men to serve the truth in the most perilous circumstances. He is the truly royal man in whom perfect love has cast out fear. Agreeable men may be applauded in seasons of calm, but they are useless when foundations are shaking and thunders rolling.

Let us "be strong in the grace that is in Christ Jesus" (2 Timothy 2:1 NKJV) and faithful servants of all the principles that can inspire and ennoble the race. When the enemy demands our crucifixion of the truth, instead of being Pilate-like, we shall reply by a louder utterance of its praise and a profounder reverence at its throne!

JOSEPH PARKER

And he said to the Jews, "Behold your King!"

John 19:14 NKJV

Everything said or done in connection with the Savior during the day of His crucifixion was full of more meaning than was intended. Pilate, the undecided spirit, uttered language as weighty as if he too had been among the prophets. If Christ was King when He was in Pilate's hands, after being scourged and spit upon and while wearing the crown of mockery, when will He not be King? If He was King at His worst, when is it that His throne can ever be shaken? They have brought Him very low, and yet He is King! Marks of royalty were present on the day of His death. He gave the dying thief a promise of an entrance into paradise. He shook the earth, opened graves, split the rocks, and darkened the sun. One voice after another, even from the ranks of His foes, proclaimed Him to be King, even when dying like a criminal. Was He a King then? When will He not be King?

If He was King before He died and was laid in the grave, what is He now that He has risen from the dead, now that He has vanquished the destroyer of our race and lives no more to die? What is He now? You angels, tell what glories surround Him now! If He was King when He stood at Pilate's court, what will He be when Pilate shall stand at His court, when He shall come on the great white throne and summon all mankind before Him to judgment? Come, let us adore and pay our humble homage to Him. And then let us go forth to our daily service in His name and make this our strong resolve, His Spirit helping us, that we will live to crown Him in our hearts and in our lives—in every place where we are—till the day break and the shadows flee away and we behold the King in His beauty.

As for us, if we wish to extend the Redeemer's kingdom, we must be prepared to deny ourselves for Christ. We must be prepared for weariness, slander, and self-denial. In this sign we conquer. The cross will have to be borne by us as well as by Him if we are to reign with Jesus. We must participate in the shame if we would participate in the glory. No thorn, no throne. The Lord grant us to be loyal subjects of the crucified that we may be favored to share His glory.

CHARLES SPURGEON

*Then he delivered Him to them to be crucified. So they
took Jesus and led Him away.*

John 19:16 NKJV

He had been all night in agony, He had spent the early morning at
the hall of Caiaphas, He had been hurried from Caiaphas to Pilate,
from Pilate to Herod, and from Herod back again to Pilate. He had,
therefore, but little strength left, and yet neither nourishment nor rest was
permitted Him. They were eager for His blood, and therefore led Him out
to die, loaded with the cross. It is no wonder that eventually we find Him
staggering beneath His load, and that another is called to bear it with Him.
O dolorous procession! He goes forth, then, bearing His cross. Well may
Jerusalem's daughters weep. My soul, do you weep also?

What do we learn here as we see our blessed Lord led forth? Do we not
perceive that truth set forth in shadow by the scapegoat on the Day of Atonement (see Leviticus 16)? Did not the high priest bring the scapegoat and put
both his hands upon its head, confessing the sins of the people, and that thus
those sins might be laid upon the goat and cease from the people? Then the
goat was led away by a man appointed to the task into the wilderness, and it
carried away the sins of the people, so that if they were sought for they could
not be found. Now we see Jesus brought before the priests and rulers, who
pronounce Him guilty; God himself imputes our sins to Him, "The LORD has
laid on Him the iniquity of us all" (Isaiah 53:6 NKJV); "He made Him who
knew no sin to be sin for us" (2 Corinthians 5:21 NKJV); and, as the substitute
for our guilt, bearing our sin upon His shoulders, represented by the cross, we
see the great Scapegoat led away by the appointed officers of justice.

Beloved, can you feel assured that He carried your sin? As you look at the
cross upon His shoulders, does it represent your sin? There is one way by
which you can tell whether He carried your sin or not. Have you laid your
hand upon His head, confessed your sin, and trusted in Him? Then your sin
lies not on you; it has all been transferred by blessed imputation to Christ,
and He bears it on His shoulder as a load heavier than the cross.

Let not the picture vanish till you have rejoiced in your own deliverance and
adored the loving Redeemer upon whom your iniquities were laid.

CHARLES SPURGEON

And He, bearing His cross, went out to a place called the
Place of a Skull, which is called in Hebrew, Golgotha.

John 19:17 NKJV

In the days to come, all eyes will be fixed on a great prince who will ride through our London streets with his royal bride. I invite your attention to another Prince, marching in another fashion through His metropolis. London shall see the glory of the one; Jerusalem beheld the shame of the other. Come close, you lovers of Immanuel, and I will show you this great sight—the King of sorrow marching to His throne of grief, the cross. I claim for the procession of my Lord an interest superior to the pageant Londoners are so anxiously expecting. Will the prince be sumptuously arrayed? Mine is adorned with garments crimsoned by His own blood. Will the prince be decorated with honors? Behold, my King is not without His crown—alas, a crown of thorns! Will the streets be thronged? So were the streets of Jerusalem, for the great multitudes followed Him. Will they raise a shout of welcome? Alas, the Lord of glory received the tumultuous yell of "Away with Him, away with Him!" (John 19:15 NKJV). High in the air they bid their banners wave about the heir of England's throne, but how shall you rival the banner of the sacred cross that day. For the thousands of eyes that shall gaze upon the youthful prince, I offer the gaze of men and angels. All nations gathered about my Lord, both great and small, clustered around His person. From the sky the angels viewed Him with wonder and amazement. The spirits of the just looked from the windows of heaven upon the scene; yes, the great God and Father watched each movement of His suffering Son.

Oh, I pray you, lend your ears to such faint words as I can write on a subject all too high for me, the march of the world's Maker along the way to His great sorrow! Your Redeemer traverses the rugged path of suffering, along which He went with heaving heart and heavy footsteps, that He might pave a royal road of mercy for His enemies.

To Golgotha He must tread. It was one of Death's castles. Here was the grim lord of that stronghold. Our great hero, the Destroyer of Death, braved the lion in his den, slew the monster in his own castle, and dragged the dragon captive from his own den. Death thought it a splendid triumph to see the Master enter the dominions of destruction. Little did he know that the grave was to be ransacked and himself destroyed by the crucified Son of Man.

CHARLES SPURGEON

Now Pilate wrote a title and put it on the cross. And the writing was: JESUS OF NAZARETH, THE KING OF THE JEWS. Then many of the Jews read this title, for the place where Jesus was crucified was near the city; and it was written in Hebrew, Greek, and Latin.

John 19:19–20 NKJV

The three tongues in which the title was written were chosen simply to make it easy to read by the crowd from every part of the empire assembled at the Passover. Pilate wanted his shaft to reach them all. It was a sign of Israel's humiliation and a flourishing of the Roman whip in their faces. Its very wording betrayed a foreign hand, for a Jew would have written "King of Israel," not "of the Jews."

But John divined a deeper meaning in this title; that the words in their three-fold garb symbolized the relation of Christ and His work to the three great types of civilization that it found possessed of the field. It bent them all to its own purposes, absorbed them into itself, used their witness, and was spread by means of them, and finally sucked the life out of them and disintegrated them. The Jew contributed the morality and monotheism of the Old Testament; the Greek, culture and the perfected language that should contain the gospel treasure, the fresh wineskin for the new wine; the Roman made the spread of the kingdom possible by the pax Romana, and at first sheltered the young plant. All three, no doubt, marred as well as helped the development of Christianity, but the prophecy of the title was fulfilled and these three tongues became heralds of the cross and with loud, uplifted trumpets blew glad tidings to the ends of the world.

That title thus became an unconscious prophecy of Christ's universal dominion. He who can deal with man's primal needs and is ready and able to meet every cry of the heart will never lack petitioners and subjects. He who can respond to our consciousness of sin and weakness and can satisfy hungry hearts will build His sway over the hearts whom He satisfies on foundations deep as life itself. The history of the past becomes a prophecy of the future. Jesus has drawn men of all sorts, of every level of culture and layer of civilization, and of every type of character to Him, and the power that has carried a peasant of Nazareth to be the acknowledged King of the civilized world is not exhausted and will not be till He is enthroned as Savior and Ruler of the whole earth. The title on the cross is forever true and is written again in nobler fashion "on His robe and on His thigh" who rides forth at last to rule the nations, "KING OF KINGS AND LORD OF LORDS" (Revelation 19:16 NKJV).

ALEXANDER MACLAREN

Now there stood by the cross of Jesus His mother, and His mother's sister, Mary the wife of Clopas, and Mary Magdalene.

John 19:25 NKJV

Mary Magdalene was the victim of a fearful evil. She had been possessed by not one demon only, but seven (see Mark 16:9). Hers was a hopeless, horrible case. She could not help herself, neither could any human help avail. But Jesus passed that way and uttered the word of power, and Mary of Magdala became a trophy of the healing power of Jesus. All the seven demons left her, never to return, forcibly ejected by the Lord of all. What a blessed deliverance! What a happy change! From delirium to delight, from despair to peace, from hell to heaven!

Straightway Mary became a constant follower of Jesus, catching His every word, following His winding steps, sharing His toilsome life; and withal she became His generous helper, first among that band of healed and grateful women "who provided for Him from their substance" (Luke 8:2–3 NKJV). How much she must have seen! She saw the most of His miracles. How much she must have heard! She heard, with her own ears, His life-changing words. When Jesus was lifted up in crucifixion, Mary remained the sharer of His shame: we find her first beholding from afar, and then drawing near to the foot of the cross. She could not die on the cross with Jesus, but she stood as near it as she could, and when His blessed body was taken down, she watched to see how and where it was laid. She was the faithful and watchful believer, last at the tomb where Jesus slept, first at the grave after He arose. Mary Magdalene's holy fidelity made her a favored beholder of her beloved Rabboni, who chose to call her by her name and to make her His messenger of good news to the trembling disciples and to Peter (see John 20:18).

Thus grace found her possessed by demons and made her a minister, cast out demons and gave her to behold angels, delivered her from Satan and united her forever to the Lord Jesus. Find me the happiest believers, and I am sure they are those who sit most often under the banner of His love and drink the deepest draughts from the cup of communion; and I am sure they will be those who give most, who serve best, and who abide closest to the bleeding heart of their dear Lord. Perhaps for this reason Mary was privileged by the grace of God to be the first to see the risen Savior. May we also be such miracles of grace!

CHARLES SPURGEON

*After this, Jesus, knowing that all things were now ac-
complished, that the Scripture might be fulfilled, said,
"I thirst!"*

John 19:28 NKJV

It is most fitting that every word of our Lord upon the cross should be preserved. The Holy Spirit took special care that each of the sacred utterances
should be recorded in the Gospels. There is a fullness of meaning in each
utterance that no man shall be able fully to bring forth or fathom.

"I thirst" is Jesus' fifth utterance from the cross, and herein we behold His
human body tormented by grievous pain, sharing in the agony of the inward
spirit. How truly man He is. He is indeed "bone of my bones and flesh of my
flesh" (Genesis 2:23 NKJV). I invite you to meditate upon the true humanity
of our Lord very reverently. Jesus, being a man, escaped none of the ills that
are experienced by man in this lifetime. Jesus endured thirst to an extreme
degree, for it was the thirst of death, the loss of blood, and the pain that was
upon Him and more, the agony of being separated from His Father as He
bore our sins.

While we admire His condescension, let our thoughts also turn with delight to His sure sympathy. If Jesus said, "I thirst," He knows all our frailties
and woes. The next time we are in pain or are suffering depression of spirit,
we will remember that our Lord understands it all, for He has had personal
experience of it. Neither in suffering of body or in sadness of heart are we
deserted by our Lord. His line is parallel with ours. The arrow that has lately
pierced you was first stained with His blood. The cup that you are made
to drink, though it is bitter, bears the mark of His lips about its brim. He
has traversed the mournful way before you, and every footprint you leave is
stamped side by side with His footmarks. Let the sympathy of Christ, then,
be fully believed in and deeply appreciated.

Beloved, if our Master said, "I thirst," do we expect every day to drink of
streams of pleasure? He was innocent, yet He bore unfathomable suffering
on our behalf. Let the gasp of your Lord, "I thirst!" touch your heart and
cause you to say, "Does He say, 'I thirst'? Then I will thirst and suffer with
Him and not complain." The power to suffer for another, the capacity to be
self-denying even to an extreme to accomplish some great work for God—this
is the thing to be sought after and gained, and in this Jesus is our example
and our strength.

CHARLES SPURGEON

So when Jesus had received the sour wine, He said, "It is finished!" And bowing His head, He gave up His spirit.

John 19:30 NKJV

While Jesus hangs there in mortal conflict with sin and Satan, His heart is broken, His limbs dislocated. "My God, my God, why have You forsaken Me?" contains the concentrated anguish of the world (Matthew 27:46 NKJV). He treads the winepress of the Almighty's wrath alone (see Revelation 19:15 NKJV); on, on, He goes, steadily determined to drink the last drops of the cup that must not pass from Him if His Father's will be done. At last He cries, "It is finished!" and He gives up His spirit. Hear this shout of triumph as it rings out today with all the force that it had centuries ago!

Not only were all of the Old Testament types, promises, and prophecies now fully accomplished in Jesus, but all the typical sacrifices of the Jewish law were now abolished as well as explained. Lo, arrayed in human flesh Jesus stands; His cross is His altar, His body and His soul the sacrifice, himself the priest. And lo! Before His Father He presents His own blood; He enters the veil, sprinkles it there, and coming forth from the midst of darkness, He cries, "It is finished!"

The satisfaction that He rendered to the justice of God was finished. The debt was now fully discharged. The atonement and payment for sin were made once for all, and forever, by the one offering made in Jesus' body on the tree. There was the cup, hell was in it, and the Savior drank it so fully that there is nothing left for any of His people. The great ten-thonged whip of the law was worn out upon His back. There is nothing left with which to strike one for whom Jesus died. The great cannon of God's justice exhausted all its ammunition. There is nothing left to be hurled against a child of God. Sheathed is your sword, O Justice! Silenced is your thunder, O Law! There remains nothing now of all the grief and pains and agonies that we should have suffered for our sins, for Christ has endured all for His own beloved, and "it is finished."

Christ has totally destroyed the power of Satan, of sin, and of death. He met Sin. Horrible, terrible, all but omnipotent Sin nailed Him to the cross. But in that deed, Christ nailed Sin also to the tree. There they both did hang—Sin and Sin's Destroyer. Sin destroyed Christ, and by that destruction, Christ destroyed Sin. The voice of the archangel rang like the silver trumpets of Jubilee, and He did say, "Let my captives go free!"

CHARLES SPURGEON

When he had received the drink, Jesus said, "It is finished." With that, he bowed his head and gave up his spirit.

John 19:30

The last act of our Lord in bowing His head and giving up His spirit was only a summing up of what He had been doing all His life. He had been offering this sacrifice, the sacrifice of himself, all the years, and in thus sacrificing He had lived the divine life. Every morning when He went out before it was day, every evening when He lingered on the mountain after His friends were gone, He was offering himself to His Father in the communion of loving words, of high thoughts, of speechless feelings; and, between, He turned to do the same thing in deed, namely, in loving word, in helping thought, in healing action toward His fellow men; for the way to worship God while the daylight lasts is to work; the service of God, the only "divine service," is the helping of our brothers and sisters.

I do not seek to point out this surrendering of our spirit to the Father as a duty: that is to turn the highest privilege we possess into a burden grievous to be borne. But I want to show that it is the simplest, most blessed thing in the human world.

For I may say to myself: "Am I going out into the business and turmoil of the day, where so many temptations may come to do less honorably, less faithfully, less kindly, less diligently than my Savior would have me do? *Father, into your hands I give my spirit.* Am I going to do a hard duty, from which I would gladly turn aside? *Father, into your hands I commend my spirit.* Am I in pain? *Take my spirit, Lord, and see, as you know best, that it has no more to bear than it can bear. I will question no more, for it is your business, not mine. You know every shade of my suffering, and you will care for me with your perfect fatherhood. If your love, which is better than life, receives my spirit, then surely your tenderness will make it great and strong."*

Think, brothers, think, sisters, we walk in the air of an eternal fatherhood. Every uplifting of the heart is a looking up to the Father. Graciousness and truth are around, above, beneath us, yes, in us. When we are least worthy, then, most tempted, hardest, unkindest, let us yet commend our spirits into His hands.

GEORGE MACDONALD

So when Jesus had received the sour wine, He said, "It is finished!" And bowing His head, He gave up His spirit.

John 19:30 NKJV

To John's words, "He gave up His spirit," Luke adds Jesus' dying words, "Father, into your hands I commit My spirit" (Luke 23:46 NKJV). Do you see our Lord? He is dying and has already declared, "It is finished!" His work here is done. His more than Herculean toil is accomplished, and the great Champion is going back to His Father's throne. He speaks, but His last words are addressed to His Father. Think of these words, and may they be your first words, too, when you return to your Father!

In His last words, we see that God is His Father, and God is our Father. In this fact lies our chief comfort. In our hour of trouble, in our time of warfare, let us say, "Father!" To help you in the difficult duty of forgiving others, cry, "Father!" To help you in a time of suffering or disappointment, cry, "Father!" Does not a child so cry when he has lost his way and is in the dark? And is not a father's heart touched by that cry? Your main strength lies in your being a child of God. Our duty, whenever anything distresses or alarms us, is to resign or commit ourselves to God.

We commit ourselves to God by faith. Our Father is the unseen Guardian of the night, the unwearied Keeper of the day. Every morning, when you get up, put yourself into God's hands. Let us enjoy the high privilege of resting in God at all times—in the face of a bad report from the doctor, in the face of an uncertain future, and in the face of death itself. He will cover you in the day of battle, and beneath His wings will you find refuge. Your duty is to resign yourself to God, commit your spirit to Him, and rest in the sense of His presence.

This privilege is also full of consummate joy. Beloved, if we know how to commit ourselves into the hands of God, what a place it is for us to be! There are the myriads of stars, and they do not fall. If we get into the hands of God, we are where all things rest, and we get home and happiness. We have moved out of the nothingness of the creature and into the all-sufficiency of the Creator. Oh, seek to be there, beloved friend, and live forever in the hands of God!

CHARLES SPURGEON

And again another Scripture says, "They shall look on
Him whom they pierced."

John 19:37 NKJV

As we approach the understanding of the Scriptures, our prayer should be, "Open my eyes, that I may see wondrous things from Your law" (Psalm 119:18 NKJV). I know of hardly anything that has been so mischievous in what is termed Christian teaching as the tearing away of little pieces of Scripture under the name of texts. Portions of Scripture so treated have been made to represent false meanings and have gone up and down the ages of the church doing all sorts of spiritual harm. There ought to be no texts in any partial sense, or in any sense that mangles and damages the integrity of Scripture. The subject is never in the text; it is always in the context. If we take a text, we should take all the texts bearing upon the subject—"again another Scripture"—so that we may know the exact evidence of Scripture in its volume and weight and applicableness. An error may be sealed by a text; a denomination may be falsely based upon a portion of Scripture torn from the context in which it is found. We ought to have grown out of the childishness of wanting a text; we should now want the Scriptures, a thousand texts, or all the texts that can be found bearing upon the subject that is to be expounded.

But herein some are dragged down. There are persons who will always insist upon having a text, one text, a little verse; they like to be surprised by it. They are not students of the divine Word; they are the victims of their own foolish curiosity. We ought to say, "What does the whole Bible declare upon a given subject?" Let us have all the evidence carefully and luminously put before us, then by the aid of the Spirit of God who wrote the testimony we may be able to come to broad, intelligible, and useful conclusions. It is that "other Scripture" we want, that supplementing, completing, and illuminating Scripture. Many of us have the one text but not the other. The devil had a set of texts. The devil said to Jesus, "It is written"; and Christ answered, "It is written again" (Matthew 4:7 NKJV). It is that "again" that explains the quotation. We must therefore have regard to the proportion of faith, or the analogy of faith, or the general balance and drift of scriptural testimony; in this way we shall clear out many misinterpretations and falsities built on rags and patches of divine testimony.

JOSEPH PARKER

NOVEMBER

30

Later, Joseph of Arimathea asked Pilate for the body of Jesus. Now Joseph was a disciple of Jesus, but secretly because he feared the Jewish leaders. With Pilate's permission, he came and took the body away. He was accompanied by Nicodemus, the man who earlier had visited Jesus at night.

John 19:38–39

While Christ lived, Joseph of Arimathea and Nicodemus had been "secret disciples," but His death, which terrified and scattered His disciples, seems to have shamed and stung them into courage. They were both members of the Jewish ruling council: the same motives of fear, no doubt, that had withheld each of them from confessing Christ now united them in this late affirmation of discipleship. Nicodemus had had the conviction, at the beginning of Christ's ministry, that He was at least a miraculously attested and God-sent teacher (see John 3:2). But the fear that made him seek out Jesus by night impeded his growth and kept him silent. Joseph of Arimathea is described as a disciple, "who had not consented" to the council's decision to put Jesus to death (Luke 23:51), which leads us to believe that his dissent had been merely silent.

Joseph and Nicodemus portray many believers today. In many areas of our daily lives, there are challenges to put into practice a real confession of our moral convictions, a real carrying out of a true discipleship. How many of us have beliefs about social and moral questions that we are ashamed to declare in certain companies for fear of the finger of ridicule being pointed at us? It is not only in the church, and in reference to purely religious belief, that we have the curse of secret discipleship, but it is everywhere. Wherever there are moral questions that are the subject of controversy and have not been enthroned with the hallelujahs of all men, you get people who carry their convictions silently when there is most need of honest declaration. The political, social, and moral conflicts of this day have their "secret disciples," who will only come out of their holes when the battle is over and then shout with the loudest.

So sometimes it is necessary that you should say, "I am a Christian," as well as that you should live like one. Ask yourself whether you have buttoned your outer coat over your uniform, that nobody may know whose soldier you are. Ask yourself whether you have sometimes held your tongue because you knew that if you spoke people would find out whom you belong to. Ask yourself if you have ever accompanied the witness of your life with the commentary of your confession. Did you ever, anywhere but in a church, stand up and say, "I believe in Jesus Christ, His only Son, my Lord"?

ALEXANDER MACLAREN

Now on the first day of the week Mary Magdalene went to the tomb early, while it was still dark, and saw that the stone had been taken away from the tomb.

John 20:1 NKJV

I t's the third day now since Jesus' death. It is in the early morning dark. A little knot of women make their way slowly along the road leading out of the city gate. Mary Magdalene is in the lead, so far ahead of the others as to be alone. They are carrying packages of perfumed ointments, thinking only of a dear dead body and of clinging fragrant memories. As she draws near the tomb, Mary's love-quickened eyes notice the stone is moved aside! She naturally thinks someone has taken the body secretly away in the night.

Yet Jesus had made an appointment. It was with these dear friends who had responded so lovingly to His love and care. It was a significant appointment, stupendous, in fact. He had appointed to meet with them three days after His death. Jesus had spoken of this indirectly but distinctly six months before, when He first told His disciples of His suffering and death. And each time afterward, when He told them of His death, the words were always added, *"and the third day rise again"* (Luke 24:7 NKJV). He spoke of it again on that never-to-be-forgotten night of the betrayal. He said it in plainest speech. And again that same night, He said, "After I have been raised, I will go before you to Galilee" (Matthew 26:32 NKJV). Could any appointment be more explicit as to time and place?

It was a sacred appointment, sacred as the love that made it, sacred to Jesus as the friendship of these men and women with whom it was made, sacred as His word that was never broken. This was a staggering appointment. He had thought much about it before He made it. The power of God was at stake in the making and the keeping of it. He made the appointment and He kept it.

But His dear friends forgot. Aye, there's the bother, this thing of forgetting. The memory is ever the index of the heart and the will and the understanding. You can tell the one by the other. Some things are never forgotten. A bit embarrassing, this thing of forgetting what Jesus said, and are we less guilty?

Jesus keeps His appointments. His Word never fails. Not even the gates of death, or the power of the evil one, can prevail against it. It reckons God's power is as big as it is. But then, that was Jesus' way. And it is the way we will be when we walk with Jesus today.

S. D. GORDON

So they both ran together, and the other disciple outran Peter and came to the tomb first.

John 20:4 NKJV

The weakest and the lowest, the roughest and the hardest, the most selfishly absorbed man and woman has lying in him and her dormant capacities for flaming up into such a splendor of devotion and magnificence of heroic self-forgetfulness and self-sacrifice as is represented in many words and scenes in the Bible. A mother will do it for her child and never think that she has done anything extraordinary; husbands will do such things for wives; friends and lovers for one another. Such is the scene of John and Peter running together to Jesus' tomb. All who love the sweetness and power of the bond of affection know that there is nothing more gladsome than to fling one's self away for the sake of those whom we love. And the capacity for such love and sacrifice lies in all of us, ordinary people as we are, with no great field on which to work out our heroisms, yet it is in all of us to love and give ourselves away thus if once the heart is stirred. If once the capacity is roused to action, it will make a man blessed and dignified as nothing else will. The joy of unselfish love is the purest joy that man can taste; the joy of perfect self-sacrifice is the highest joy that humanity can possess—and it lies open for us all.

And wherever, in some humble measure, these emotions are realized, there you get weakness springing up into strength and the fallen and low down into loftiness. All have this capacity in them, and all are responsible for the use of it. What have you done with it? Is there any person or thing in this world that has ever been able to lift you up out of your self-centeredness? Is there any magnet that has proved strong enough to raise you from the low levels along which your life creeps? Have you ever known the thrill of resolving to become the bondservant of some great cause not your own? Or are you, as so many are, like spiders living in the midst of your web, mainly intent upon what it can catch for you? Have you ever set a light to that inert mass of enthusiasm that lies in you? Have you ever awakened the sleeper? Learn the lesson that there is nothing that so ennobles and dignifies a common nature as enthusiasm for a great cause, a self-sacrificing love for a worthy heart.

ALEXANDER MACLAREN

Then the other disciple, who came to the tomb first, went in also; and he saw and believed. For as yet they did not know the Scripture, that He must rise again from the dead.

John 20:8–9 NKJV

In the account, we may observe, first, the characteristic conduct of each of the two. Peter is first to set out, and John follows, both men doing according to their nature. The younger runs faster than his companion. He looked into the tomb and saw the wrappings lying, but the reverent awe that holds back finer natures kept him from venturing in. Peter is not said to have looked before entering. He loved with all his heart, but his love was impetuous and practical, and he went straight in, feeling no reason why he should pause. His boldness encouraged his friend, as the example of a strong nature does. They found the tomb empty with only the folded handkerchief and linen clothes. What did it mean?

Observe, too, the birth of the apostle's faith. John connects it with the sight of the folded garments. *Believed* here must mean more than recognition of the fact that the grave was empty. The next clause seems to imply that it means belief in the resurrection. The Scripture, which they "knew" as Scripture, was for John suddenly interpreted, and he was lifted out of the ignorance of its meaning, which till that moment he had shared with his fellow disciples. Their failure to understand Christ's frequent distinct prophecies that He would rise again the third day has been thought incredible, but is surely understandable enough if we remember how unparalleled such a thing was, and how marvelous is our power of hearing and yet not hearing the plainest truth. We all in the course of our lives are lost in astonishment when things happen to us that we have been plainly told will happen. The fulfilment of all divine promises . . . and warnings . . . is a surprise, and no warnings beforehand teach one tenth so clearly as experience.

John believed, but Peter was still in the dark. Again, the former had outrun his friend. His more sensitive nature, not to say his deeper love—for that would be unjust, since their love differed in quality more than in degree—had gifted him with a more subtle and swifter-working perception. Perhaps if Peter's heart had not been overwhelmed by his sin, he would have been more ready to feel the sunshine of the wonderful hope. We condemn ourselves to the shade when we deny our Lord by deed or word.

ALEXANDER MACLAREN

And she saw two angels in white sitting, one at the head and the other at the feet, where the body of Jesus had lain. Then they said to her, "Woman, why are you weeping?"

John 20:12–13 NKJV

Truly this was no occasion for Mary's tears. Though she was speaking to angels, she left God out of the equation, and consequently her words were only feverish with personal disappointment. She speaks as if the whole question lay between certain other people and herself; thus, "Because they have taken away my Lord, and I do not know where they have laid Him" (v. 13 NKJV). She is lost in the murky region of second causes—and thus she is unable to see the divine hand far above all human meddling and strife.

Many of us are like Mary. To many of us human history is but a disorderly and haphazard movement, a scrabbling race. Where is the spiritual eye that sees God above it all and can trace His hand in all the incongruous and violent features of the course? Mary said that somebody had taken away her Lord; the idea never occurred to her that He had taken himself away; and thus she missed the point. She saw the Jewish leaders, the executors, the mob, clearly enough; but the divine hand was hidden from her eyes. And what is human history but a chaos without that hand? However, when His hand is seen, the whole spectacle is changed—it is a chaos out of which order will come and last forever. In the meantime, we are victimized by our own senses; and so life has become an enigma without an answer, and a fight in which the strong wins all, and that all is less than nothing and vanity.

Are not God's angels often asking why we weep? The angels see the things that are hidden from us. In the seed they see the coming harvest. Behind the wintry snow they see the fair spring ready to spread her flowers at our feet. We see the underside of the pattern that God is weaving; they see the upper side in all the charm of its celestial color and all the beauty of its infinite perfection. God's providence may be full of mystery, a path through a jungle where beasts lurk in cruel patience for their prey; yet it leads onward to the summer landscape and the harvest plain. When Mary knew but part of the case, she wept; when she knew it all, her joy became almost a pain by its very keenness. So shall it be with us in the revelations that are to come. We cannot stop the tears now—they must come; but out of every tear shed over the unknown or misknown way of God, there will come a new and surprising joy.

JOSEPH PARKER

At this, she turned around and saw Jesus standing there, but she did not realize that it was Jesus. He asked her, "Woman, why are you crying? Who is it you are looking for?"

John 20:14–15

Here we have the first manifestation of the risen Savior, to Mary Magdalene, the woman who loved much. Think of what the morning watch meant to Mary. Was it not a proof of the intense longing of a love that would not rest until it had found the Lord it sought? It meant a separation from everything else, even from the chief of the apostles, in her longing to find Christ. It meant a struggle of fear against a faith that refused to let go its hold of the wonderful promise. It meant Christ's coming and fulfilling the promise: "The one who loves me will be loved by my Father, and I too will love them and show myself to them" (John 14:21). It meant that her love was met by the love of Jesus, and she found Him, the living Lord, in all the power of His resurrection life. It meant that she now understood what He said about ascending to the Father, to the life of divine and omnipotent glory. It meant, too, that she received her commission from her Lord to go and tell His brethren what she had heard from Him (see John 20:17).

That first morning watch, waiting for the risen Lord to reveal himself, what a prophecy and a pledge of what the morning watch has been to thousands of souls! In fear and doubt, and yet with a burning love and strong hope, they waited until He whom they had known but little, by reason of their human feeble apprehension, should breathe upon them in the power of His resurrection life and manifest himself as the Lord of glory. And there they learned, not in words or thought, but in the reality of a divine experience, that He, to whom all power had been given on earth and in heaven, had then taken them up into the keeping of His abiding presence.

And what are we now to learn? That there is nothing that can prove a greater attraction to our Lord than the love that sacrifices everything and rests satisfied with nothing less. It is to such a love that Christ manifests himself. He loved us and gave himself for us. Christ's love is revealed through our love. It is to our love that He speaks the word, "And surely I am with you always" (Matthew 28:20). It is love that accepts and rejoices in and lives in that word.

ANDREW MURRAY

*She turned around and saw Jesus standing there, and
did not know that it was Jesus. . . . She, supposing Him
to be the gardener . . .*

John 20:14–15 NKJV

If Mary had seen the dead Christ in the grave, the recognition of His face
probably would have brought a comfort to her bereaved heart. But the
idea of death having been turned to life never occurred to her. She little
thought that all the signs and wonders of Christ's ministry could culminate
in the magnificent miracle of His resurrection. Christ was infinitely larger in
spiritual influence than Mary had imagined, and He is infinitely larger and
grander than any church has conceived Him to be.

I would to God I could adequately rebuke all theological and church narrowness. There are people who would rather have a dead Christ in their own
tradition than a living Savior outside of their own approved boundaries. There
are others who care more for their own idealized pictures of Christ than they
would for the living Man himself, were He to look upon them face-to-face.
Christ is not a theory; He is a divine and infinite life, infusing himself into
our spirit and history in innumerable and unnamable ways, covering and
absorbing all theories, and honoring all honest thought, reverent doubt, and
pure aspiration. What man has seen all the truth of God? Into what church
has God crowded all the riches of heaven? You may find Christ everywhere if
you seek Him with a true heart—not, perhaps, just in the way you expected,
not nominally, not formally, but in all the subtlety of His spiritual power and
all the tenderness of His recovering and comforting grace.

Now, at the very moment of Mary's complaint that Christ had been taken
away, He was looking at her! She thought He was the gardener! How clearly
this shows that though we may think we know Christ, we know Him only in
one aspect, and if we happen to see Him in any other we actually know nothing
about Him. We only know Christ in one place, in one tradition, in one theology,
in one church. Take Him out of these, and He becomes an unknown gardener!
Probably there is not in all history so striking an illustration of not knowing
Christ except in one particular form and guise. Some people do not know Christ
except from the lips of their favorite preacher. Others do not think they have
kept Sunday properly unless they have attended a particular place of worship.
Some people can only see Christ in church. I would that we could see Him and
hear Him everywhere: in history, in communions, in commerce, in art, in all the
endeavors and enterprises of civilization.

JOSEPH PARKER

Jesus said to her, "Mary."
John 20:16

N ear the cross of Jesus stood his mother, his mother's sister, Mary the wife of Clopas, and Mary Magdalene" (John 19:25). Were there ever women's hearts with such emotions in them as these women? Did you ever try to put yourself into His mother's heart that day, or into Mary Magdalene's heart, from whom Jesus had cast out seven demons? (See Luke 8:2.) They stood and wept as no other women have wept since. But Mary Magdalene would not be dismissed, and she stood near to His crucified feet. All His disciples had forsaken Him and fled. It was no place for a woman, but this was no ordinary woman. The outposts of hell had been stormed and driven from her life, and no darkness could drive her from the One whom she loved.

The supreme lesson to me out of all Mary Magdalene's marvelous history is that she was the first one to whom Jesus appeared. It was not Peter, James, John, nor even to His own mother. It was to Mary Magdalene. It was to her who loved Him best, and had the best reason to love Him best, of all the men and women then living in the world. While this world lasts, let Mary Magdalene be often preached upon, and let this lesson be always taught out of her experience—that no depth of sin, no possession of demons even, shall separate us from the love of Christ. That repentance and love will outlive and overcome everything; there is no honor too high, and no communion too close, for the love of Christ on His side, and for the soul's love on her side, between them to enjoy. Only repent deep enough and to tears enough, only love as Mary Magdalene loved Him, and He will appear to you also and will call you by your name. And He will employ you in His service even more and even better than He honored and employed Mary Magdalene on the morning after His resurrection.

Mary Magdalene! You are my sister, my forerunner into heaven till I come! But remember, only till I come. Cease not to kiss His feet till I come, but give up your place to me when I come. For to whom little is forgiven the same loves little. Give place to me before His feet!

ALEXANDER WHYTE

She turned to him and cried out in Aramaic, "Rabboni!"
(which means "Teacher").

John 20:16

This is the very epitome of love. Love understands love; it needs no talk. Sunlight needs no light bulbs or switches; it just shines out in its fullness. And the dewdrop flashes it back in the same way. The sparkle may be tiny, but it is true and immediate. Christ had called Mary's name, focusing the powerful sunshine of His love into a beam of sevenfold light, and her whole soul was concentrated into the responsive love-flash, "Rabboni!" When that word has truly gone up from the soul to Christ, we have felt what can never be put into any other words.

Love. There is a great hush; we have no words to express what we feel. We cannot tell Him we love Him, because we are dazzled with a glimpse of His love and overwhelmed with our unworthiness of it. Our eyes fill, and our chests heave. The tide has risen too high for verbal prayer or praise; we have to be silent in love—the very silence being an echo of the eternal depth of calmness of the exceeding great love in which He rests. There is only one word that does not disturb the still music of such a moment—*Rabboni!*

Adoration. For the breathing of the name is all we can do to express the unexplainable recognition of His glory, the admiration, the astonishment. *We praise you, we bless you, we worship you, we glorify you, we give thanks to you for your great glory!* And yet we only utter one word, *Rabboni!*

Allegiance. The true utterance of it is the very oath of allegiance. We cannot, we must not, we dare not, will not serve two masters, nor the still more subtle many masters. The word has been breathed into His heart, and He will treasure it there and keep it for us. It has been said, and the sound waves can never be retracted. God grant no traitorous whisper!

Obedience. Not only our lips, but our lives must say, "Rabboni!" By His grace the name shall be emblazoned on every page of our lives. Jesus himself will make it plain upon our tablets. This is the test, the fruit, the manifestation of love. But oh, how sweet that we may fearlessly say the word, knowing that the Master will enable us to fill it up with the practical obedience that we want so intensely to yield to Him!

FRANCES RIDLEY HAVERGAL

"Go to My brethren and say to them, 'I am ascending to My Father and your Father, and to My God and your God.'"

John 20:17 NKJV

G od's people are doubly His children: we are His offspring by creation, and we are His sons and daughters by adoption in Christ. Hence we are privileged to call Him "Our Father in heaven."

Father! Oh, what a precious word is that. He is our Father because He has the deepest love to protect us—and if we doubt whether His power is equal to His love, let us notice what Jesus says: "I am ascending . . . to My God and your God." And inasmuch as God is omnipotent, and the Father is love, you have all the love you need and all the power equal to that love! It seems sweet to hear Christ calling His Father His God. As He was a Man, the Father was His God. As He was Christ, the God-man, the Father was God over Him and, speaking as a Man, He could say, "My Father is greater than I" (John 14:28 NKJV). God the Father being greater than the Mediator, who said, in effect, "As Man, I worship Him as my Father the same as you do. He is my Father as He is your Father."

How beautifully the Savior refers to the believer's union with himself! The whole Bible points to the believer's union with Christ, and this sweet verse is full of that blessed truth. When Christ calls God His Father, we may call God "our Father" too. In His inheritance we have a joint interest—He is Heir of all things, and we are joint heirs with Him. Christ's brethren are our brethren—His Father is our Father. Even in service, as Christ was Man, as He was the Servant of God for our sakes, so the Master whom He served is the Master whom we serve—and we together take the same service upon ourselves, believing that we together shall have the same kingdom conferred upon us and shall reign with Christ forever and ever.

Father! How great is a father's love to His children! They are his offspring, he must bless them; they are his children, he must show himself strong in their defense. If an earthly father watches over his children with unceasing love and care, how much more does our heavenly Father?

Abba, Father! He who can say this has uttered better music than cherubim can reach. There is heaven in the depth of that word *Father*! There is all I can ask, all my necessities can demand, all my wishes can desire. I have all eternity to say, "Father."

CHARLES SPURGEON

Then, the same day at evening, being the first day of the week, when the doors were shut where the disciples were assembled, for fear of the Jews, Jesus came and stood in the midst, and said to them, "Peace be with you."

John 20:19 NKJV

Look at these people to whom Jesus spoke. Remember what they were between the Friday afternoon and the Sunday morning: utterly frightened and defeated, while sharing their sorrow, also touched by despair at the perceived end of all the hopes that they had been building upon Christ's official character and position. They were on the point of parting. Then *something* happened and those who had been cowards, dissolved in sorrow and despair, in forty-eight hours became heroes. From that time, when, by all reasonable logic and common sense applied to men's motives, the crucifixion should have crushed their dreams and dissolved their society, a precisely opposite effect ensues, and not only did the church continue, but the men's characters changed and became full of the very two things intrinsic to what Christ wished for them: joy and peace.

Now, I want to know—what bridged that gulf? How did the Peter of the four gospels become the Peter of the book of Acts? Is there any way of explaining the revolution of character that occurred in him, and all of them, except the one that says the *something* that happened *was* the resurrection of Jesus Christ and the consequent gift of joy and peace, a joy that no troubles or persecutions could shake, a peace that no conflicts could for a moment disturb?

It seems to me that every theory of Christianity that questions the resurrection of Jesus Christ as a plain fact is shattered to pieces on this sharp-pointed rock. You will never get a reasonable theory of these two undeniable facts until you believe that He rose from the dead. In His right hand He carried peace, and in His left, joy. He gave these to them, and therefore they "out of weakness were made strong, became valiant in battle, turned to flight the armies of the aliens," and when the time came, "were tortured, not accepting deliverance, that they might obtain a better resurrection" (Hebrews 11:34–35 NKJV).

There is omnipotent efficiency in Christ's greetings. Christ's wishes are gifts, and when He speaks "peace" to us, it is done. When He desires for us joy, it is a deed of transference and invests us with the joy that He desires if we observe the conditions. Christ's wishes to us are omnipotent.

ALEXANDER MACLAREN

When He had said this, He showed them His hands and His side. Then the disciples were glad when they saw the Lord.

John 20:20 NKJV

Two things stand out sharply. First, the resurrection was not expected, despite Jesus' repeated promise to rise again. It came to the disciples as the most tremendous surprise. The news was received at first by those most interested with utter unbelief. Then the evidence was so clear and incontestable that these same men staked their lives on it. They suffered to the extreme for their witness that Jesus had indeed risen from the dead.

Jesus rose from the dead. His body was reinhabited by His spirit. The spirit didn't die. Spirits neither sleep nor die. The body died. Then life came into it again. It was a real body that could eat and be touched. It was recognized as the same one they had known, but it was changed. The old limitations were gone. New powers had come.

The second thing that stands out sharply is that Jesus keeps His appointments. His pledged word never fails. Not a word He has spoken can ever be broken. Someday He is coming back. It is an appointment. "For the Lord Himself will descend from heaven with a shout, with the voice of an archangel, and with the trumpet of God. And the dead in Christ will rise first. Then we who are alive and remain shall be caught up together with them in the clouds to meet the Lord in the air. And thus we shall always be with the Lord" (1 Thessalonians 4:16–17 NKJV). That's His sacred promise to us, someday. And He will keep it.

And meanwhile, everything He has promised us in the Scripture is sure, as being His pledged word. His resurrection is our bond, our guarantee. As surely as He rose on that third morning, He will keep His word regarding every matter to you and me.

His appointments never fail, whether of guidance, of bodily health and strength, of supplies for every sort of need, of peace, of power, of victory. The power that raised Jesus up from the dead is pledged to us for every promise of this Book for today's life. He will do an act of creation before He will let His Word fail. He will leave no power unused to keep the appointment of His Word with us.

Let us trust fully His Word to us. And let us live faithfully our trust in Him.

S. D. GORDON

So Jesus said to them again, "Peace to you! As the Father has sent Me, I also send you." And when He had said this, He breathed on them, and said to them, "Receive the Holy Spirit."

John 20:21–22 NKJV

The time at which these words were spoken should be considered in attempting to estimate their meaning and value. Jesus was rapidly drawing His personal ministry upon earth to a close, and it was time to disclose how He would provide for the future and the very highest phases of the great work that He came to accomplish. The relationships subsisting between the Father and Him, and between Him and the disciples, were now formally specified, and the divine Agent under whose direction that method was to be carried out was spoken of by Jesus Christ himself.

This address, it must be borne in mind, was not spoken to one disciple, but was delivered to all the disciples in their corporate capacity. We have no reason to infer that any one of the disciples received a larger measure of the Holy Spirit than his brethren. They were sent forth by Jesus, as Christ had been sent by the Father. Here is the divine commission of the church in terms most precise and emphatic: "As the Father has sent Me, I also send you." The question then arises, "How did the Father send Jesus Christ?" He himself says, "For I have come down from heaven, not to do My own will, but the will of Him who sent Me" (John 6:38 NKJV). The answer is comprehensive: the church is sent to do God's will, not her own; she is God's servant, God's representative, God's light in a dark world.

It appears perfectly clear that the disciples were divinely commissioned; that, in short, they had their authority from God. To these words, however, is added a special gift—"Receive the Holy Spirit." The possession of the Holy Spirit separated and distinguished the disciples from all other men. It was distinctively a Christian gift; it was given to all who received the faith of Jesus Christ, conferred upon all believers. From the day of Pentecost onward, events recorded in the Acts of the Apostles leave no doubt that the Holy Spirit was not confined to the apostles, nor do we anywhere find a hint that the apostles claim to have the Holy Spirit in any degree superior to all believers in Jesus. We have the same spiritual privileges, powers, and responsibilities as the first disciples of the Lord. But do we believe it and live accordingly?

JOSEPH PARKER

*Now Thomas (also known as Didymus), one of the
Twelve, was not with the disciples when Jesus came. So
the other disciples told him, "We have seen the Lord!"
But he said to them, "Unless I see the nail marks in his
hands and put my finger where the nails were, and put
my hand into his side, I will not believe."*

John 20:24–25

The character of Thomas is an examination of melancholy. He was such a melancholic soul that he seldom spoke, and when he did speak it was always out of the depths of a depressed heart. And a whole lifetime of melancholy, constitutional and circumstantial, had by this time settled on Thomas. Terrible questions arose in the hearts of all the disciples as their Master spiraled down through Gethsemane and Calvary. But all that doubt and fear, despondency and despair, met in Thomas's melancholic heart until it took absolute possession of him. His earlier expression, "Let us also go, that we may die with him" (John 11:16), may have been more that of resignation than of willing discipleship.

How was it that Thomas was not with the other disciples that glorious Sabbath evening when Jesus appeared to them all? It could not have been by accident. He must have been told the remaining astounded disciples were to be all together that wonderful night, after the overwhelming events of the morning. What conceivable cause could have kept Thomas away? Whatever it was, he paid dearly for it, for he lost the first and best sight of his risen Master, and His first and best benediction of peace. It seems the joy of the other disciples who had received it was the final blow that cast Thomas down into the darkness, bitterness, and sullenness that had its roots so deep in his heart. He would have none of their joy. He would not believe it. Unbelief, obstinacy, loss of opportunity, and then increased unbelief took its toll on him. And the same has taken its toll on our lives. Yet Jesus came to him, as He comes to us.

Do you clearly understand the blessedness of believing without seeing, of a strong and an easy acting faith in the things of Christ? Faith is always easy where love and hope are strong. What we live for and hope to see, what we love with our whole heart, what we pray for night and day, what our whole future is anchored upon, that we easily believe. Let us never allow in the deadly thoughts that darkened the heart of Thomas, who ran the risk of never seeing his Master again in this world.

ALEXANDER WHYTE

Then He said to Thomas, "Reach your finger here, and look at My hands; and reach your hand here, and put it into My side. Do not be unbelieving, but believing."

John 20:27 NKJV

We are, all of us, apt to fall into a wrong state of heart, simply because of our natural weaknesses. So long as we are in this body, exposed to trial and temptation, we shall be prone to doubt and sin. Thomas was a true-hearted follower of Jesus. He loved his Master. It had been a severe shock to his sensitive disposition and his thoughtful mind to see his Master crucified, dead, and buried. He could not, at once, rally to think it possible that Jesus could have risen from the dead. He would require, he said, very clear proofs before he would believe it. In like manner, you and I have, each of us, our characteristic faults. Let no man exalt himself. He who rejoices in God today may be in spiritual poverty tomorrow, having felt his feet slide from under him and so fallen from his steadfastness as to have dishonored God!

How exquisitely touching is Jesus' gentleness! Does He upbraid Thomas? Is there anger in His tone? No, far from it! He rather takes Thomas on his own ground, considers his weaknesses, and meets them precisely as they are, without a single word of rebuke until the close—and even then He puts it very lovingly. The God of all patience would not desert him . . . or us! The love that our Lord Jesus Christ bears to His people is so great that He passes by our unbelief and sin! No, there is no anger on His part to divide you from your Lord. Behold! He comes over the mountains of your sins! He leaps over the hills of your follies. Since He thus graciously comes to you, will you not gladly come to Him?

Notice also, beloved, that Thomas did not seek his Master. Therein He was just like we are! It is prevenient grace—it is grace that is beforehand with us—even with our faint desires, that comes to us from Jesus Christ. Oh, how our Lord outruns us! Our sense of need is not as swift of foot as His perception of our need! Long before we know we need Him, He understands that we require Him and He comes to us to bless us! It was for one He came, and for that one who did not seek Him! He was found of one who sought Him not! There is no kindness too costly for Christ to show—to Thomas, and to you and me!

CHARLES SPURGEON

Then Jesus told him, "Because you have seen me, you have believed; blessed are those who have not seen and yet have believed."

John 20:29

We all count the blessedness of Thomas as something very wonderful. Christ manifested himself and allowed Thomas to touch His hands and His side. No wonder that this blessedness can find no words but those of holy adoration: "My Lord and my God!" Has there ever been higher expression of the overwhelming nearness and glory of God?

And yet Christ said: "Because you have seen me, you have believed; blessed are those who have not seen and yet have believed." True, living faith gives a sense of Christ's divine nearness far deeper and more intimate than even the joy that filled the heart of Thomas. Here, even now, after the lapse of all these centuries, we may have experienced the presence and power of Christ in a far deeper reality than Thomas did. To those who see not, yet believe—simply, only, truly, fully believe—in what Christ is and can be to them every moment, He has promised that He will manifest himself, and that the Father and He will come and dwell in them.

Have we not often been inclined to think of this full life of faith as something beyond our reach? Such a thought robs us of the power to believe. Let us turn to take hold of Christ's word: "Blessed are those who have not seen and yet have believed." This is indeed the heavenly blessing, filling the whole heart and life, the faith that receives the love and the presence of the living Lord.

You ask how to come to this childlike faith. The answer is very simple: Where Jesus Christ is the one object of our desire and our confidence, He will manifest himself in divine power. Thomas had proved his intense devotion to Christ when he said, "Let us also go, that we may die with him" (John 11:16). To such a love, even when it is struggling with unbelief, Jesus Christ will manifest himself. He will make His holy promise an actual reality in our conscious experience. Let us see to it that our faith in His blessed Word, in His divine power, in His holy abiding presence, is the one thing that masters our whole being—Christ will in reality manifest himself, abide with us, and dwell in our hearts as His home.

ANDREW MURRAY

Jesus said to him, "Thomas, because you have seen Me, you have believed. Blessed are those who have not seen and yet have believed."

John 20:29 NKJV

What a blessing it was for the people who lived in our Savior's day and saw and heard what kings and prophets had long desired to see and hear. But our text tells us that we who now believe in Jesus Christ have a blessing superior to theirs, so do not diminish it by desiring what is based on sight. Some have said, "Oh, but if God would reveal himself to me by a voice, a vision, a revelation, or a remarkable providence, I would never doubt again. I expect God to do something wonderful for me or I cannot trust Him." They do not feel content to swim in the pure sea of faith. To them, our Lord says, "My child, instead of wanting to see, believe, trust, follow me in the dark, for it is better for you not to see. Even if you did see, you would only obtain an inferior gift, for the blessing is for those who have not seen and yet have believed."

Without our seeing Him, God deserves to be believed. Apart from every other consideration, His own personal character is such that He should be believed. If God has spoken to us in the Scriptures and revealed a truth that is not supported by the judgment of learned men, and to which our own experience seems to be a contradiction, still God must be believed. Surely you are not going to set the evidence of your eyes against the declaration of God who cannot lie. If you trust Him based on His word alone, you shall realize the blessedness of which our text speaks.

It is a poor character who lives only on what he sees. There is no great character that can ever come to a man who has no faith. The heroes among men, even concerning common matters, are all men of faith. It was faith of some sort that braced them up and made them superior to those around them. No man could have been a Martin Luther who did not completely trust in his God. What a wondrous thing if after paddling our canoe of faith along the shore, we are carried out to sea by a big rolling wave, and there taught to be a mariner who braves the tempest and laughs at the hurricane. We would always remain children if we did not have trials and troubles. God often hides himself in order to teach us to trust Him more, and so we grow to be men of faith.

CHARLES SPURGEON

And truly Jesus did many other signs in the presence of His disciples, which are not written in this book; but these are written that you may believe that Jesus is the Christ, the Son of God, and that believing you may have life in His name.

John 20:30–31 NKJV

The silence of Scripture is quite as eloquent as its speech. For instance, of how many things in the Bible are taken for granted that you would not expect to be taken for granted in a book of religious instruction. It takes for granted the Being of God. It takes for granted our relationship to Him. It takes for granted our moral nature. In its later portions, at all events, it takes for granted the future life. Look at how the Bible, as a whole, passes by, without one word of explanation, a great many of the difficulties that gather round some of its teaching. For instance, we find no attempt to explain the divine nature of our Lord or the existence of the three persons in the Godhead or of the mystery of prayer. It has not a word to explain, though many a word to proclaim and enforce, the fact of Christ's death as the payment for the sins of the whole world. Observe, too, how scanty the information on points on which the heart craves for more light, such as the veil that is kept over the future life! How many questions that are not prompted by mere curiosity our sorrow and our love ask in vain!

Nor is the incompleteness of Scripture as a historical book less marked. Nations and men appear on its pages abruptly, rending the curtain of oblivion, and striding to the front of the stage for a moment, and then they disappear. It has no care to tell the stories of any of its heroes, except as they were the mouthpieces of that divine breath, which, breathed through the weakest reed, makes music. The self-revelation of God, not the acts and fortunes of even His noblest servants, is the theme of the Book. It is full of gaps about matters that any philosopher or theologian would have filled up. There it stands—a book unique in the world's history, unique in what it says and no less in what it does not say.

And yet, put the four gospels down beside thick books written about well-known people, and you will feel the incompleteness of these biographies. They are but pen-and-ink drawings! And although you might sit down and read all four gospels in an evening, is it not strange that they have stamped on the whole world an image so deep and so sharp of such a One as the modern world never saw?

ALEXANDER MACLAREN

*But these are written that you may believe that Jesus
is the Messiah, the Son of God, and that by believing
you may have life in his name.*

John 20:31

This was John's whole thought in telling the story of Jesus. The practical
gripped him wholly and hard. This is the thing that guides his selection
of incidents. This purpose shapes the book. It explains everything told,
and just why it is told in just the way it is told.

John lets Jesus walk before our eyes fresh from His Father's presence. The
mere fact of His presence, the beauty of His personality, the clearness of His
teaching, the power of His actions, the uncompromising purity of His character amid sin-stained crowds and sin-stained surroundings, the unflinching
rigidity of His ideals, the persuasiveness of His very manner and tone of
speech, the patience and gentleness, the rugged granite strength, the mother
tenderness, above all the willingness to suffer so terribly—all this is a plea, a
tremendous overpowering plea, all the stronger because presented so simply
and briefly. Jesus is a lover and this is His wooing.

And John's one thought in writing is the same as the one thought in the
Lover's heart. John has become simply an echo of Jesus. It is this, that you—
whoever you are, wherever, whatever—may believe. You look and listen, question, puzzle a bit, maybe, but keep on listening, looking, thinking, weighing,
till you are clear these things are just as John tells them. You accept them as
trustworthy. Then you accept Him, Jesus, as He comes to you, your wooing
Lover, your God, your Savior, and Lord.

You believe; that is, you love. The word works itself out inside you in this
way: *believe, trust, love.* The truth comes in through the eyes and ears and
feeling, into the brain and will, then through the emotions clear down into
your heart. You love. You cannot help yourself. You love Him, Jesus the Messiah, the Son of God so lovable.

Only let this sift through your thought and heart; who would not believe,
trust, love, and fall on his face in the utter devotion of a voluntary slave before
such a God!

S. D. GORDON

After these things Jesus showed Himself again to the disciples at the Sea of Tiberias, and in this way He showed Himself.

John 21:1 NKJV

J ohn's story seemed finished. With the skill of a seasoned lawyer he drew up a clear full line of evidence and plainly stated his case. His whole purpose is that those who read his book shall come into a warm, personal touch of life with the Lord Jesus. That ties the knot on tight at the end of chapter twenty—"that you may believe that Jesus is the Christ" (v. 31 NKJV). John's case has gone to the jury of his readers.

But now the guiding Spirit has put another word into his heart to write down. In this final chapter we have an unrecognized Stranger who turns out to be Jesus; an unusual haul of fish gotten in a very unusual way; a warm fire and tasty breakfast for cold, hungry men; a tender talk about love and service and sacrifice, and about Jesus' return. All this is a picture illustration of the key word to this added chapter, occurring three times: Jesus *showed* or *manifested* himself to them. What was hidden to them is allowed to be seen. He did not come; He was there, but their eyes couldn't see Him. Now He is seen and known.

This is the tremendous thing Jesus is burning into their hearts: He, whose power they had felt so stupendously and whose warm sympathy so tenderly, *He is always present with them.* And He is just the same Jesus in His warm love and power.

It was an advance illustration of the promised coming of the Holy Spirit in the book of Acts. The Spirit would be as Jesus' other self, as Jesus himself. The one thing the Spirit would do is manifest, to openly show, the power of Jesus. He would be with them continually manifesting himself in rarest power of action, in tenderest personal care, in talking and walking with them.

They would see the power plainly at work; then they would say with a soft hush, "He is here." They would find new strength, new guidance in perplexity, new peace in the midst of confusion, and they would say to one another in awed tones, "He is here: it's the Master's touch." And so it would come to be a habit to anticipate His presence. They would factor Him in, and factor Him in big, as big as He is, in all sorts of circumstances and planning and meeting of difficulties.

Jesus is present with us, all the while walking along the shore of our common ground of life, clothed with matchless power, and devoting himself to us as we to Him.

S. D. GORDON

Simon Peter said to them, "I am going fishing." They said to him, "We are going with you also."

John 21:3 NKJV

What sent them back to fishing? Not doubt or despair, because they had seen Jesus Christ in Jerusalem and had come down to Galilee at His command on purpose to meet Him. "There you will see Him. Behold, I have told you" was ringing in their ears, and they went back in full confidence of His appearance there (Matthew 28:7 NKJV). It is very like Peter to suggest filling the hours of waiting time with manual labor. The time would be hanging heavily on his hands. Peter thought that the best thing they could do, till Jesus chose to come, was to get back to their work, and he was right. The best preparation for Christ's appearance, and the best attitude to be found in by Him, is doing our daily work, however common it may be. A dirty, wet fishing boat, all slimy with scales, was a strange place in which to wait for the risen Savior. But it was the right place.

They went out to do their work, and to them was fulfilled the old saying, "I, being in the way, the Lord met me." Jesus Christ will come to you and me in the street if we carry the waiting heart there, and in the grocery store, the workplace, the gym, and the kitchen, or wherever we may be. For all things are sacred when done with a hallowed heart, and He chooses to make himself known to us amid the dusty common places of daily life.

He had said to them before the crucifixion: "'When I sent you without money bag, knapsack, and sandals, did you lack anything?' So they said, 'Nothing'" (Luke 22:35 NKJV). And then He said, changing the conditions: "But now, he who has a money bag, let him take it, and likewise a knapsack" (v. 36). As long as He was with them, they didn't need these common things. Now that He had left them, they were back to the normal order. And the order of things for His servants in all time henceforth was therein declared to be: no shirking of daily tasks on the plea of seeking divine communication; keep at your work, and if it lasts all night, stick to it; and if there are no fish in the net, never mind; go out again. And be sure that sooner or later you will see Him standing on the beach, hear His voice, and be blessed by His smile.

ALEXANDER MACLAREN

And He said to them, "Cast the net on the right side of the boat, and you will find some." So they cast, and now they were not able to draw it in because of the multitude of fish.

John 21:6 NKJV

Think of them as the darkness fell, and the Syrian sky was mirrored with all its stars sparkling in the still lake. All the night long cast after cast was made, and time after time the net was drawn in with nothing in it but tangle and mud. And when the first streak of the morning breaks over the eastern hills, they hear a voice that hails them from the nearer shore: "Children, have you any food?" And they answer it with a half surly and wholly disappointed monosyllabic "No!" It is a picture of us all: weary and wet, exhausted at the oars of life, and often seeming to fail. What then? You cannot expect that your nets will always be full. Failure and disappointment mingle in the most successful lives.

And so, there stands the risen Lord on the beach, interested in, caring about, directing and crowning with His own blessing the obedient work of His servants. Jesus Christ, who had been down into those dark regions of mystery where the dead sleep and wait, and had come back into this world, and was on the eve of ascending to the Father, takes an interest in seven poor men's fishing. It teaches us that anything that interests us is not without interest to Christ. Anything that is big enough to occupy our thoughts and our efforts is large enough to be taken into His. All our toils and anxieties touch a chord that vibrates in that deep and tender heart. The risen Lord is interested in our poor fishing and our disappointments.

And not only that: here is a promise of certain guidance and direction, if only we will come to Him and acknowledge our dependence upon Him. Christ's command regarding the nets is followed by swift unquestioning obedience, which in its turn is immediately succeeded by the largest blessing. We may be sure that while we are toiling on the tossing sea, He watches from the shore, is interested in all our weary efforts, will guide us if we own to Him our weakness, and will give us to see at last issues greater than we had dared to hope from our poor service. Though we are on the tossing sea and He on the quiet shore, between us there is a true union and communion, His heart is with us, if our heart is with Him, and from Him will pass over all strength, grace, and blessing to us.

ALEXANDER MACLAREN

*Therefore that disciple whom Jesus loved said to Peter,
"It is the Lord!"*

John 21:7 NKJV

A s always, as in that morning sunrise on the Galilean lake, Christ comes to us. Everywhere He is present, everywhere revealing himself. Now, as then, our eyesight is restricted by our own fault, so that we recognize not the merciful presence that is all around us. Now, as then, those who are nearest to Christ by love see Him first. Now, as then, those who are nearest to Him by love are so because He loves them, and because they know and believe the love He has to them. Only those who love see Christ. John, the apostle of love, knew Him first. In spiritual matters, love is the foundation of knowledge. A man cannot argue his way into knowing Christ. The treasures of earthly wisdom are powerless in that area. Man's natural understanding and capacity is strong and good, but in the area of knowing God and Christ, his understanding is not the means by which he can know Christ.

"He who does not love does not know God, for God is love" (1 John 4:8 NKJV). It is the force and the depth of our love to the great Friend and Lover of our souls that determines our knowledge of Christ. Love will follow Him everywhere. Love's quick eye pierces through disguises impenetrable to a colder scrutiny. Love has in it a longing for His presence that makes us eager and quick to note the faintest sign that He for whom it longs is near. Love to Him strips from our eyes the veil that self and sin, reason and tradition, have drawn over them. It is these that hide Him from us. It is because men are so indifferent to, so forgetful of, their best Friend that they fail to behold Him.

They who love Him know Him, and they who know Him love Him. The true salve for our blinded eyes is applied when we have turned our hearts to Christ. The simple might of faithful love opens them to behold the glorious vision and ever-present form of the Lord of life. When they who love Jesus turn to see the voice that speaks with them, they ever behold the Son of man in His glory; and where others see but the dim beach and a mysterious stranger, it is to their lips that the glad cry first comes, "It is the Lord!"

ALEXANDER MACLAREN

Jesus said to them, "Come and eat breakfast."

John 21:12 NKJV

Notice that it was Jesus who provides the fire and meal as well as the invitation. Jesus is Master of the feast. He condescends to the feast. Is it not wonderful that the Holy Lord should have communion with His faulty followers? Yet He will breakfast with us—with us who doubted Him, as Thomas did; with us who denied Him, as Peter did; with us who forsook Him and fled, as the rest did.

In these words the believer is invited to a holy nearness to Jesus. "Come and eat breakfast" implies the same table, the same food; yes, and sometimes it means to sit side by side and lean our head upon the Savior's bosom. It is being brought into the banqueting house, where waves the banner of redeeming love. "Come and eat" gives us a vision of union with Jesus, because the only food that we can feast upon when we dine with Jesus is himself. Oh, what union is this! It is a depth that reason cannot fathom, that we thus feed upon Jesus. "He who eats My flesh and drinks My blood abides in Me, and I in him" (John 6:56 NKJV).

It is also an invitation to enjoy fellowship with the saints. Christians may differ on a variety of points, but they have all one spiritual appetite; if we cannot all think alike, we can all feed alike on the bread of life sent down from heaven. At the table of fellowship with Jesus we are one bread and one cup. As the loving cup goes round, we pledge one another wholeheartedly therein. Get nearer to Jesus, and you will find yourself linked more and more in spirit to all who are like yourself, supported by the same heavenly manna. If we were nearer to Jesus, we should be nearer to one another.

We likewise see in these words the source of strength for every Christian. To look at Christ is to live, but for strength to serve Him you must "come and eat." We labor under much unnecessary weakness on account of neglecting this precept of the Master. We should fatten on the marrow and fatness of the gospel that we may accumulate strength therein, and urge every power to its full strength in the Master's service. Thus, then, if you would realize nearness to Jesus, union with Jesus, love to His people, and strength from Jesus, "come and eat" with Him by faith.

CHARLES SPURGEON

*So when they had eaten breakfast, Jesus said to Simon
Peter, "Simon, son of Jonah, do you love Me more than
these?"*

John 21:15 NKJV

There is an obvious intention in these words to recall Peter's denial of
Christ, and so they would pierce to his heart. The fact of his risen Lord
coming to him with a question about his love upon His lips would be
a dagger in his soul; all the more because he knew that the question was a
reasonable one. Now, all this deliberate raking up of Peter's failure gives the
appearance of being cruel. How was it prophesied of Jesus, "A bruised reed He
will not break, and smoking flax He will not quench" (Matthew 12:20 NKJV)?
Would not Christ have been nearer the ideal of divine and perfect forgiveness
if He had not put Peter through this torture of remembrance?

No! For the happiest love and the deepest to Him must always rest upon the
contrite remembrance of sins forgiven. Therefore the tenderest and divinest
work of Christ is to help His conscience-stricken servant to a true repentance.
He cannot give His love or honor with service unless we acknowledge and
abandon our sin before Him. He will make sure work. The keenest cut of the
surgeon's knife is not cruel. The malignant tumors have to be removed, and it
will always be painful. Therefore does Christ hold the man right up against
his past and make him, as the preliminary to the fullest communication and
reception of His love, feel intensely and bitterly the reality of his wrongdoing.

Now, take these two figures just as they stand before us. Look! There is Jesus
Christ, fresh from the cross, coming to you for a double purpose, to remind
you of your unworthiness, your failures, your denials, and your forgetfulness
of Him and to entreat you for your love. What a depth of perfect forgiveness
there is in that, that He comes to the denier with only these gentle and delicate
reminders, with no spoken rebuke, with no uttered word in reference to the
past! His questions imply this: "Whatever the past has been, if you can only
say in truth that you love me now, it is all right, and there will never be another
word said about your falls!" And if the answer to that is swift and real, then
no more need be said about the fault. When a penitent denier comes back to
the Master, and in humble faith in His pardoning mercy clasps His feet and
washes them with tears, the believing love is all that Christ asks, before He
reinstates him in all the forfeited privileges.

ALEXANDER MACLAREN

He said to him again a second time, "Simon, son of Jonah, do you love Me?"

John 21:16 NKJV

What questions Christ might have asked! "Simon, have you humbled yourself and repented?" Nothing of that kind was said by the gentle Jesus; rather, He uses the word that is paramount in the Christian vocabulary—"Simon, son of Jonah, do you love Me?"—a question you might put to a child; the deepest question of all. This was profound, because love carries everything; it is a furnace that purges the gold of all its dross; it is a passion that means prophetic insight, and a sympathetic identification with all things pure, true, and lovely. This is the question that He asks all of us—"Do you love Me?" We are not made theologians, but we can answer the question as to our love. Love sees in the darkness, walks on the water, is cast down but not destroyed, persecuted but not forsaken, in continual peril and yet in continual security. When there is love, there will be progress. Love opens the door of every difficulty, and love makes our faith a daily delight.

This was practical as well as gracious and profound, because love is the true qualification for service: "Feed My lambs" (v. 15 NKJV). A man cannot labor for Christ if he does not love Christ. If love fails, service goes down. But the heart will not confess this; the heart is prolific in excuses for the lapses of life. Why do we forsake the assembling together with other believers or not give as liberally as we used to give? Then will follow a list of excuses and lies, anything but a confession of the truth. What is the truth? That love has gone down. When we fail in love, we cannot attain to service, and we begin to think that something of another kind is needed, and thus we lie, not to man, but to God. Could we speak the truth, we should have at least a statement made credible by its obvious truth. Peter gave a great heart-answer at the last, and his voice trembled when he said it. It was a noble voice, Peter's, accustomed to giving orders while the wind was raging out in the open sea, but when this inquiry touched his heart, that great voice shrank into a tearful whisper, and he said, "Lord, You know all things; You know that I love You" (v. 17 NKJV). Until we get a heart testimony like that, the church will hesitate and flounder, will aim at nothing, and will beat the air.

JOSEPH PARKER

"Simon, son of Jonah, do you love Me?"

John 21:16 NKJV

Not as a mere echo from the morning gilded shore of Tiberias, but as an ever new, ever sounding note of divinest power, come the familiar words to each of us, "Do you love Me?" He who asks it has loved us with an everlasting love. He has died for us. He has washed us from our sins in His own blood. He has waited for our love, waited patiently all through our coldness.

And if by His grace we have said, "Take my love," which of us has not felt that part of His very answer has been to make us see how little there was to take, and how little of that little has been kept for Him? And yet we *do* love Him! He knows that! The very grieving and longing to love Him more proves it. But we want more than that, and so does our Lord.

He has created us to love. We have a sealed treasure of love, which either remains sealed, and then gradually dries up and wastes away, or is unsealed and poured out, and yet is the fuller and not the emptier for the outpouring. The more love we give, the more we have to give. So far it is only natural. But when the Holy Spirit reveals the love of Christ and sheds abroad the love of God in our hearts, this natural love is penetrated with a new principle as it discovers a new Object. Everything that it beholds in that Object gives it new depth and new color. As it sees the holiness, beauty, and glory, it takes the deep hues of conscious sinfulness, unworthiness, and nothingness. As it sees even a glimpse of the love that surpasses knowledge, it takes the glow of wonder and gratitude. And when it sees that love drawing close to its deepest need with blood-purchased pardon, it is intensified and stirred, and there is no more time for weighing and measuring; we must pour it out, all there is of it, with our tears, at the feet that were pierced for love of us.

The love of Christ is not an absorbing, but a radiating love. The more we love Him, the more we shall most certainly love others. He is so gracious that He puts back an even larger measure of the love into our hand, sanctified with His own love, energized with His blessing, and strengthened with His new commandment, "That you love one another, as I have loved you."

Frances Ridley Havergal

"Feed My sheep."

John 21:17 NKJV

The command to Peter, first of all to care for the sustenance of the least, then to guide and direct the more advanced, and then to open the deepest stores of God's truth and impart wisdom as well as guidance to all, of all stages—these are the responsibilities that love wins for its honor and its crown. Of course, these duties apply primarily to the apostles, and subordinately to the teachers of the church, but they also apply to all of us, in our measure and degree. The lesson is just this: the source of all service to men is love to Christ. Historically it has been so. A wider and a wiser philanthropy has sprung up within the Christian church more than anywhere else. That love is the great antagonist of selfishness; that love fills men with Christ's own spirit; that love leads me to care for all that Christ cares for. It is a poor affection that does not cherish the property of an absent friend. If one who is dear to us, going away on an extended trip, says to us, "Will you take care of my house till I come back again?" We shall care for it if we care for him. And when He says to us, "Feed My lambs" (v. 15) and "Tend My sheep" (v. 16), we shall not have much love for the Shepherd if we forget the flock.

Therefore, let us further learn that all so-called Christian service that does not rest on the basis of love to Jesus Christ is nothing and profitless. People complain that after all the preaching and Sunday-school teaching and the like, so few results should be found. My belief is that we get as much success as we work for, and that if some power could make inaudible every word of our preaching that had been spoken from other motives than love to Jesus Christ, many an eloquent sermon would have little left. And if every line in our Christian books that had been written from other motives were deleted, what gaps on the page there would be! How many of your Christian activities would disappear if that test were applied to them! And do you expect God to bless the work that is no Christian service at all—unless its foundation has been laid in love to the Master?

ALEXANDER MACLAREN

"Most assuredly, I say to you, when you were younger, you girded yourself and walked where you wished; but when you are old, you will stretch out your hands, and another will gird you and carry you where you do not wish." This He spoke, signifying by what death he would glorify God. And when He had spoken this, He said to him, "Follow Me."

John 21:18–19 NKJV

As Christ foresaw all His own sufferings, so He foresaw the sufferings of His followers, and He specifically foretells Peter, having charged him to feed His sheep, to expect trouble and persecution. Most commentators think that the stretching out of his hands points to the manner of his death by crucifying, and the tradition of the ancients informs us that Peter was crucified in Rome under Nero. A violent death, in this awful form, could not be approached without extreme reluctance. And to this, Christ compares Peter's former liberty. When trouble comes, we are apt to worsen it and to fret the more at the grievances of restraint, sickness, and poverty, because we have known the sweetness of liberty, health, and abundance.

Christ lovingly warns Peter he will suffer thus in his old age. The explanation of this prediction was to signify by what death he should glorify God. Observe, that whether Peter's death would be natural or violent, easy or painful, the great concern, whatever death he dies, is to glorify God in it; for what is our chief end but this, to die to the Lord, "according to the word of the LORD" (Deuteronomy 34:5 NKJV)? When we die patiently, submitting to the will of God, rejoicing in the hope of the glory of God, and die witnessing to the truth and goodness of our faith and encouraging others, we glorify God in dying. The grace of God, which carried us with so much constancy through our sufferings, is hereby magnified. And the consolations of God, which have abounded toward us in our sufferings, and His promises, the sources of our consolations, have hereby been commended to the faith and joy of all the saints.

After the prediction of his sufferings, Jesus then tells Peter, "Follow Me." He is saying to Peter, "While you feed my sheep, expect to be treated as I have been and to tread the same path that I have trod." Let Peter set his Master before him as an example of pastoral care. Let the under shepherds study to imitate the Chief Shepherd. They had followed Christ while He was here upon the earth, and still they must follow the rules He had given them and the example He had set them. Those who faithfully follow Christ in grace shall certainly follow Him to glory.

MATTHEW HENRY

Then Peter, turning around, saw the disciple whom Jesus loved following, who also had leaned on His breast at the supper.

John 21:20 NKJV

Our Lord loved all His disciples, and yet within that circle of love there was an innermost place in which the beloved John was favored to dwell. Let us not, because John was specially loved, think less, even in the slightest degree, of the love that Jesus Christ had for the rest of His chosen. All believers are the dear objects of the Savior's choice, the purchase of His blood, His portion and inheritance, the jewels of His crown. If, in John's case, one is greater in love than another, yet all are eminently great. Our Lord's love to each of us has in it heights immeasurable and depths unfathomable. It passes knowledge.

Yet I encourage you to rise to the highest point of love. Why should you not, before long, be styled as Daniel, a "man greatly beloved" (Daniel 10:11 NKJV)? Or like John, "the disciple whom Jesus loved"? To be loved as John was is an innermost form of that same grace with which all believers have been favored. It was all grace—the supposition of anything else is out of place! But I look upon this special form of our Lord's love as one of those "best gifts" that we are instructed to earnestly desire (1 Corinthians 12:31 NKJV)—but most emphatically a gift and not a wage for works done. Love is not bought. Its atmosphere is free favor. The most supreme love is to be sought for, then, after the analogy of grace, as gracious men seek greater grace. If ever we reach the upper chambers of Love's palace, Love himself must lead us up the stairs!

At the same time, the love of Jesus was shed abroad in John's heart, and there was created in John much that was a fit object for the love of Christ. The fitness for love is love. To enjoy the love of Jesus we must overflow with love. Pray for earnest, eager, intense affection. If you want to be the man or woman whom Jesus loves, cultivate strong affection and let your nature be tender and kind. Forgive your fellow man as if you never had anything to forgive. When others hurt you, hope that it was unintentional, or else think that if they knew you better, they would treat you worse! Be willing to lay down not only your comfort, but even your life for the brethren! Live for the joy of others, even as the saints in heaven. So shall you become one greatly loved.

CHARLES SPURGEON

Jesus said to him, "If I will that he remain till I come, what is that to you? You follow Me."

John 21:22 NKJV

Only a moment before, our Lord had said to Peter, "Follow Me," yet He found it necessary to repeat that command, from which it is clear that the Lord Jesus himself might be here and might speak to us in the most plain terms, and yet His words might not make the impression upon our hearts that we sometimes think they would. Peter's mind seems to have been distracted from the command to follow the Savior by something as simple as his awakened curiosity as to John's future. To which the Master replied, in the words of my text, "What is that to you? You follow Me."

The main business of our life is still to follow Christ. The one thing we are to aim at is to walk in Christ's footsteps, to do what He did, and, as far as He is imitable by us, to do it as He did it and to be as He was in the midst of the sons and daughters of men. If I am a Christian, I am to mold my thoughts, words, character, and actions after the model of Christ!

I believe that every Christian was created to serve God in whatever he is doing. Every person is such a noble work of God that he cannot have been intended merely to work at a job. There is something grander than that for them to do! To every believer, Christ has given a position, a special vocation in which he can follow Christ that nobody else can so well occupy, and from that position he can influence some other person or persons whom God will bless through him. Every man has his own particular calling, and every Christian's calling should be especially for God. One beauty of Christ's life was that He kept to His calling and did not go beyond His commission. And you will be wise if you do the same.

Our life has an outlook toward the infinite—there are windows in our life that look toward God. Look out of them, dear Christian! With your windows open toward God, live in the light of His countenance and seek in all things to please and honor Him! It is your lifework to honor God, to glorify the Lord Jesus Christ, to be the instrument by which God shall illustrate His almighty power, but you cannot do this unless you follow Christ.

CHARLES SPURGEON

And there are also many other things that Jesus did,
which if they were written one by one, I suppose that
even the world itself could not contain the books that
would be written. Amen.

John 21:25 NKJV

Jesus Christ, the Son of God, is the center of Scripture, and the Book—whatever are the historical facts about its origin, its authorship and dates of composition—is a unity, because there is driven right through it, like a core of gold, either in the way of prophecy and forward-looking anticipation or in the way of history and grateful retrospect, the reference to the one "name which is above every name . . . the name of Jesus" (Philippians 2:9–10 NKJV). Christ towers above the history of the world and the process of revelation like Mount Everest among the Himalayas. To that great peak all the country on the one side runs upward, and from it all the valleys on the other descend, and the springs are born there that carry abundance and life over the world.

Our Father God—for God is the Author of the Bible—has painted on this great canvas of the Bible much in sketching outline, and left out many details that some suggest make it flawed, that every eye may be fixed on the central Figure, the Christ of God, on whose head comes down the dove and round whom echoes the divine declaration: "You are My beloved Son; in You I am well pleased" (Luke 3:22 NKJV).

But it is not merely in order to represent Jesus as the Christ of God that these are written, but it is that this representation may become the object of our faith. If the intention of Scripture had been simply to establish the fact that Jesus was the Christ and the Son of God, a theological paper would have been enough to do that. But, if the object is that men should not only accept with their understanding the truth concerning Christ's office and nature, but that their hearts and souls should rest upon Him as the Son of God and the Christ, then there is no other way to accomplish that but by the history of His life and the manifestation of His heart. If the object is to lead us to put our faith in Him, we must have what we have here, the infinitely touching and tender figure of Jesus Christ himself set forth before us in all its sweetness and beauty, as He lived and moved and died for us.

Give thanks that all God's lavish revelation has been expended on the world that you and all mankind might believe that Jesus is the Christ, the Son of God.

ALEXANDER MACLAREN

LANCE WUBBELS began his publishing career with Bethany House Publishers, where he served for eighteen years as its managing editor, before becoming the vice president of literary development for fifteen years at Koechel Peterson & Associates, a Minneapolis-based design firm. He presently runs his own literary service to publishers and many bestselling authors, both in the development of new books as well as the writing of derivative study guides, journals, and daily reading books.

Wubbels has authored several fiction and nonfiction books, including five gift books with Hallmark that sold well over a million copies. He authored seven fiction books for Bethany House Publishers, including the Angel Award-winning novel *One Small Miracle*. Two of his books have won Gold Medallion awards from the Evangelical Christian Publishers Association, one for best gift book of 2005 and one for best devotional of 1999.

Combining the skills of teacher, researcher, and editor, Wubbels discovered a wealth of classic writings, sermons, and biblical expositors from legendary Christians that are very difficult to access for most believers. With a desire to make these extraordinary writings and ageless messages available to today's readers, he became the compiler/editor of twelve Charles Spurgeon books under the CHRISTIAN LIVING CLASSICS series and DISCOVERING THE POWER series, which were followed with a six-book 30-DAY DEVOTIONAL TREASURY series. It is his belief that the readings selected for this volume, *Day by Day through the Gospel of John*, represent some of the most profound expositions ever given regarding the life of Christ.

Wubbels resides in Bloomington, Minnesota, with his wife, Karen.